OF BITTER SOULS

A mysterious New Orleans Pastor named Secord adorns four individuals with powers that are directly related to their character flaws.

It begs the question, what do we do with the gifts we are given?

Under the guidance of Pastor Secord, the four flawed heroes will be set loose on the supernatural threats that are so prevalent in New Orleans' legends. They will be a force for good...that is if they don't destroy themselves with their own powers first.

Of Bitter Souls

chapter 1
A Stroll Through the Cities of the Dead

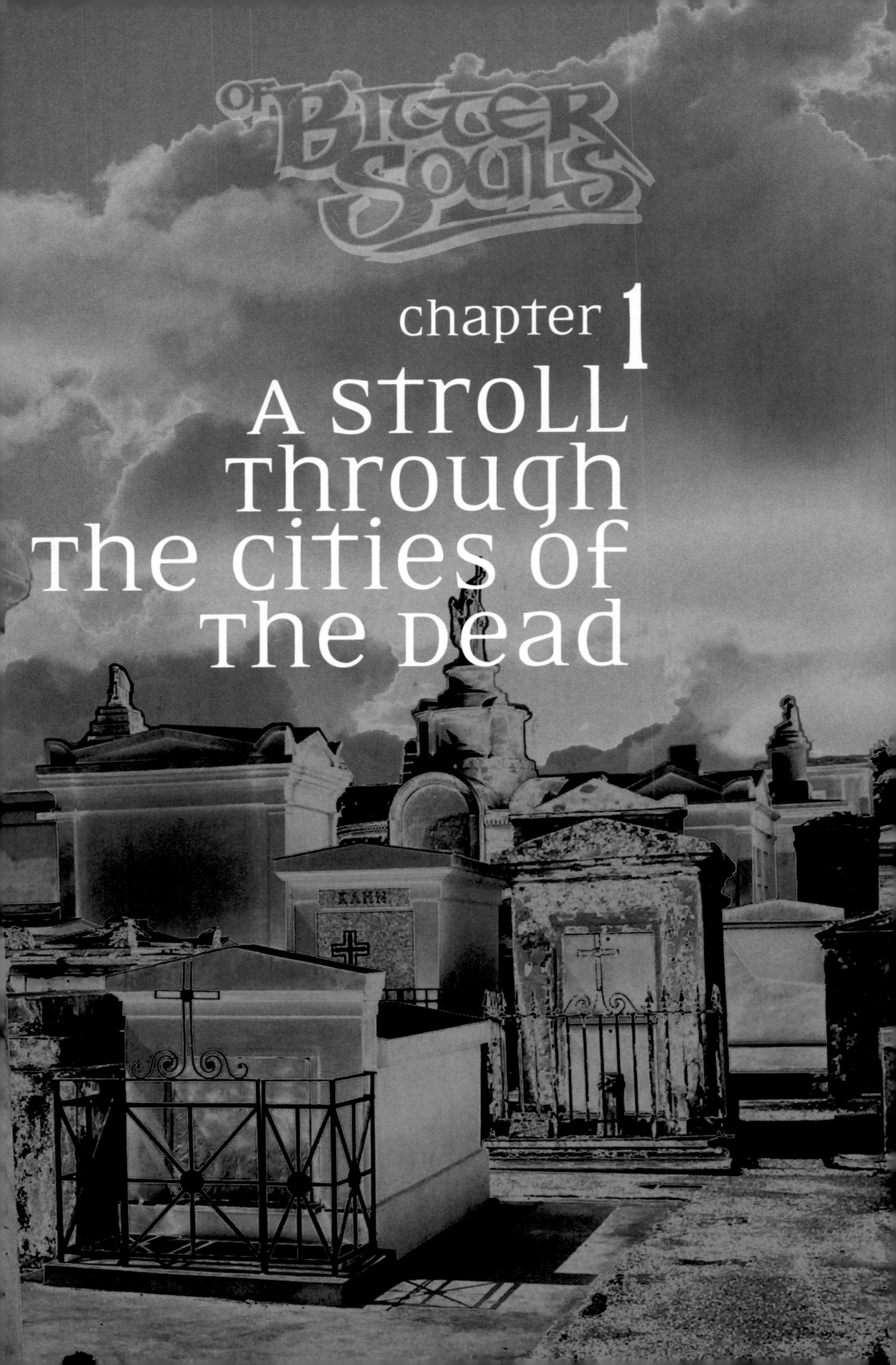
KAHN

table of
contents:

mark waid

introduction:

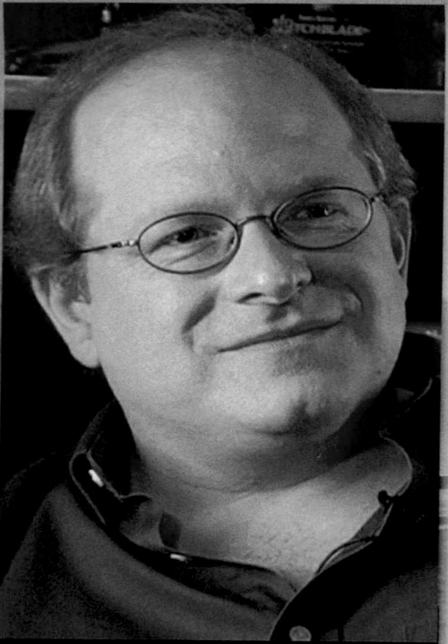

Mark Waid is a comic industry legend. He has written for all of the major publishers and is responsible for such smash hits as KINGDOM COME and HUNTER/KILLER. Mark is also the world's leading Superman trivia expert.

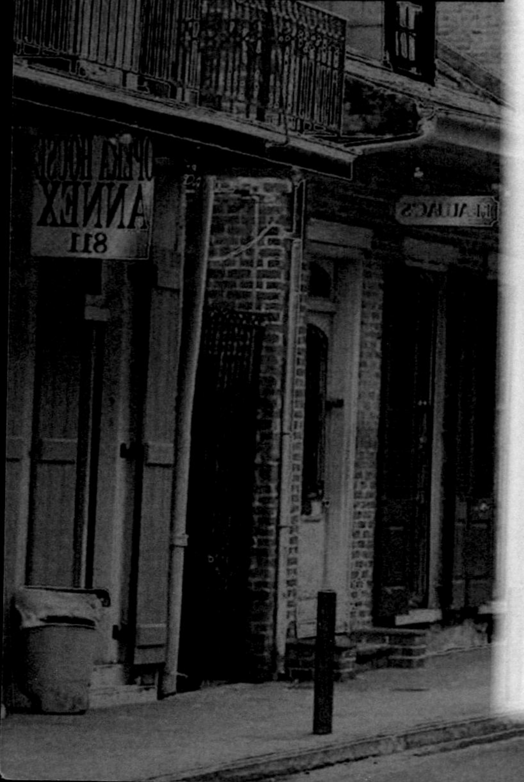

Here's what blows about redemption: it requires effort and sacrifice. The main reason I'm a hellbound soul with nothing to look forward to in my future save decades of spiraling further down a path of self-loathing pity? I'm too lazy to put on my pants.

Chuck and Norm's heroes wear pants.

Seriously, Chuck Satterlee and Norm Breyfogle's OF BITTER SOULS is probably the most candid, certainly the most honest, foray into combining super-heroes and spirituality that I've ever read. No one here is born with powers and abilities far beyond those of mortal men; no one is gifted with a magic word that allows them to fly and takes away all their problems. In the pages following, you'll meet four men and women, utterly lost and utterly without hope, who have through divine intervention been given a second chance to find the meaning in their lives--but never guaranteed success or an easy path. In order to create the energy for their own redemption, they're going to have to face devils and demons both within and without. Along the way, we're going to learn one by one just how each of them got to this point in their lives, and these heroes' individual tales-poignant and well-told within the context of a larger adventure--are a testament to the inspirational power of good, moral fiction.

The concept that redemption, like anything worth having, must be earned through blood and toil and tears isn't a light and breezy message, but it makes for great drama. Struggle always does. And if reading OF BITTER SOULS affects you the way it has affected me...well, let's just say that I've started looking around the room for my pants.

March 2006, California

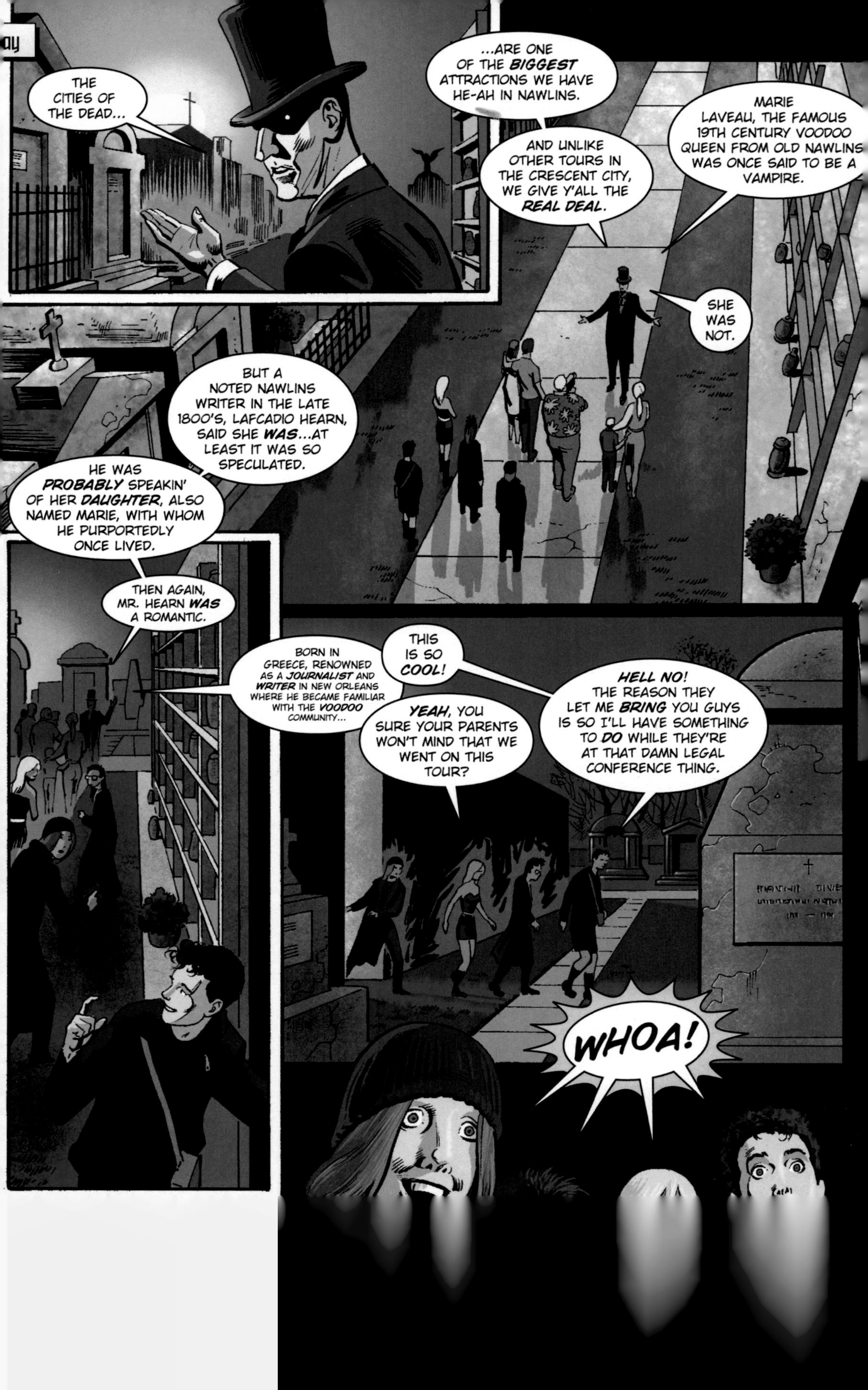
THE CITIES OF THE DEAD...
...ARE ONE OF THE BIGGEST ATTRACTIONS WE HAVE HE-AH IN NAWLINS.
AND UNLIKE OTHER TOURS IN THE CRESCENT CITY, WE GIVE Y'ALL THE REAL DEAL.
MARIE LAVEAU, THE FAMOUS 19TH CENTURY VOODOO QUEEN FROM OLD NAWLINS WAS ONCE SAID TO BE A VAMPIRE.
SHE WAS NOT.
BUT A NOTED NAWLINS WRITER IN THE LATE 1800'S, LAFCADIO HEARN, SAID SHE WAS...AT LEAST IT WAS SO SPECULATED.
HE WAS PROBABLY SPEAKIN' OF HER DAUGHTER, ALSO NAMED MARIE, WITH WHOM HE PURPORTEDLY ONCE LIVED.
THEN AGAIN, MR. HEARN WAS A ROMANTIC.
BORN IN GREECE, RENOWNED AS A JOURNALIST AND WRITER IN NEW ORLEANS WHERE HE BECAME FAMILIAR WITH THE VOODOO COMMUNITY...
THIS IS SO COOL!
YEAH, YOU SURE YOUR PARENTS WON'T MIND THAT WE WENT ON THIS TOUR?
HELL NO! THE REASON THEY LET ME BRING YOU GUYS IS SO I'LL HAVE SOMETHING TO DO WHILE THEY'RE AT THAT DAMN LEGAL CONFERENCE THING.
WHOA!

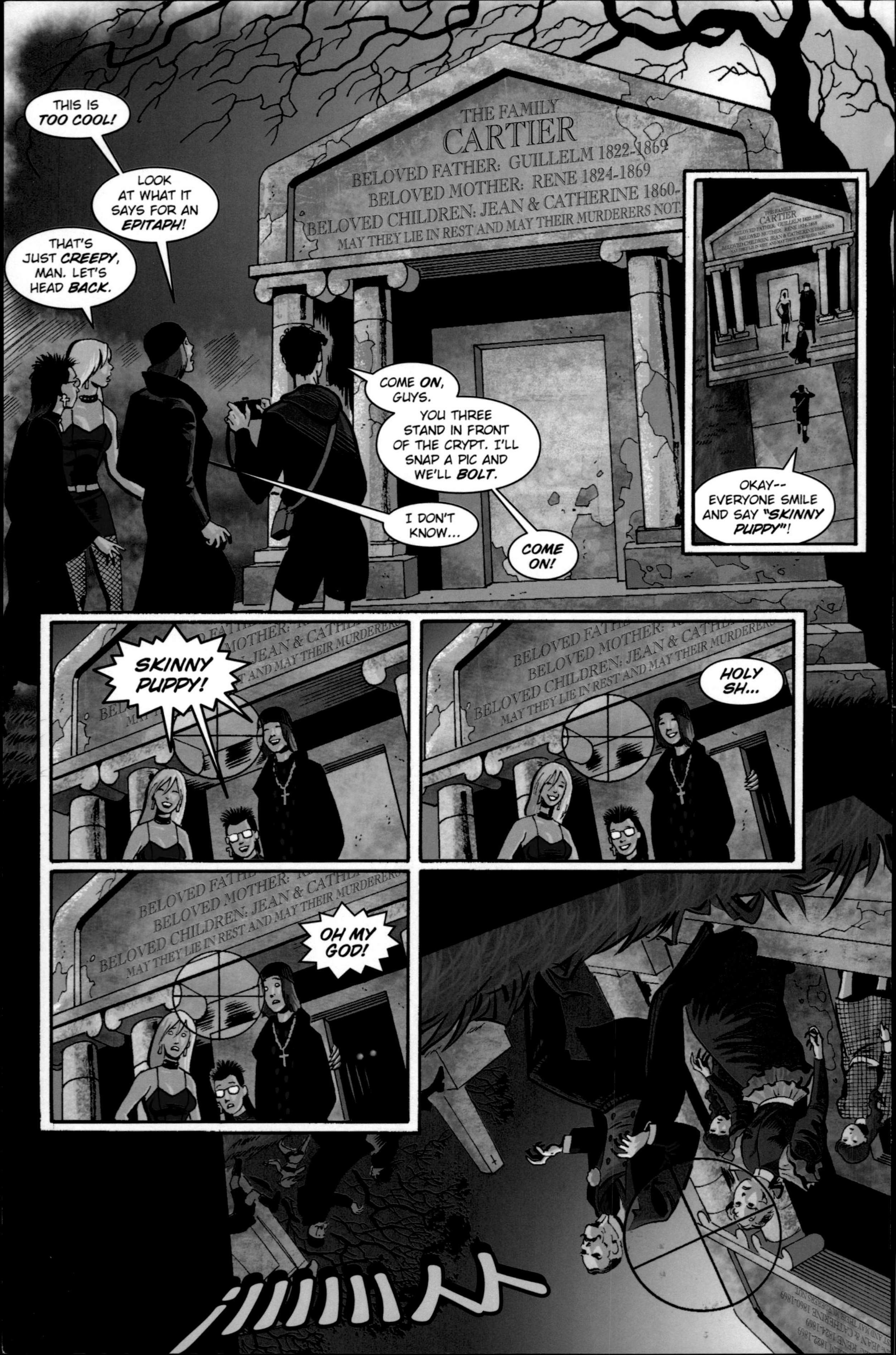
THE FAMILY
CARTIER
BELOVED FATHER: GUILLELM 1822-1869
BELOVED MOTHER: RENE 1824-1869
BELOVED CHILDREN: JEAN & CATHERINE 1860-
MAY THEY LIE IN REST AND MAY THEIR MURDERERS NOT.
THIS IS TOO COOL!
LOOK AT WHAT IT SAYS FOR AN EPITAPH!
THAT'S JUST CREEPY, MAN. LET'S HEAD BACK.
COME ON, GUYS.
YOU THREE STAND IN FRONT OF THE CRYPT. I'LL SNAP A PIC AND WE'LL BOLT.
I DON'T KNOW...
COME ON!
OKAY-- EVERYONE SMILE AND SAY "SKINNY PUPPY"!
SKINNY PUPPY!
HOLY SH...
OH MY GOD!

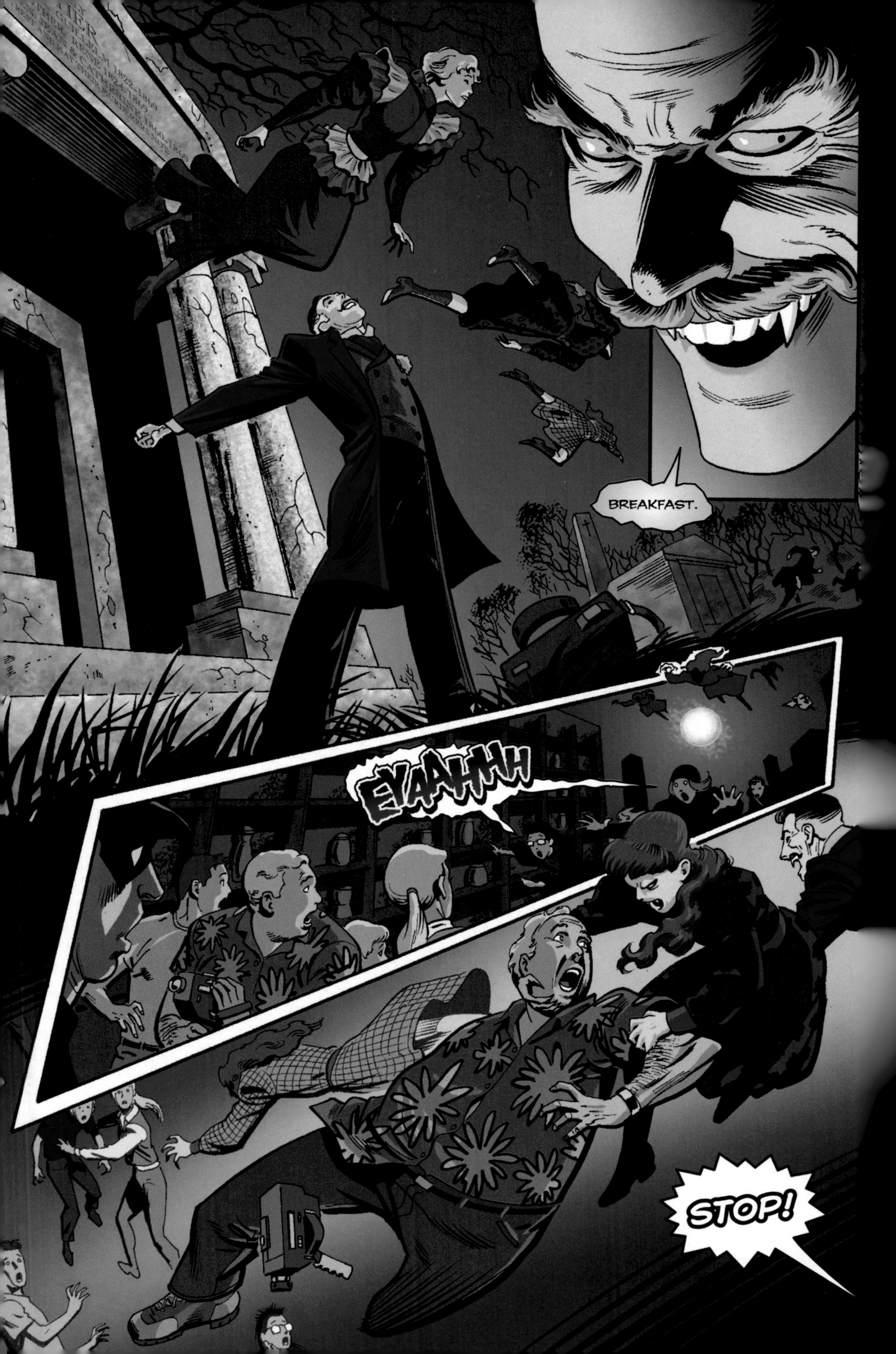
BREAKFAST.
EYAAHHH
STOP!

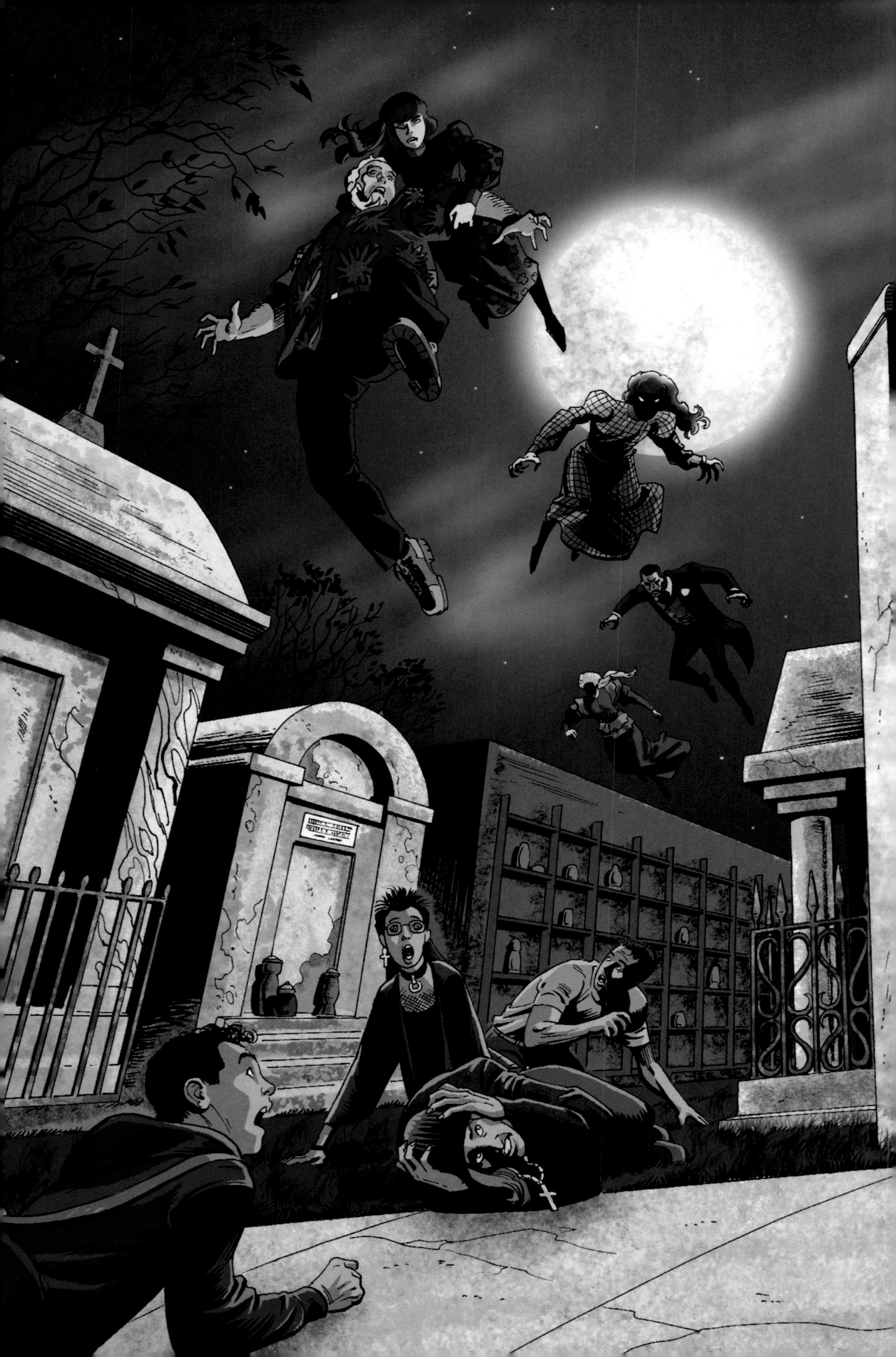

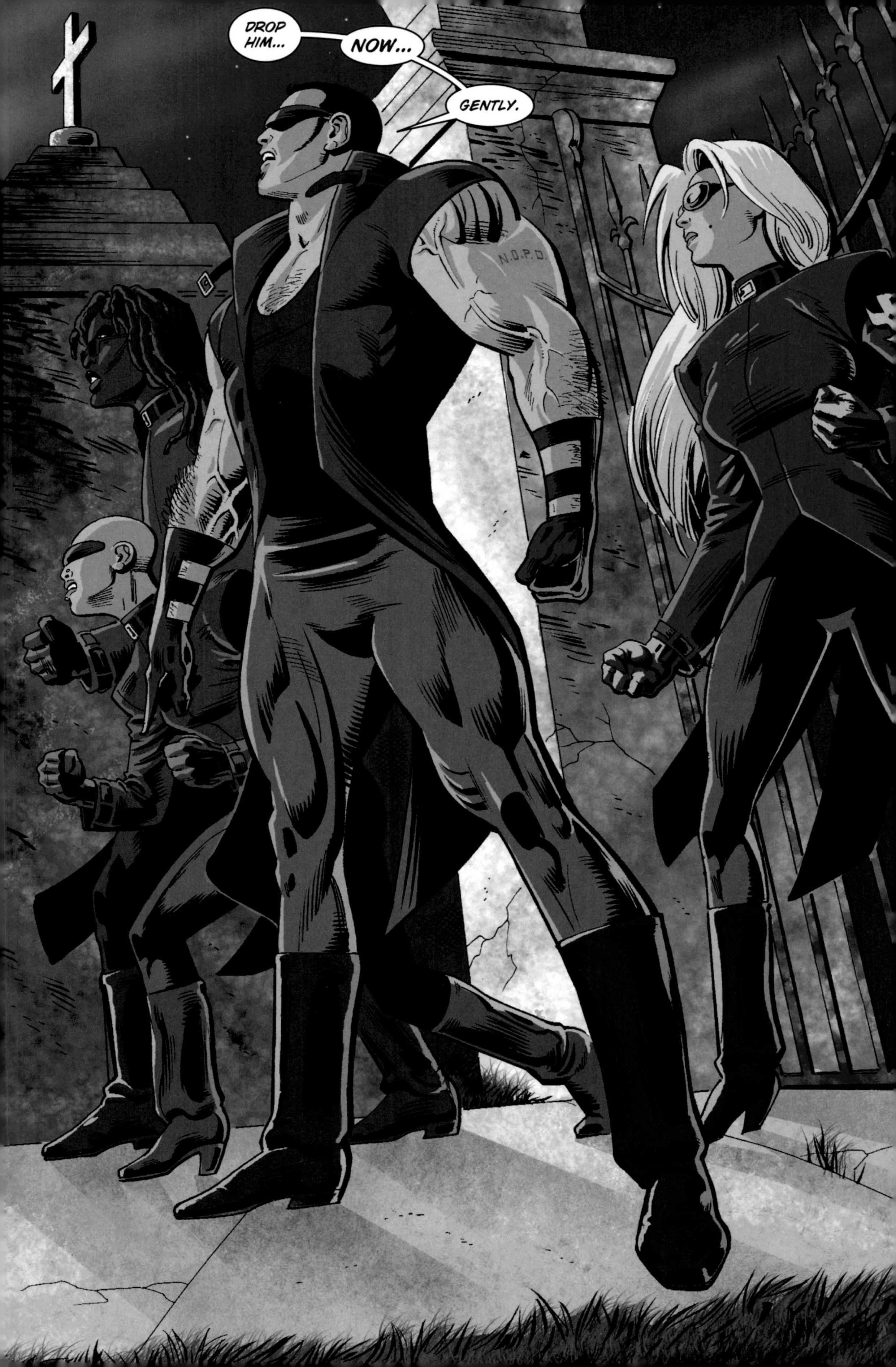
DROP HIM...
NOW...
GENTLY.
N.O.P.D.

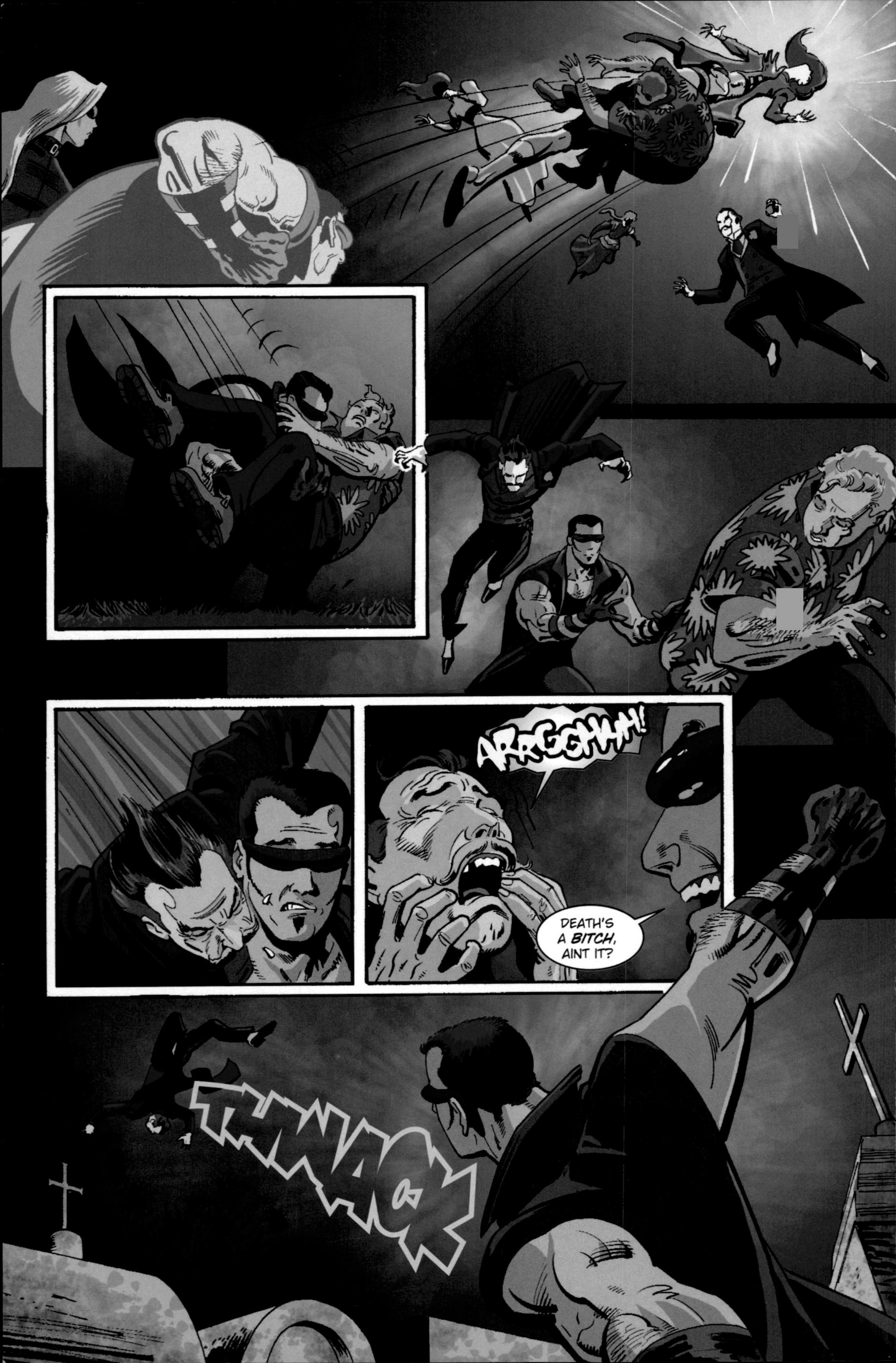
ARRGGHHH!
DEATH'S A *BITCH*, AINT IT?
THWACK

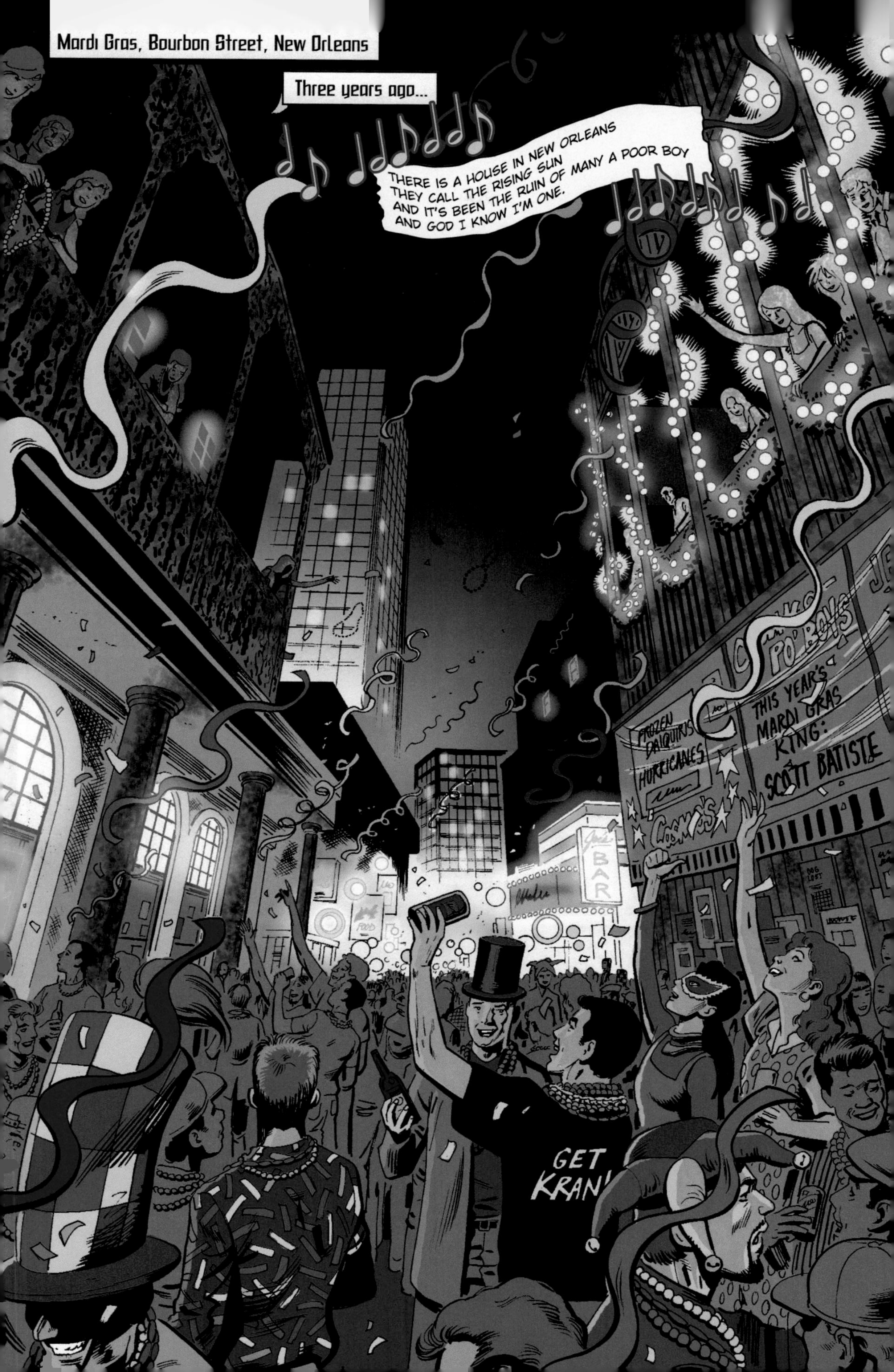
Mardi Gras, Bourbon Street, New Orleans
Three years ago...
THERE IS A HOUSE IN NEW ORLEANS
THEY CALL THE RISING SUN
AND IT'S BEEN THE RUIN OF MANY A POOR BOY
AND GOD I KNOW I'M ONE.
PO' BOYS
THIS YEAR'S MARDI GRAS KING: SCOTT BATISTE
FROZEN DAIQUIRIS
HURRICANES
COSMO'S
BAR
GET KRAN

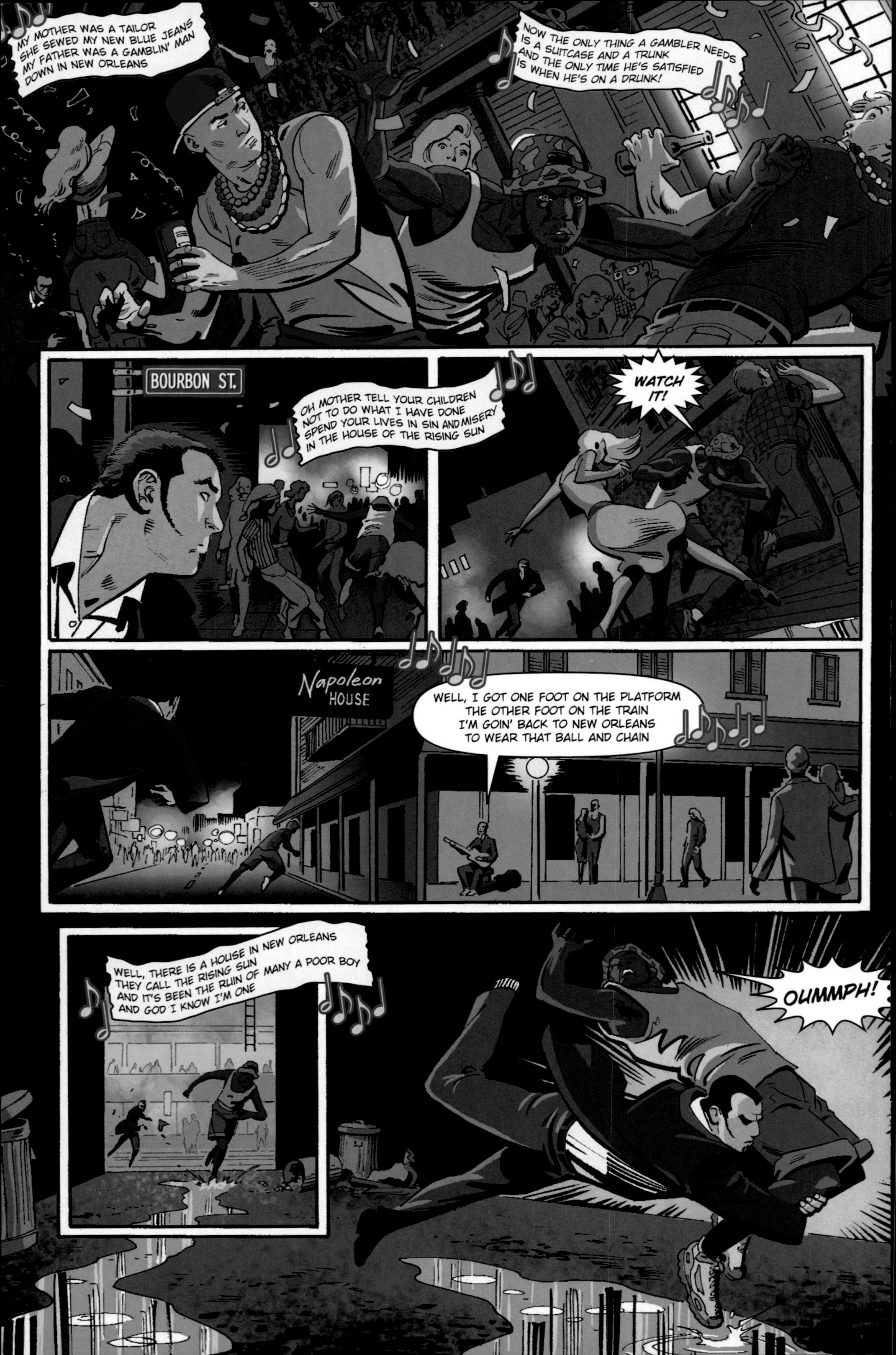

MY MOTHER WAS A TAILOR
SHE SEWED MY NEW BLUE JEANS
MY FATHER WAS A GAMBLIN' MAN
DOWN IN NEW ORLEANS
NOW THE ONLY THING A GAMBLER NEEDS
IS A SUITCASE AND A TRUNK
AND THE ONLY TIME HE'S SATISFIED
IS WHEN HE'S ON A DRUNK!
BOURBON ST.
OH MOTHER TELL YOUR CHILDREN
NOT TO DO WHAT I HAVE DONE
SPEND YOUR LIVES IN SIN AND MISERY
IN THE HOUSE OF THE RISING SUN
WATCH IT!
Napoleon HOUSE
WELL, I GOT ONE FOOT ON THE PLATFORM
THE OTHER FOOT ON THE TRAIN
I'M GOIN' BACK TO NEW ORLEANS
TO WEAR THAT BALL AND CHAIN
WELL, THERE IS A HOUSE IN NEW ORLEANS
THEY CALL THE RISING SUN
AND IT'S BEEN THE RUIN OF MANY A POOR BOY
AND GOD I KNOW I'M ONE
OUMMPH!

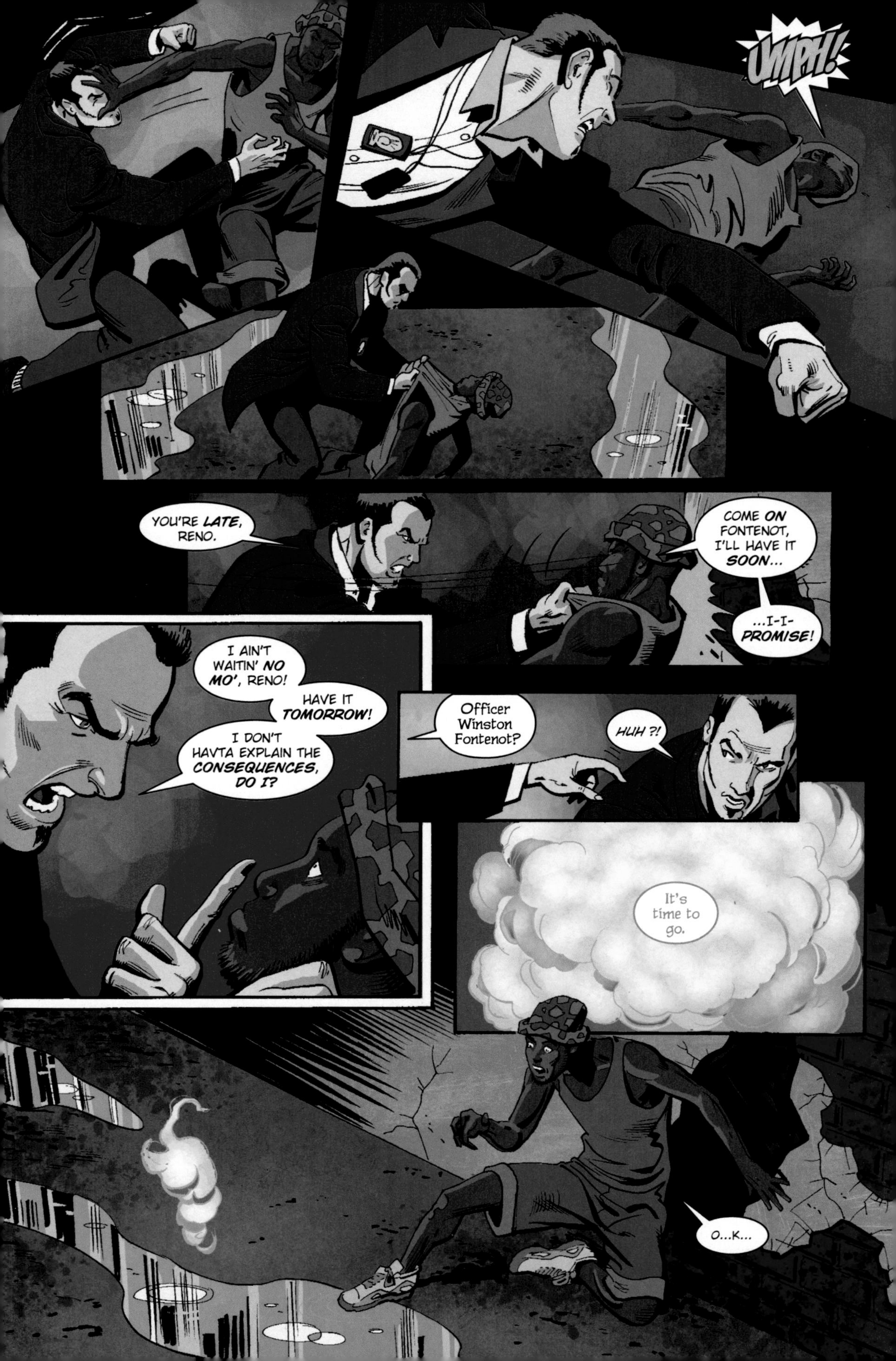
UMPH!
YOU'RE LATE, RENO.
COME ON FONTENOT, I'LL HAVE IT SOON...
...I-I-PROMISE!
I AIN'T WAITIN' NO MO', RENO!
HAVE IT TOMORROW!
I DON'T HAVTA EXPLAIN THE CONSEQUENCES, DO I?
Officer Winston Fontenot?
HUH ?!
It's time to go.
O...K...

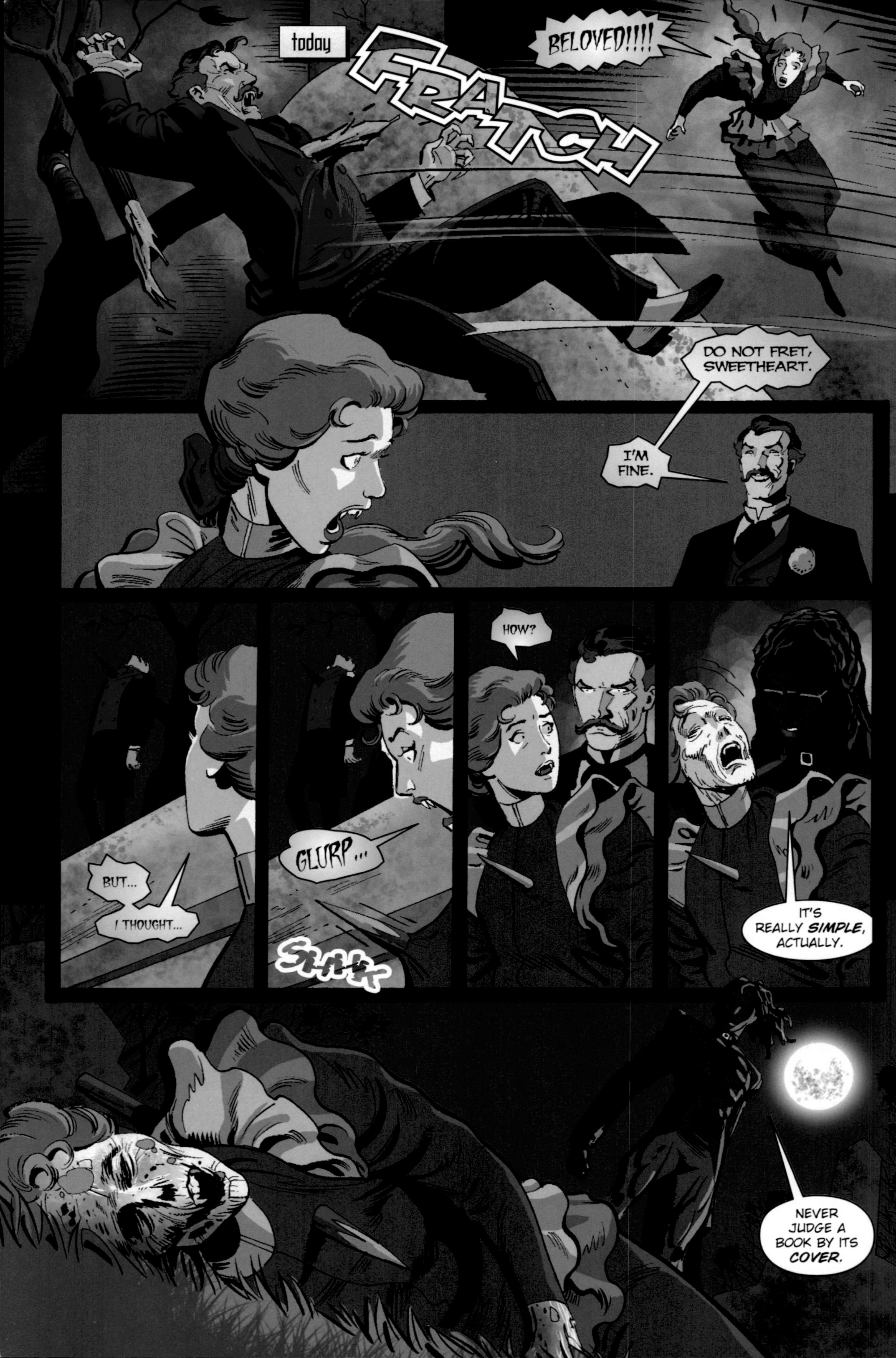
today
FRATCH
BELOVED!!!!
DO NOT FRET, SWEETHEART.
I'M FINE.
BUT...
I THOUGHT...
GLURP...
SHTIKK
HOW?
IT'S REALLY SIMPLE, ACTUALLY.
NEVER JUDGE A BOOK BY ITS COVER.

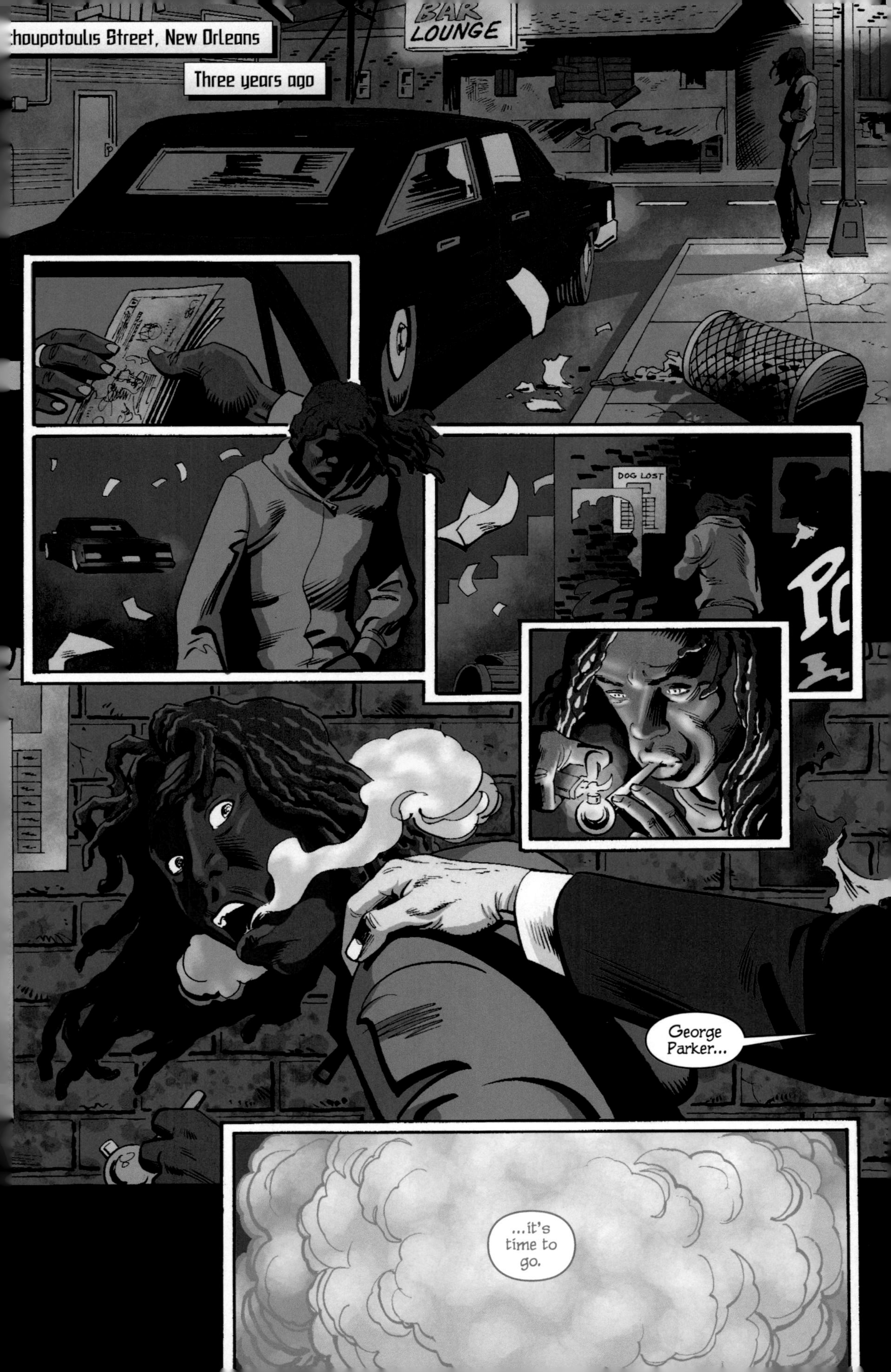

choupotoulis Street, New Orleans
Three years ago
BAR
LOUNGE
DOG LOST
George Parker...
...it's time to go.

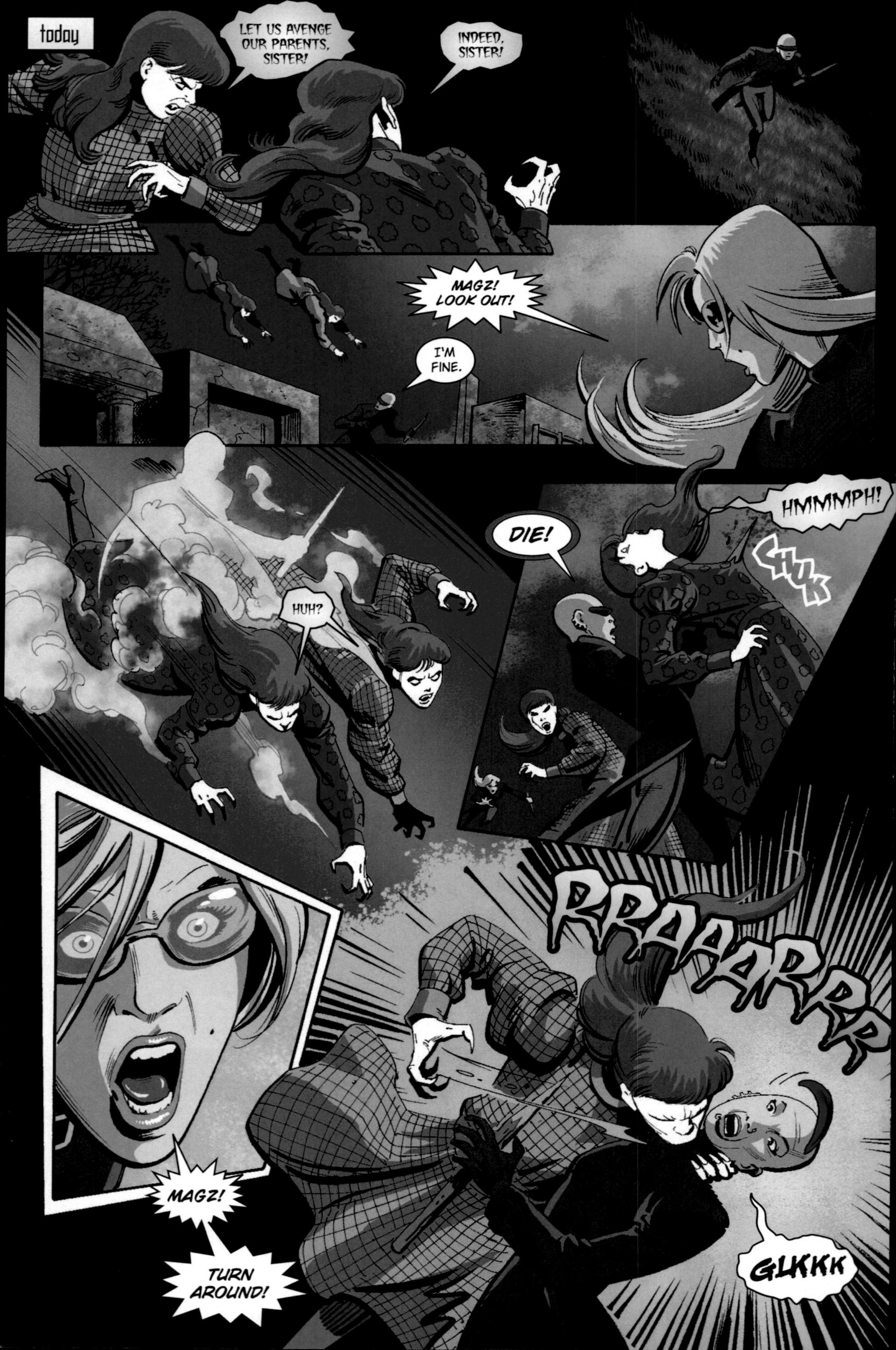
today
LET US AVENGE OUR PARENTS, SISTER!
INDEED, SISTER!
MAGZ! LOOK OUT!
I'M FINE.
HUH?
DIE!
HMMMPH!
CHUK
RRAAARRR
MAGZ!
TURN AROUND!
GLKKK

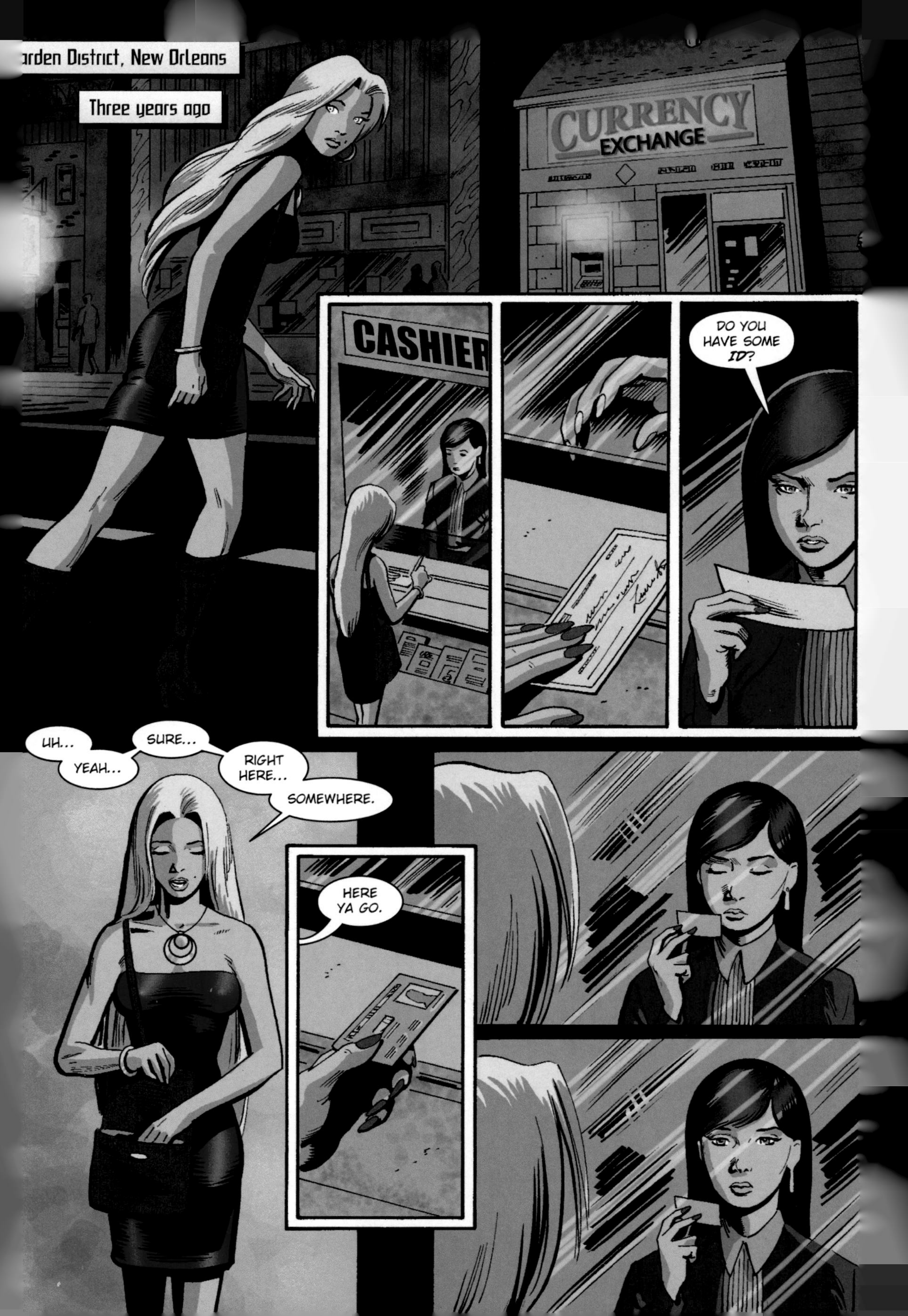

arden District, New Orleans
Three years ago
CURRENCY EXCHANGE
CASHIER
DO YOU HAVE SOME ID?
UH...
YEAH...
SURE...
RIGHT HERE...
SOMEWHERE.
HERE YA GO.

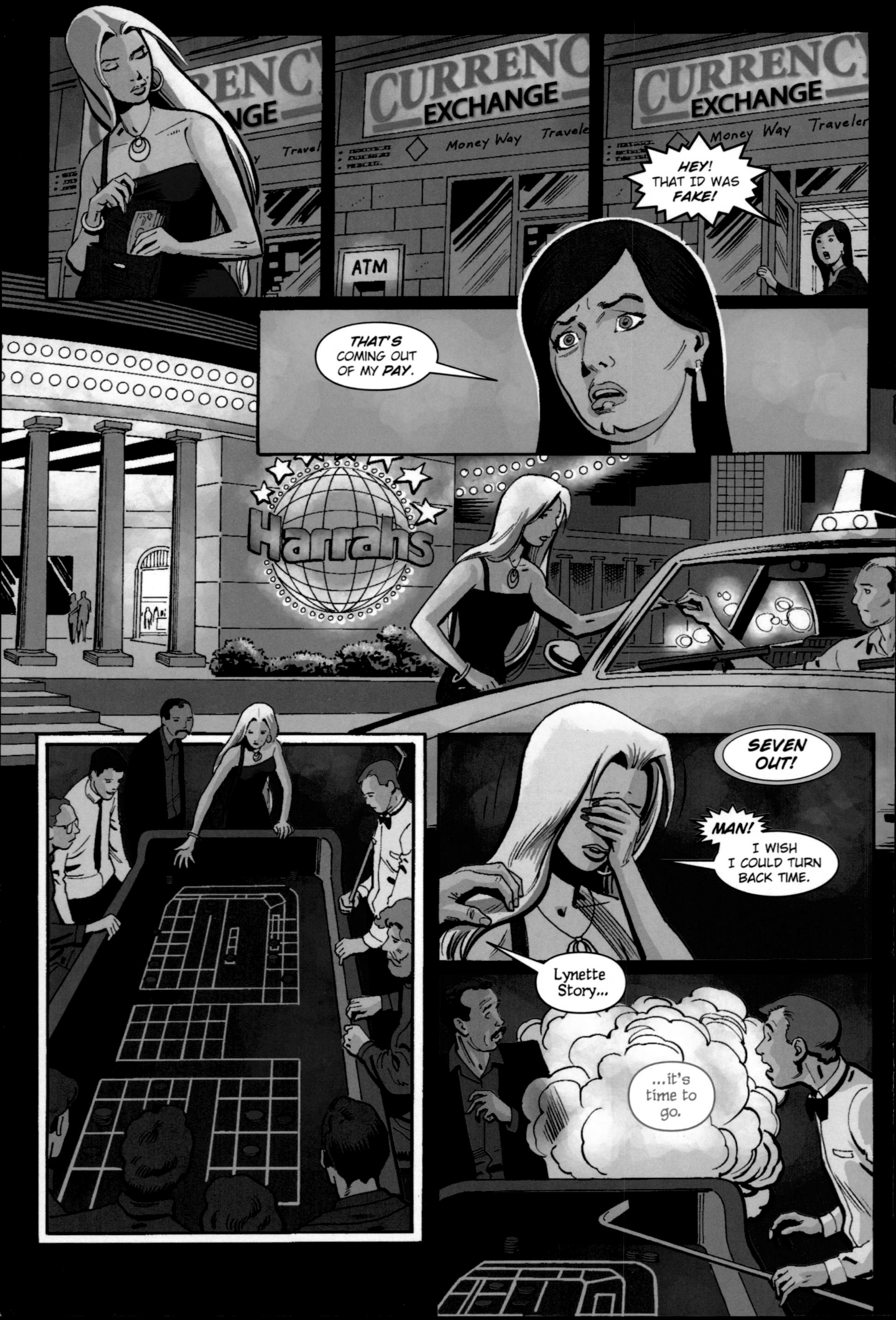
CURRENCY EXCHANGE
Money Way
Traveler
ATM
HEY! THAT ID WAS FAKE!
THAT'S COMING OUT OF MY PAY.
Harrahs
SEVEN OUT!
MAN! I WISH I COULD TURN BACK TIME.
Lynette Story...
...it's time to go.

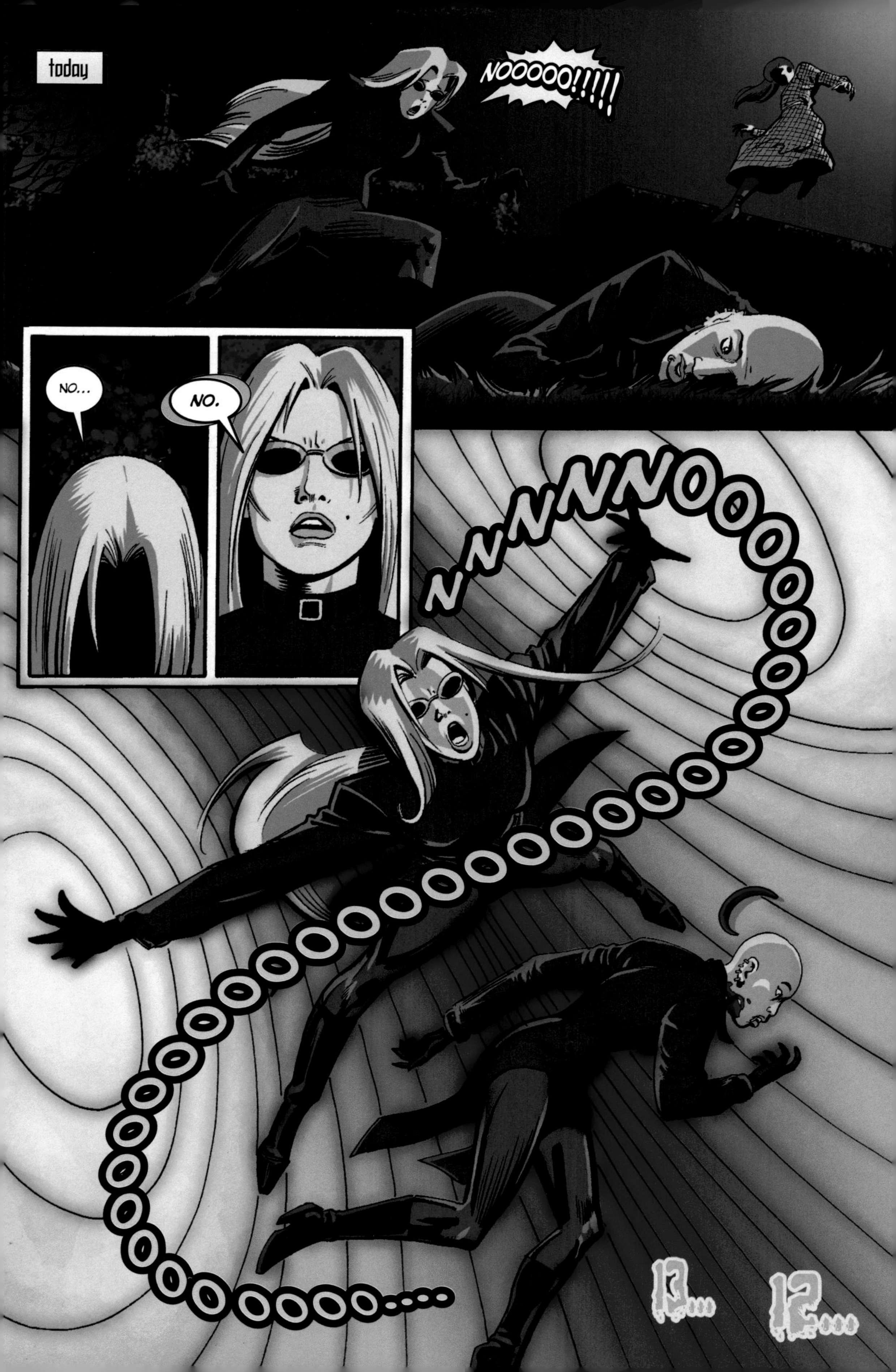
today
NOOOOO!!!!!
NO...
NO.
NNNNNOOOOOOOOOOOOOOOOOOOOOOOOOOOOOOOOOOOOOOOOOOOOOOOO....
13...
12...

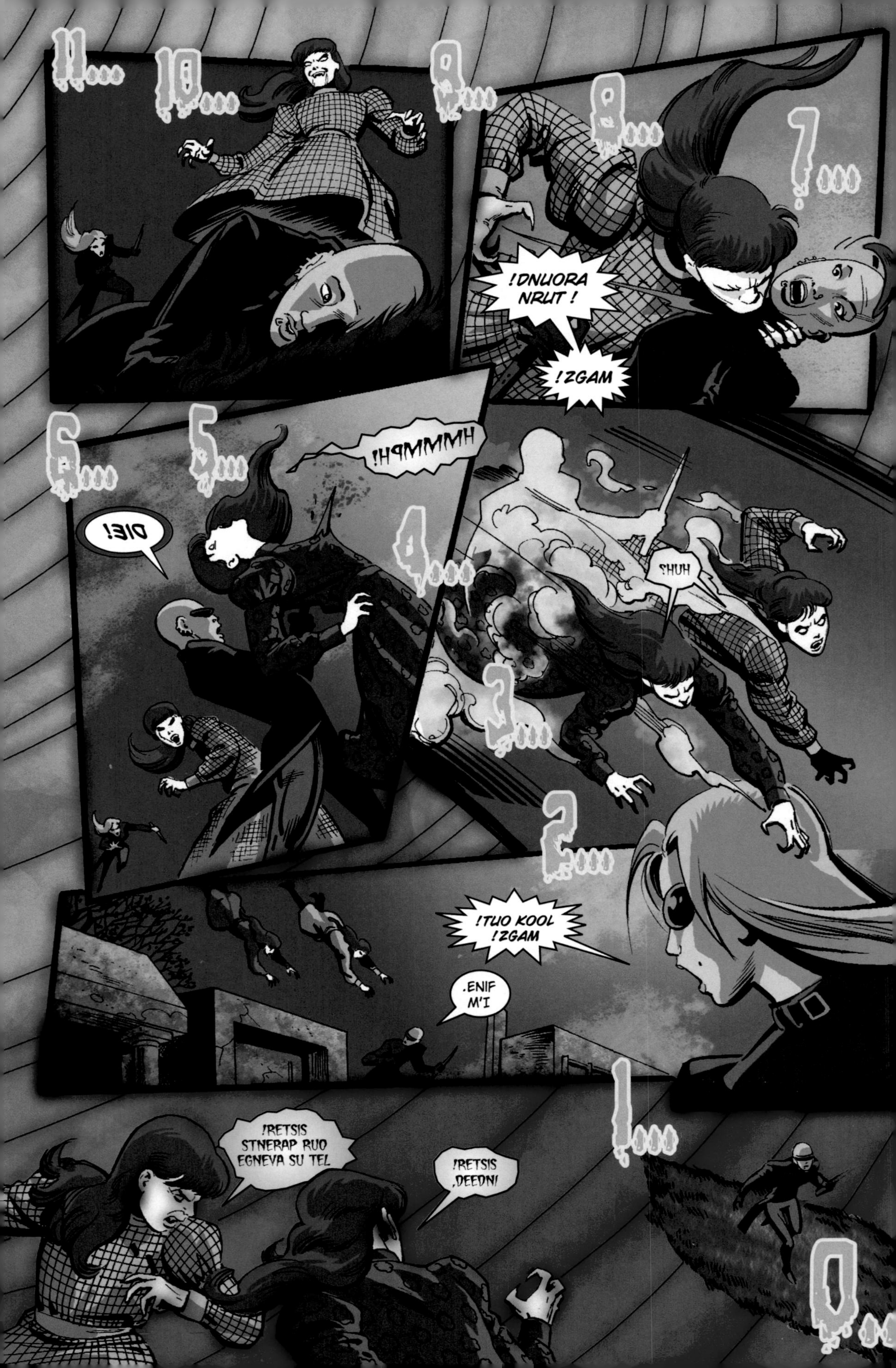

11...
10...
9...
8...
7...
!DNUORA NRUT !
!ZGAM
6...
5...
HMMMMPH!
DIE!
4...
HUH?
3...
2...
!TUO KOOL !ZGAM
.ENIF M'I
1...
!RETSIS STNERAP RUO EGNEVA SU TEL
!RETSIS ,DEEDNI
0...

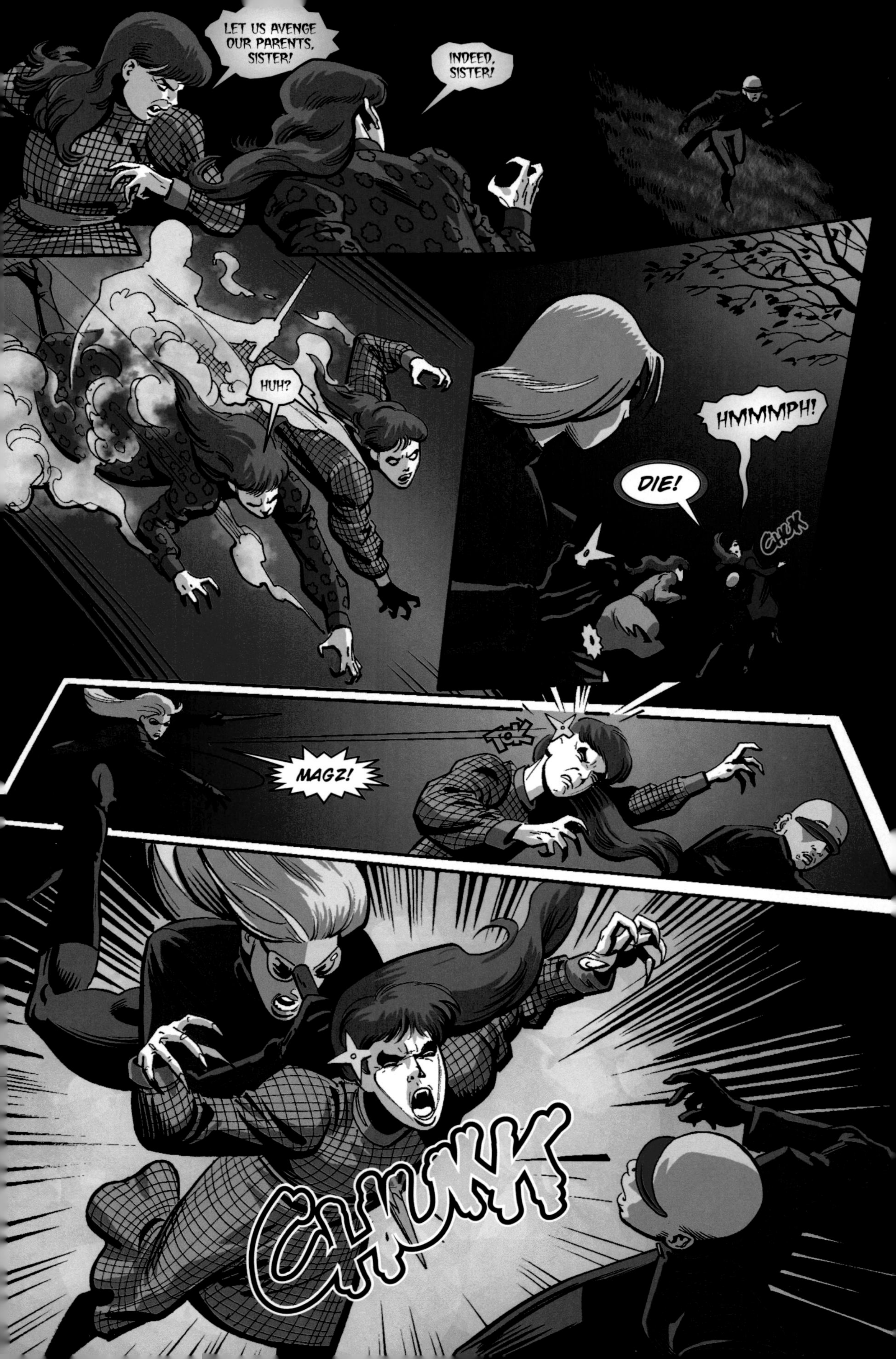

LET US AVENGE OUR PARENTS, SISTER!
INDEED, SISTER!
HUH?
HMMMPH!
DIE!
CHUK
TOK
MAGZ!
CHUNK

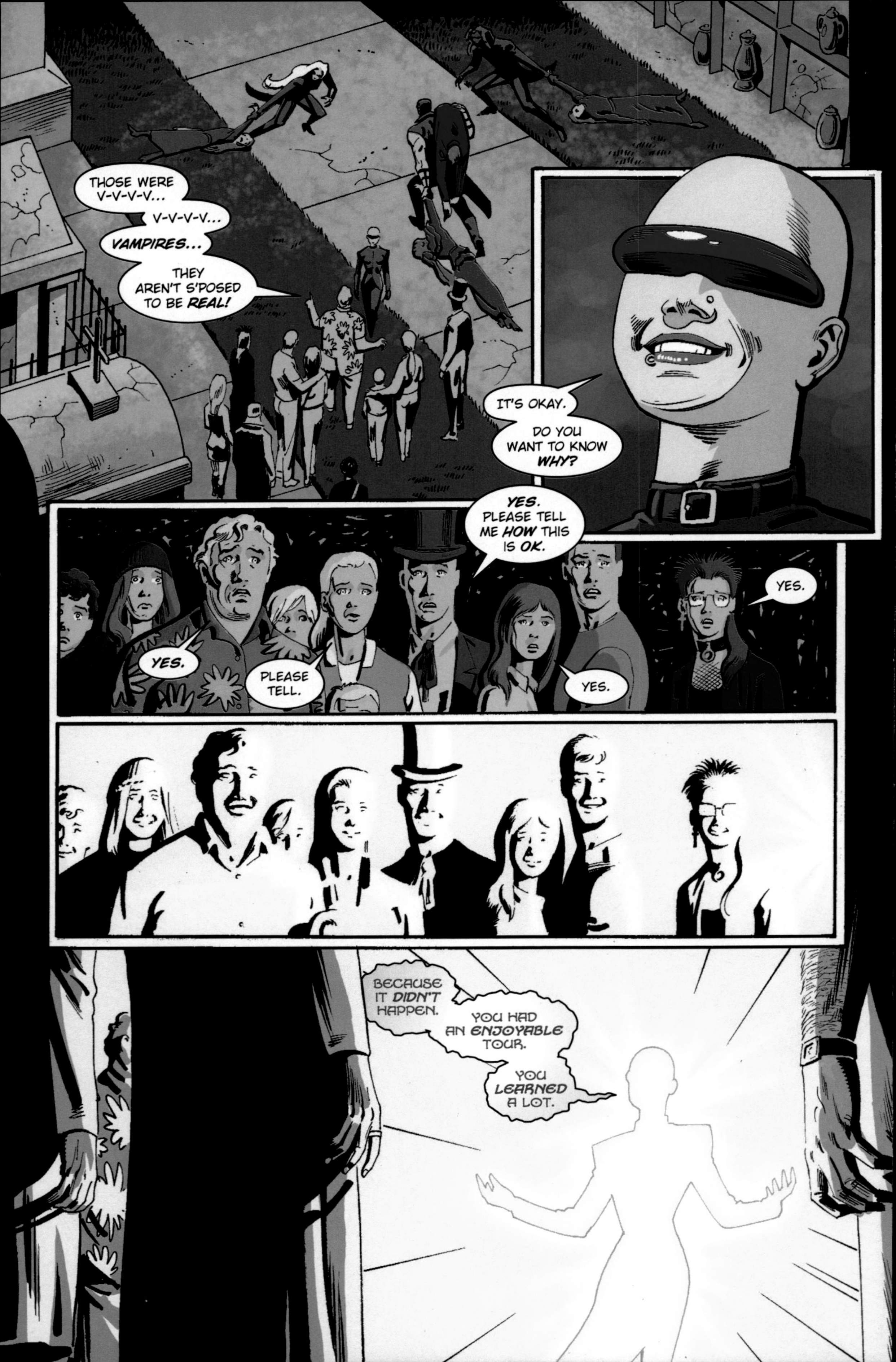
THOSE WERE V-V-V-V...
V-V-V-V...
VAMPIRES...
THEY AREN'T S'POSED TO BE REAL!
IT'S OKAY.
DO YOU WANT TO KNOW WHY?
YES. PLEASE TELL ME HOW THIS IS OK.
YES.
YES.
PLEASE TELL.
YES.
BECAUSE IT DIDN'T HAPPEN.
YOU HAD AN ENJOYABLE TOUR.
YOU LEARNED A LOT.

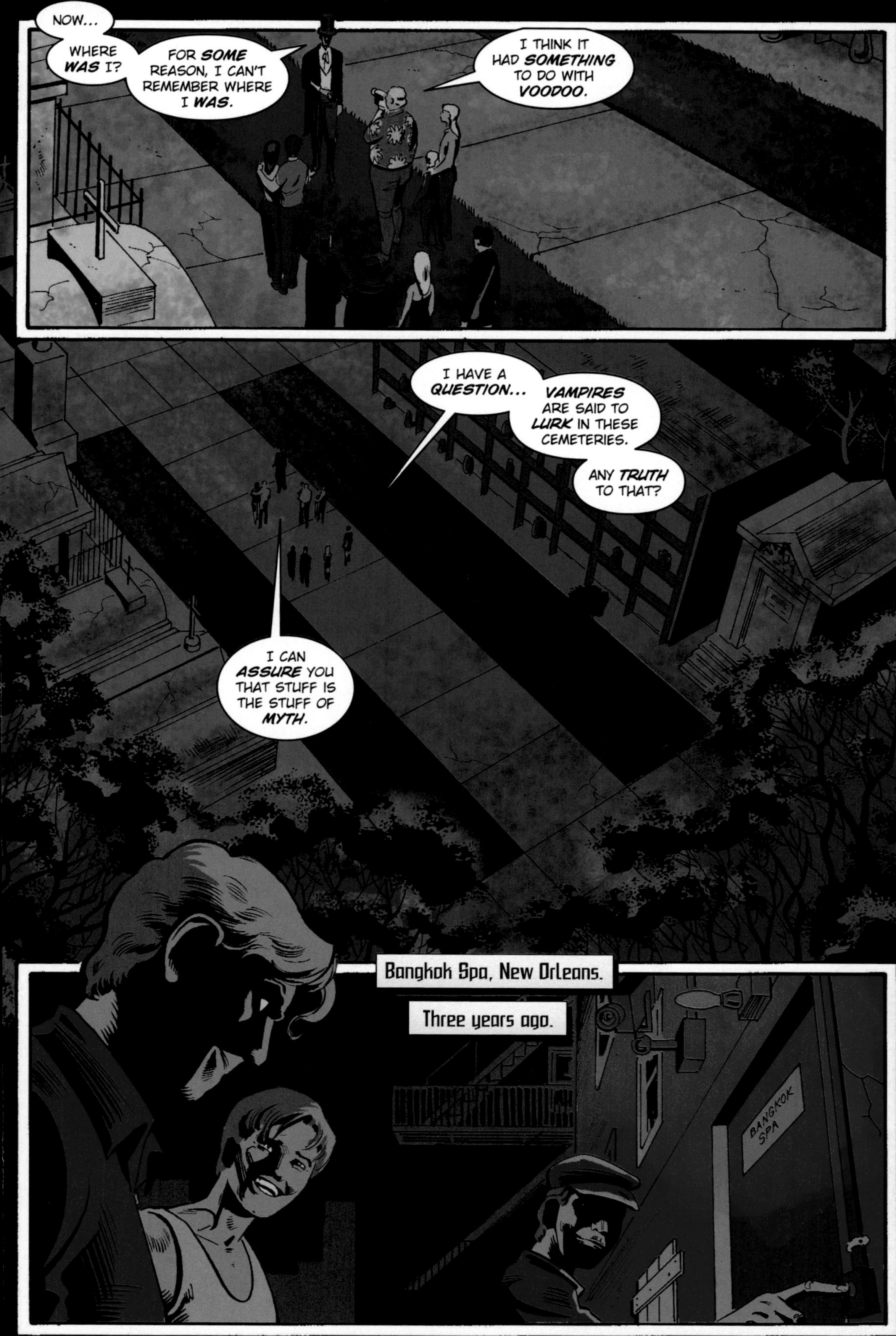
NOW...
WHERE WAS I?
FOR SOME REASON, I CAN'T REMEMBER WHERE I WAS.
I THINK IT HAD SOMETHING TO DO WITH VOODOO.
I HAVE A QUESTION...
VAMPIRES ARE SAID TO LURK IN THESE CEMETERIES.
ANY TRUTH TO THAT?
I CAN ASSURE YOU THAT STUFF IS THE STUFF OF MYTH.
Bangkok Spa, New Orleans.
Three years ago.
BANGKOK SPA

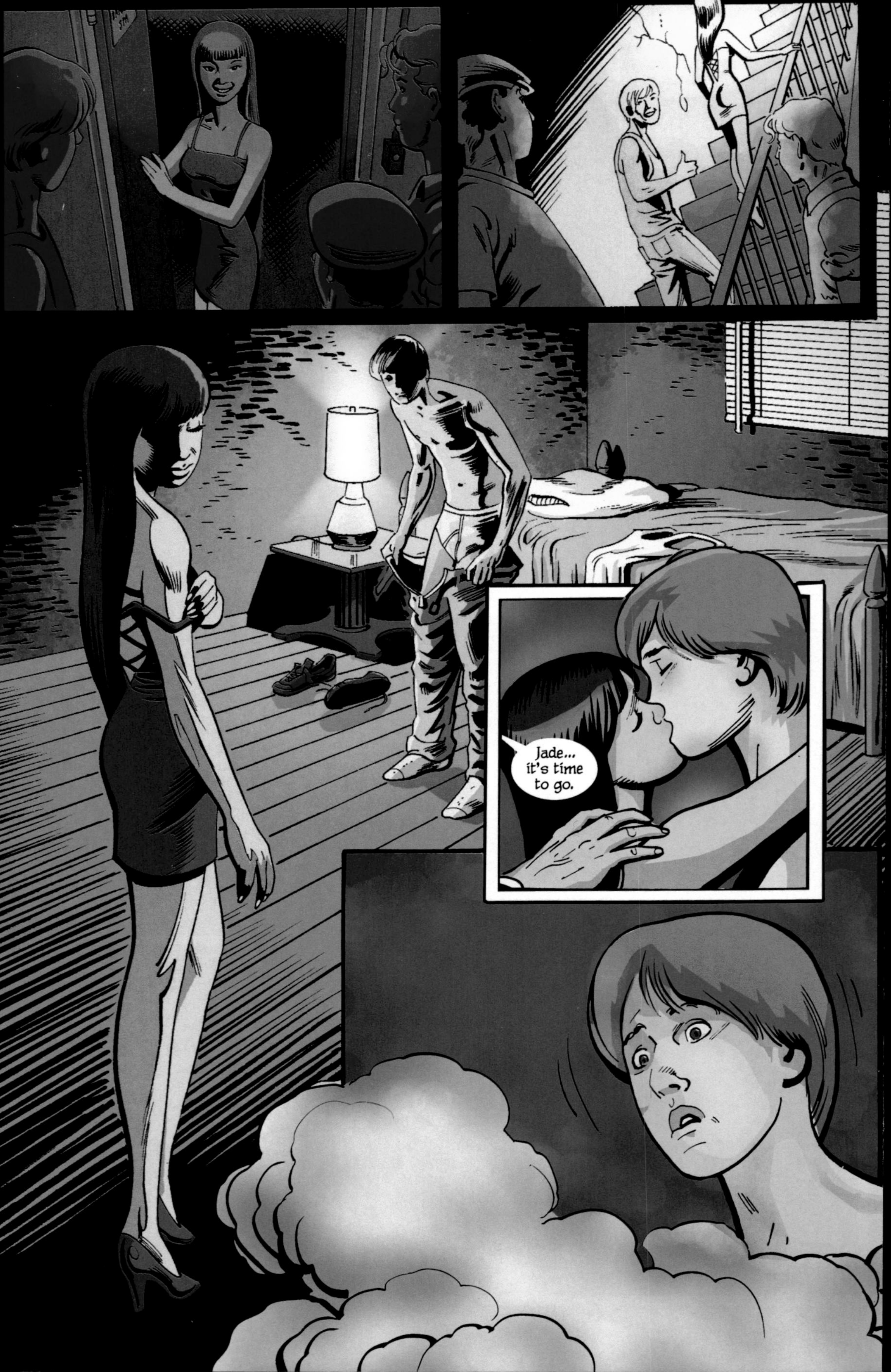
Jade... it's time to go.

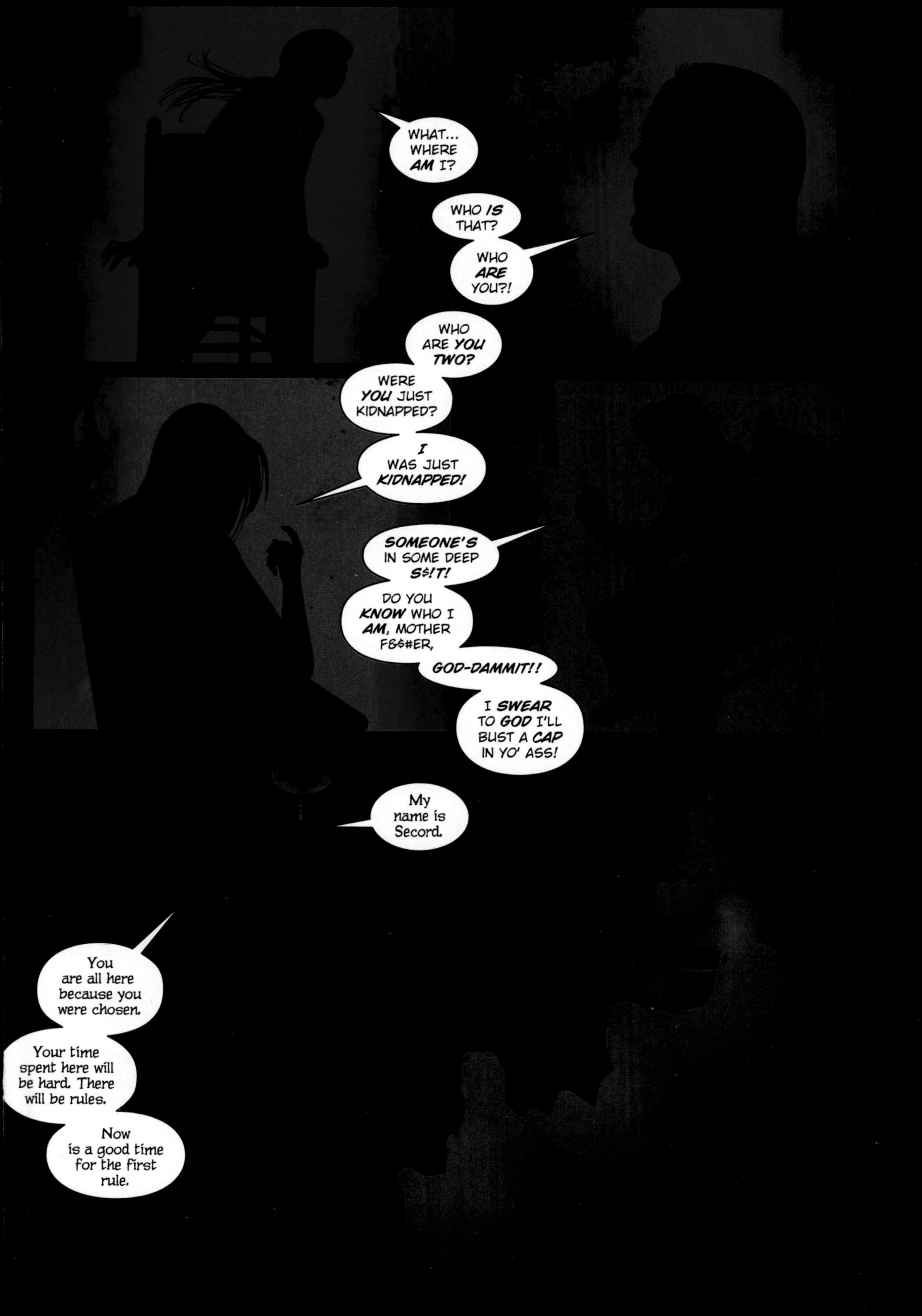
WHAT... WHERE AM I?
WHO IS THAT?
WHO ARE YOU?!
WHO ARE YOU TWO?
WERE YOU JUST KIDNAPPED?
I WAS JUST KIDNAPPED!
SOMEONE'S IN SOME DEEP S$!T!
DO YOU KNOW WHO I AM, MOTHER F&$#ER,
GOD-DAMMIT!!
I SWEAR TO GOD I'LL BUST A CAP IN YO' ASS!
My name is Secord.
You are all here because you were chosen.
Your time spent here will be hard. There will be rules.
Now is a good time for the first rule.

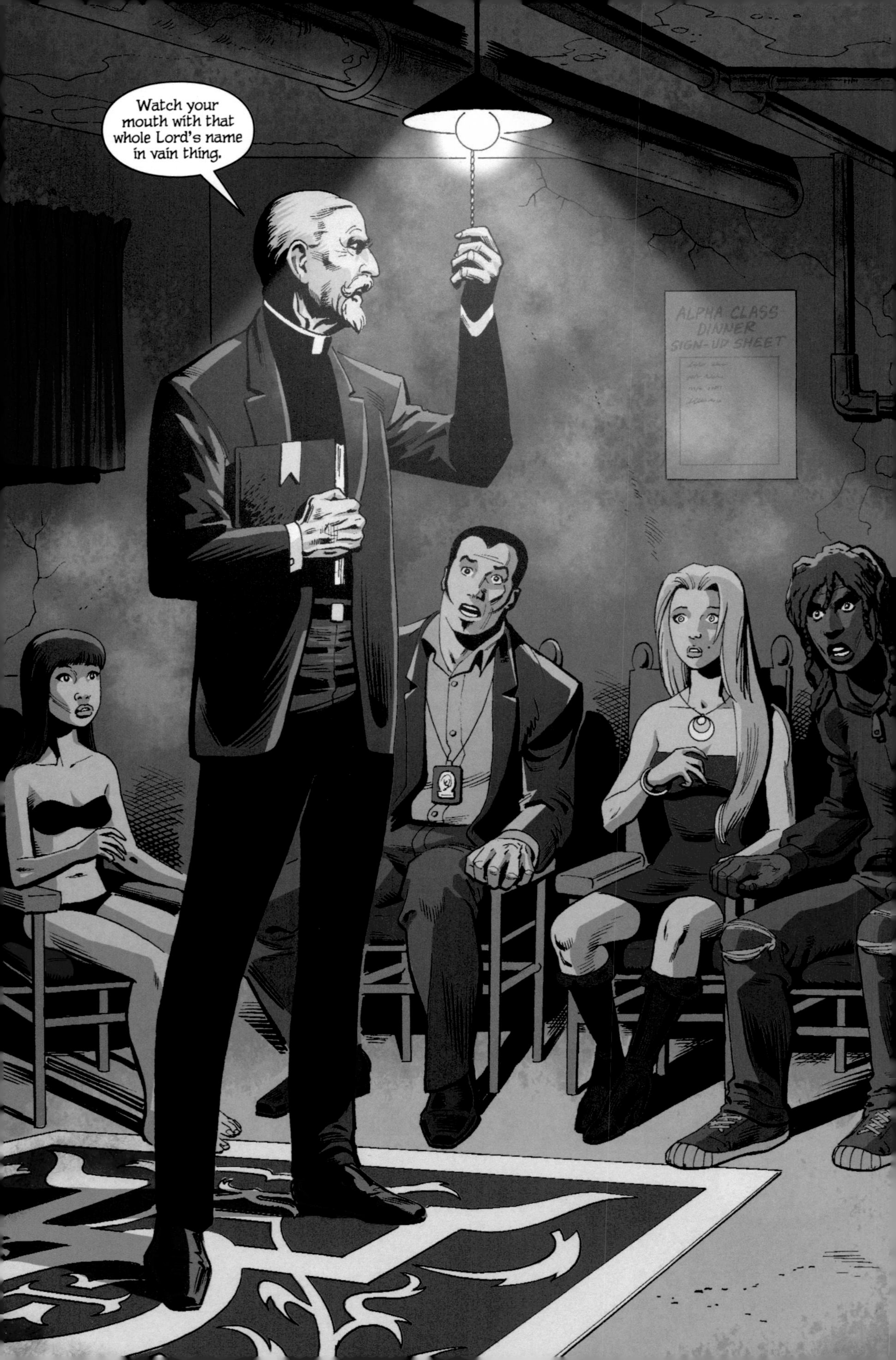
Watch your mouth with that whole Lord's name in vain thing.
ALPHA CLASS DINNER SIGN-UP SHEET

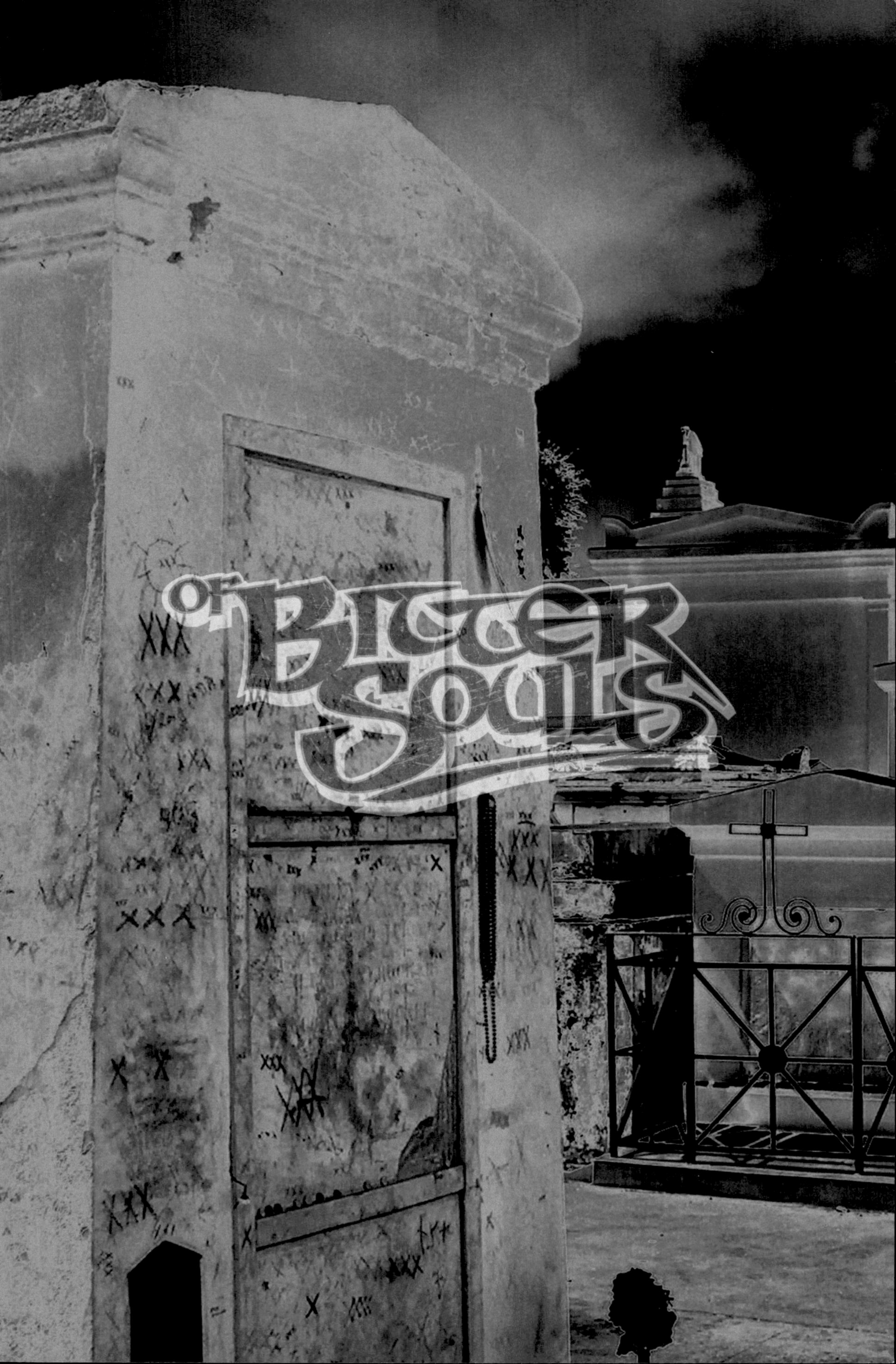
Of Bitter Souls

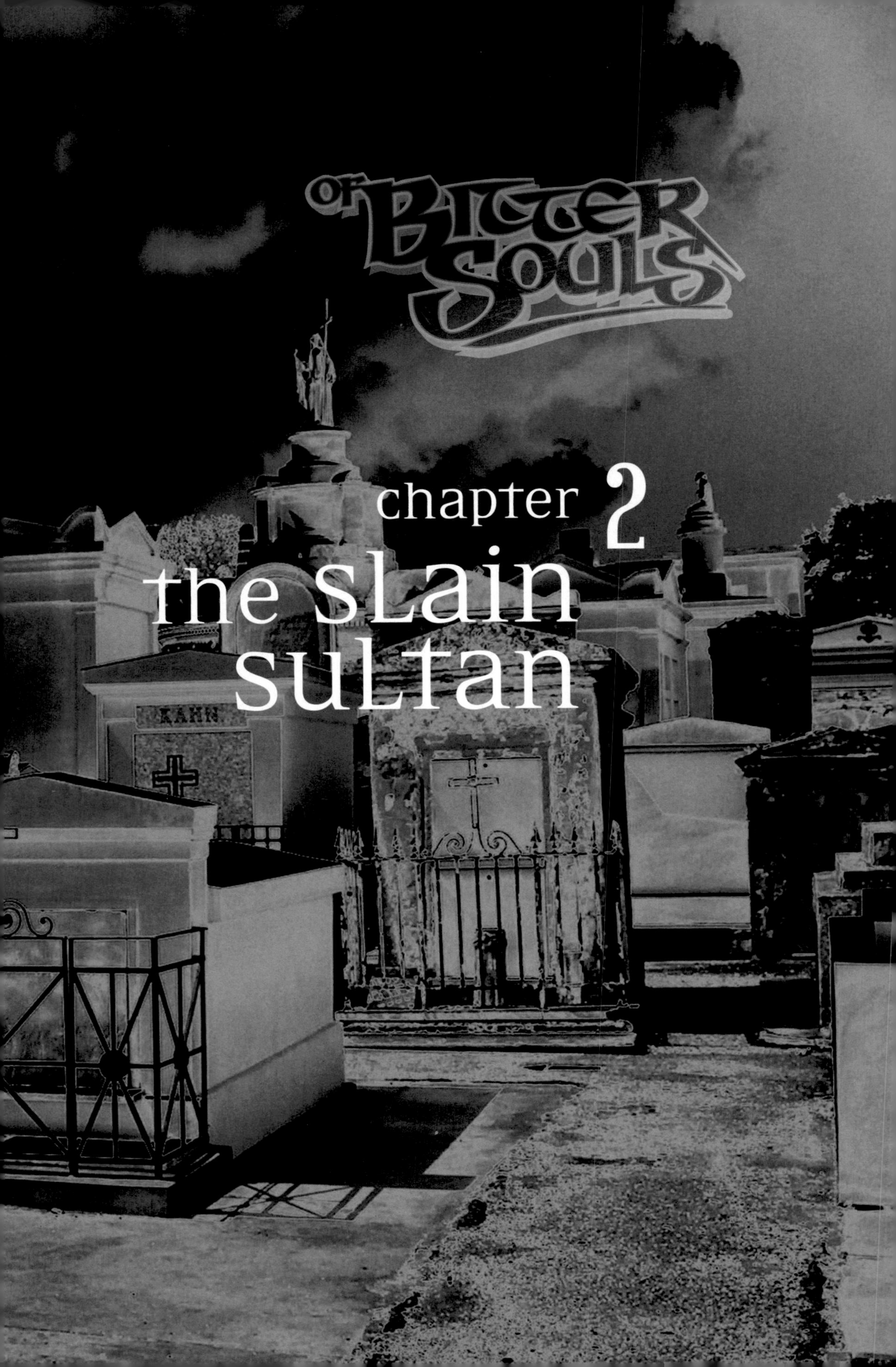
KAHN

Of Bitter Souls

chapter 2
the slain sultan

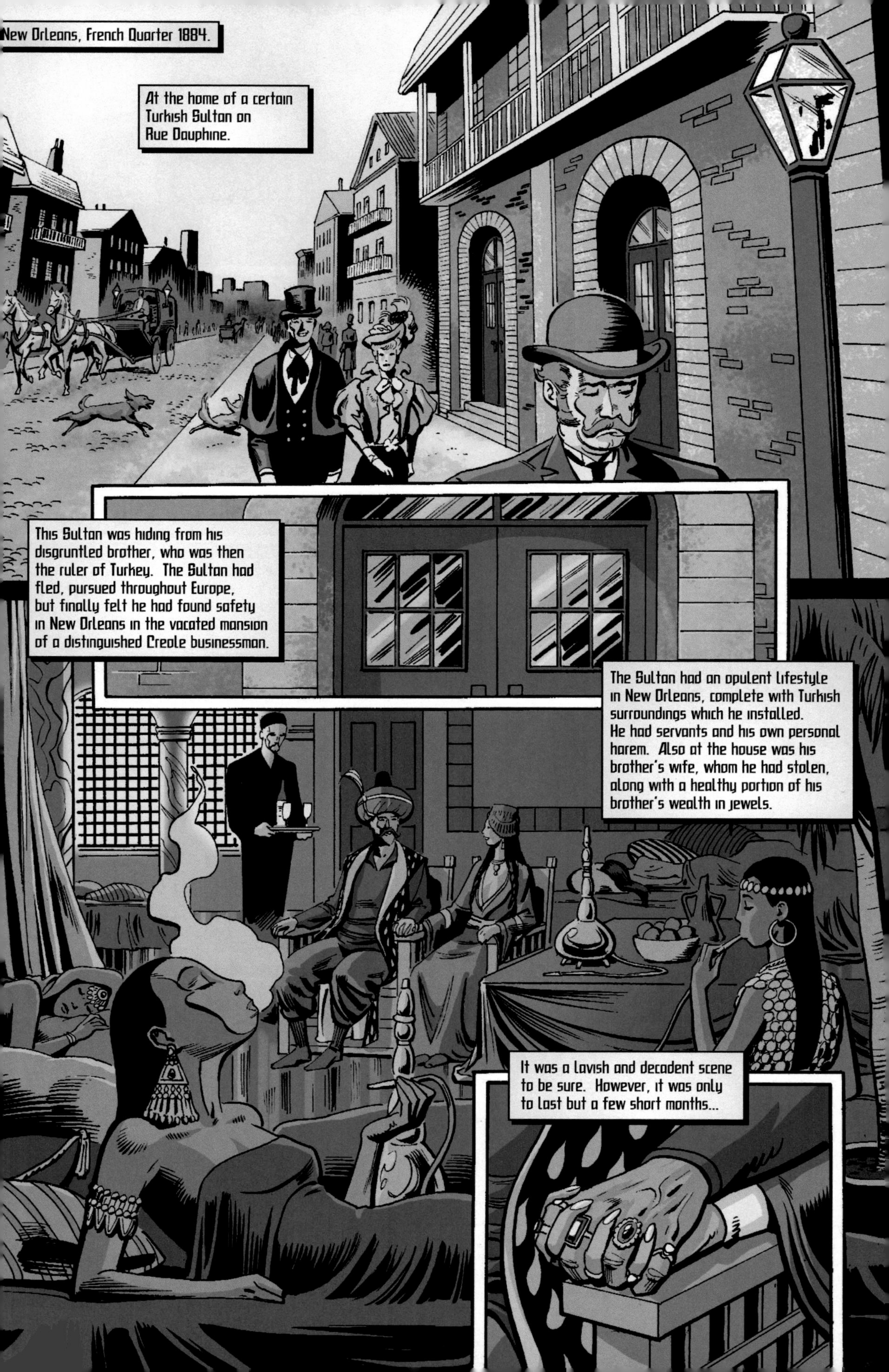
New Orleans, French Quarter 1884.
At the home of a certain Turkish Sultan on Rue Dauphine.
This Sultan was hiding from his disgruntled brother, who was then the ruler of Turkey. The Sultan had fled, pursued throughout Europe, but finally felt he had found safety in New Orleans in the vacated mansion of a distinguished Creole businessman.
The Sultan had an opulent lifestyle in New Orleans, complete with Turkish surroundings which he installed. He had servants and his own personal harem. Also at the house was his brother's wife, whom he had stolen, along with a healthy portion of his brother's wealth in jewels.
It was a lavish and decadent scene to be sure. However, it was only to last but a few short months...

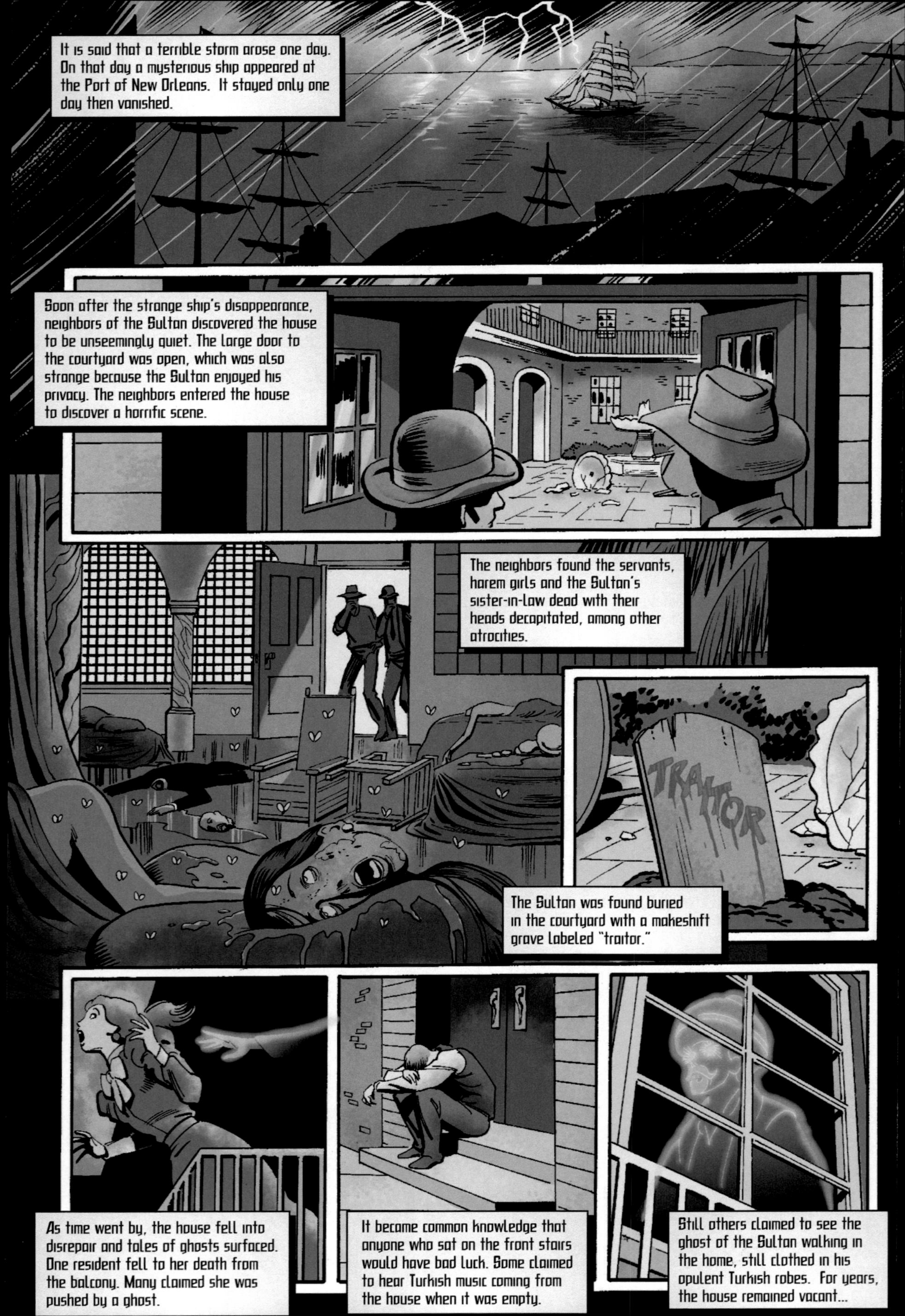
It is said that a terrible storm arose one day. On that day a mysterious ship appeared at the Port of New Orleans. It stayed only one day then vanished.
Soon after the strange ship's disappearance, neighbors of the Sultan discovered the house to be unseemingly quiet. The large door to the courtyard was open, which was also strange because the Sultan enjoyed his privacy. The neighbors entered the house to discover a horrific scene.
The neighbors found the servants, harem girls and the Sultan's sister-in-law dead with their heads decapitated, among other atrocities.
TRAITOR
The Sultan was found buried in the courtyard with a makeshift grave labeled "traitor."
As time went by, the house fell into disrepair and tales of ghosts surfaced. One resident fell to her death from the balcony. Many claimed she was pushed by a ghost.
It became common knowledge that anyone who sat on the front stairs would have bad luck. Some claimed to hear Turkish music coming from the house when it was empty.
Still others claimed to see the ghost of the Sultan walking in the home, still clothed in his opulent Turkish robes. For years, the house remained vacant...

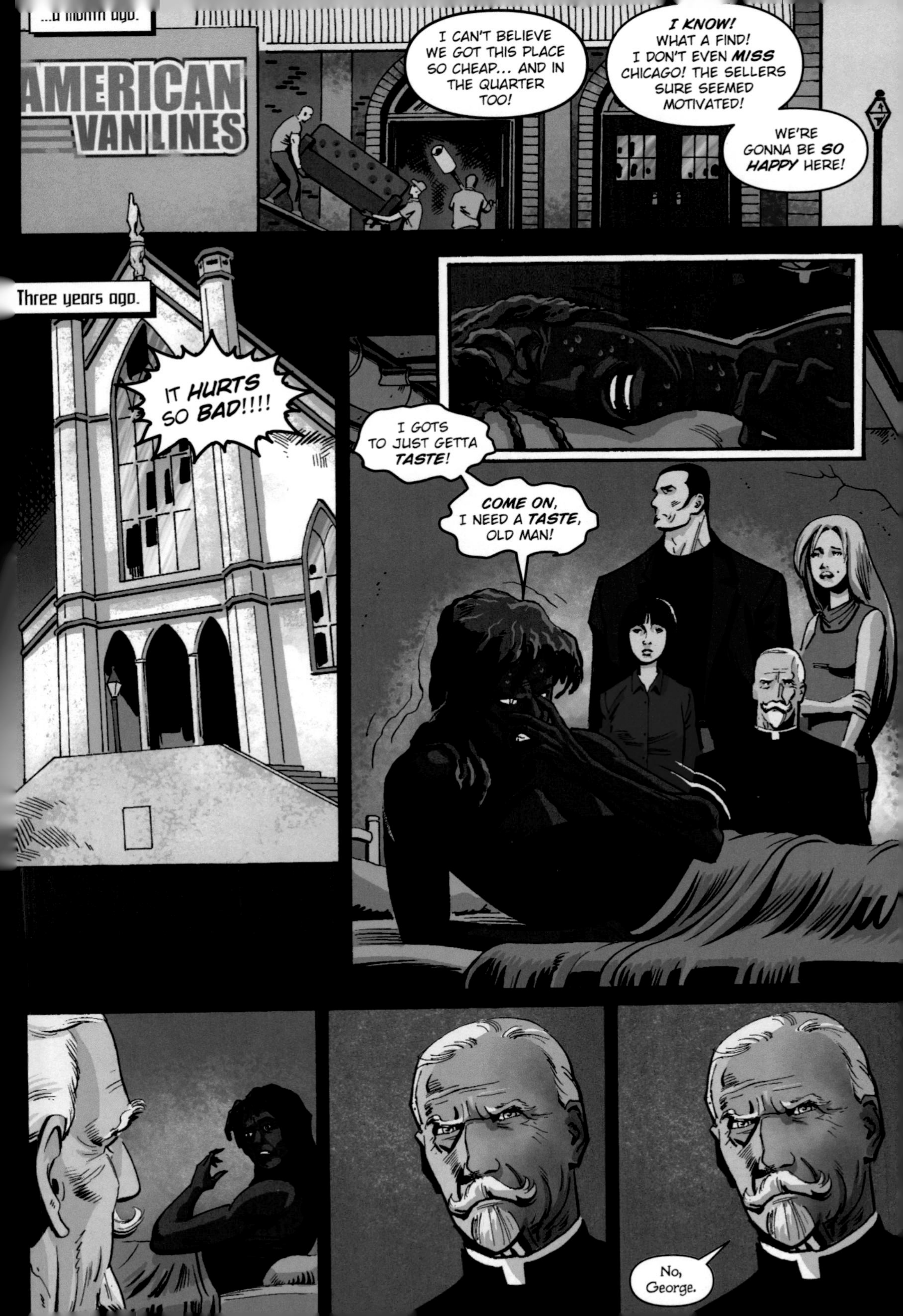

...a month ago.
AMERICAN VAN LINES
I CAN'T BELIEVE WE GOT THIS PLACE SO CHEAP... AND IN THE QUARTER TOO!
I KNOW! WHAT A FIND! I DON'T EVEN MISS CHICAGO! THE SELLERS SURE SEEMED MOTIVATED!
WE'RE GONNA BE SO HAPPY HERE!
Three years ago.
IT HURTS SO BAD!!!!
I GOTS TO JUST GETTA TASTE!
COME ON, I NEED A TASTE, OLD MAN!
No, George.

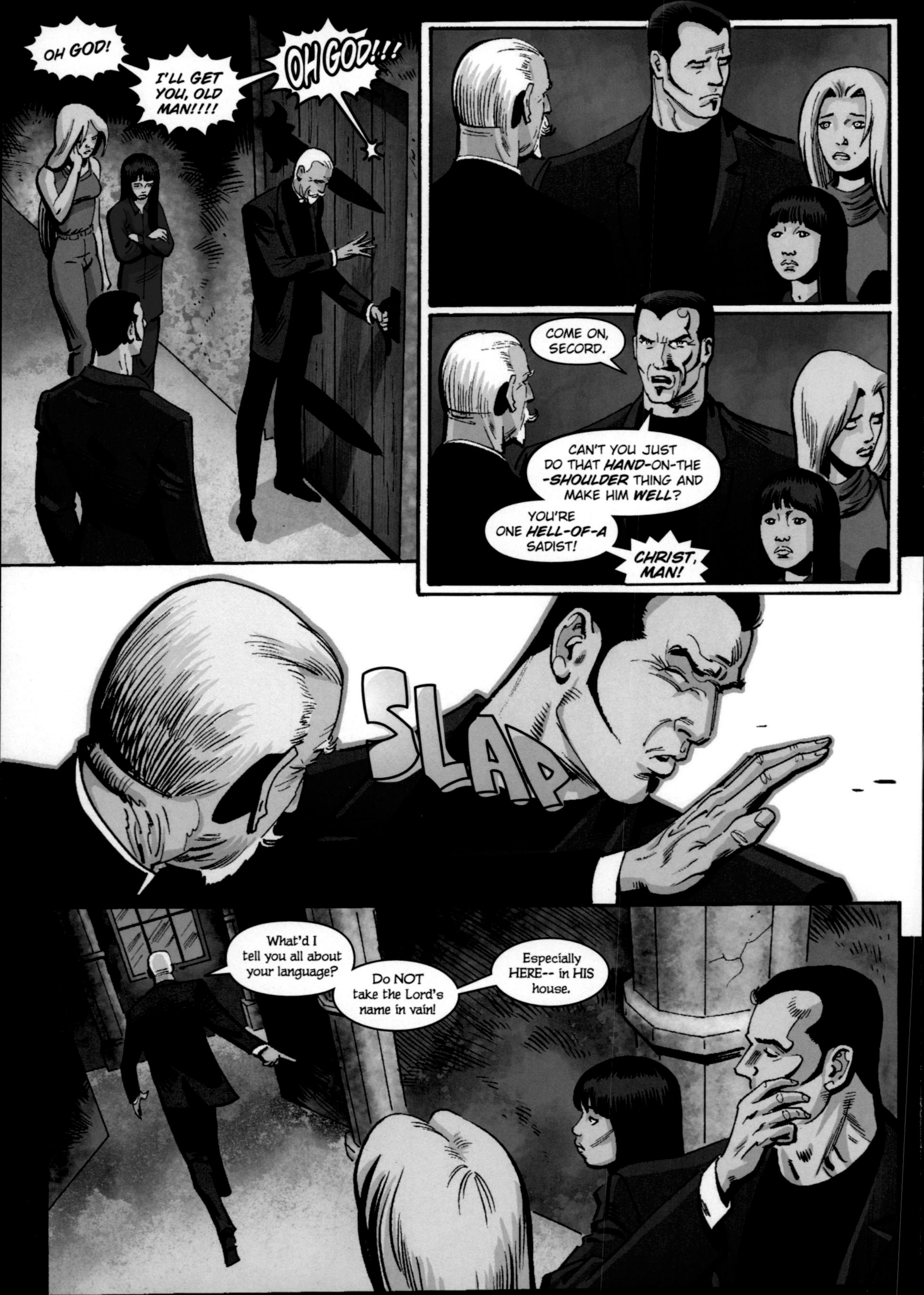
OH GOD!
I'LL GET YOU, OLD MAN!!!!
OH GOD!!!
COME ON, SECORD.
CAN'T YOU JUST DO THAT HAND-ON-THE -SHOULDER THING AND MAKE HIM WELL?
YOU'RE ONE HELL-OF-A SADIST!
CHRIST, MAN!
SLAP
What'd I tell you all about your language?
Do NOT take the Lord's name in vain!
Especially HERE-- in HIS house.

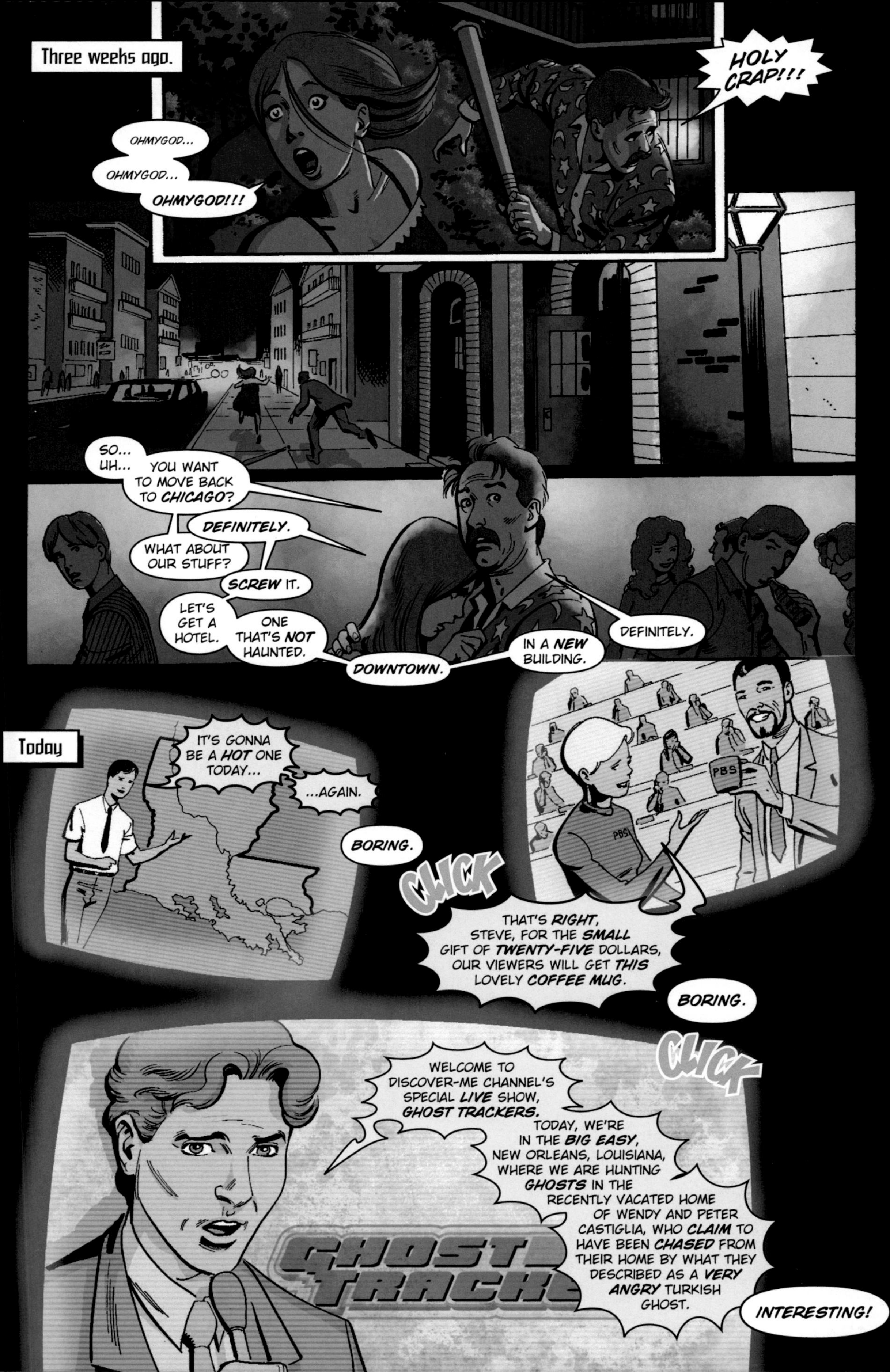
Three weeks ago.
HOLY CRAP!!!
OHMYGOD...
OHMYGOD...
OHMYGOD!!!
SO... UH... YOU WANT TO MOVE BACK TO CHICAGO?
DEFINITELY.
WHAT ABOUT OUR STUFF?
SCREW IT.
LET'S GET A HOTEL.
ONE THAT'S NOT HAUNTED.
DOWNTOWN.
IN A NEW BUILDING.
DEFINITELY.
Today
IT'S GONNA BE A HOT ONE TODAY...
...AGAIN.
BORING.
CLICK
PBS
THAT'S RIGHT, STEVE, FOR THE SMALL GIFT OF TWENTY-FIVE DOLLARS, OUR VIEWERS WILL GET THIS LOVELY COFFEE MUG.
BORING.
CLICK
WELCOME TO DISCOVER-ME CHANNEL'S SPECIAL LIVE SHOW, GHOST TRACKERS.
TODAY, WE'RE IN THE BIG EASY, NEW ORLEANS, LOUISIANA, WHERE WE ARE HUNTING GHOSTS IN THE RECENTLY VACATED HOME OF WENDY AND PETER CASTIGLIA, WHO CLAIM TO HAVE BEEN CHASED FROM THEIR HOME BY WHAT THEY DESCRIBED AS A VERY ANGRY TURKISH GHOST.
INTERESTING!

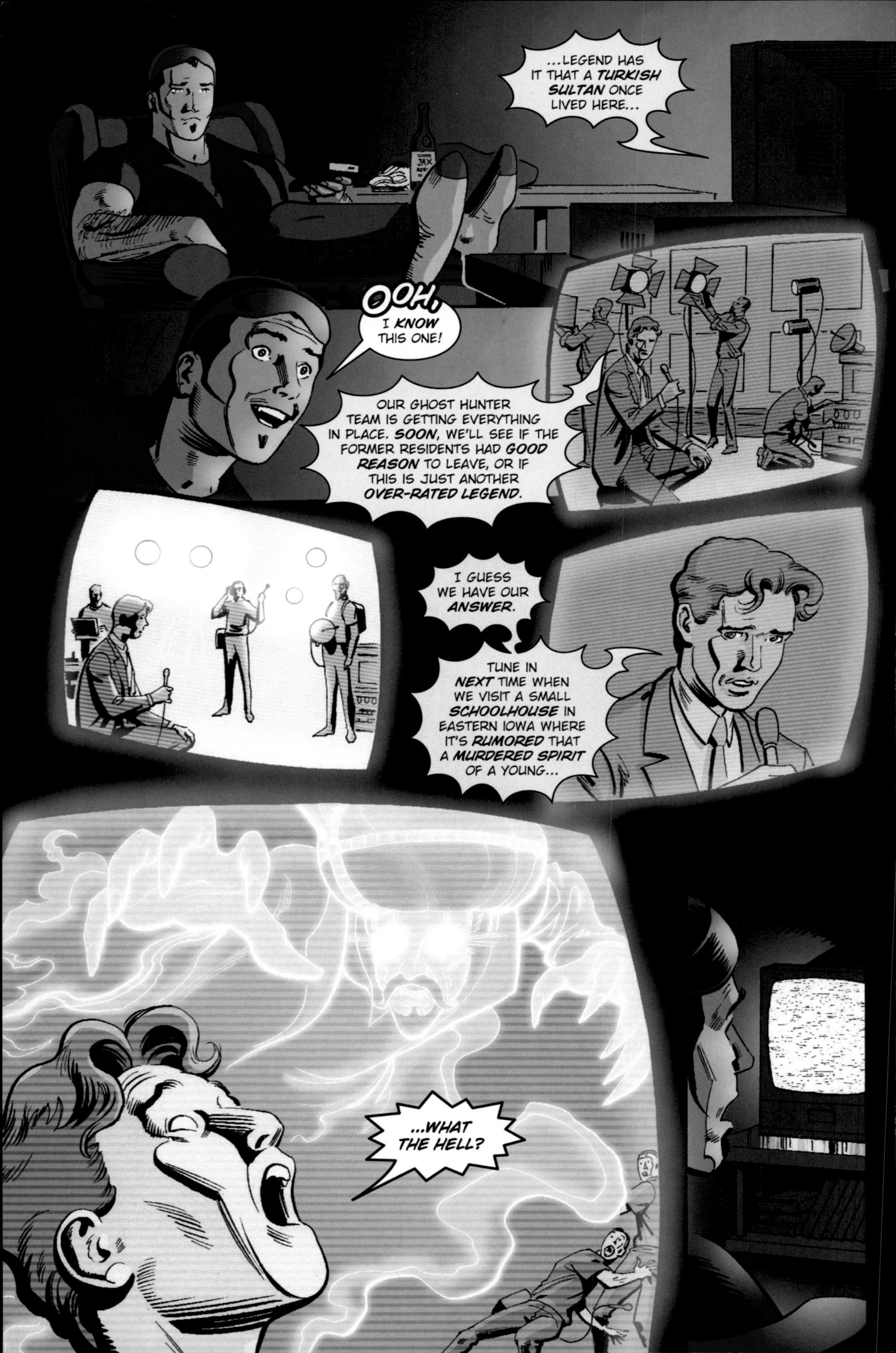
...LEGEND HAS IT THAT A TURKISH SULTAN ONCE LIVED HERE...
OOH, I KNOW THIS ONE!
OUR GHOST HUNTER TEAM IS GETTING EVERYTHING IN PLACE. SOON, WE'LL SEE IF THE FORMER RESIDENTS HAD GOOD REASON TO LEAVE, OR IF THIS IS JUST ANOTHER OVER-RATED LEGEND.
I GUESS WE HAVE OUR ANSWER.
TUNE IN NEXT TIME WHEN WE VISIT A SMALL SCHOOLHOUSE IN EASTERN IOWA WHERE IT'S RUMORED THAT A MURDERED SPIRIT OF A YOUNG...
...WHAT THE HELL?

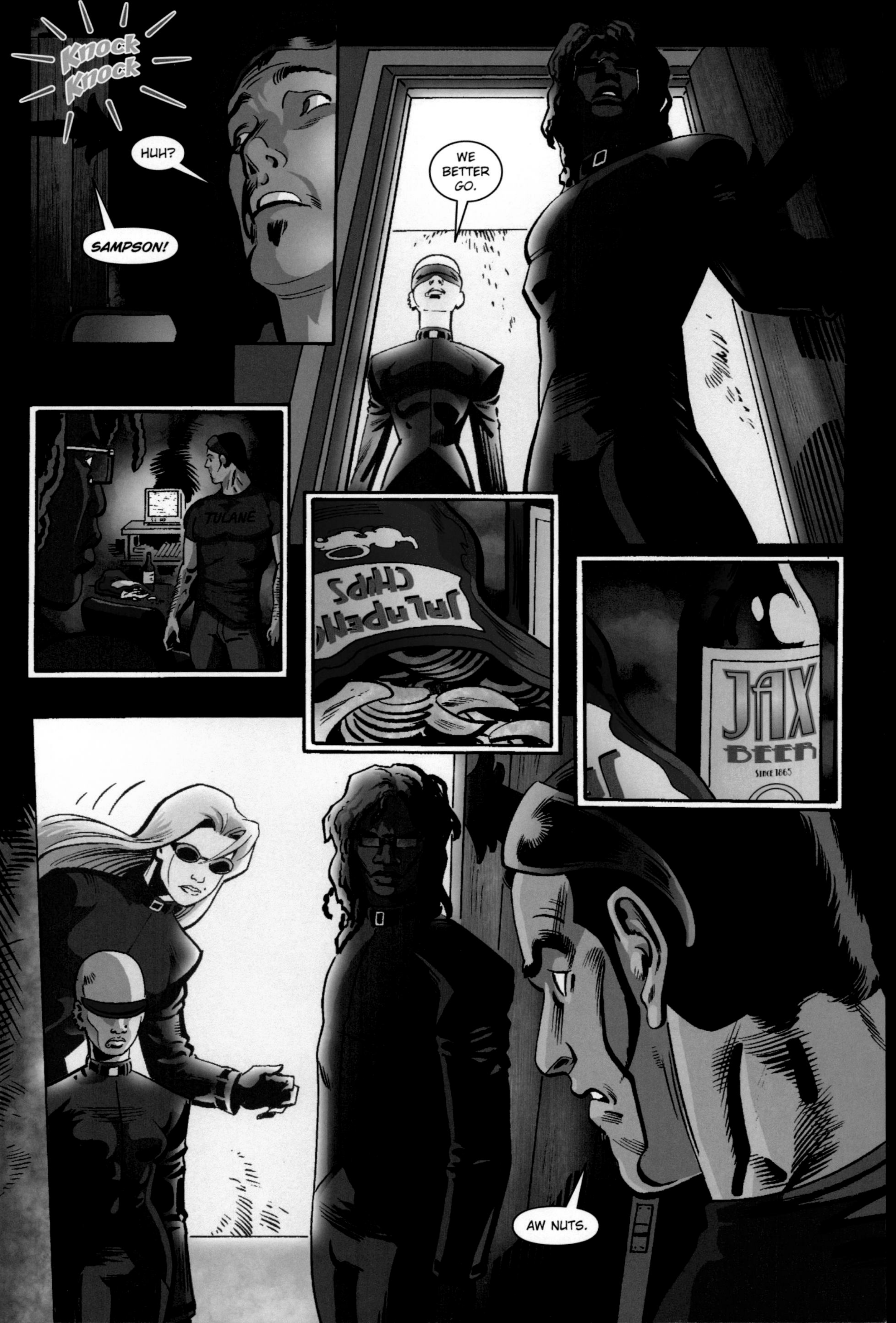
Knock Knock
HUH?
SAMPSON!
WE BETTER GO.
TULANE
JALAPENO CHIPS
JAX BEER SINCE 1865
AW NUTS.

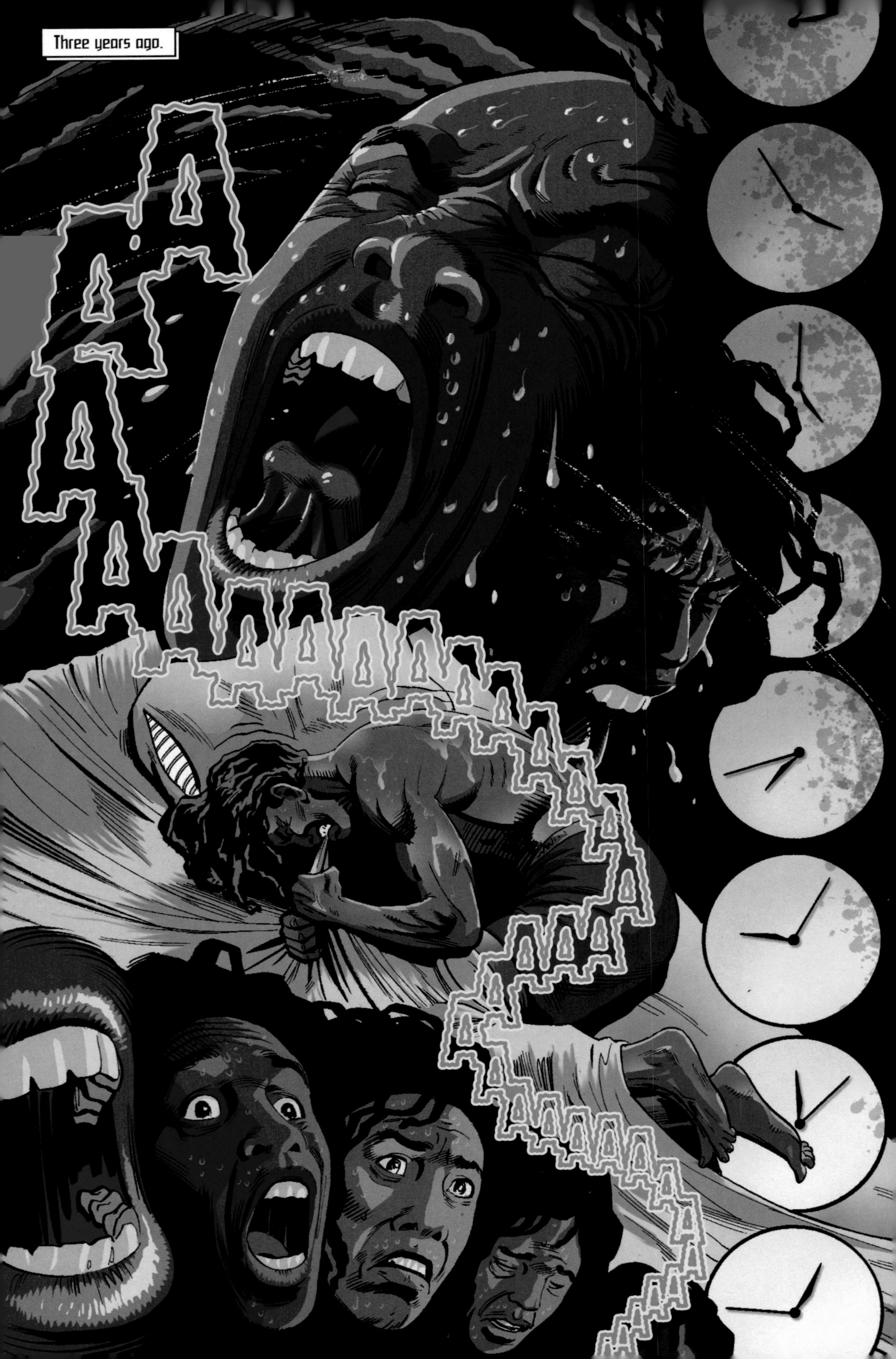

Three years ago.
AAAAAAAAAAAAAAAAAAAAAAAAAAAAAA

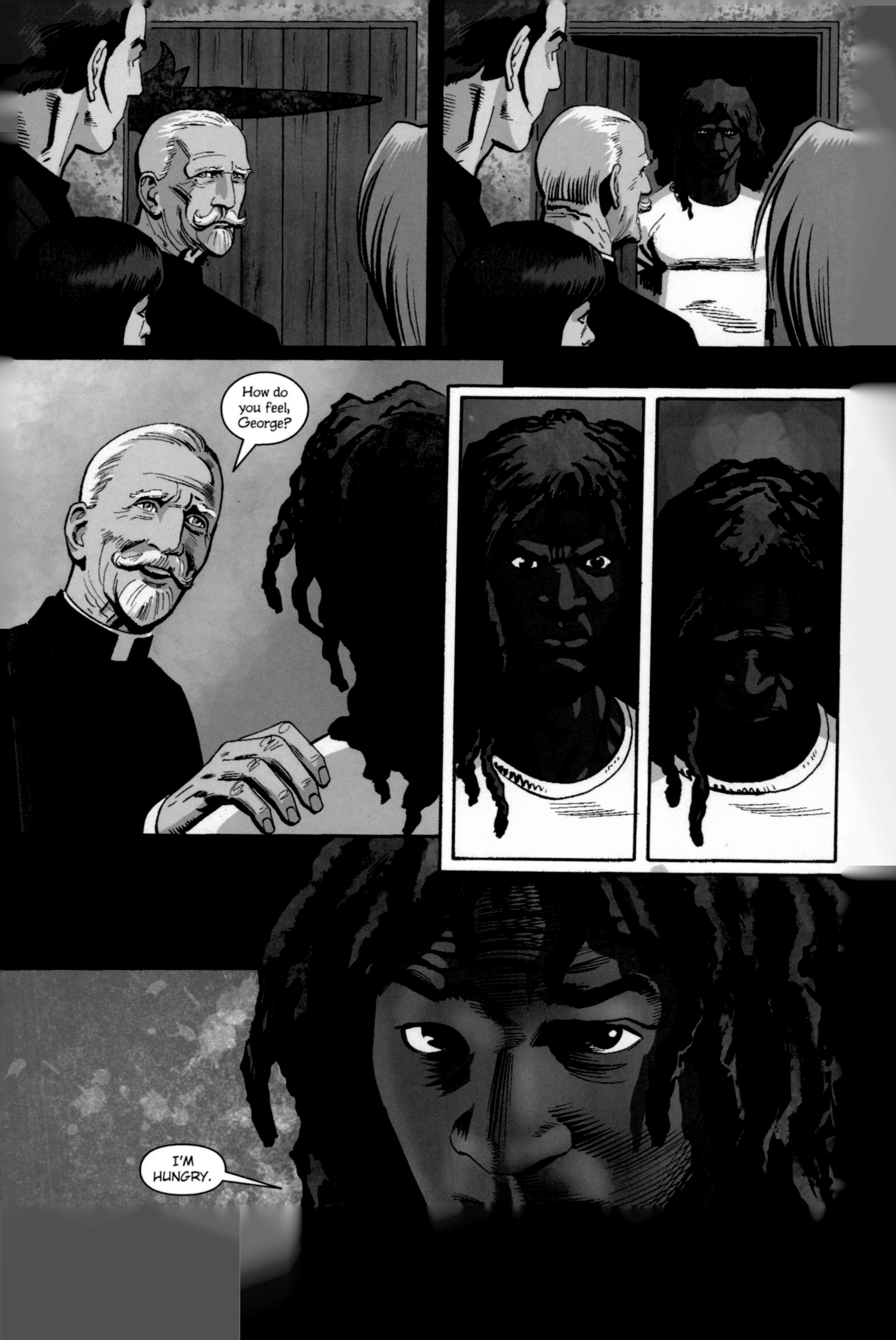
How do you feel, George?
I'M HUNGRY.

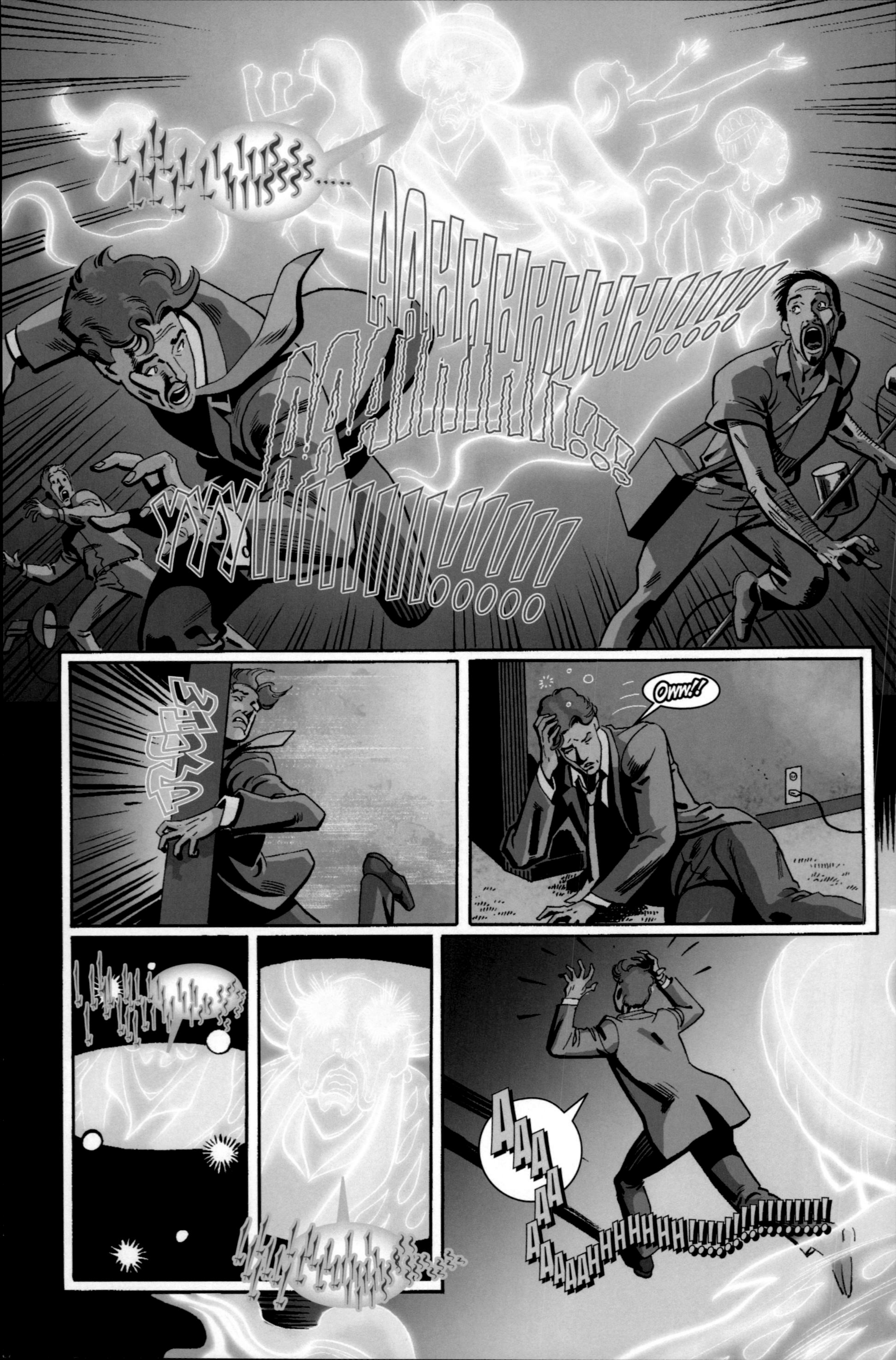
Oww!!
AAAAAAAHHHHHH!!!!!!!!!!!!!!!!

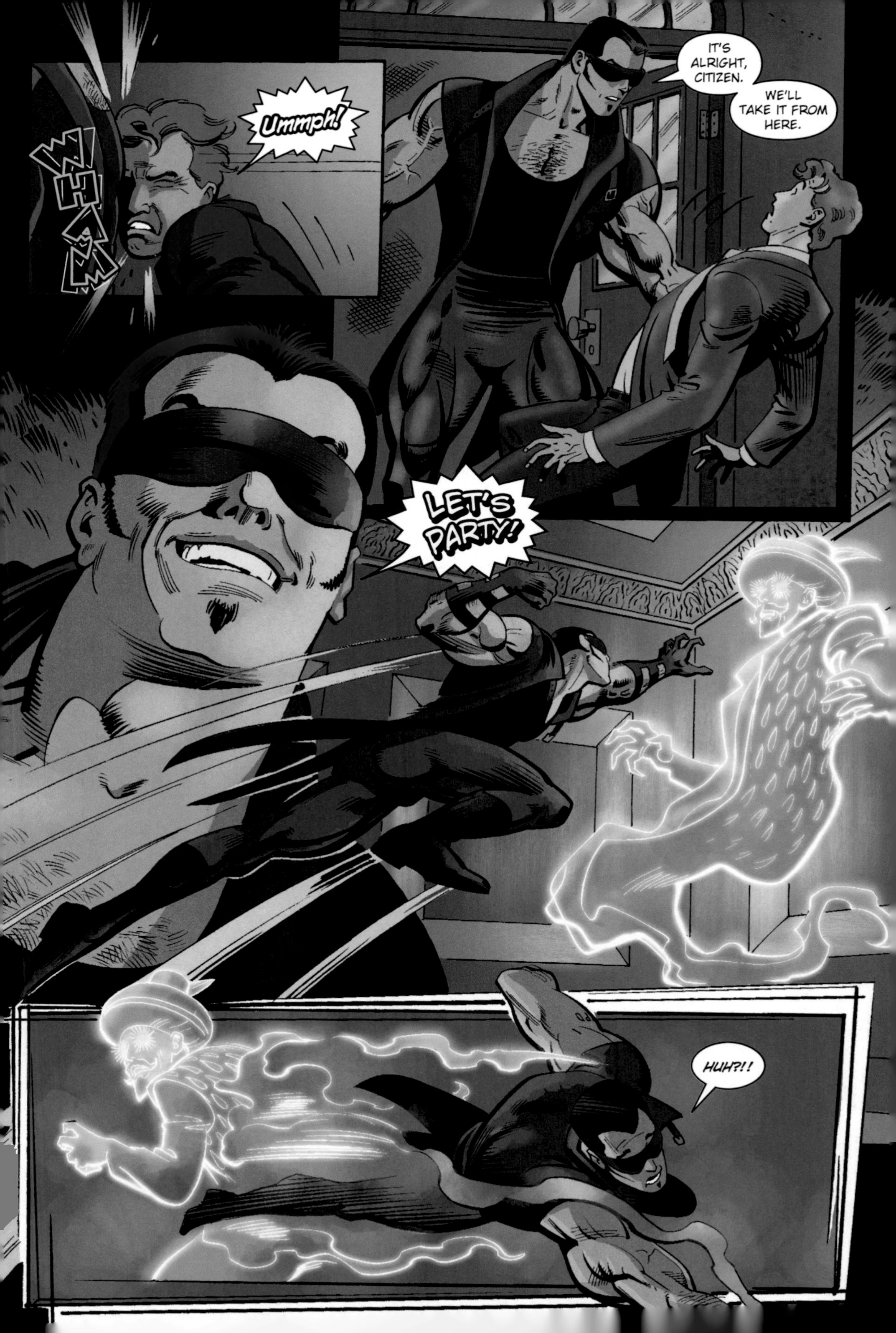
WHAM
Ummph!
IT'S ALRIGHT, CITIZEN.
WE'LL TAKE IT FROM HERE.
LET'S PARTY!
HUH?!!

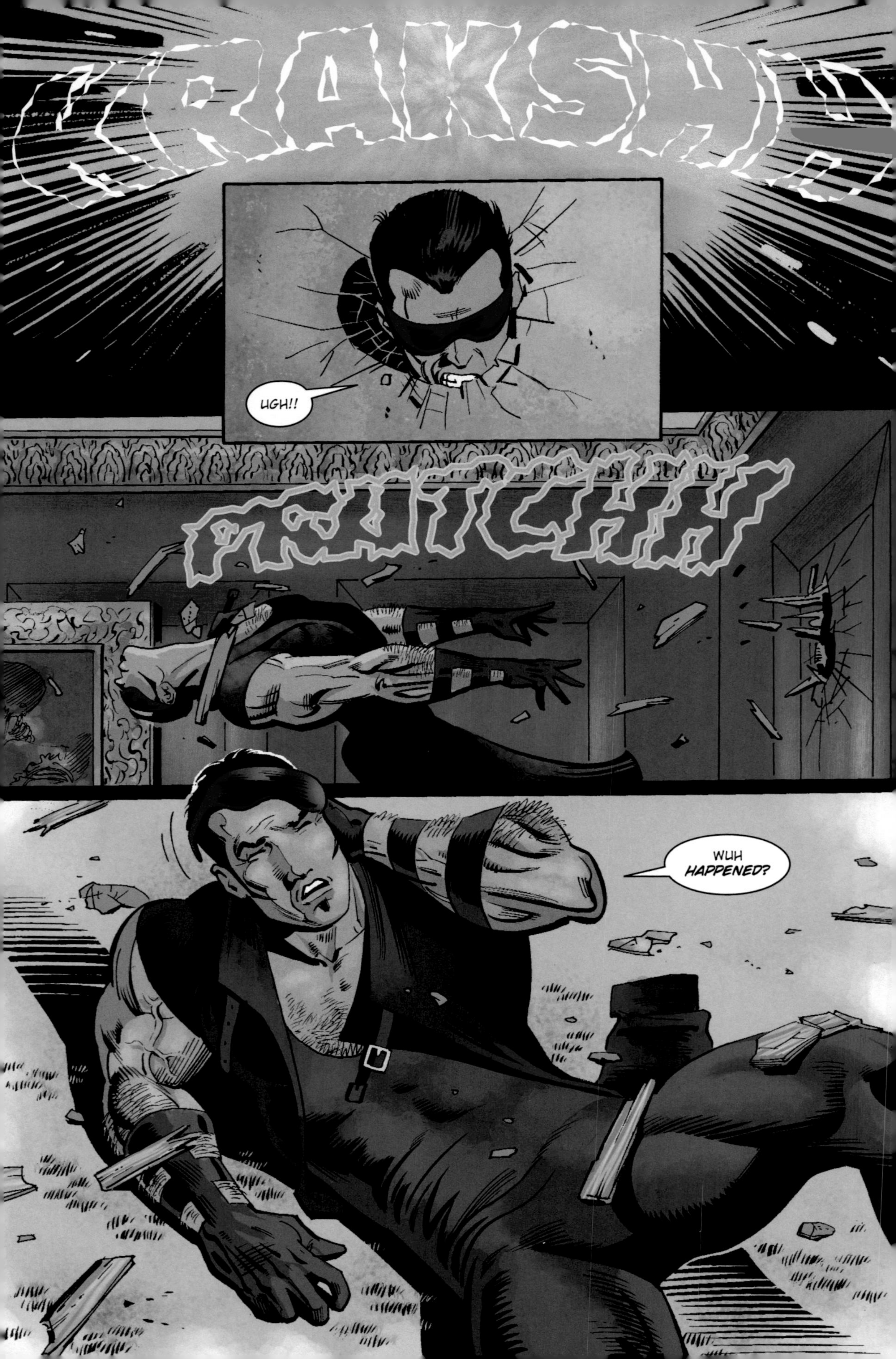
UGH!!
WUH HAPPENED?

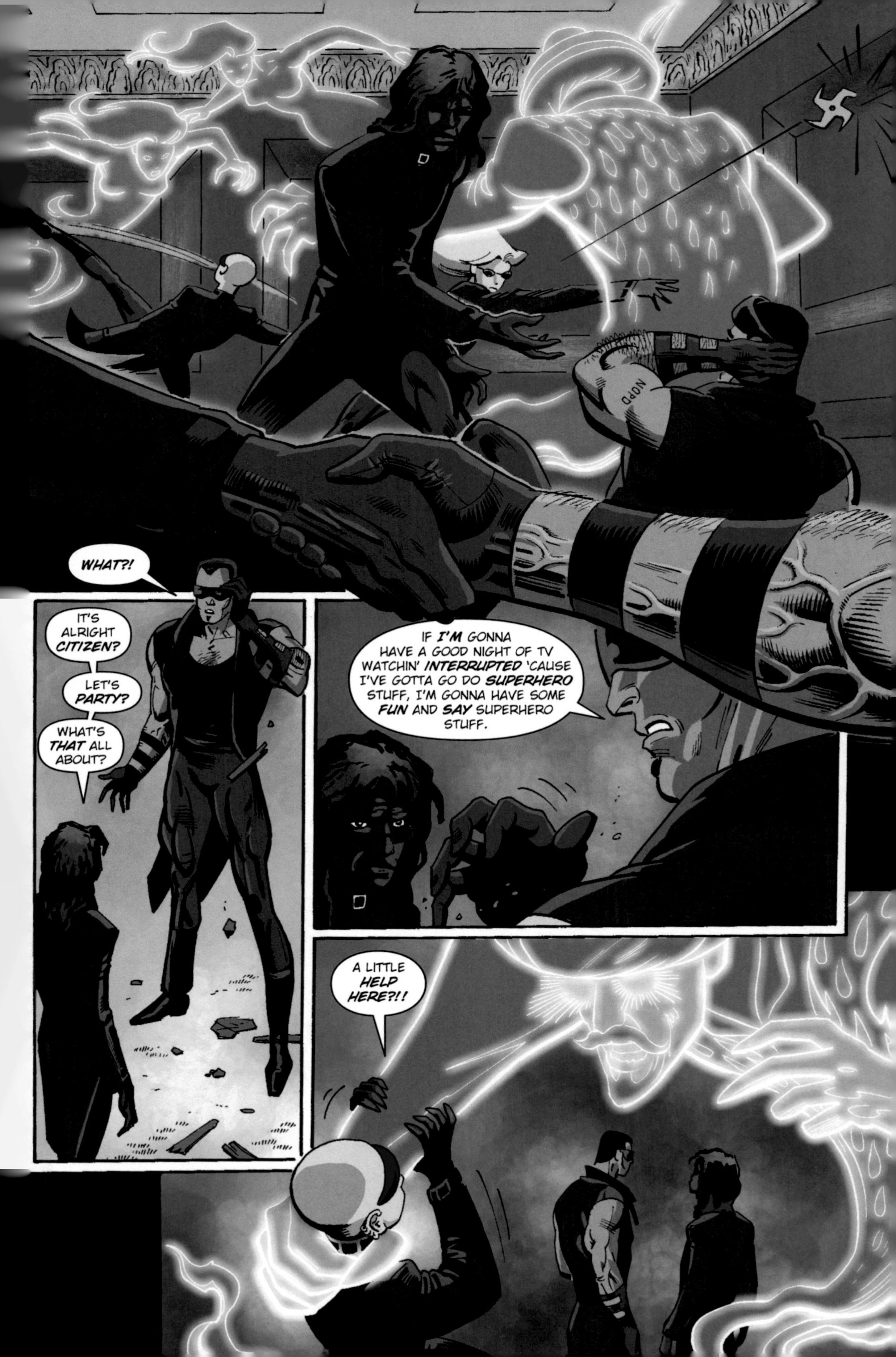
NOPD
WHAT?!
IT'S ALRIGHT *CITIZEN?*
LET'S *PARTY?*
WHAT'S *THAT* ALL ABOUT?
IF *I'M* GONNA HAVE A GOOD NIGHT OF TV WATCHIN' *INTERRUPTED* 'CAUSE I'VE GOTTA GO DO *SUPERHERO* STUFF, I'M GONNA HAVE SOME *FUN* AND *SAY* SUPERHERO STUFF.
A LITTLE *HELP HERE?!!*

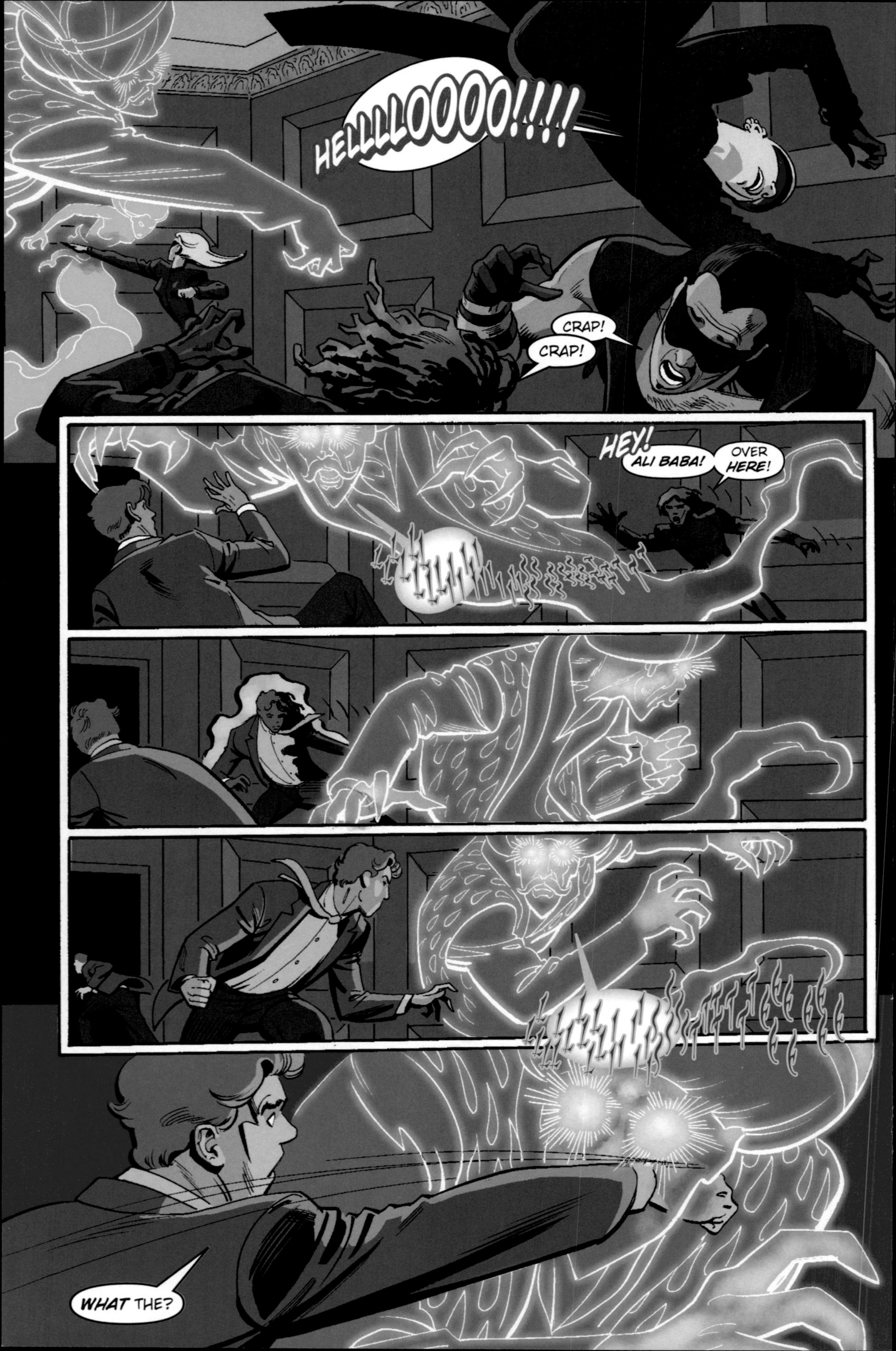
HELLLLOOOO!!!!!
CRAP!
CRAP!
HEY!
ALI BABA!
OVER HERE!
WHAT THE?

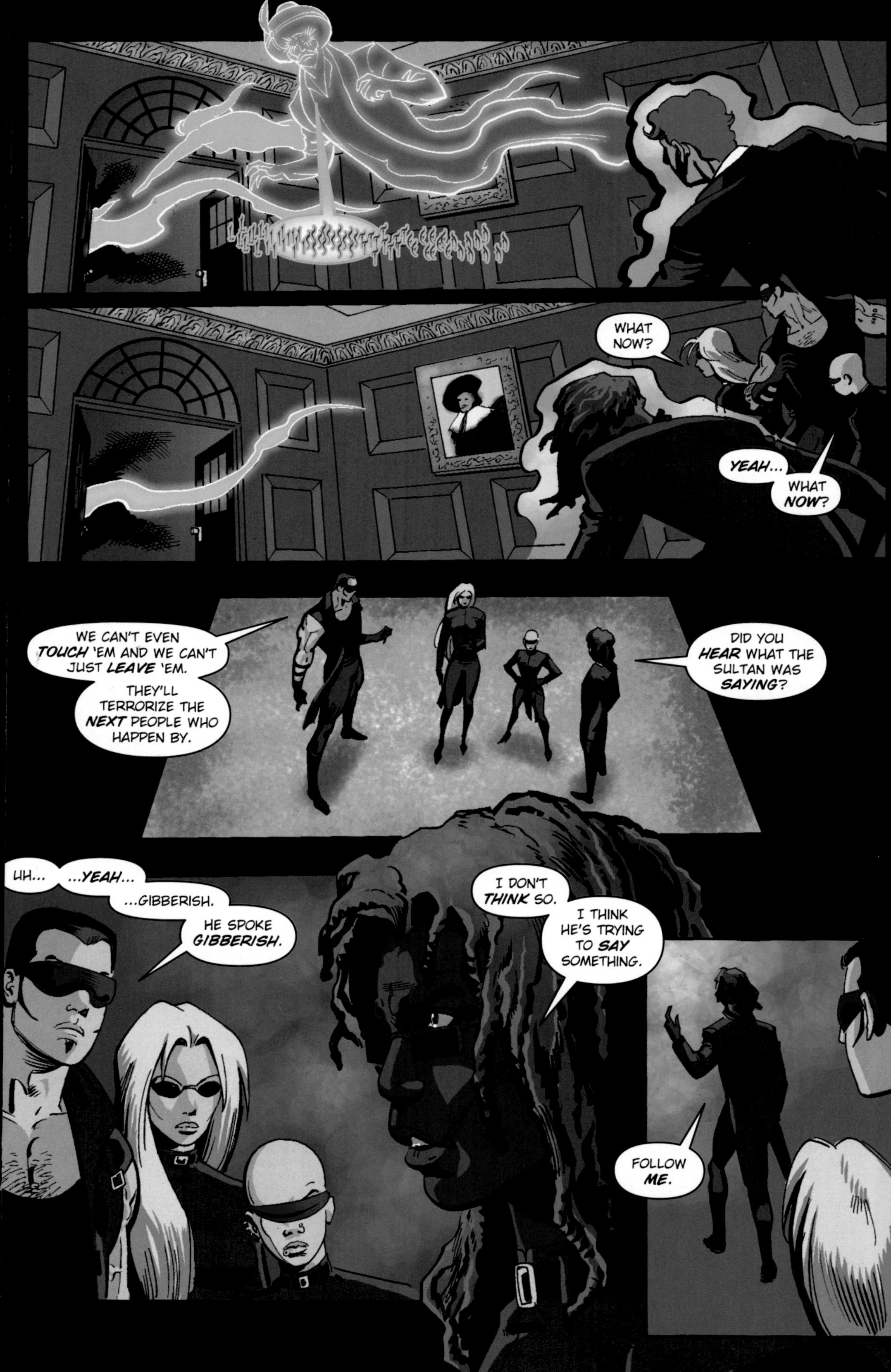
WHAT NOW?
YEAH... WHAT NOW?
WE CAN'T EVEN TOUCH 'EM AND WE CAN'T JUST LEAVE 'EM.
THEY'LL TERRORIZE THE NEXT PEOPLE WHO HAPPEN BY.
DID YOU HEAR WHAT THE SULTAN WAS SAYING?
UH...
...YEAH...
...GIBBERISH.
HE SPOKE GIBBERISH.
I DON'T THINK SO.
I THINK HE'S TRYING TO SAY SOMETHING.
FOLLOW ME.

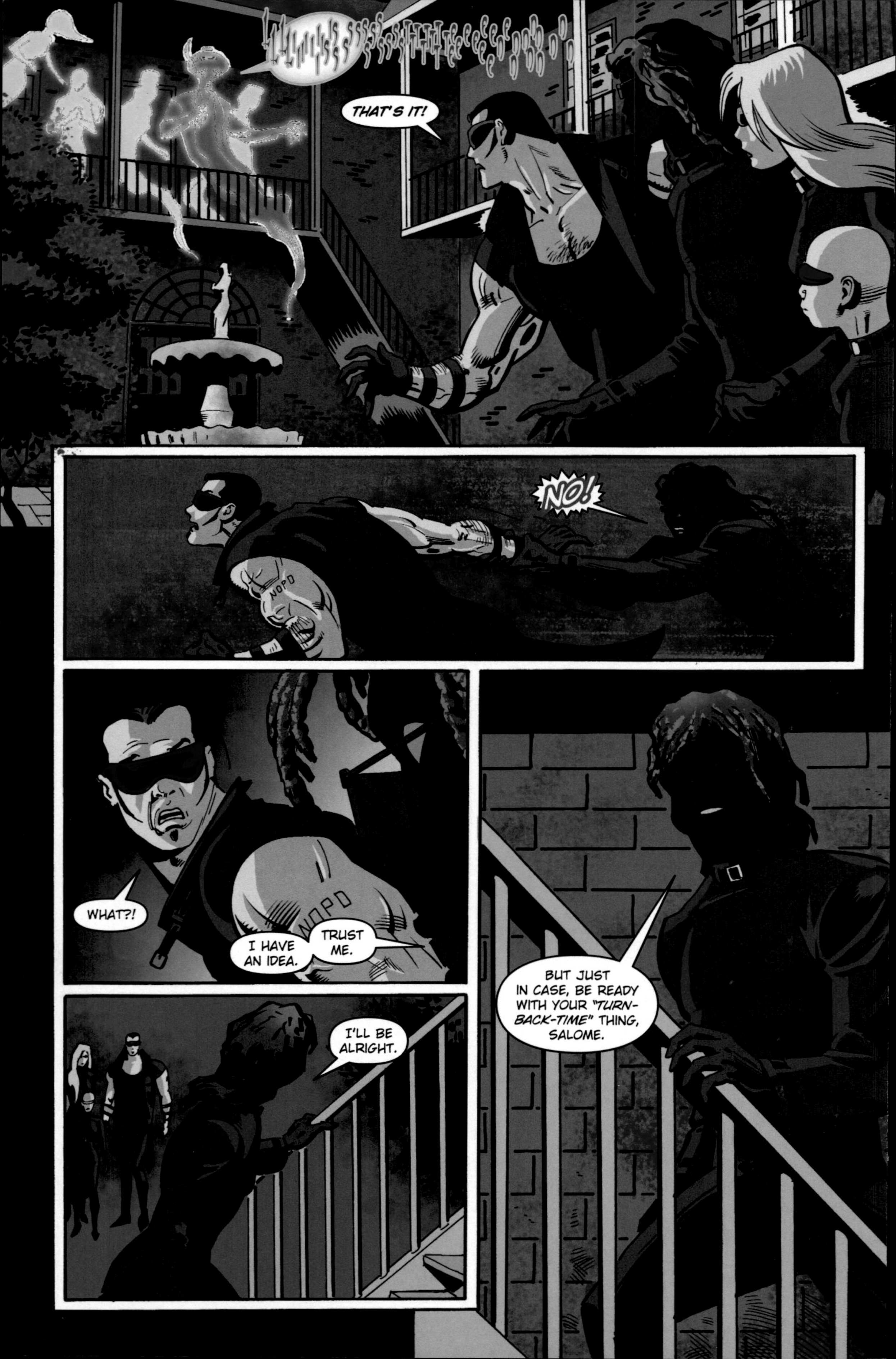
THAT'S IT!
NO!
WHAT?!
I HAVE AN IDEA.
TRUST ME.
BUT JUST IN CASE, BE READY WITH YOUR "TURN-BACK-TIME" THING, SALOME.
I'LL BE ALRIGHT.

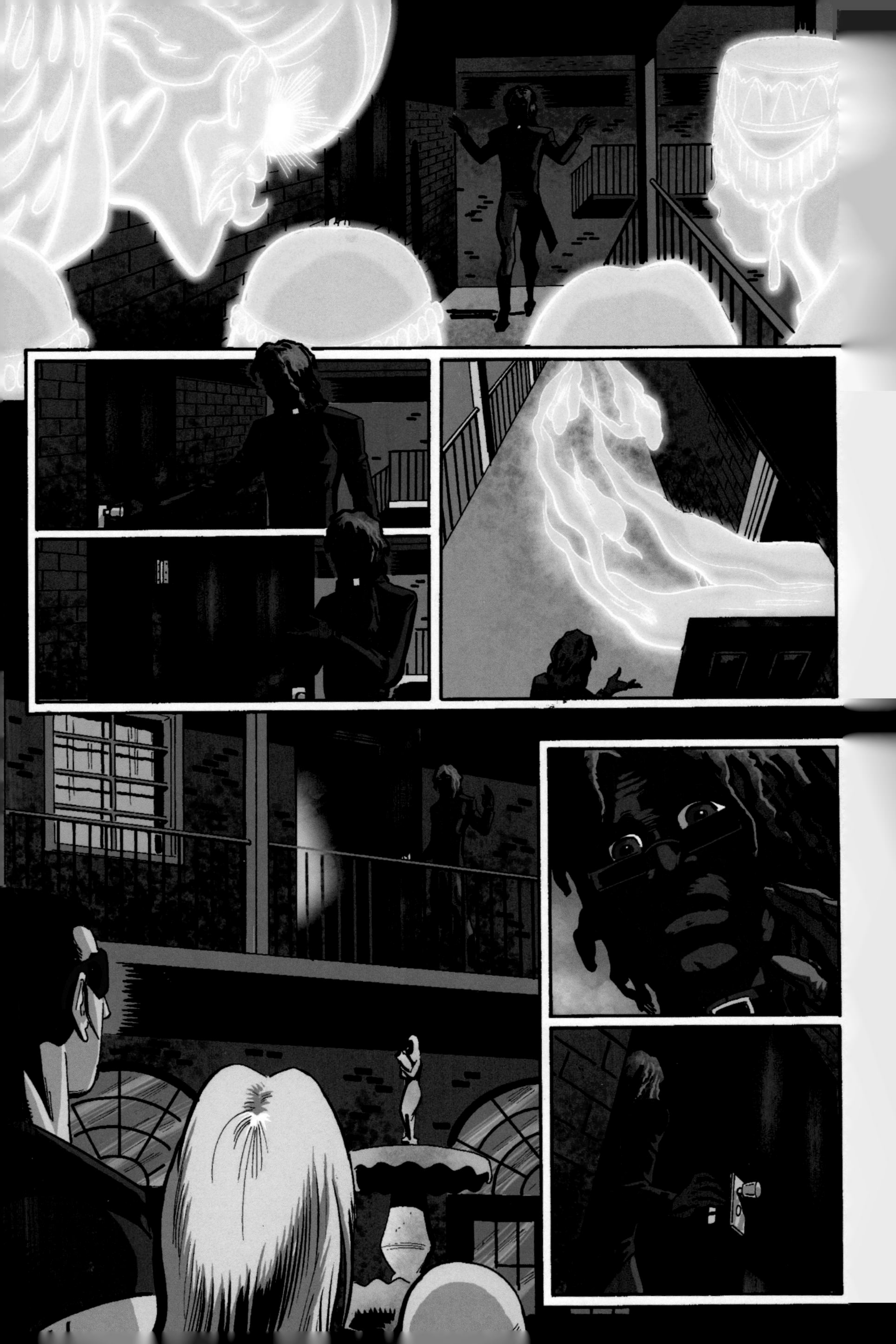

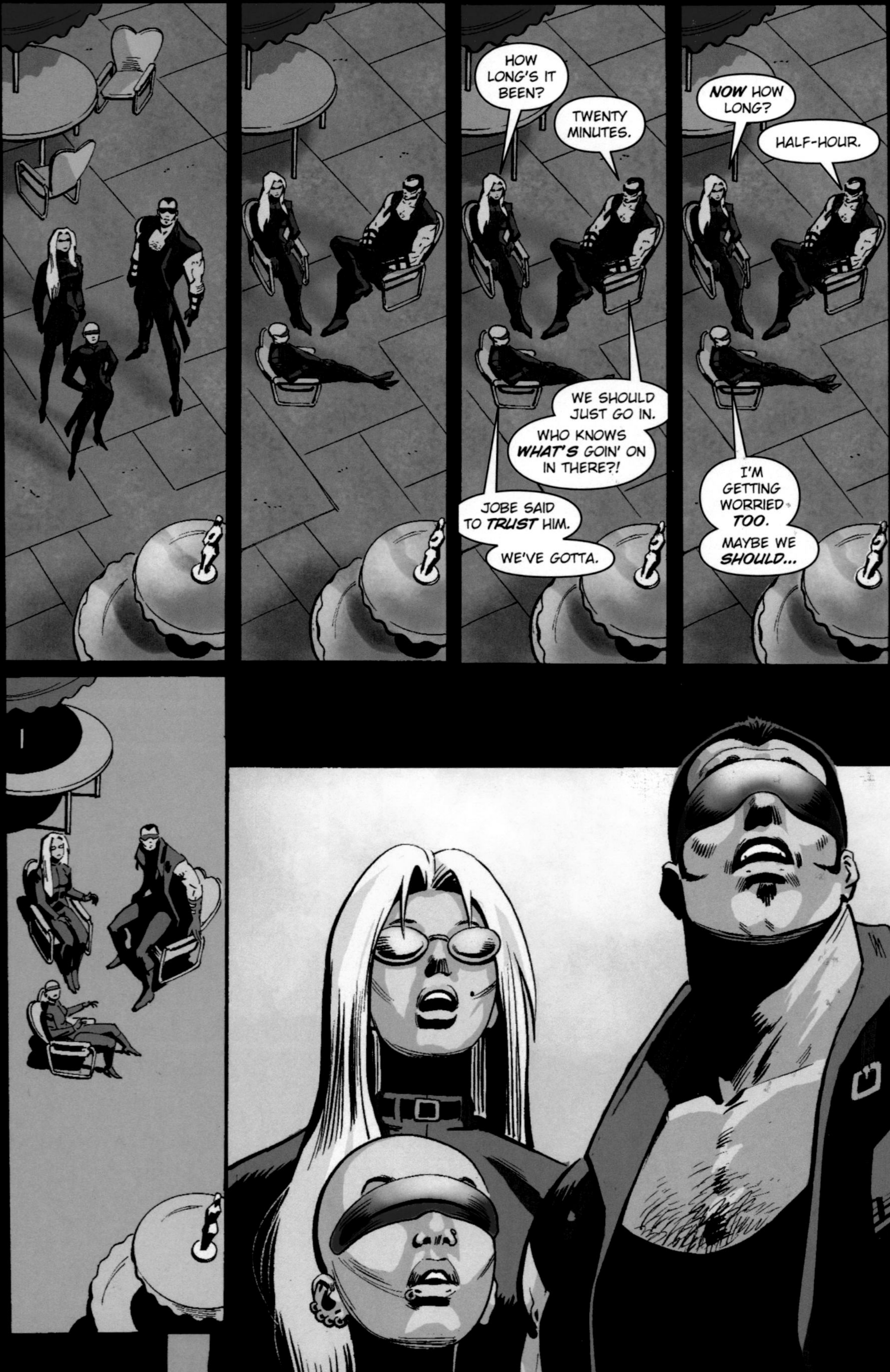
HOW LONG'S IT BEEN?
TWENTY MINUTES.
WE SHOULD JUST GO IN.
WHO KNOWS WHAT'S GOIN' ON IN THERE?!
JOBE SAID TO TRUST HIM.
WE'VE GOTTA.
NOW HOW LONG?
HALF-HOUR.
I'M GETTING WORRIED TOO.
MAYBE WE SHOULD...

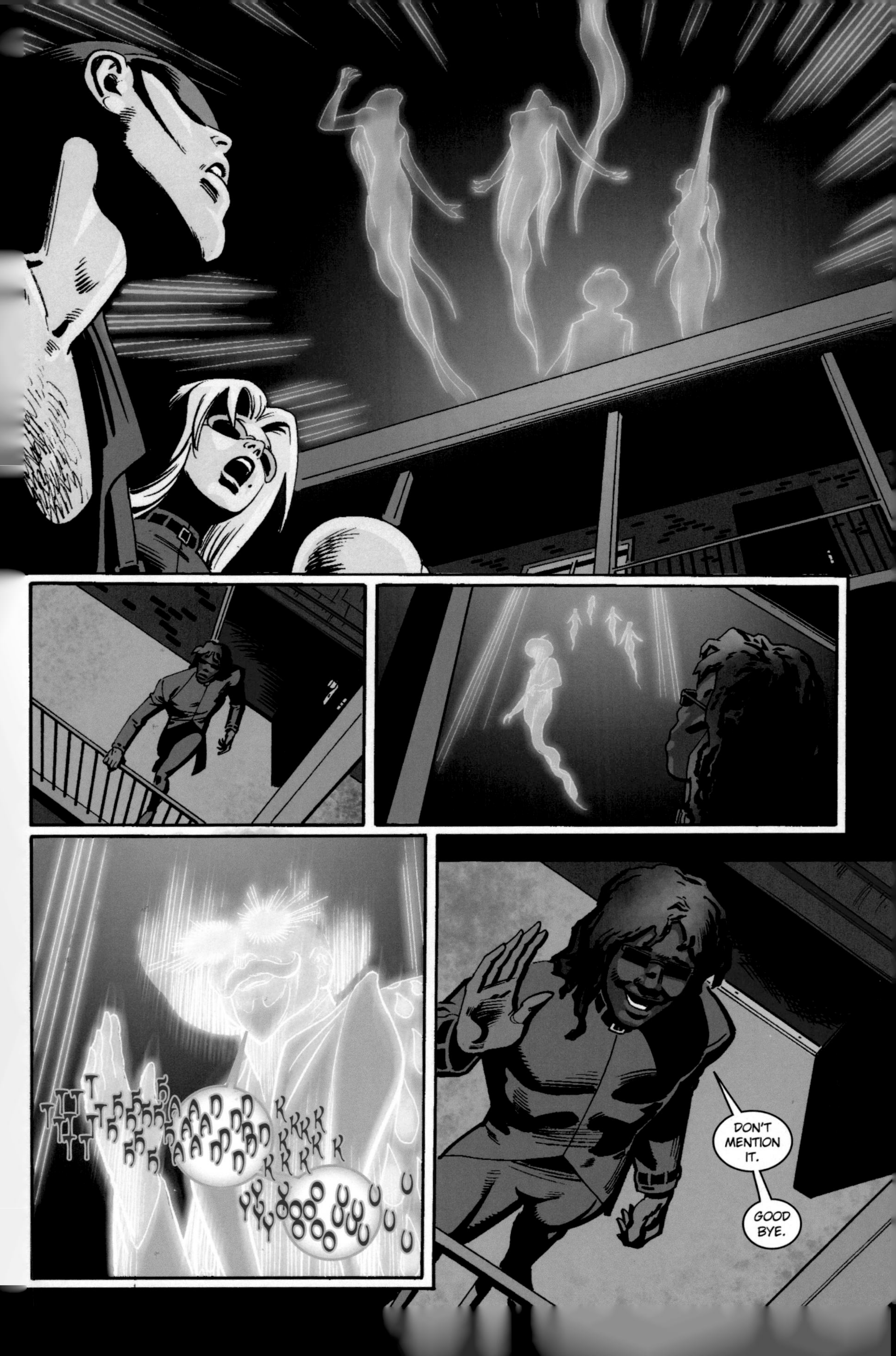
DON'T MENTION IT.
GOOD BYE.

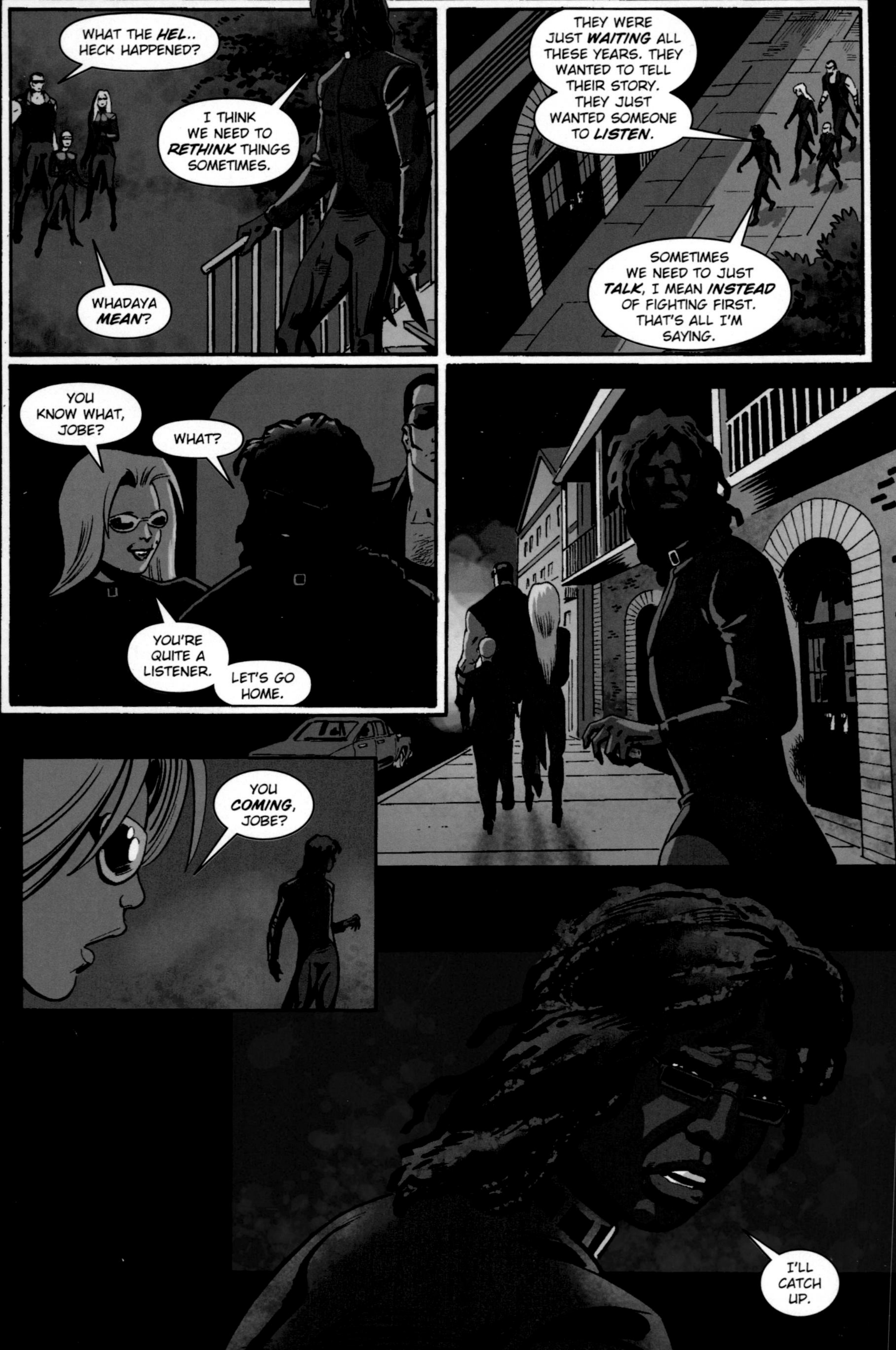
WHAT THE **HEL**.. HECK HAPPENED?
I THINK WE NEED TO **RETHINK** THINGS SOMETIMES.
WHADAYA **MEAN**?
THEY WERE JUST **WAITING** ALL THESE YEARS. THEY WANTED TO TELL THEIR STORY. THEY JUST WANTED SOMEONE TO **LISTEN**.
SOMETIMES WE NEED TO JUST **TALK**, I MEAN **INSTEAD** OF FIGHTING FIRST. THAT'S ALL I'M SAYING.
YOU KNOW WHAT, JOBE?
WHAT?
YOU'RE QUITE A LISTENER.
LET'S GO HOME.
YOU **COMING**, JOBE?
I'LL CATCH UP.

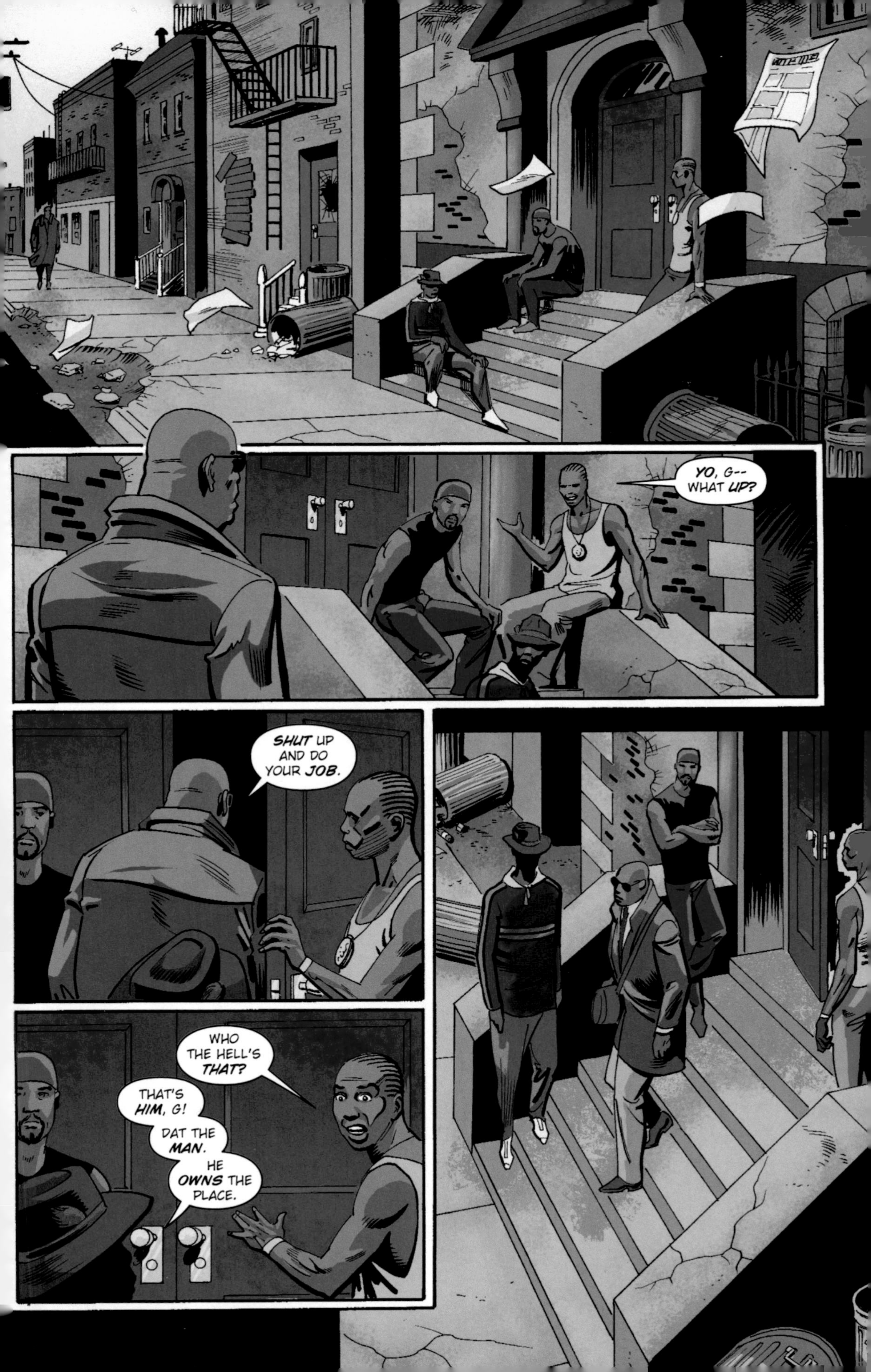
YO, G--
WHAT UP?
SHUT UP
AND DO
YOUR JOB.
WHO
THE HELL'S
THAT?
THAT'S
HIM, G!
DAT THE
MAN.
HE
OWNS THE
PLACE.

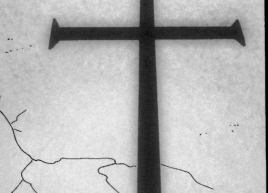

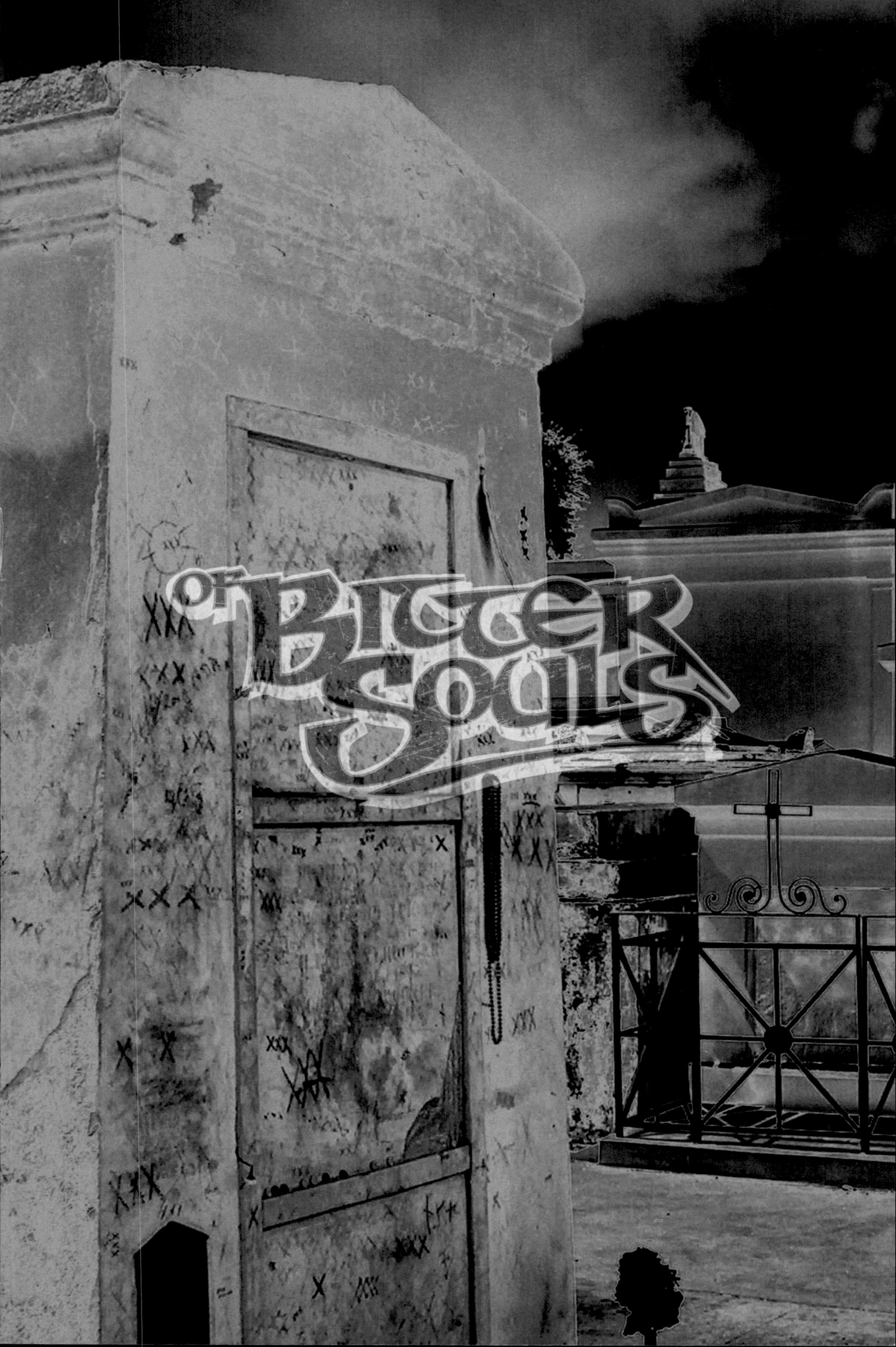
OF BITTER SOULS

chapter 3
the Axeman's Jazz

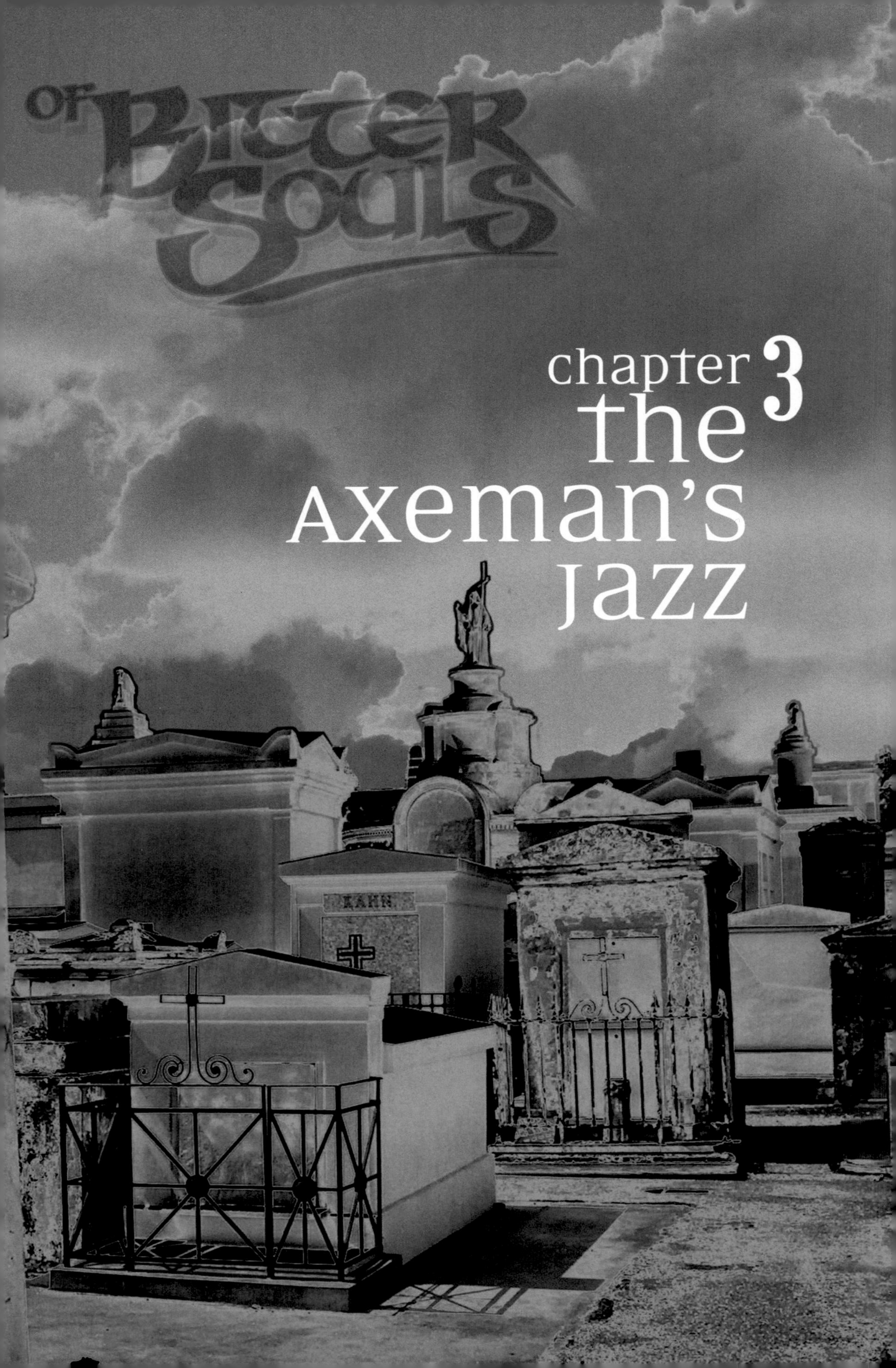
Of Bitter Souls
KAHN

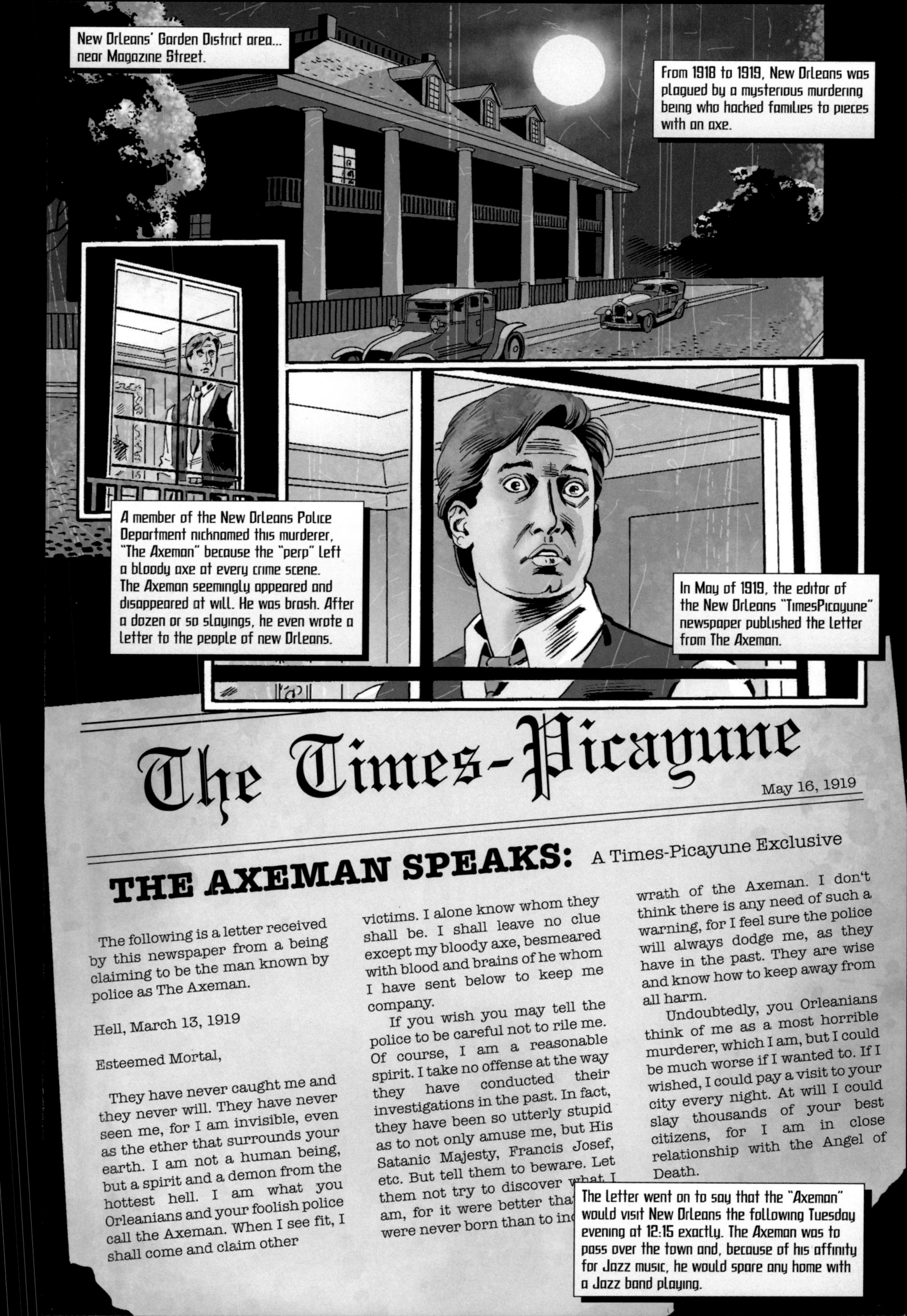
New Orleans' Garden District area... near Magazine Street.
From 1918 to 1919, New Orleans was plagued by a mysterious murdering being who hacked families to pieces with an axe.
A member of the New Orleans Police Department nicknamed this murderer, "The Axeman" because the "perp" left a bloody axe at every crime scene. The Axeman seemingly appeared and disappeared at will. He was brash. After a dozen or so slayings, he even wrote a letter to the people of new Orleans.
In May of 1919, the editor of the New Orleans "TimesPicayune" newspaper published the letter from The Axeman.
The Times-Picayune
May 16, 1919
THE AXEMAN SPEAKS: A Times-Picayune Exclusive
The following is a letter received by this newspaper from a being claiming to be the man known by police as The Axeman.
Hell, March 13, 1919
Esteemed Mortal,
They have never caught me and they never will. They have never seen me, for I am invisible, even as the ether that surrounds your earth. I am not a human being, but a spirit and a demon from the hottest hell. I am what you Orleanians and your foolish police call the Axeman. When I see fit, I shall come and claim other victims. I alone know whom they shall be. I shall leave no clue except my bloody axe, besmeared with blood and brains of he whom I have sent below to keep me company.
If you wish you may tell the police to be careful not to rile me. Of course, I am a reasonable spirit. I take no offense at the way they have conducted their investigations in the past. In fact, they have been so utterly stupid as to not only amuse me, but His Satanic Majesty, Francis Josef, etc. But tell them to beware. Let them not try to discover what I am, for it were better tha were never born than to in
wrath of the Axeman. I don't think there is any need of such a warning, for I feel sure the police will always dodge me, as they have in the past. They are wise and know how to keep away from all harm.
Undoubtedly, you Orleanians think of me as a most horrible murderer, which I am, but I could be much worse if I wanted to. If I wished, I could pay a visit to your city every night. At will I could slay thousands of your best citizens, for I am in close relationship with the Angel of Death.
The letter went on to say that the "Axeman" would visit New Orleans the following Tuesday evening at 12:15 exactly. The Axeman was to pass over the town and, because of his affinity for Jazz music, he would spare any home with a Jazz band playing.

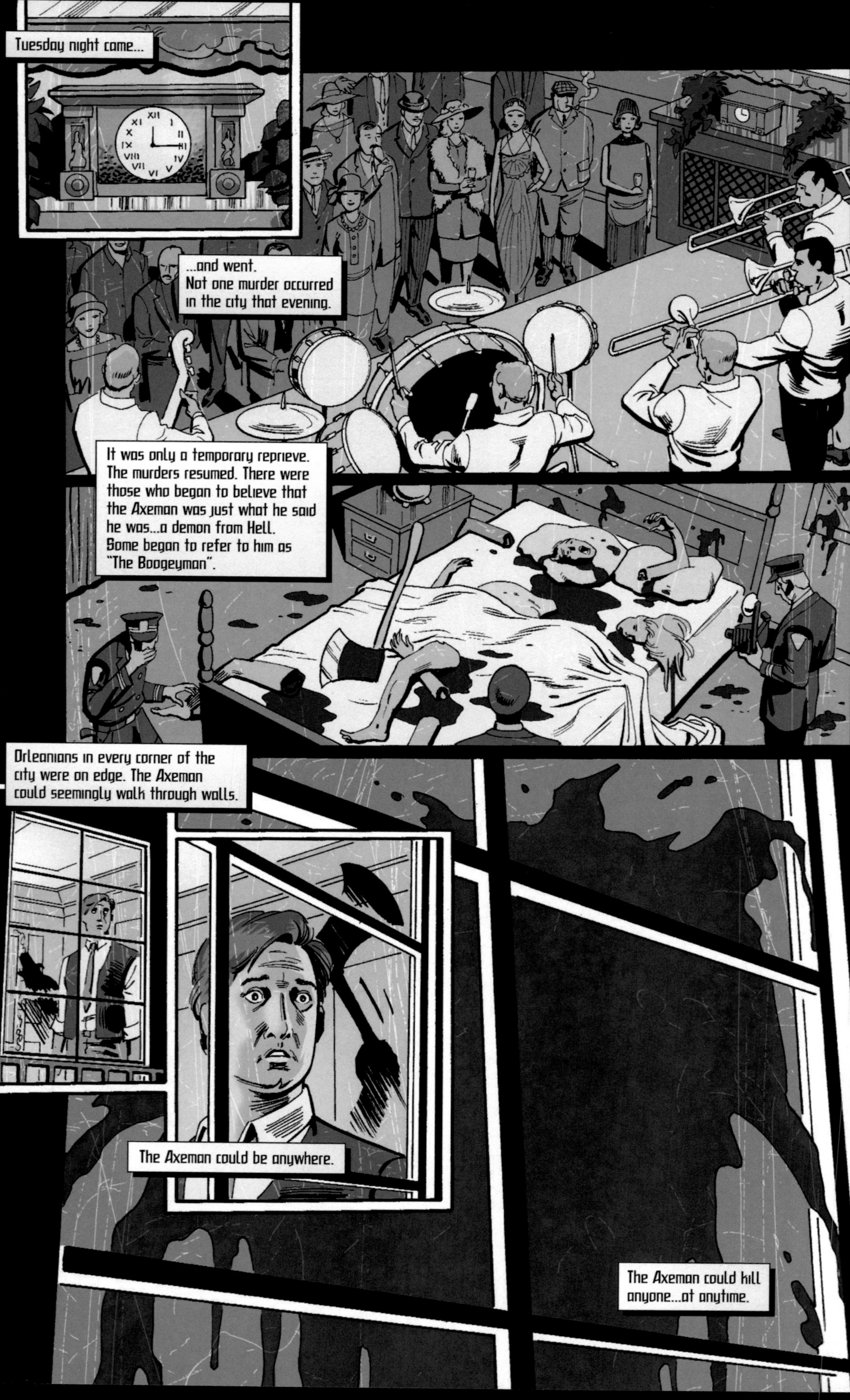
Tuesday night came...
...and went.
Not one murder occurred in the city that evening.
It was only a temporary reprieve. The murders resumed. There were those who began to believe that the Axeman was just what he said he was...a demon from Hell. Some began to refer to him as "The Boogeyman".
Orleanians in every corner of the city were on edge. The Axeman could seemingly walk through walls.
The Axeman could be anywhere.
The Axeman could kill anyone...at anytime.

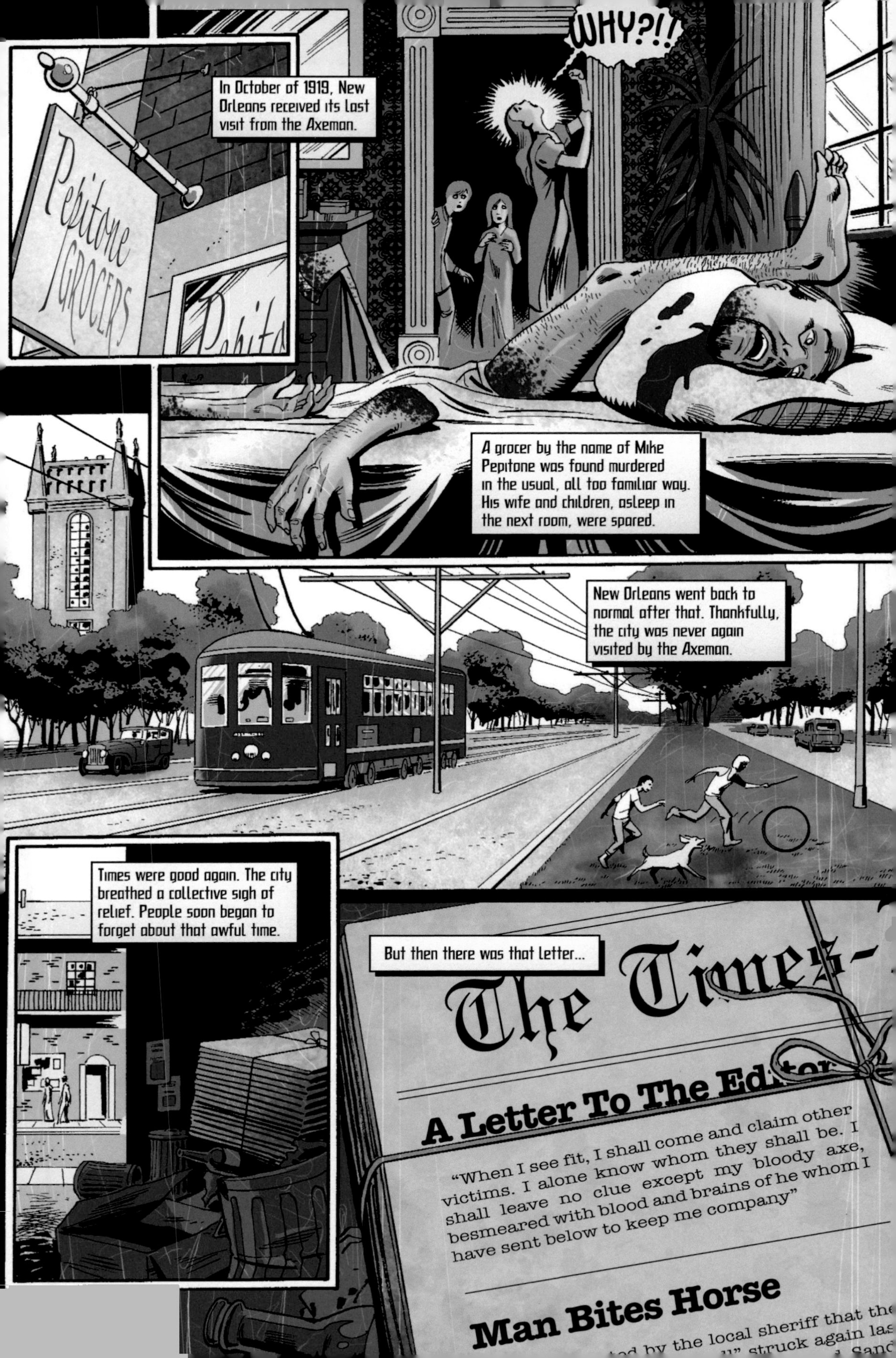
Pepitone GROCERS
In October of 1919, New Orleans received its last visit from the Axeman.
WHY?!!
A grocer by the name of Mike Pepitone was found murdered in the usual, all too familiar way. His wife and children, asleep in the next room, were spared.
New Orleans went back to normal after that. Thankfully, the city was never again visited by the Axeman.
Times were good again. The city breathed a collective sigh of relief. People soon began to forget about that awful time.
But then there was that letter...
The Times
A Letter To The Edit
"When I see fit, I shall come and claim other victims. I alone know whom they shall be. I shall leave no clue except my bloody axe, besmeared with blood and brains of he whom I have sent below to keep me company"
Man Bites Horse

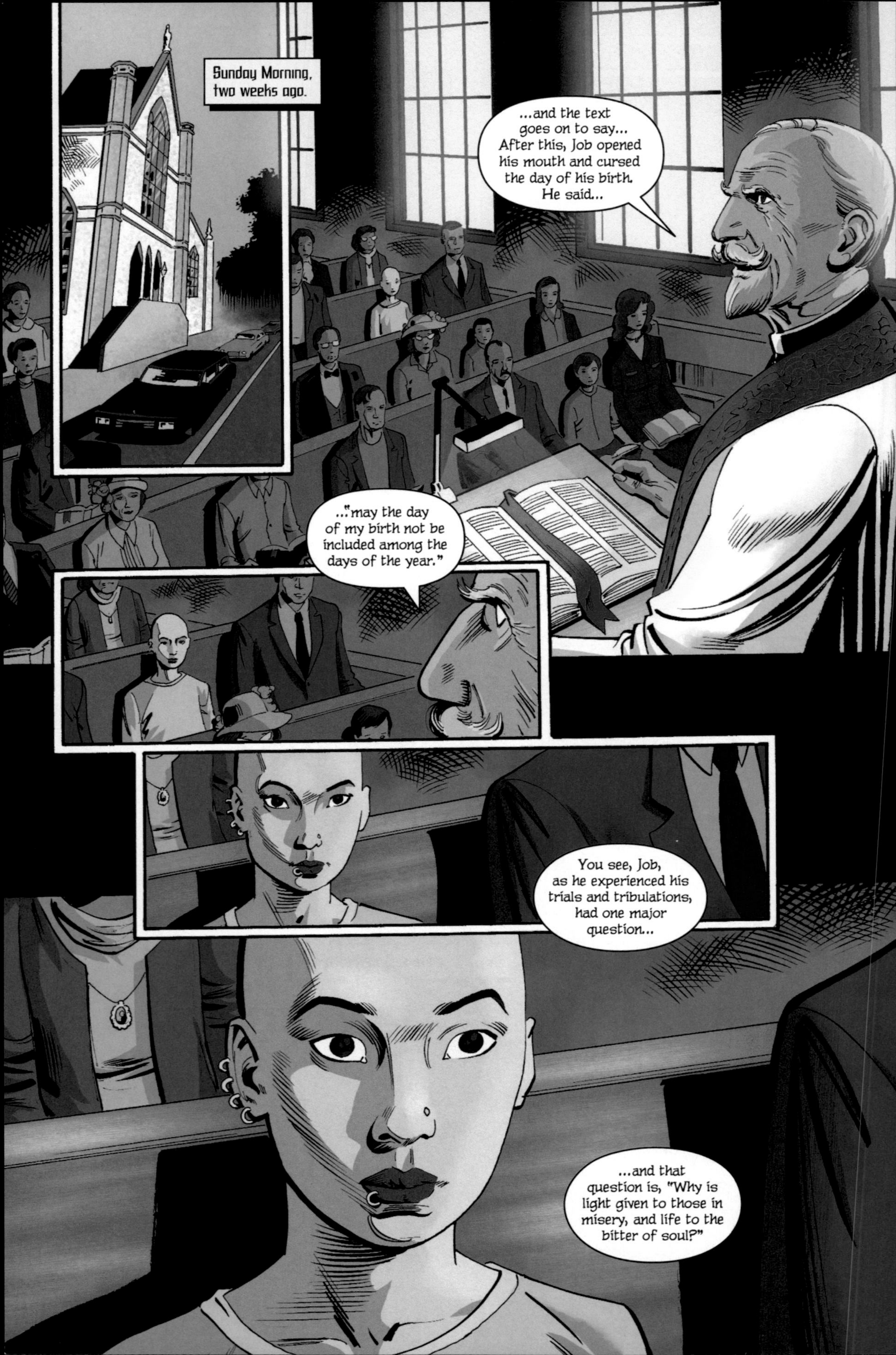
Sunday Morning, two weeks ago.
...and the text goes on to say... After this, Job opened his mouth and cursed the day of his birth. He said...
..."may the day of my birth not be included among the days of the year."
You see, Job, as he experienced his trials and tribulations, had one major question...
...and that question is, "Why is light given to those in misery, and life to the bitter of soul?"

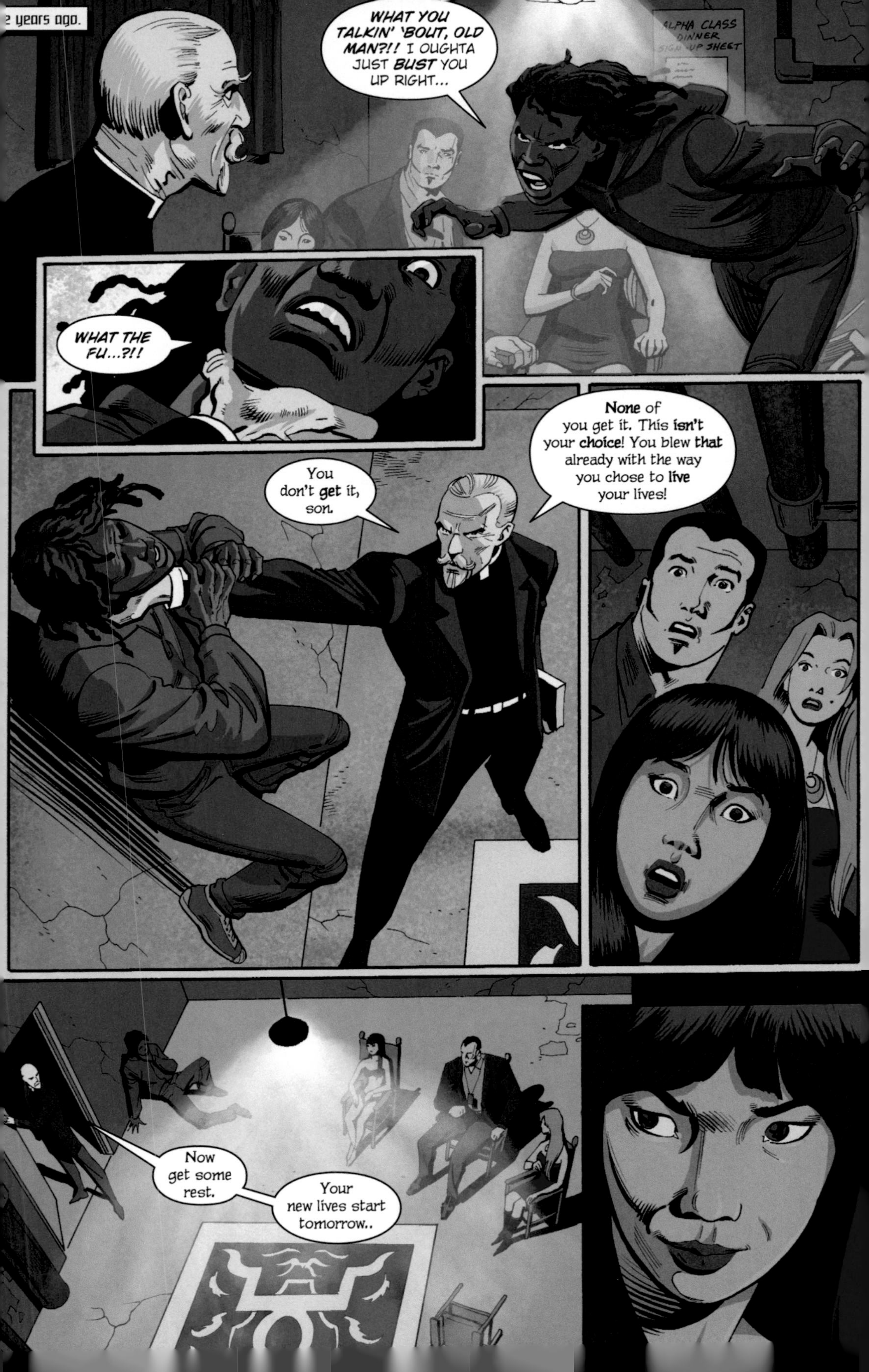
...e years ago.
ALPHA CLASS DINNER SIGN-UP SHEET
WHAT YOU TALKIN' 'BOUT, OLD MAN?!! I OUGHTA JUST BUST YOU UP RIGHT...
WHAT THE FU...?!!
You don't get it, son.
None of you get it. This isn't your choice! You blew that already with the way you chose to live your lives!
Now get some rest.
Your new lives start tomorrow..

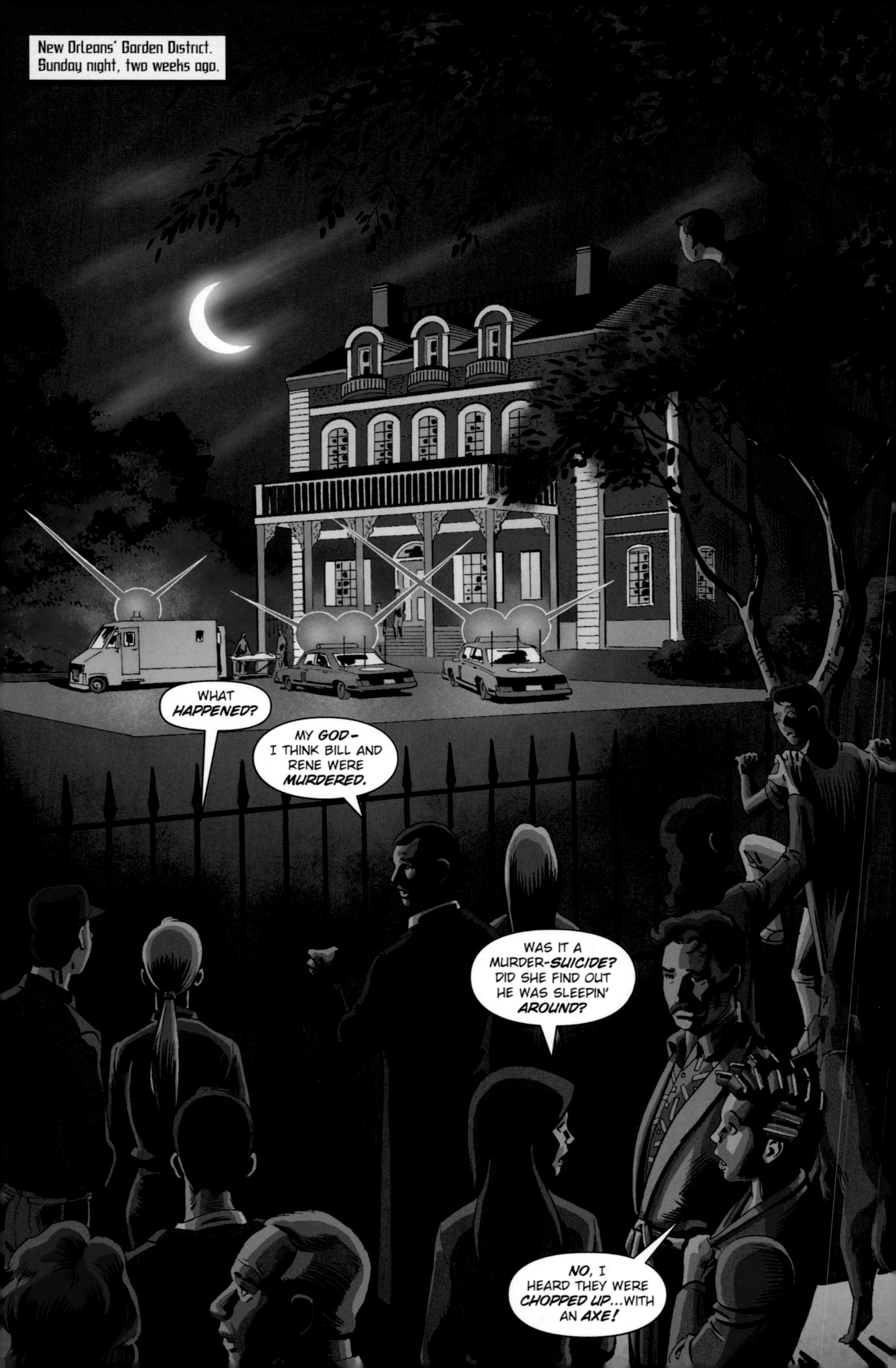
New Orleans' Garden District.
Sunday night, two weeks ago.
WHAT HAPPENED?
MY GOD- I THINK BILL AND RENE WERE MURDERED.
WAS IT A MURDER-SUICIDE? DID SHE FIND OUT HE WAS SLEEPIN' AROUND?
NO, I HEARD THEY WERE CHOPPED UP...WITH AN AXE!

The
TIMES PICAYUNE

TIMES PICAYUNE

PICAYUNE

PRICE:
50¢
DAILY
75¢
SATURDAY

The TIMES PICAY

THIRD BRUTAL SLAYING IN A WEEK TERRIFIES ORLENIAN

By Chuck Mah
NEW ORLE

High court vacancy behind Senate fight

By JESSE J. HOLLAND
Associated Press Writer
WASHINGTON — While senators argue over Texas jurist
Priscilla Owen's blocked federal appeals court nomination on the Senate floor, the driving force in backroom negotiations in the Capitol is how senators will treat a future Supreme Court nominee if a vacancy opens up in the next two years.

"This whole debate, for me, is about the Supreme Court," said Sen. Lindsey Graham, R-S.C., one of the Senate negotiators who scurried from office to office Wednesday trying to work out a deal that would avoid a show-down whether judicial

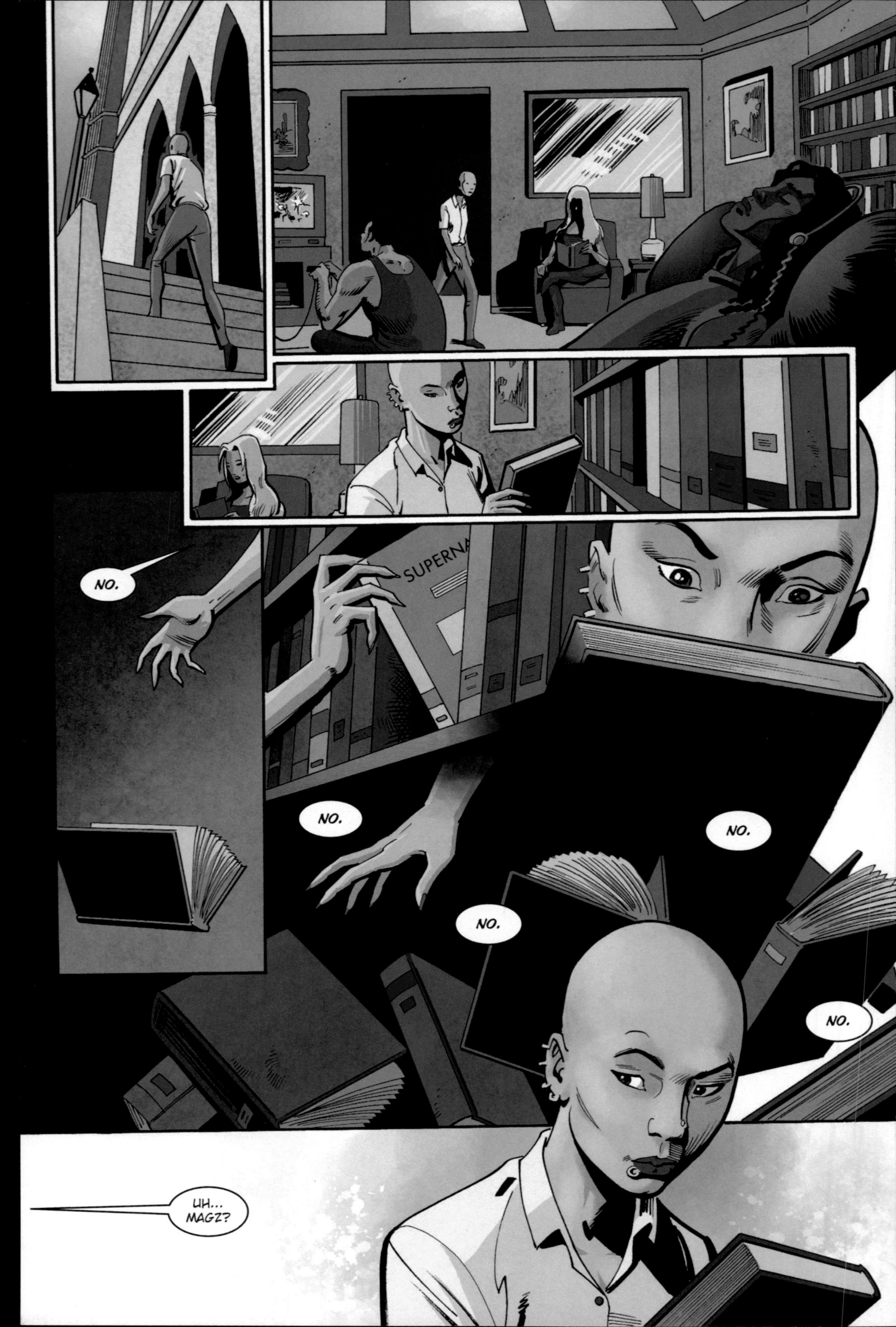
SUPERNA
NO.
NO.
NO.
NO.
NO.
UH... MAGZ?

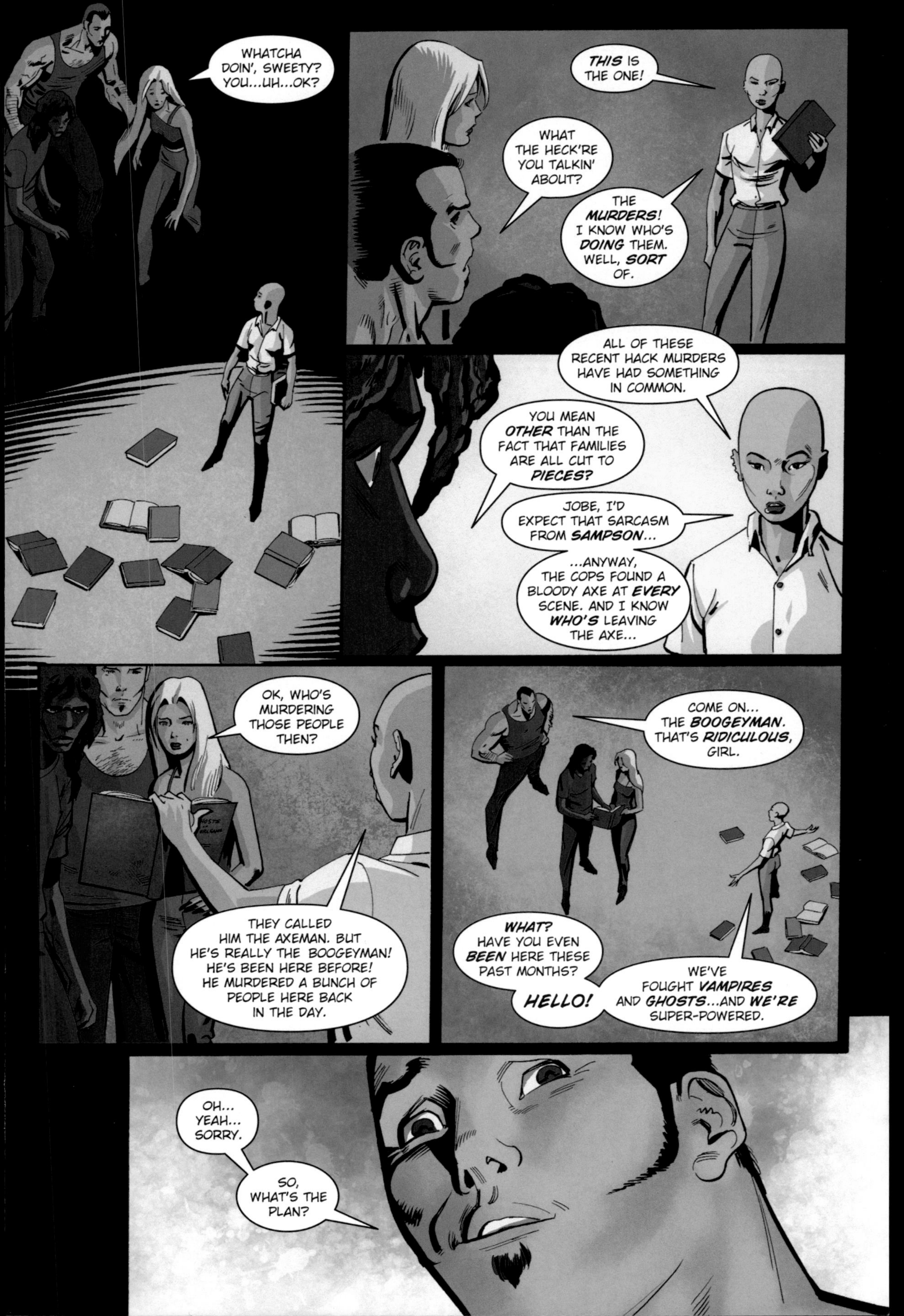
WHATCHA DOIN', SWEETY? YOU...UH...OK?
THIS IS THE ONE!
WHAT THE HECK'RE YOU TALKIN' ABOUT?
THE MURDERS! I KNOW WHO'S DOING THEM. WELL, SORT OF.
ALL OF THESE RECENT HACK MURDERS HAVE HAD SOMETHING IN COMMON.
YOU MEAN OTHER THAN THE FACT THAT FAMILIES ARE ALL CUT TO PIECES?
JOBE, I'D EXPECT THAT SARCASM FROM SAMPSON...
...ANYWAY, THE COPS FOUND A BLOODY AXE AT EVERY SCENE. AND I KNOW WHO'S LEAVING THE AXE...
OK, WHO'S MURDERING THOSE PEOPLE THEN?
THEY CALLED HIM THE AXEMAN. BUT HE'S REALLY THE BOOGEYMAN! HE'S BEEN HERE BEFORE! HE MURDERED A BUNCH OF PEOPLE HERE BACK IN THE DAY.
COME ON... THE BOOGEYMAN. THAT'S RIDICULOUS, GIRL.
WHAT? HAVE YOU EVEN BEEN HERE THESE PAST MONTHS?
HELLO!
WE'VE FOUGHT VAMPIRES AND GHOSTS...AND WE'RE SUPER-POWERED.
OH... YEAH... SORRY.
SO, WHAT'S THE PLAN?

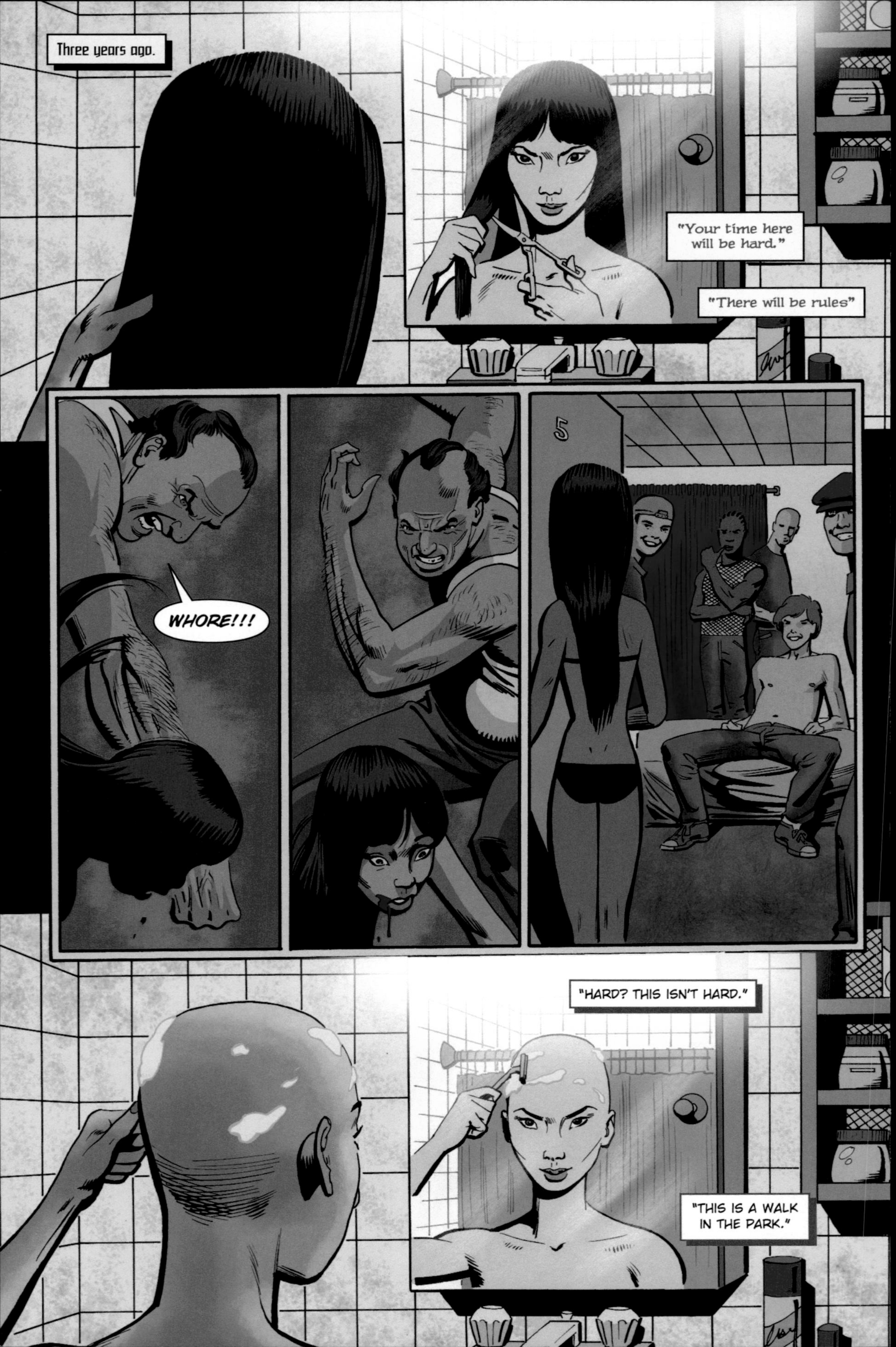
Three years ago.
"Your time here will be hard."
"There will be rules"
WHORE!!!
"HARD? THIS ISN'T HARD."
"THIS IS A WALK IN THE PARK."

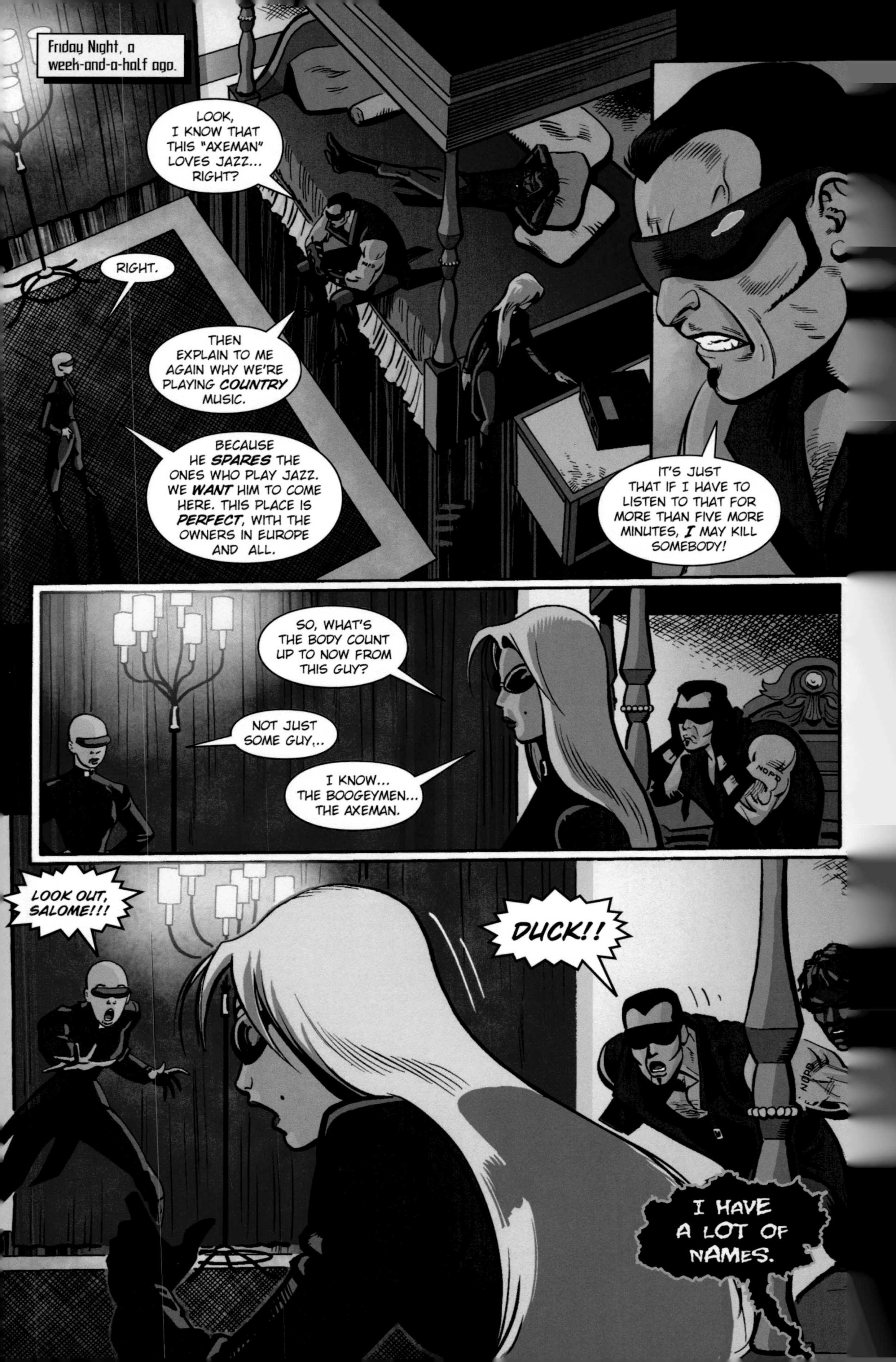

Friday Night, a week-and-a-half ago.
LOOK, I KNOW THAT THIS "AXEMAN" LOVES JAZZ... RIGHT?
RIGHT.
THEN EXPLAIN TO ME AGAIN WHY WE'RE PLAYING COUNTRY MUSIC.
BECAUSE HE SPARES THE ONES WHO PLAY JAZZ. WE WANT HIM TO COME HERE. THIS PLACE IS PERFECT, WITH THE OWNERS IN EUROPE AND ALL.
IT'S JUST THAT IF I HAVE TO LISTEN TO THAT FOR MORE THAN FIVE MORE MINUTES, I MAY KILL SOMEBODY!
SO, WHAT'S THE BODY COUNT UP TO NOW FROM THIS GUY?
NOT JUST SOME GUY,..
I KNOW... THE BOOGEYMEN... THE AXEMAN.
LOOK OUT, SALOME!!!
DUCK!!
I HAVE A LOT OF NAMES.

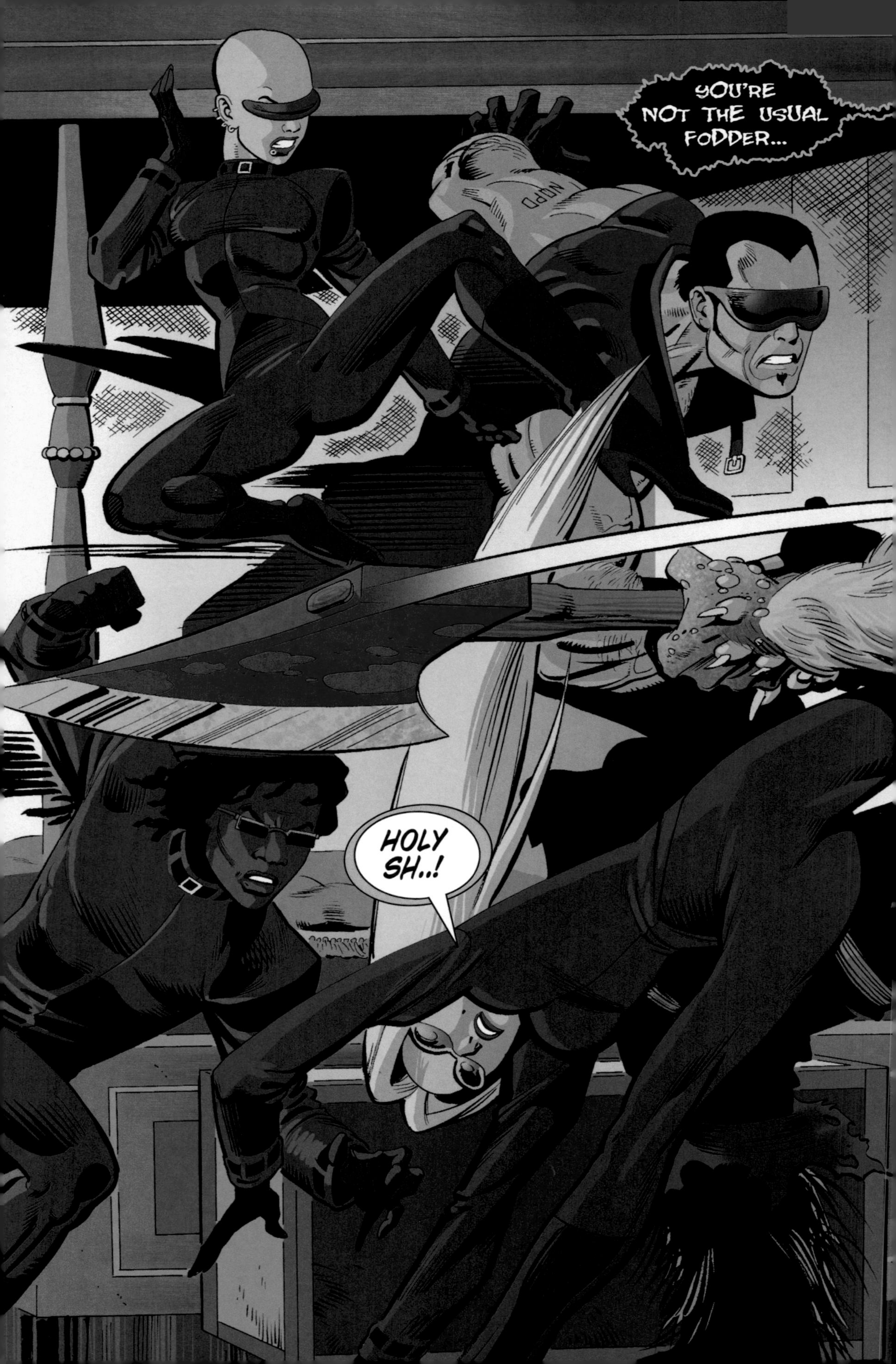
YOU'RE NOT THE USUAL FODDER...
HOLY SH..!
NOPD

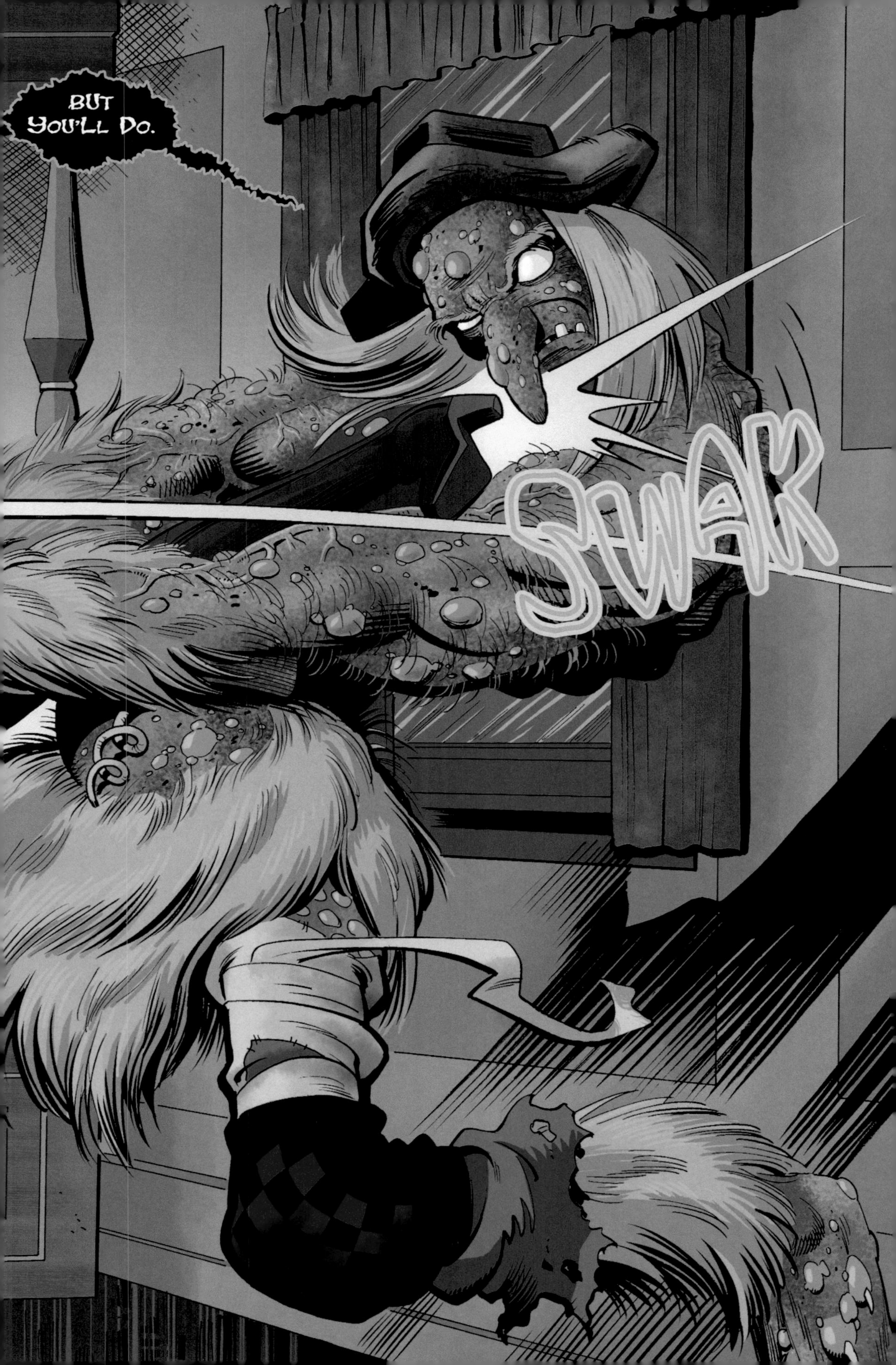
BUT YOU'LL DO.
SWAK

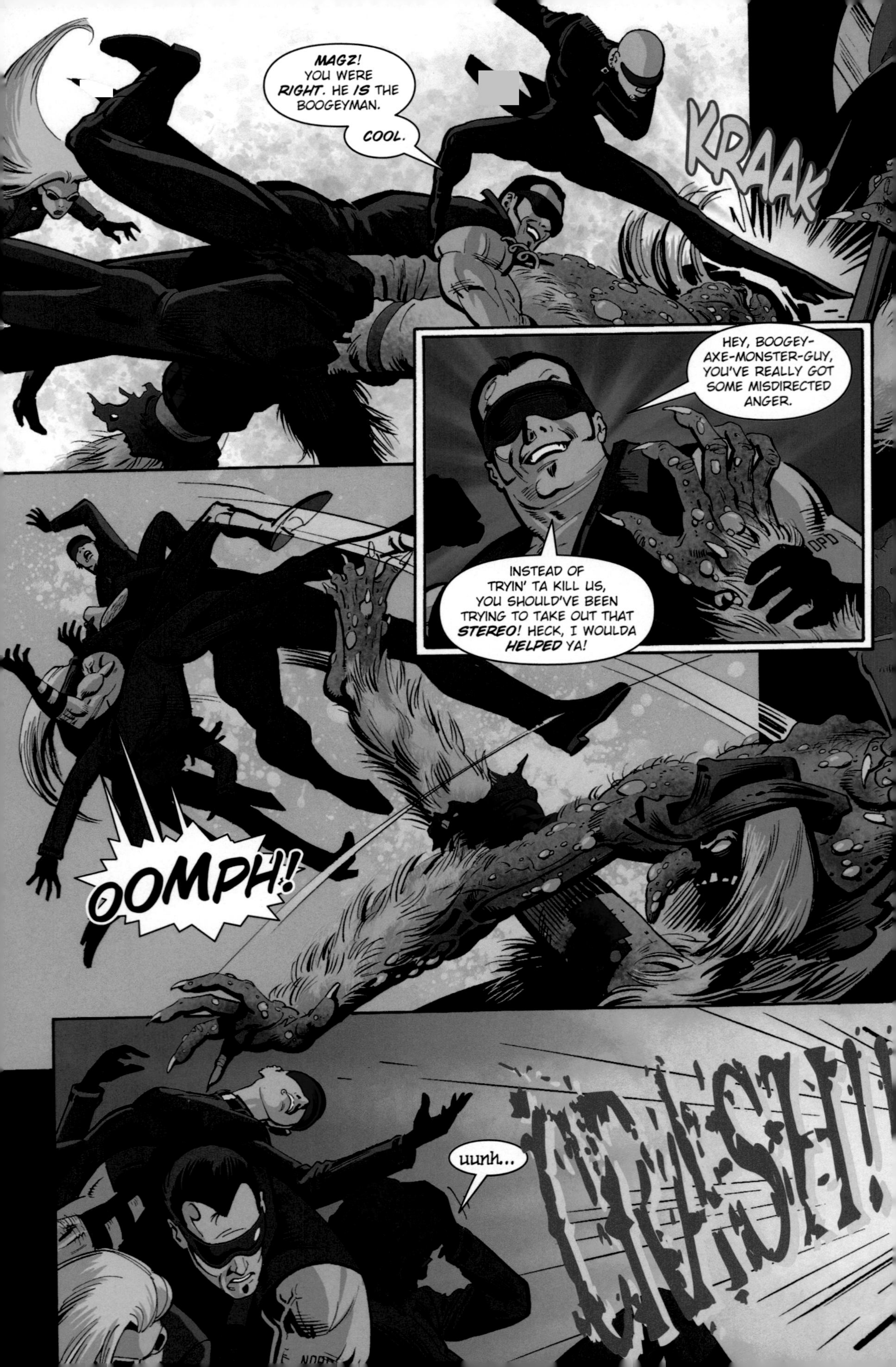
MAGZ! YOU WERE RIGHT. HE IS THE BOOGEYMAN.
COOL.
KRAAK
HEY, BOOGEY-AXE-MONSTER-GUY, YOU'VE REALLY GOT SOME MISDIRECTED ANGER.
INSTEAD OF TRYIN' TA KILL US, YOU SHOULD'VE BEEN TRYING TO TAKE OUT THAT STEREO! HECK, I WOULDA HELPED YA!
OOMPH!
uunh...

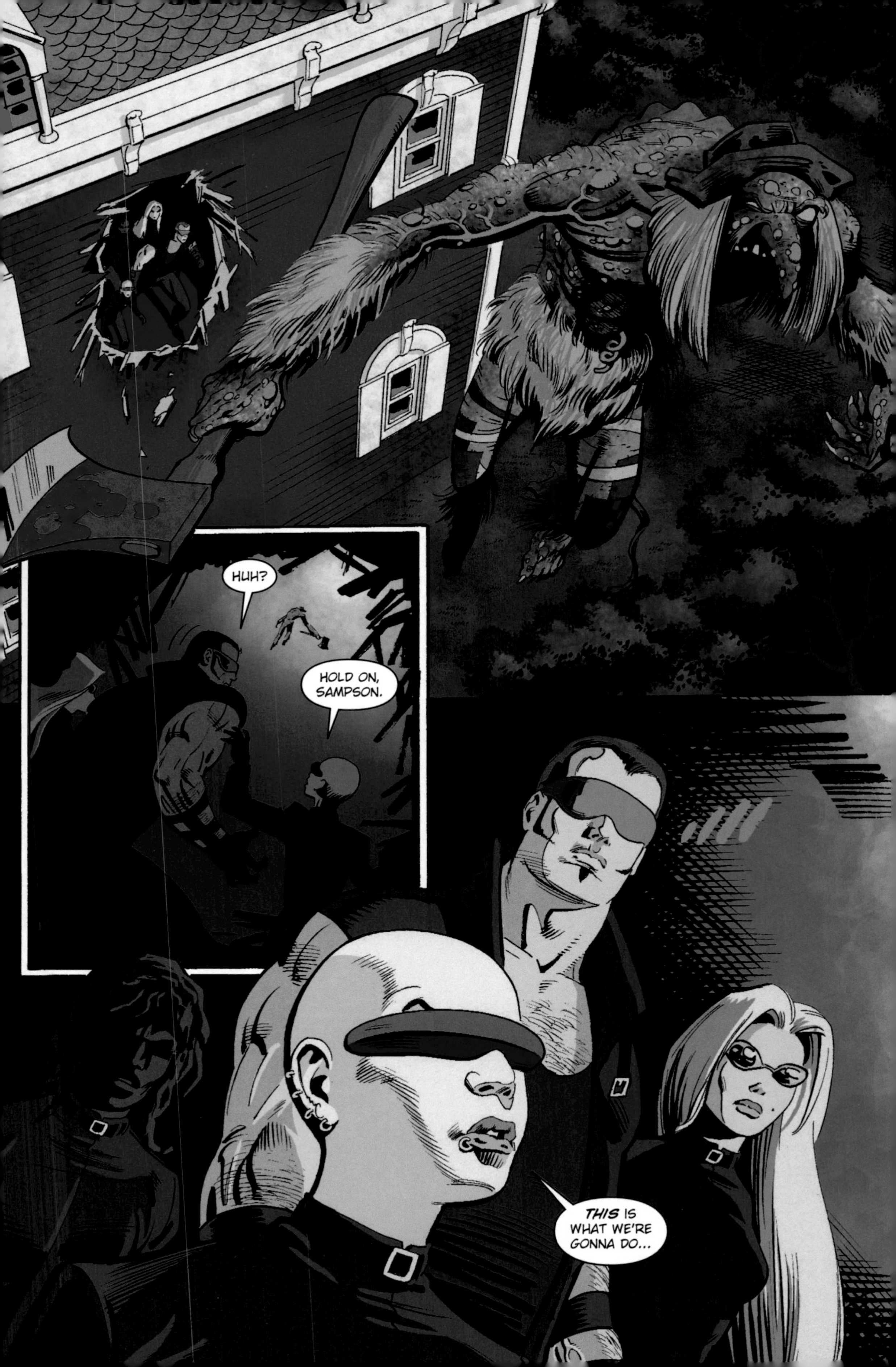
HUH?
HOLD ON, SAMPSON.
THIS IS WHAT WE'RE GONNA DO...

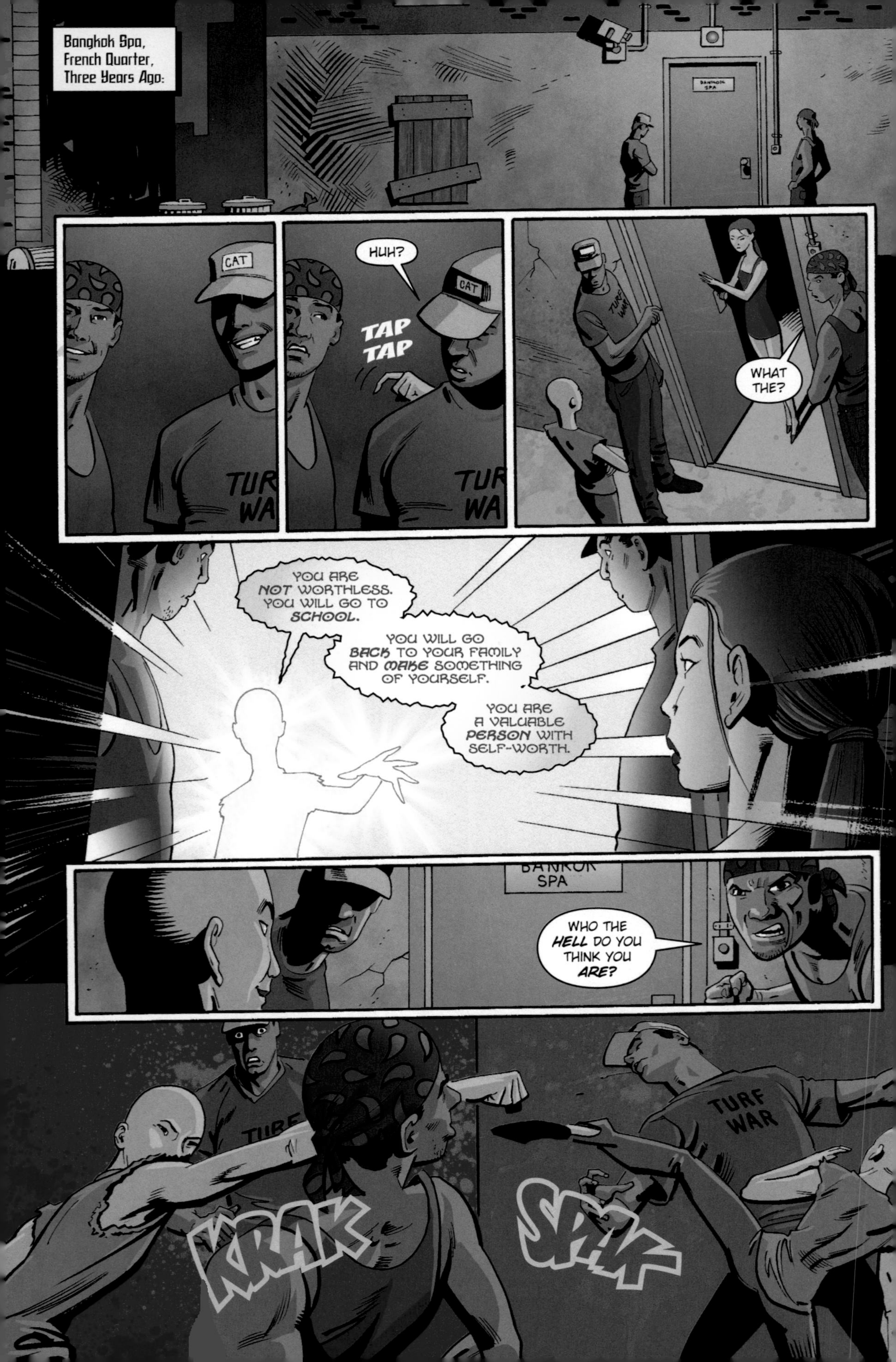

Bangkok Spa, French Quarter, Three Years Ago:
BANGKOK SPA
CAT
TURF WAR
HUH?
TAP TAP
CAT
TURF WAR
TURF WAR
WHAT THE?
YOU ARE NOT WORTHLESS. YOU WILL GO TO SCHOOL.
YOU WILL GO BACK TO YOUR FAMILY AND MAKE SOMETHING OF YOURSELF.
YOU ARE A VALUABLE PERSON WITH SELF-WORTH.
BANKOK SPA
WHO THE HELL DO YOU THINK YOU ARE?
TURF WAR
KRAK
SPAK

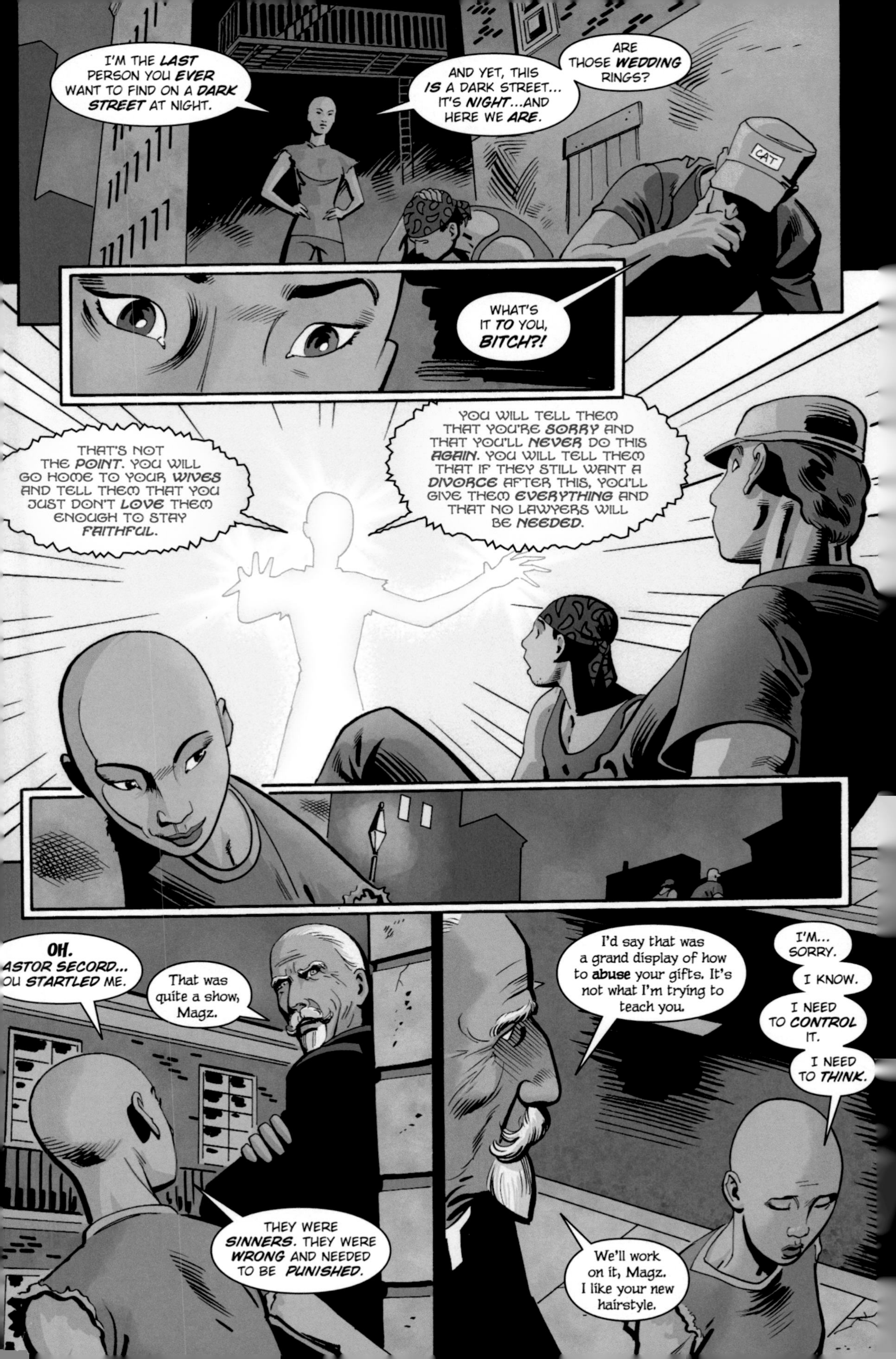

I'M THE LAST PERSON YOU EVER WANT TO FIND ON A DARK STREET AT NIGHT.
AND YET, THIS IS A DARK STREET... IT'S NIGHT...AND HERE WE ARE.
ARE THOSE WEDDING RINGS?
WHAT'S IT TO YOU, BITCH?!
THAT'S NOT THE POINT. YOU WILL GO HOME TO YOUR WIVES AND TELL THEM THAT YOU JUST DON'T LOVE THEM ENOUGH TO STAY FAITHFUL.
YOU WILL TELL THEM THAT YOU'RE SORRY AND THAT YOU'LL NEVER DO THIS AGAIN. YOU WILL TELL THEM THAT IF THEY STILL WANT A DIVORCE AFTER THIS, YOU'LL GIVE THEM EVERYTHING AND THAT NO LAWYERS WILL BE NEEDED.
OH.
ASTOR SECORD... OU STARTLED ME.
That was quite a show, Magz.
THEY WERE SINNERS. THEY WERE WRONG AND NEEDED TO BE PUNISHED.
I'd say that was a grand display of how to abuse your gifts. It's not what I'm trying to teach you.
I'M... SORRY.
I KNOW.
I NEED TO CONTROL IT.
I NEED TO THINK.
We'll work on it, Magz. I like your new hairstyle.

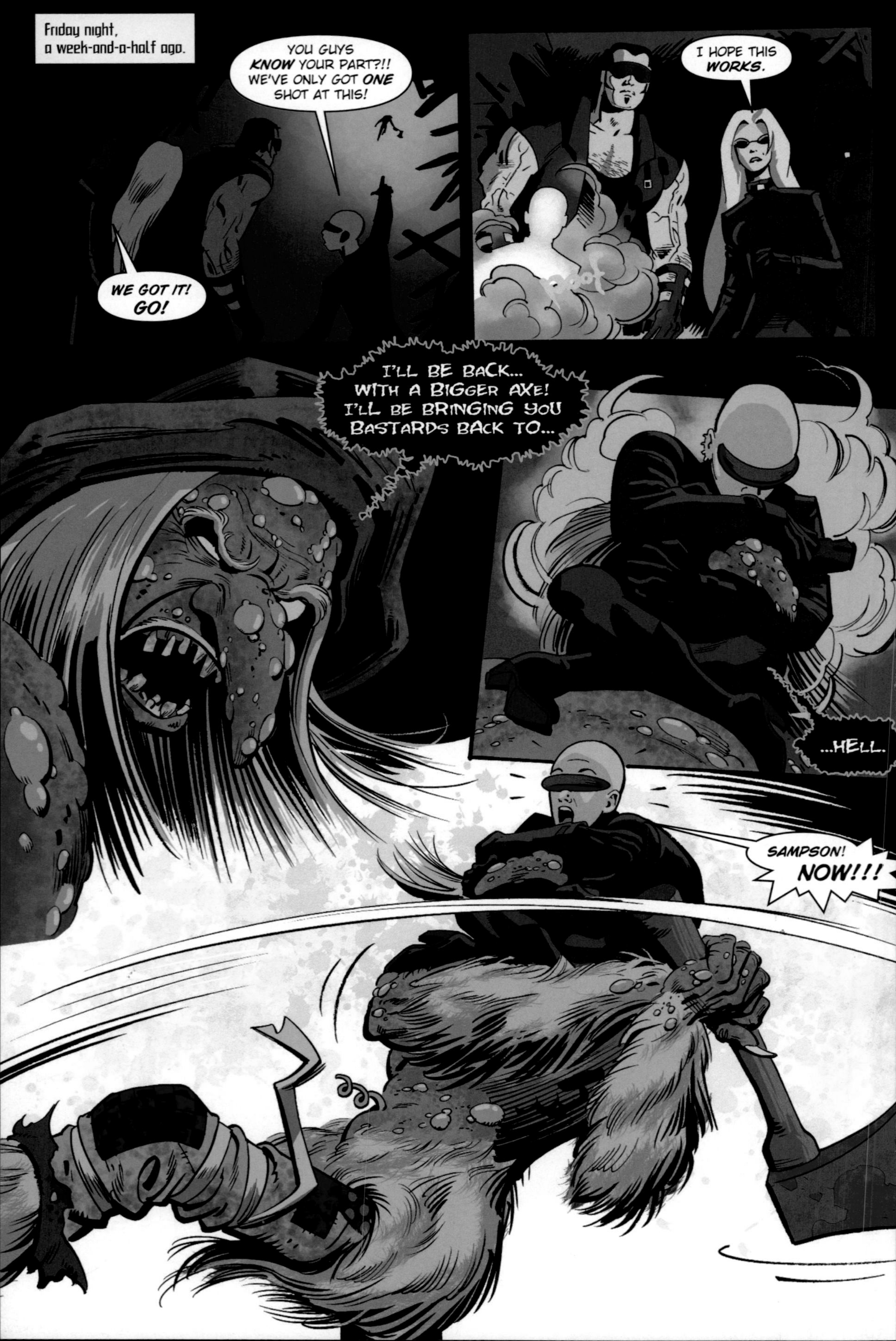
Friday night,
a week-and-a-half ago.
YOU GUYS KNOW YOUR PART?!! WE'VE ONLY GOT ONE SHOT AT THIS!
WE GOT IT! GO!
I HOPE THIS WORKS.
poof
I'LL BE BACK... WITH A BIGGER AXE! I'LL BE BRINGING YOU BASTARDS BACK TO...
...HELL.
SAMPSON! NOW!!!

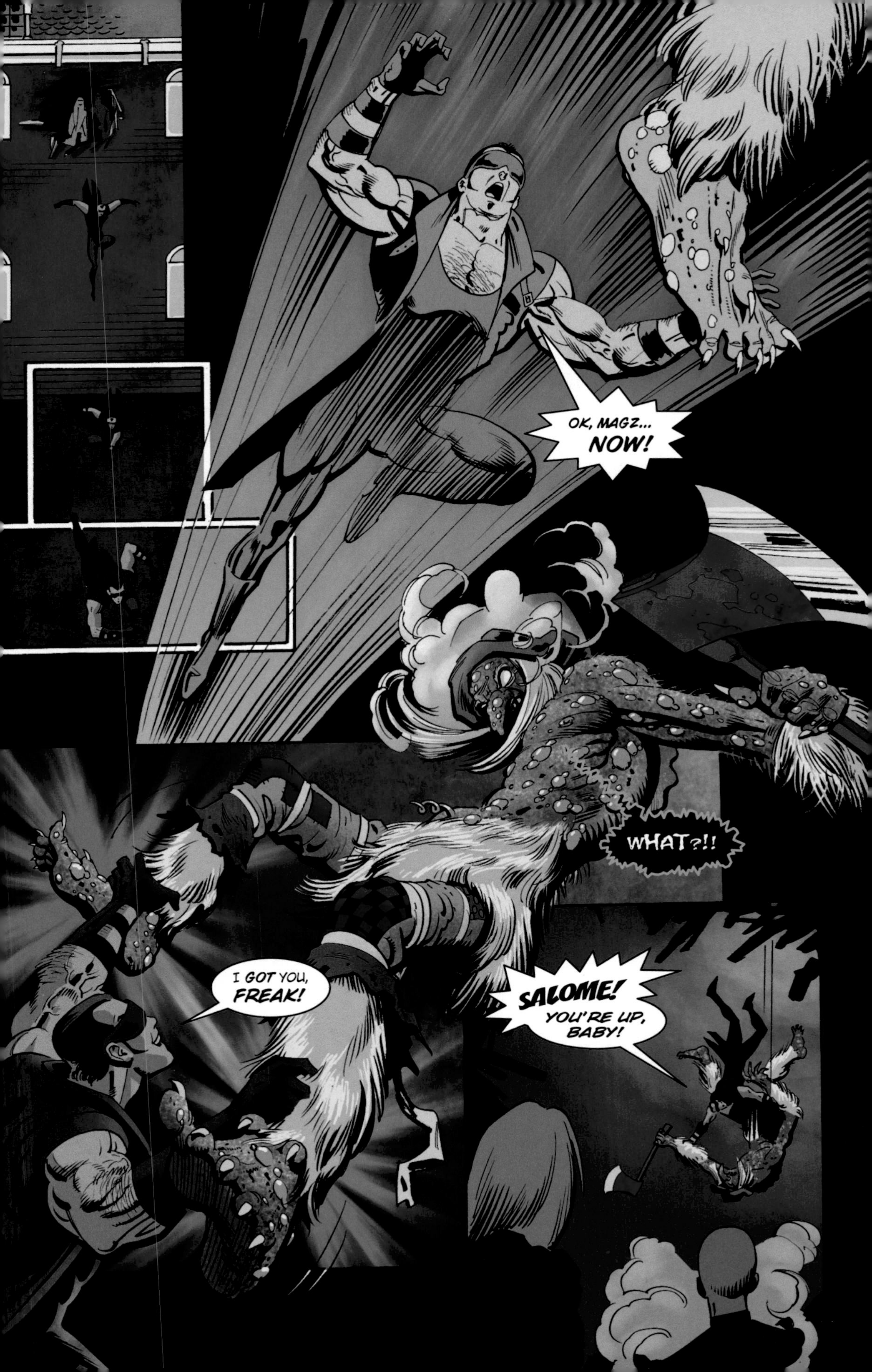
OK, MAGZ... NOW!
WHAT?!!
I GOT YOU, FREAK!
SALOME! YOU'RE UP, BABY!

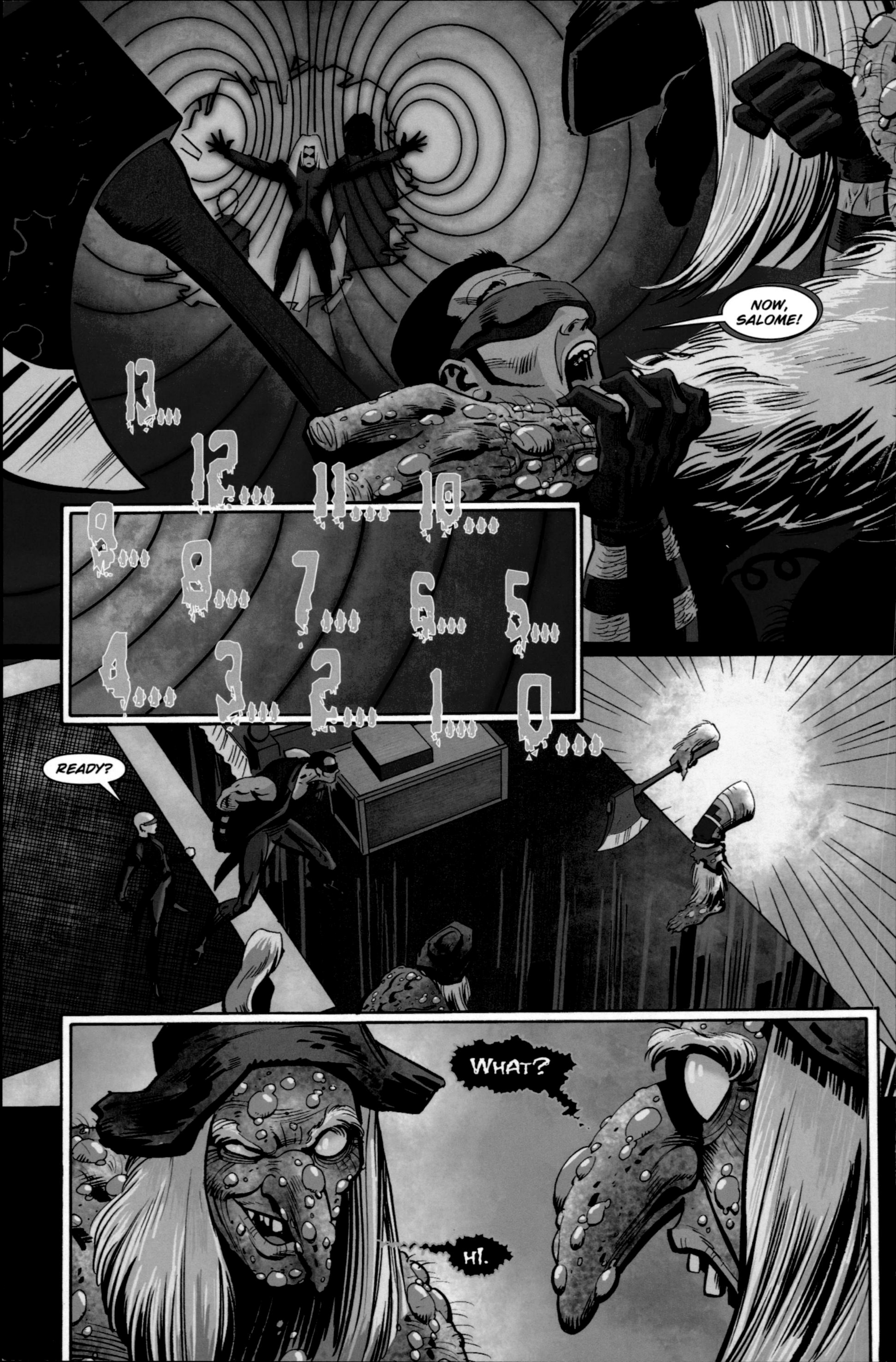
NOW, SALOME!
13...
12... 11... 10...
9... 8... 7... 6... 5...
4... 3... 2... 1... 0...
READY?
WHAT?
HI.

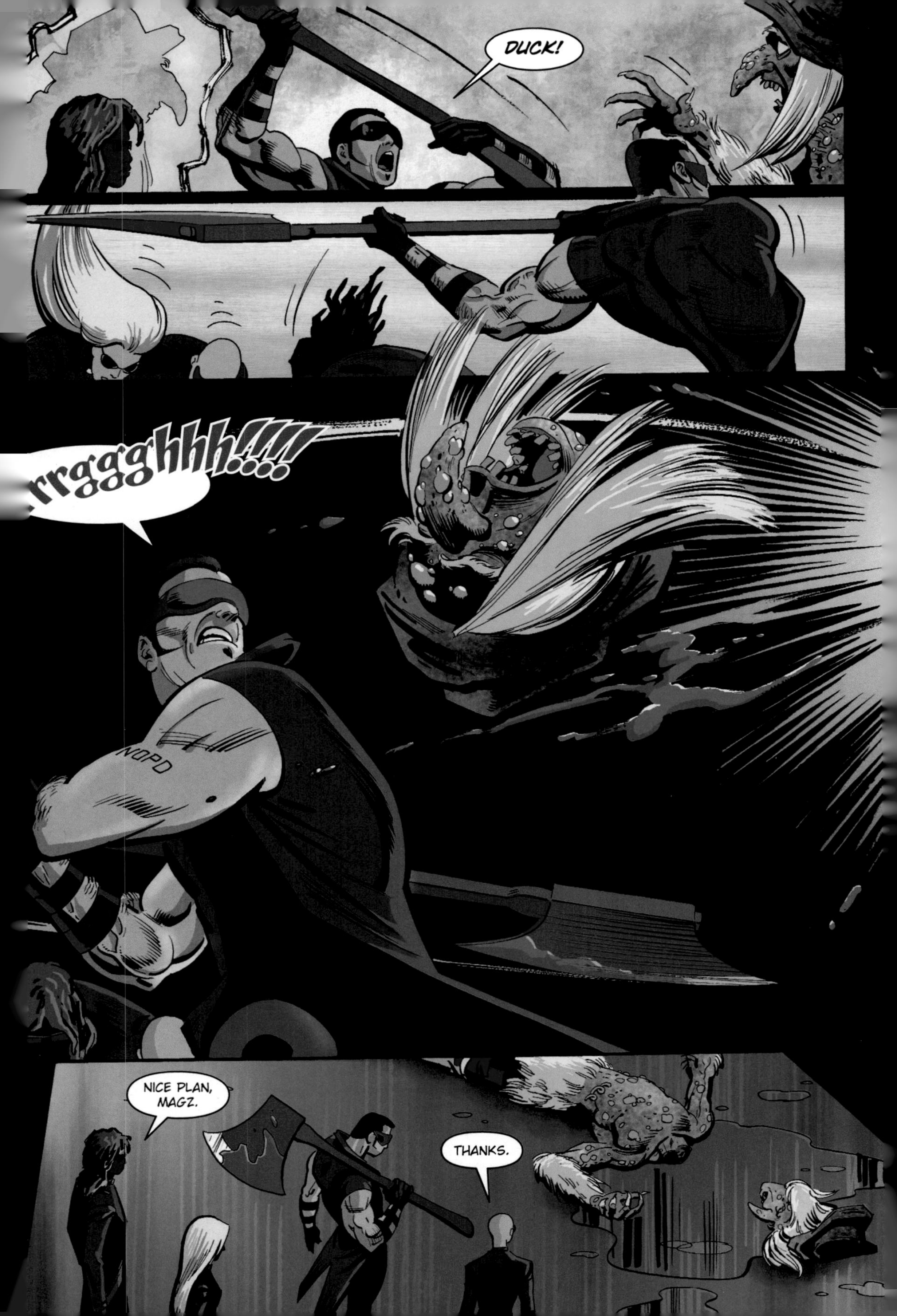
DUCK!
rrrggghhh!!!!
NOPD
NICE PLAN, MAGZ.
THANKS.

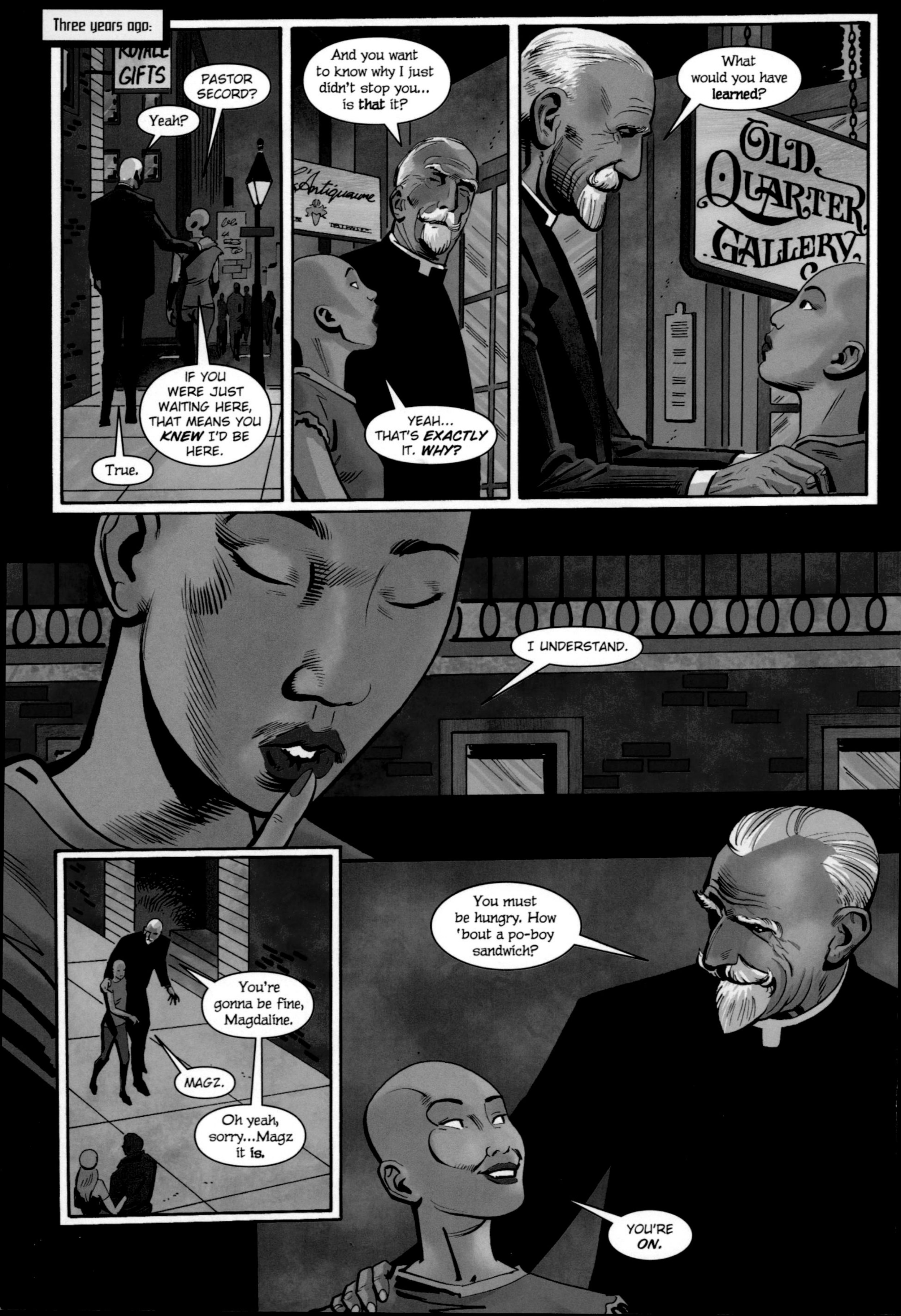

Three years ago:
ROYALE GIFTS
PASTOR SECORD?
Yeah?
IF YOU WERE JUST WAITING HERE, THAT MEANS YOU KNEW I'D BE HERE.
True.
And you want to know why I just didn't stop you... is that it?
YEAH... THAT'S EXACTLY IT. WHY?
What would you have learned?
OLD QUARTER GALLERY
I UNDERSTAND.
You must be hungry. How 'bout a po-boy sandwich?
YOU'RE ON.
You're gonna be fine, Magdaline.
MAGZ.
Oh yeah, sorry...Magz it is.

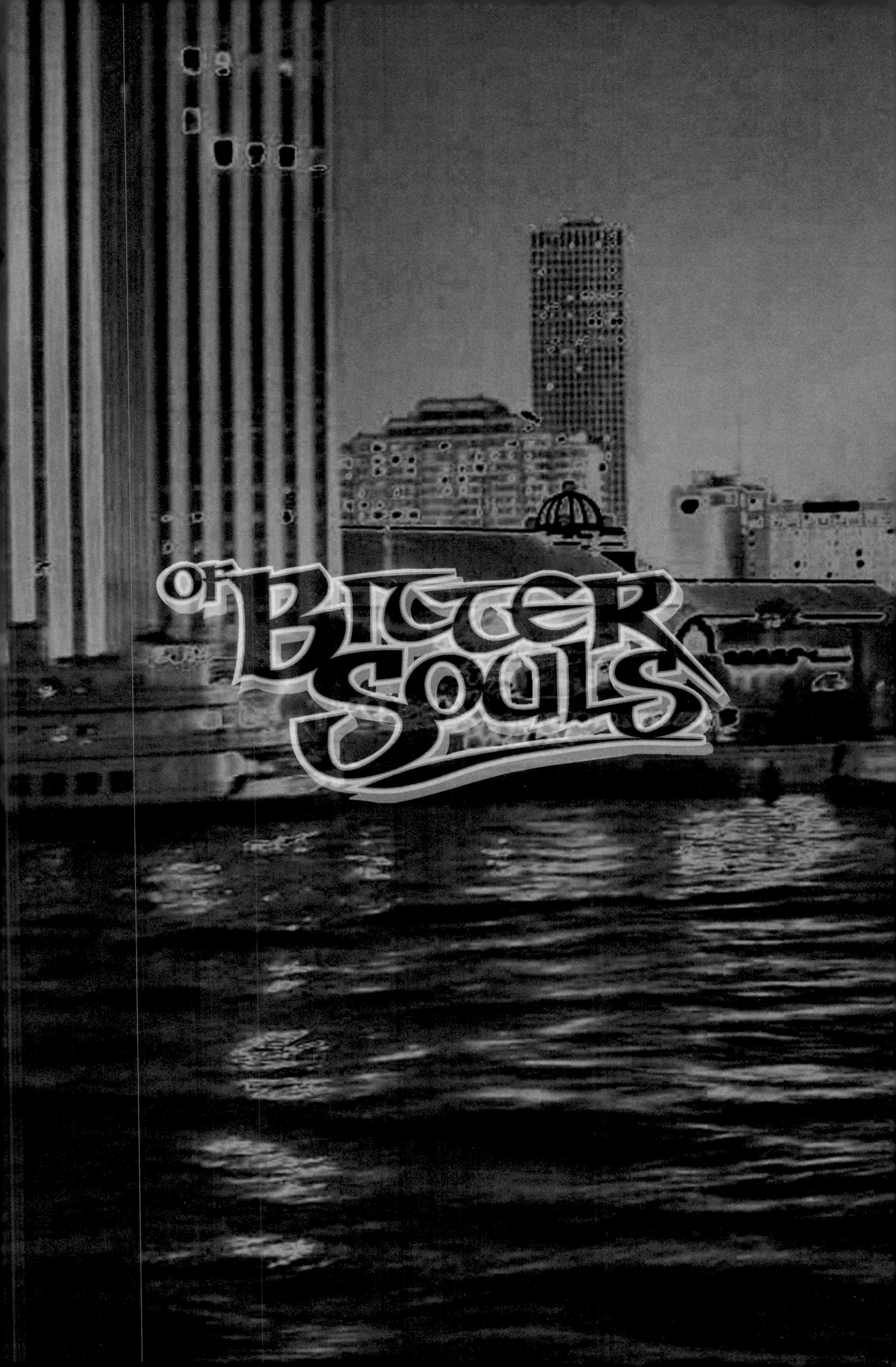
Of Bitter Souls

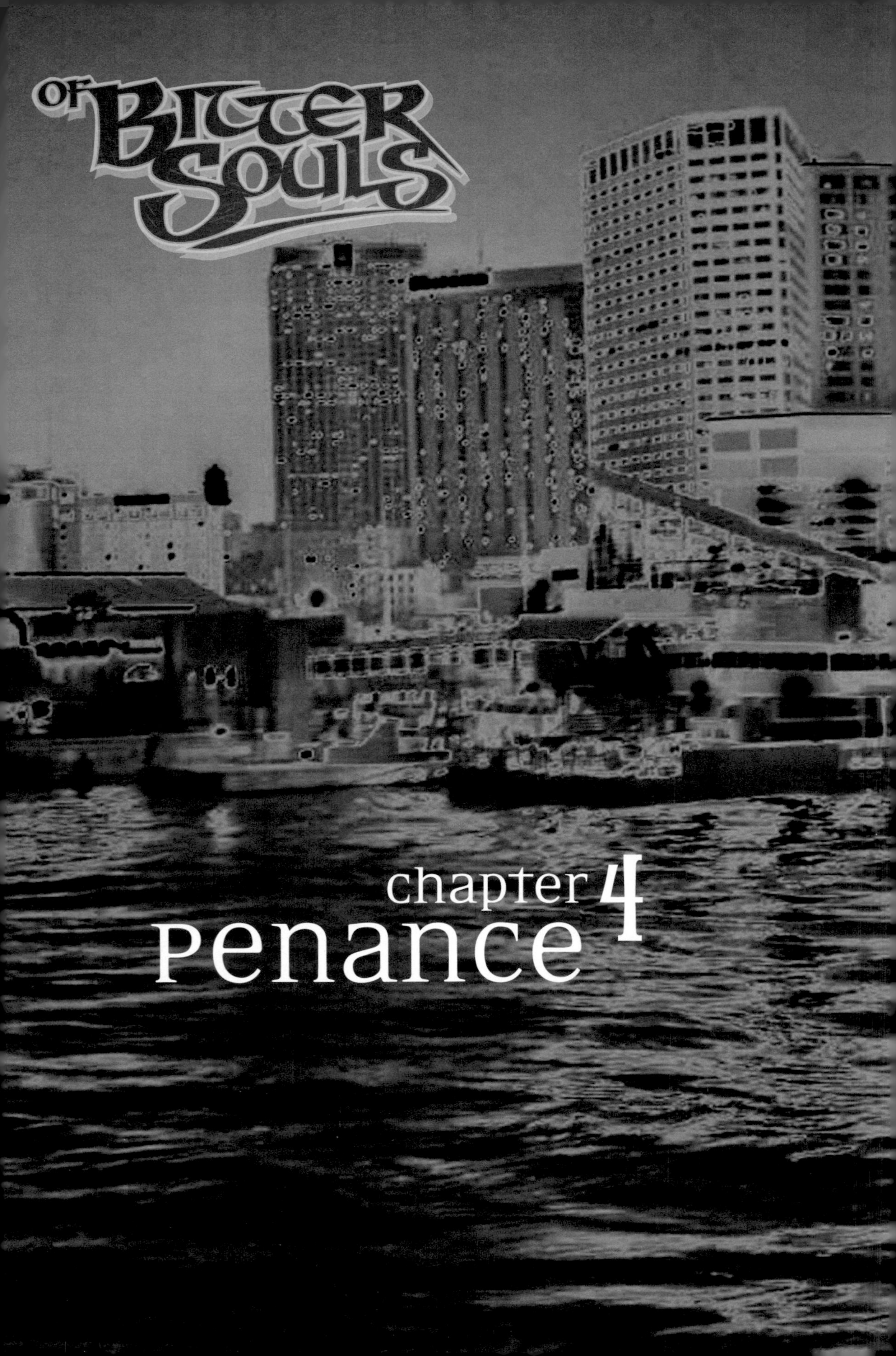
Of Bitter Souls

chapter 4
Penance

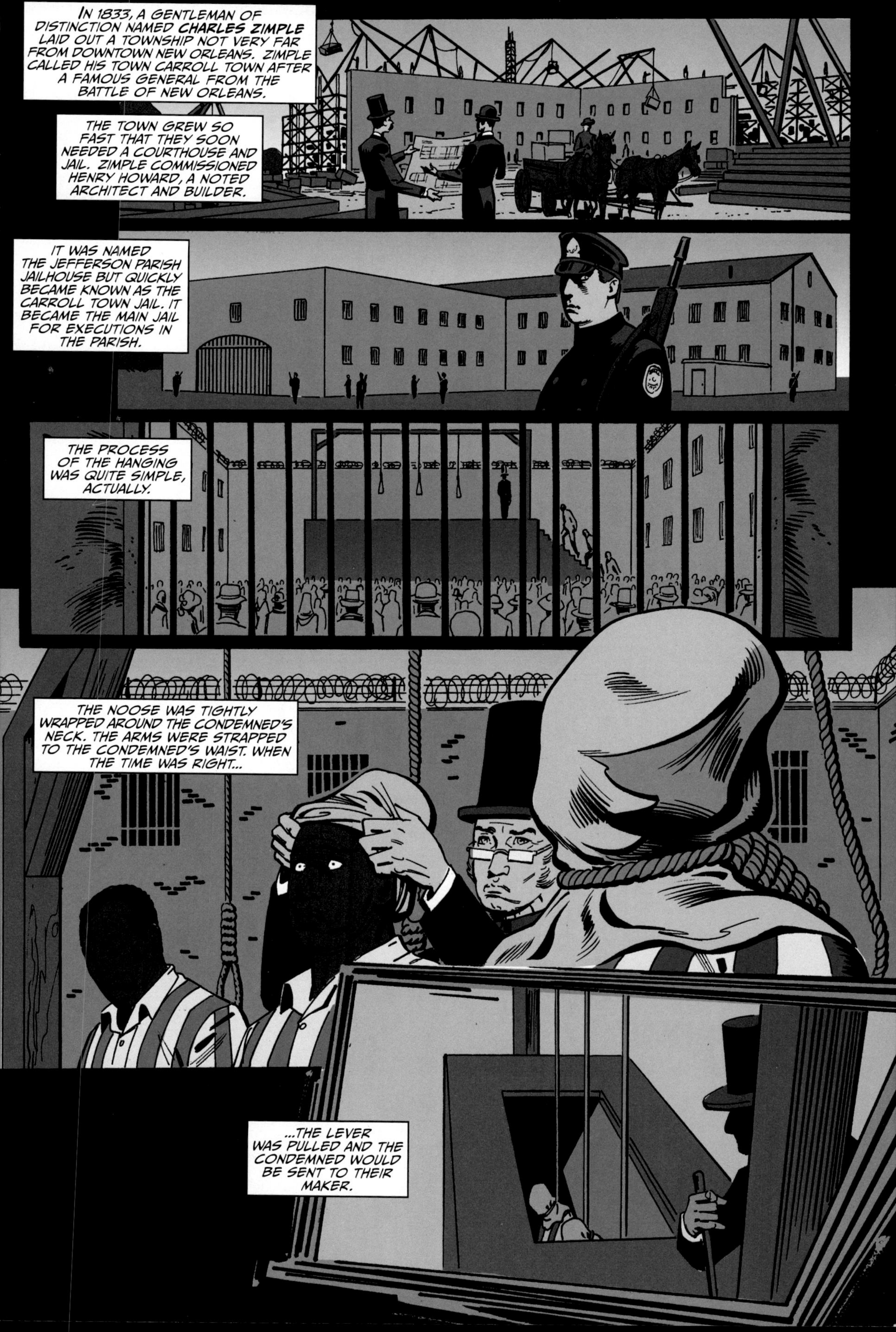

IN 1833, A GENTLEMAN OF DISTINCTION NAMED CHARLES ZIMPLE LAID OUT A TOWNSHIP NOT VERY FAR FROM DOWNTOWN NEW ORLEANS. ZIMPLE CALLED HIS TOWN CARROLL TOWN AFTER A FAMOUS GENERAL FROM THE BATTLE OF NEW ORLEANS.
THE TOWN GREW SO FAST THAT THEY SOON NEEDED A COURTHOUSE AND JAIL. ZIMPLE COMMISSIONED HENRY HOWARD, A NOTED ARCHITECT AND BUILDER.
IT WAS NAMED THE JEFFERSON PARISH JAILHOUSE BUT QUICKLY BECAME KNOWN AS THE CARROLL TOWN JAIL. IT BECAME THE MAIN JAIL FOR EXECUTIONS IN THE PARISH.
THE PROCESS OF THE HANGING WAS QUITE SIMPLE, ACTUALLY.
THE NOOSE WAS TIGHTLY WRAPPED AROUND THE CONDEMNED'S NECK. THE ARMS WERE STRAPPED TO THE CONDEMNED'S WAIST. WHEN THE TIME WAS RIGHT...
...THE LEVER WAS PULLED AND THE CONDEMNED WOULD BE SENT TO THEIR MAKER.

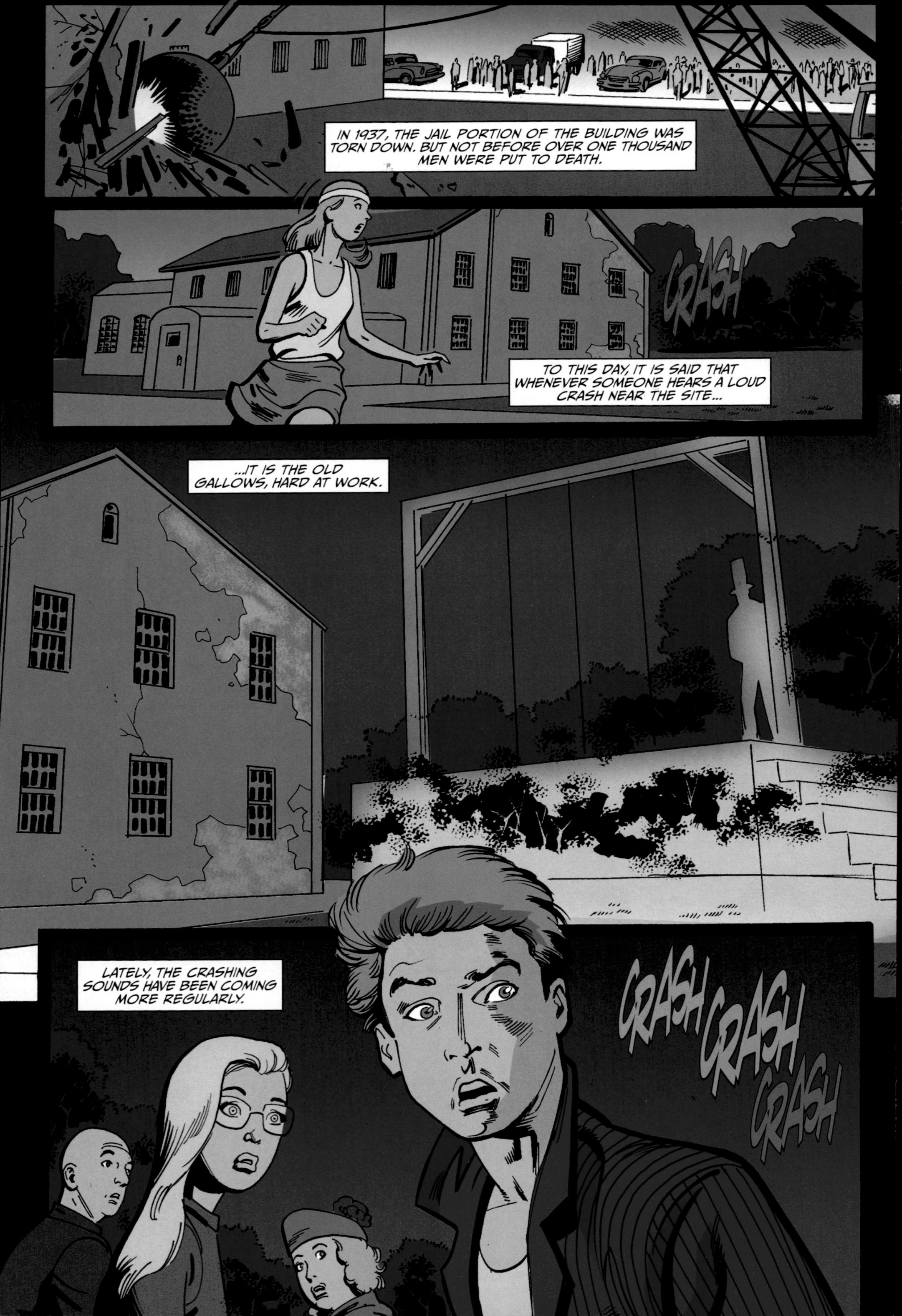
IN 1937, THE JAIL PORTION OF THE BUILDING WAS TORN DOWN. BUT NOT BEFORE OVER ONE THOUSAND MEN WERE PUT TO DEATH.
CRASH
TO THIS DAY, IT IS SAID THAT WHENEVER SOMEONE HEARS A LOUD CRASH NEAR THE SITE...
...IT IS THE OLD GALLOWS, HARD AT WORK.
LATELY, THE CRASHING SOUNDS HAVE BEEN COMING MORE REGULARLY.
CRASH CRASH CRASH

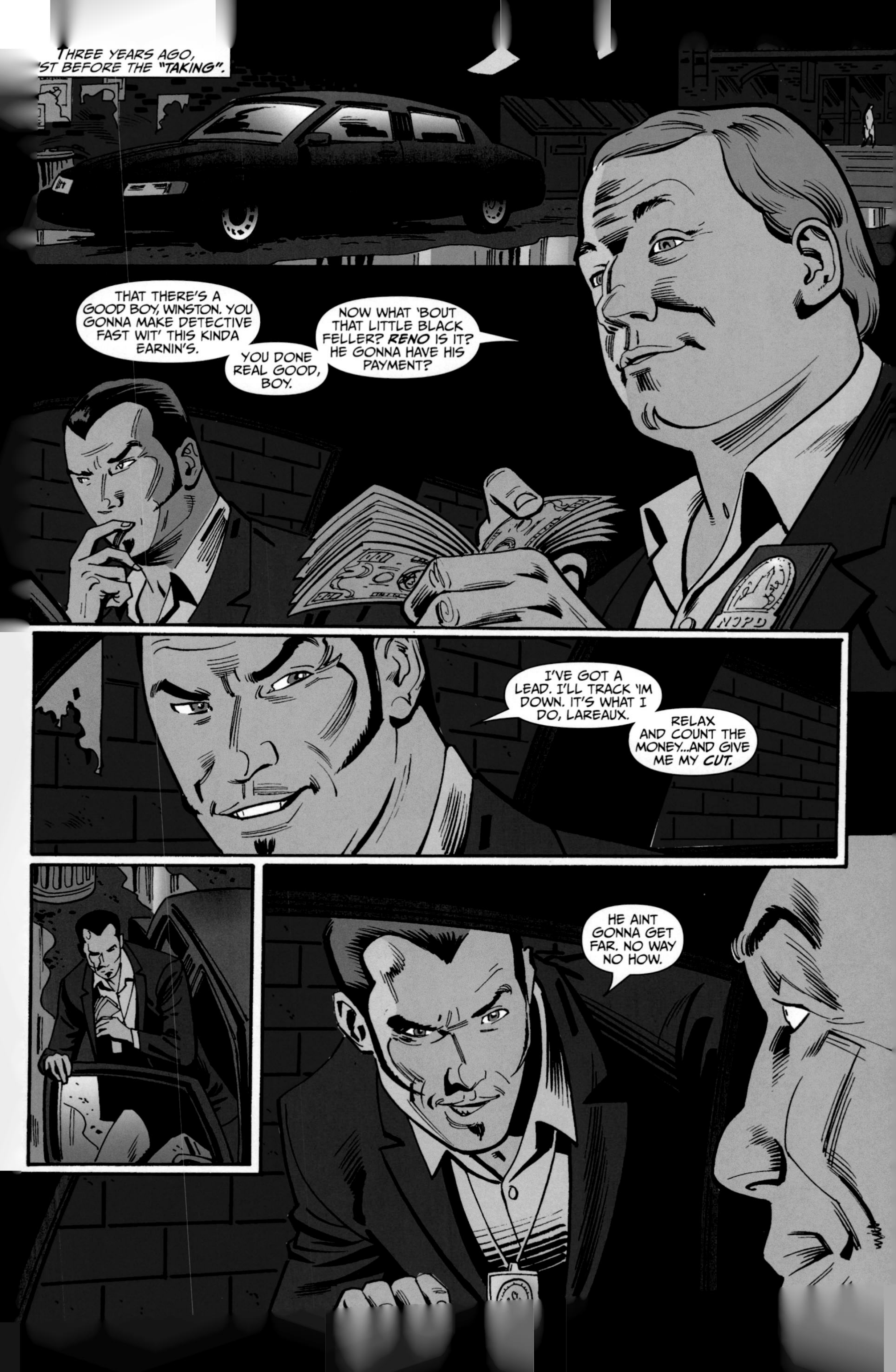
THREE YEARS AGO, ST BEFORE THE "TAKING".
THAT THERE'S A GOOD BOY, WINSTON. YOU GONNA MAKE DETECTIVE FAST WIT' THIS KINDA EARNIN'S.
YOU DONE REAL GOOD, BOY.
NOW WHAT 'BOUT THAT LITTLE BLACK FELLER? RENO IS IT? HE GONNA HAVE HIS PAYMENT?
I'VE GOT A LEAD. I'LL TRACK 'IM DOWN. IT'S WHAT I DO, LAREAUX.
RELAX AND COUNT THE MONEY...AND GIVE ME MY CUT.
HE AINT GONNA GET FAR. NO WAY NO HOW.

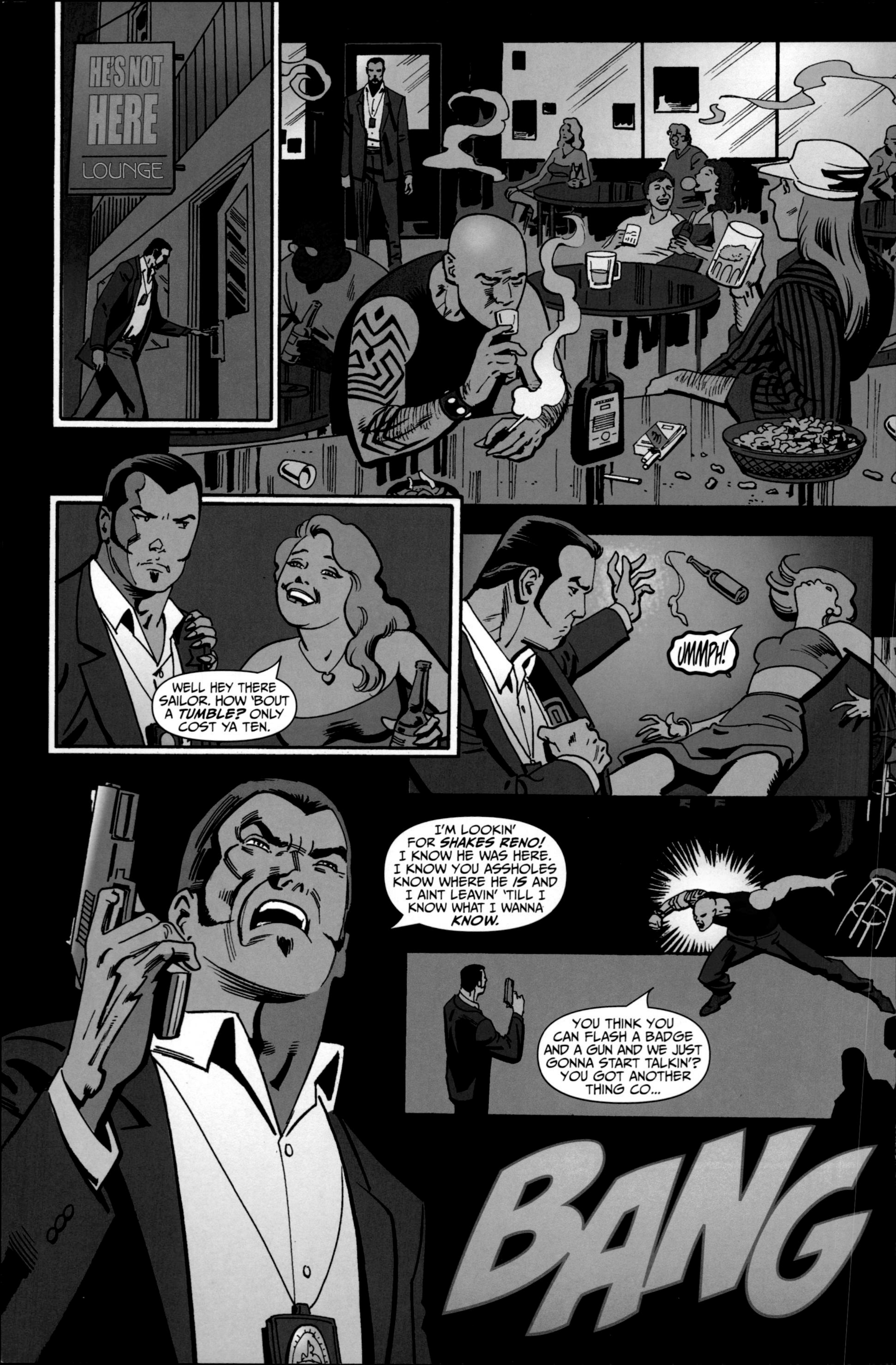
HE'S NOT HERE
LOUNGE
WELL HEY THERE SAILOR. HOW 'BOUT A TUMBLE? ONLY COST YA TEN.
UMMPH!
I'M LOOKIN' FOR SHAKES RENO! I KNOW HE WAS HERE. I KNOW YOU ASSHOLES KNOW WHERE HE IS AND I AINT LEAVIN' 'TILL I KNOW WHAT I WANNA KNOW.
YOU THINK YOU CAN FLASH A BADGE AND A GUN AND WE JUST GONNA START TALKIN'? YOU GOT ANOTHER THING CO...
BANG

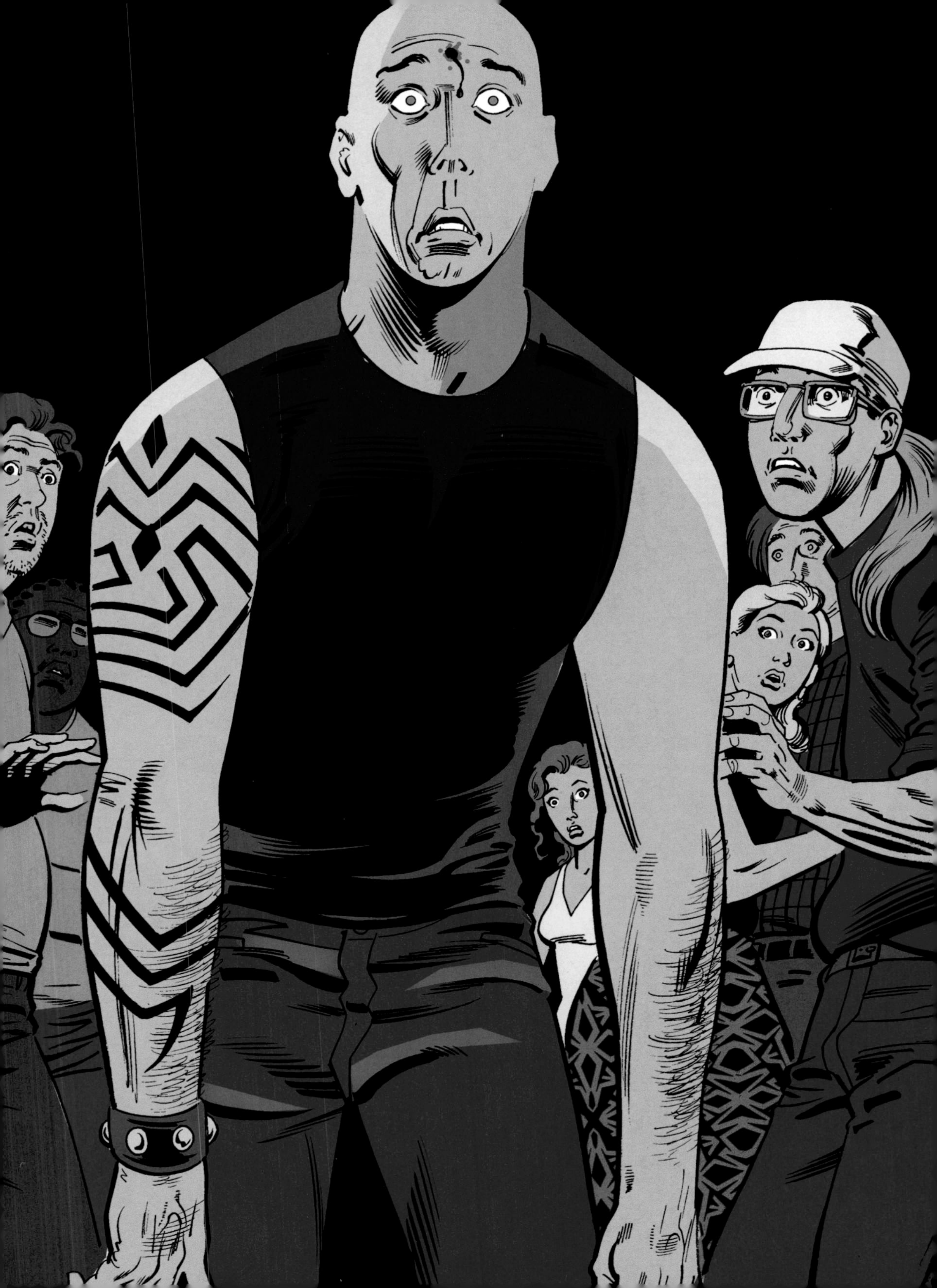

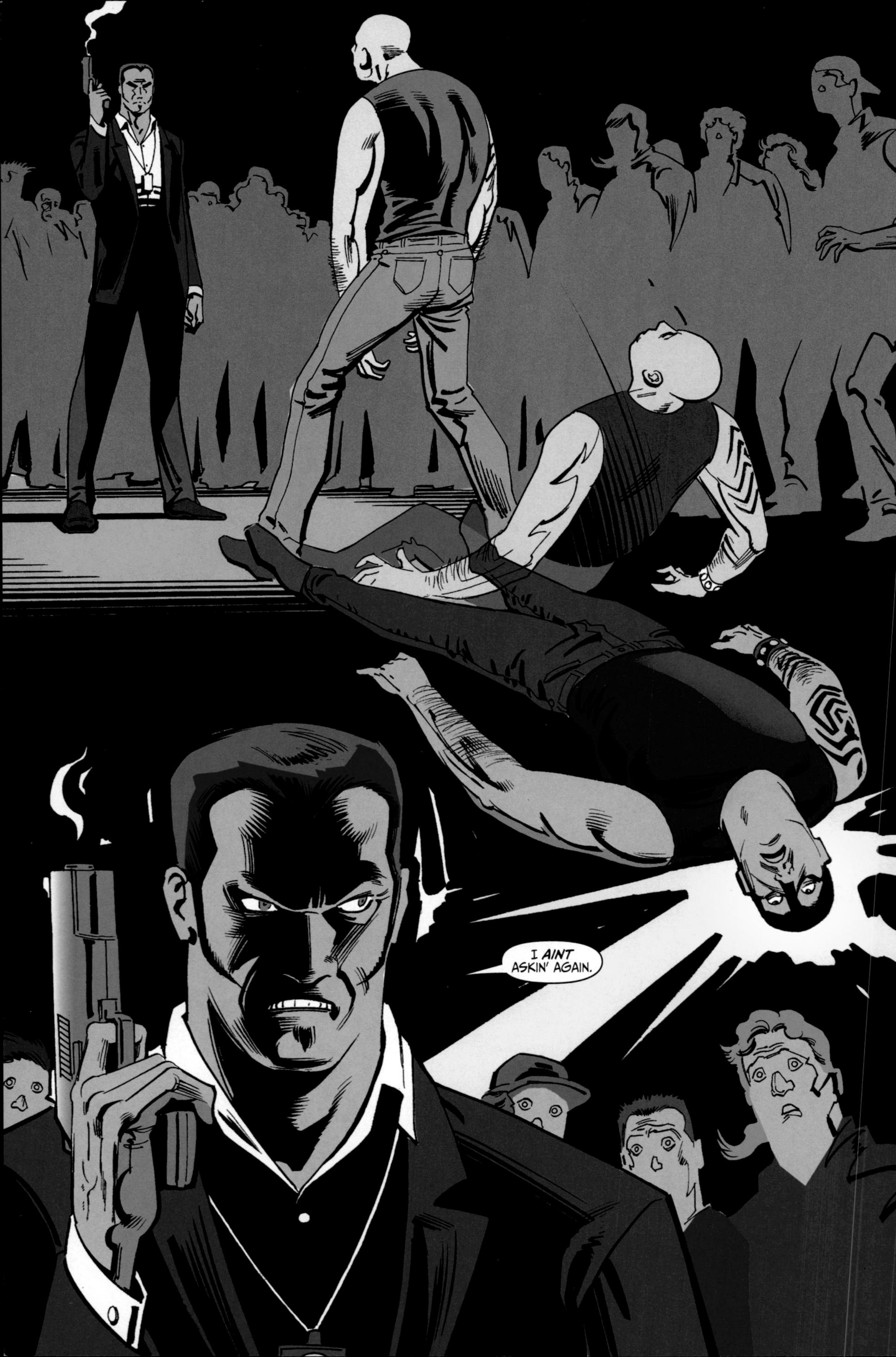
I AINT ASKIN' AGAIN.

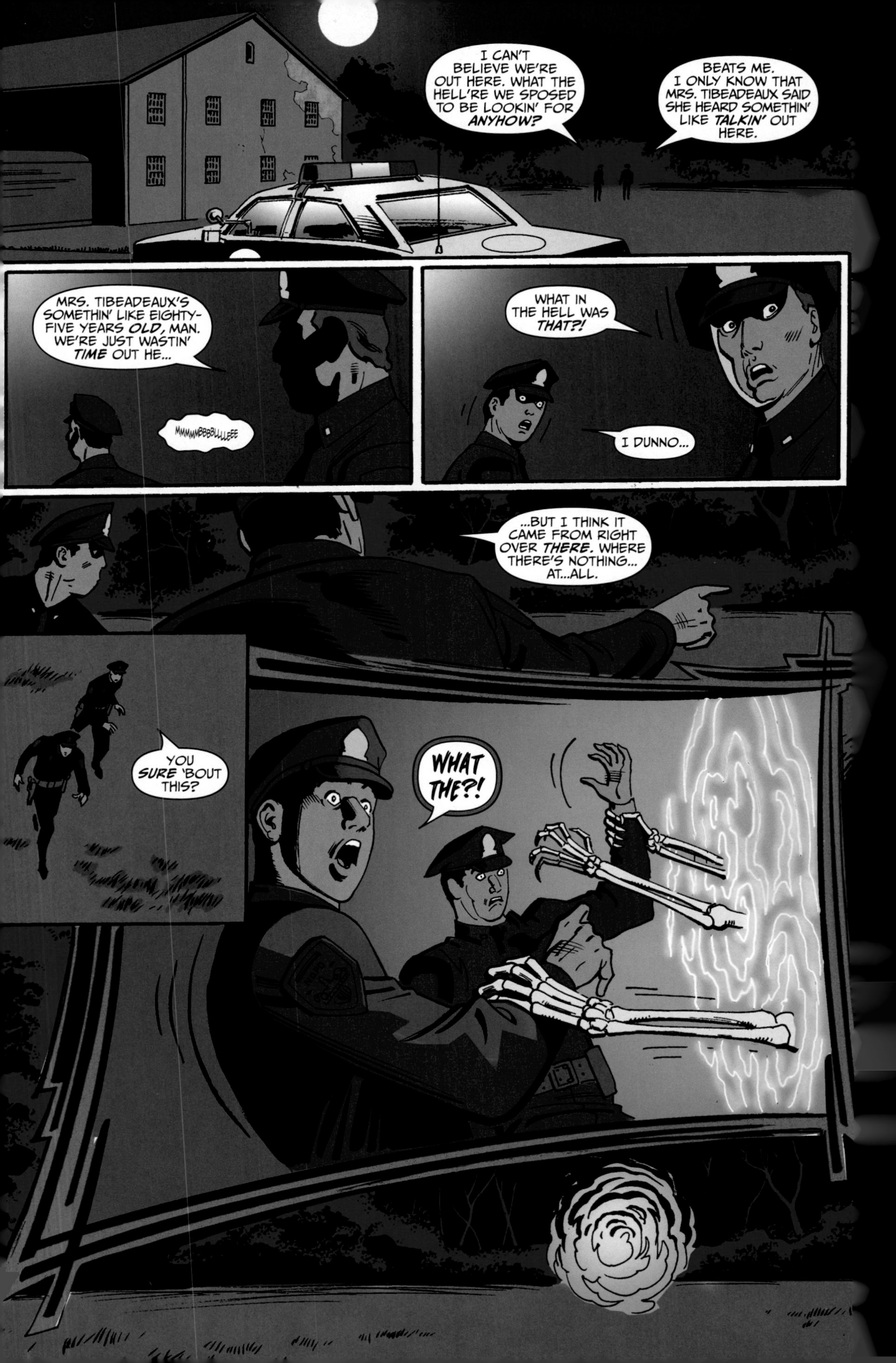
I CAN'T BELIEVE WE'RE OUT HERE. WHAT THE HELL'RE WE SPOSED TO BE LOOKIN' FOR ANYHOW?
BEATS ME. I ONLY KNOW THAT MRS. TIBEADEAUX SAID SHE HEARD SOMETHIN' LIKE TALKIN' OUT HERE.
MRS. TIBEADEAUX'S SOMETHIN' LIKE EIGHTY-FIVE YEARS OLD, MAN. WE'RE JUST WASTIN' TIME OUT HE...
MMMMMBBBBLLLLEEE
WHAT IN THE HELL WAS THAT?!
I DUNNO...
...BUT I THINK IT CAME FROM RIGHT OVER THERE. WHERE THERE'S NOTHING... AT...ALL.
YOU SURE 'BOUT THIS?
WHAT THE?!

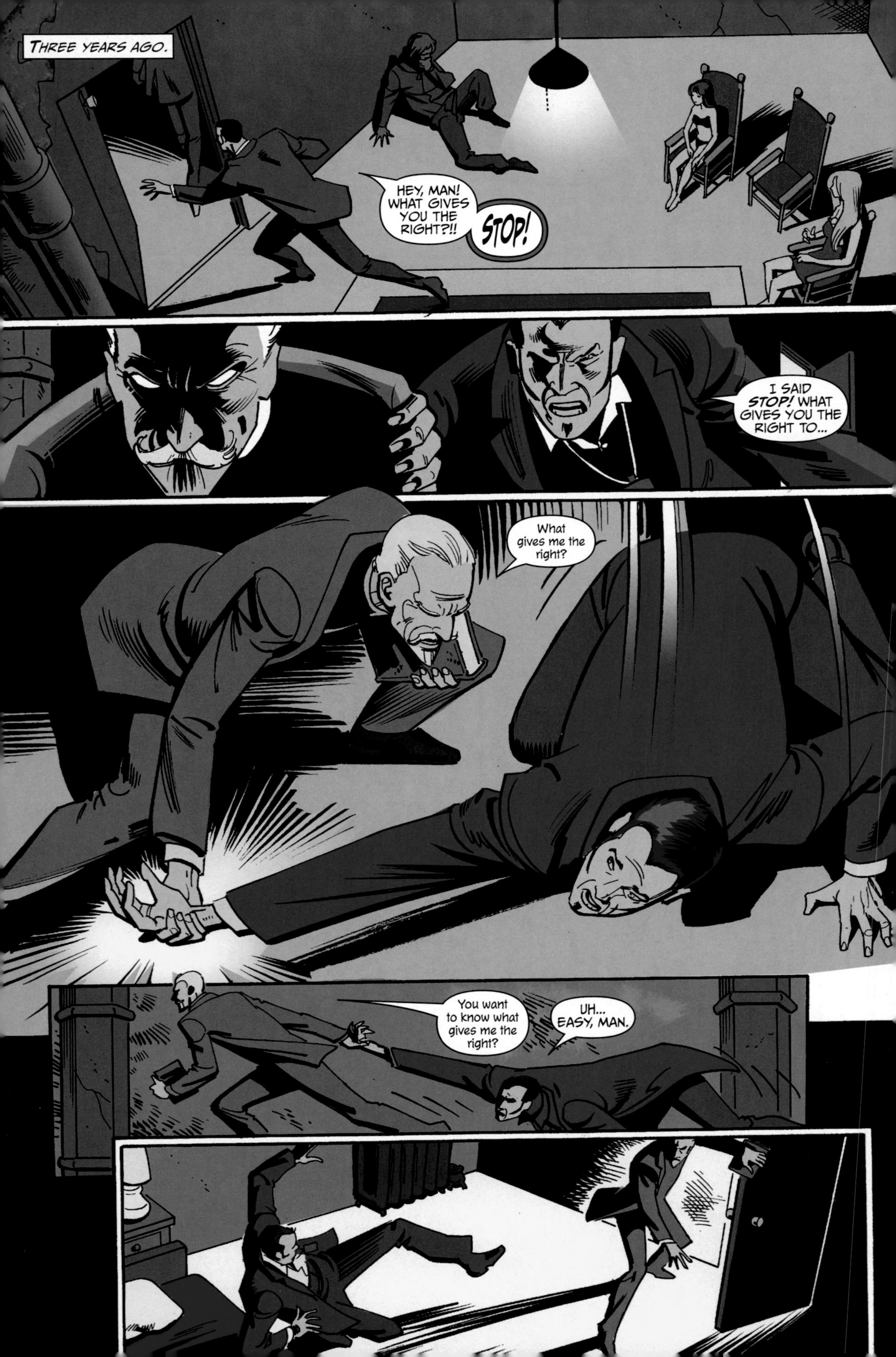
THREE YEARS AGO.
HEY, MAN! WHAT GIVES YOU THE RIGHT?!!
STOP!
I SAID STOP! WHAT GIVES YOU THE RIGHT TO...
What gives me the right?
You want to know what gives me the right?
UH... EASY, MAN.

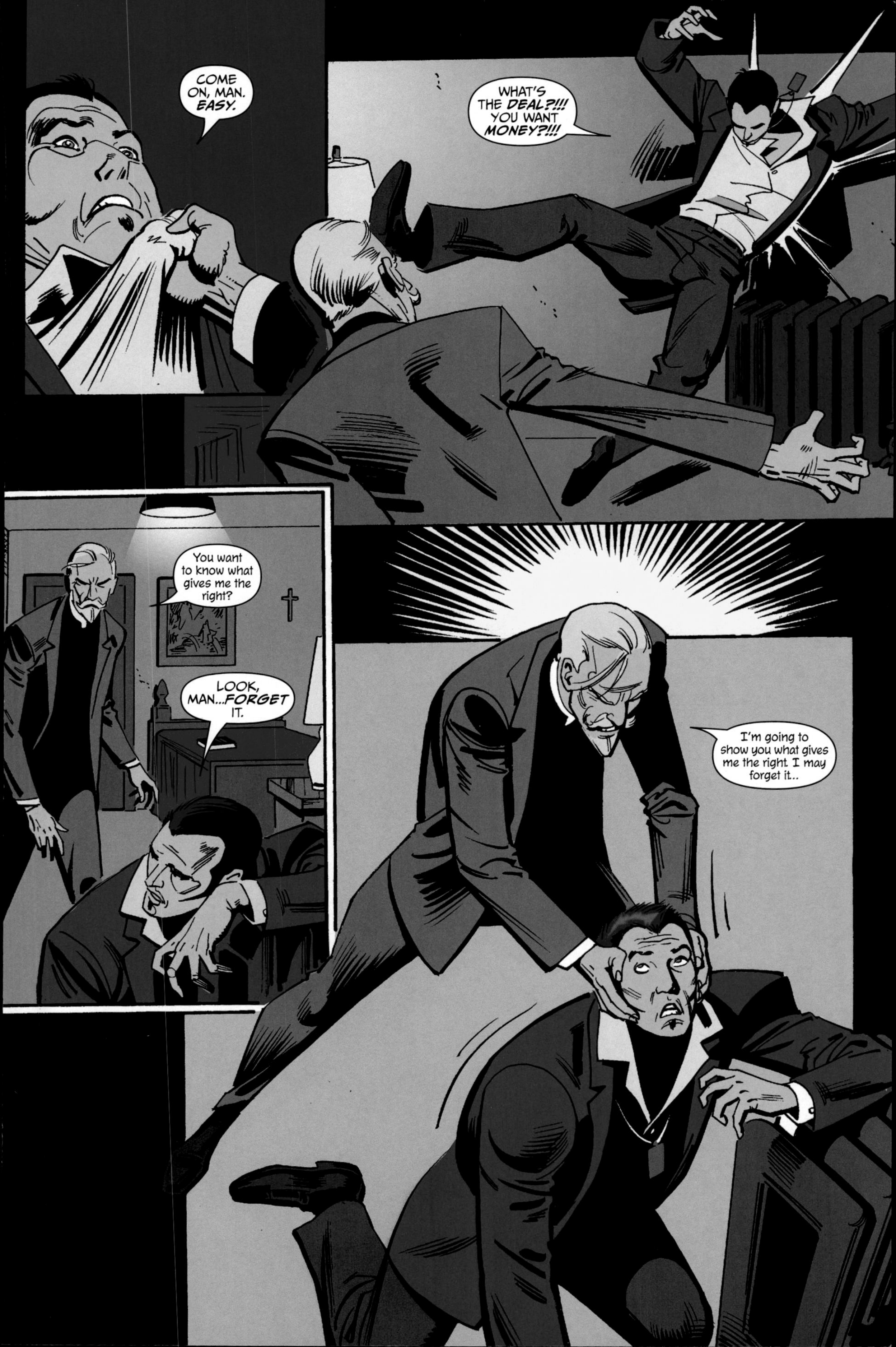
COME ON, MAN. EASY.
WHAT'S THE DEAL?!!! YOU WANT MONEY?!!!
You want to know what gives me the right?
LOOK, MAN...FORGET IT.
I'm going to show you what gives me the right. I may forget it...

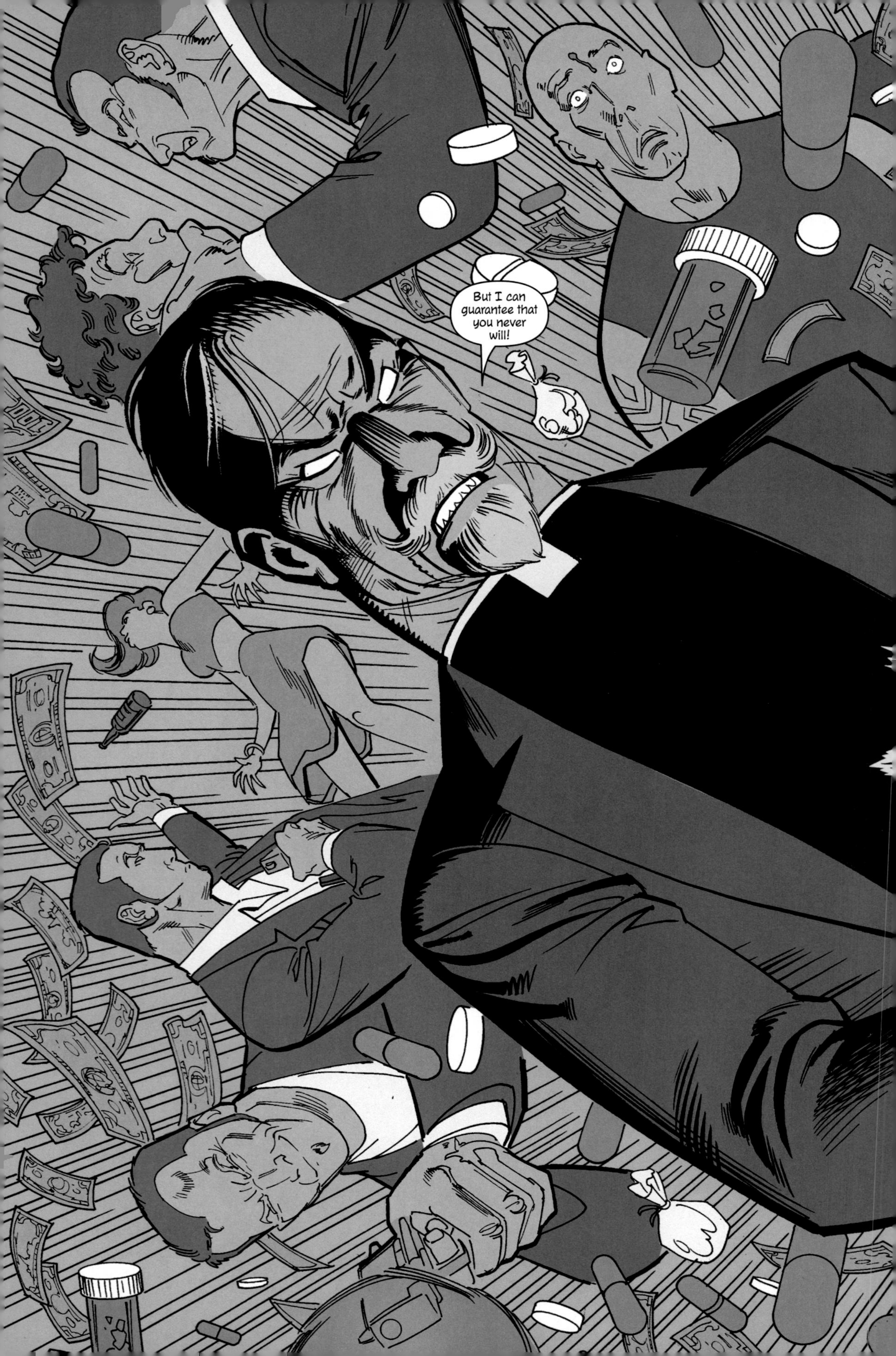
But I can guarantee that you never will!

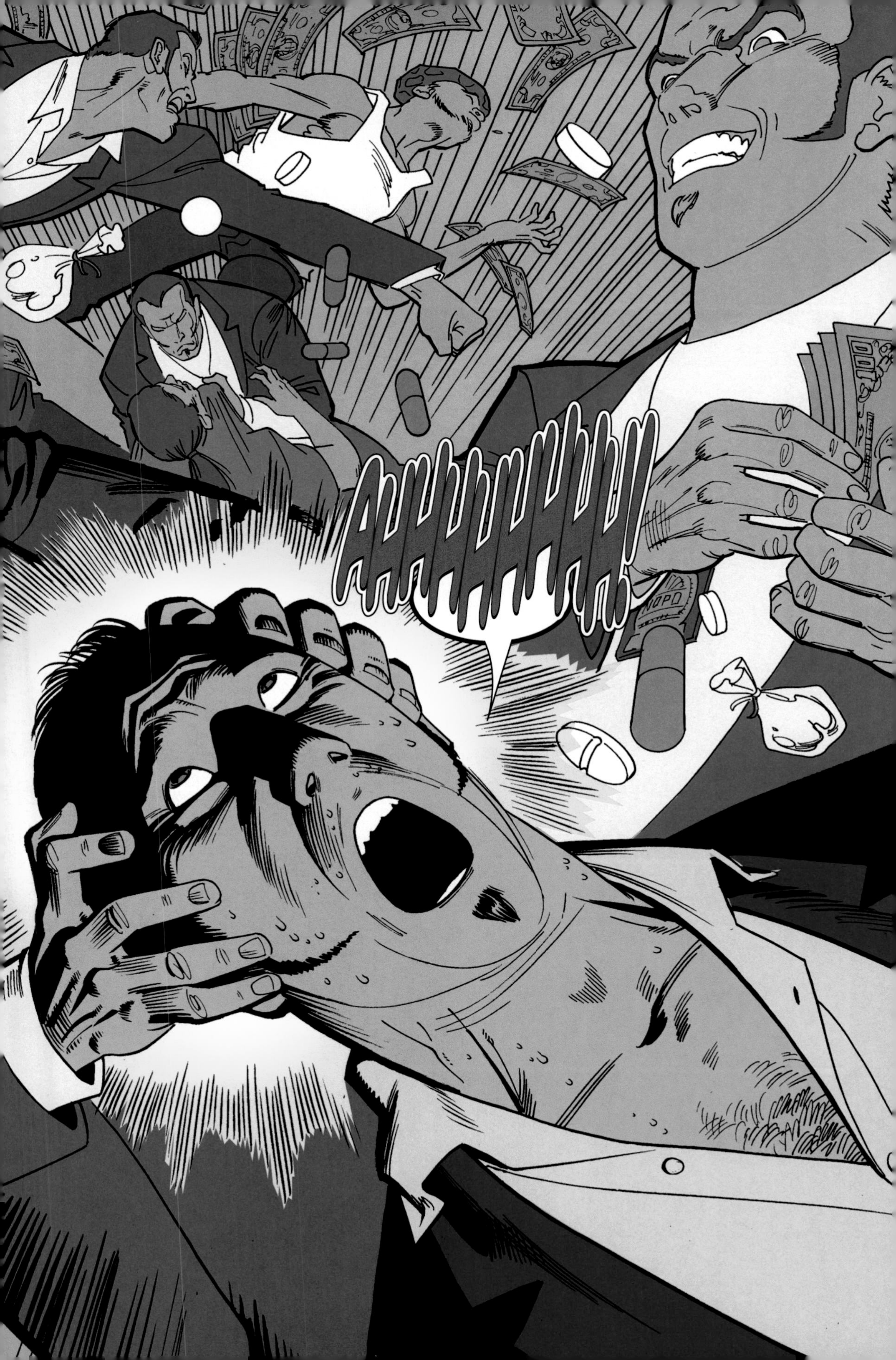
AHHHHHHH!

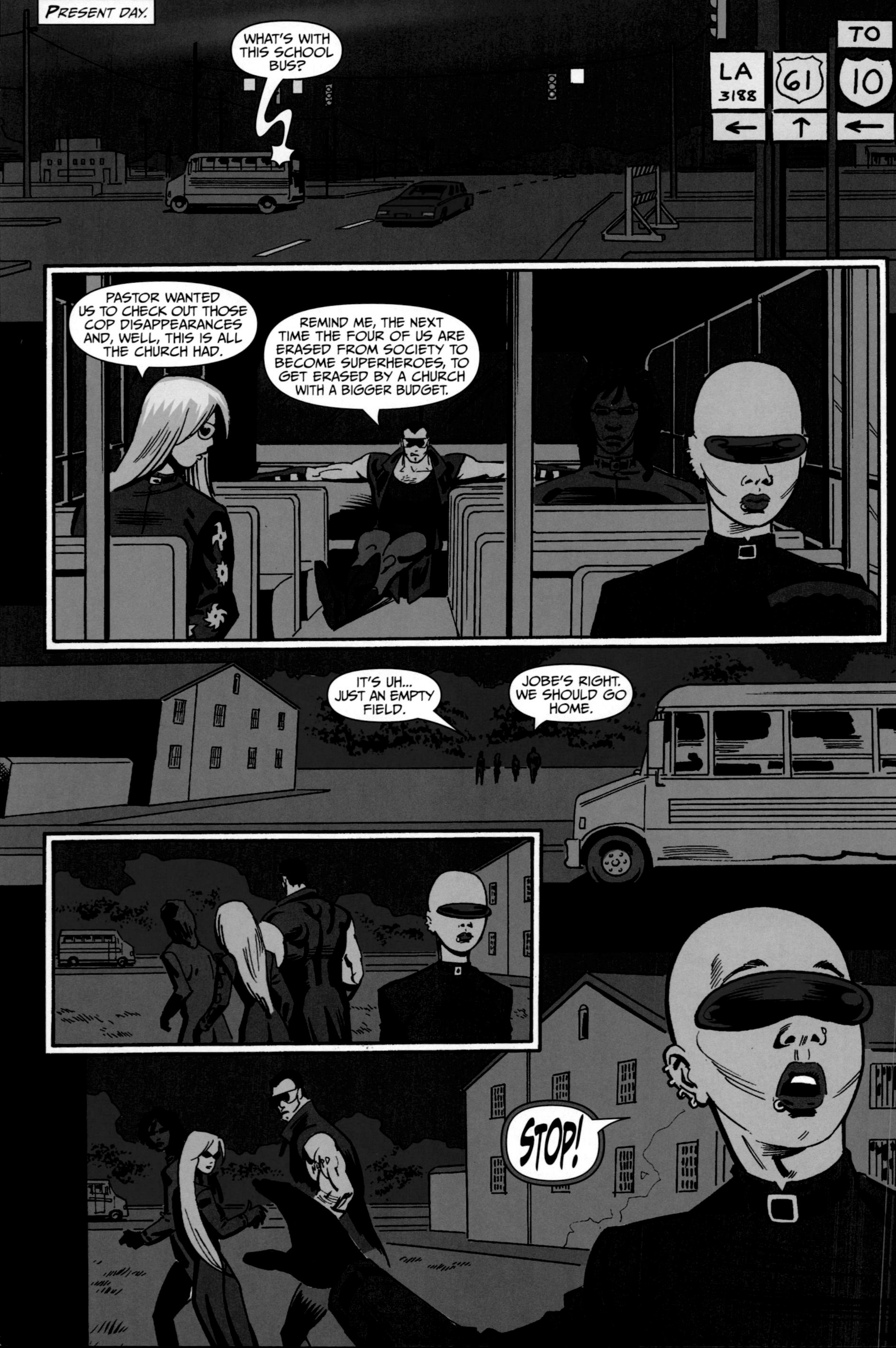
PRESENT DAY.
WHAT'S WITH THIS SCHOOL BUS?
TO
LA 3188
61
10
PASTOR WANTED US TO CHECK OUT THOSE COP DISAPPEARANCES AND, WELL, THIS IS ALL THE CHURCH HAD.
REMIND ME, THE NEXT TIME THE FOUR OF US ARE ERASED FROM SOCIETY TO BECOME SUPERHEROES, TO GET ERASED BY A CHURCH WITH A BIGGER BUDGET.
IT'S UH... JUST AN EMPTY FIELD.
JOBE'S RIGHT. WE SHOULD GO HOME.
STOP!

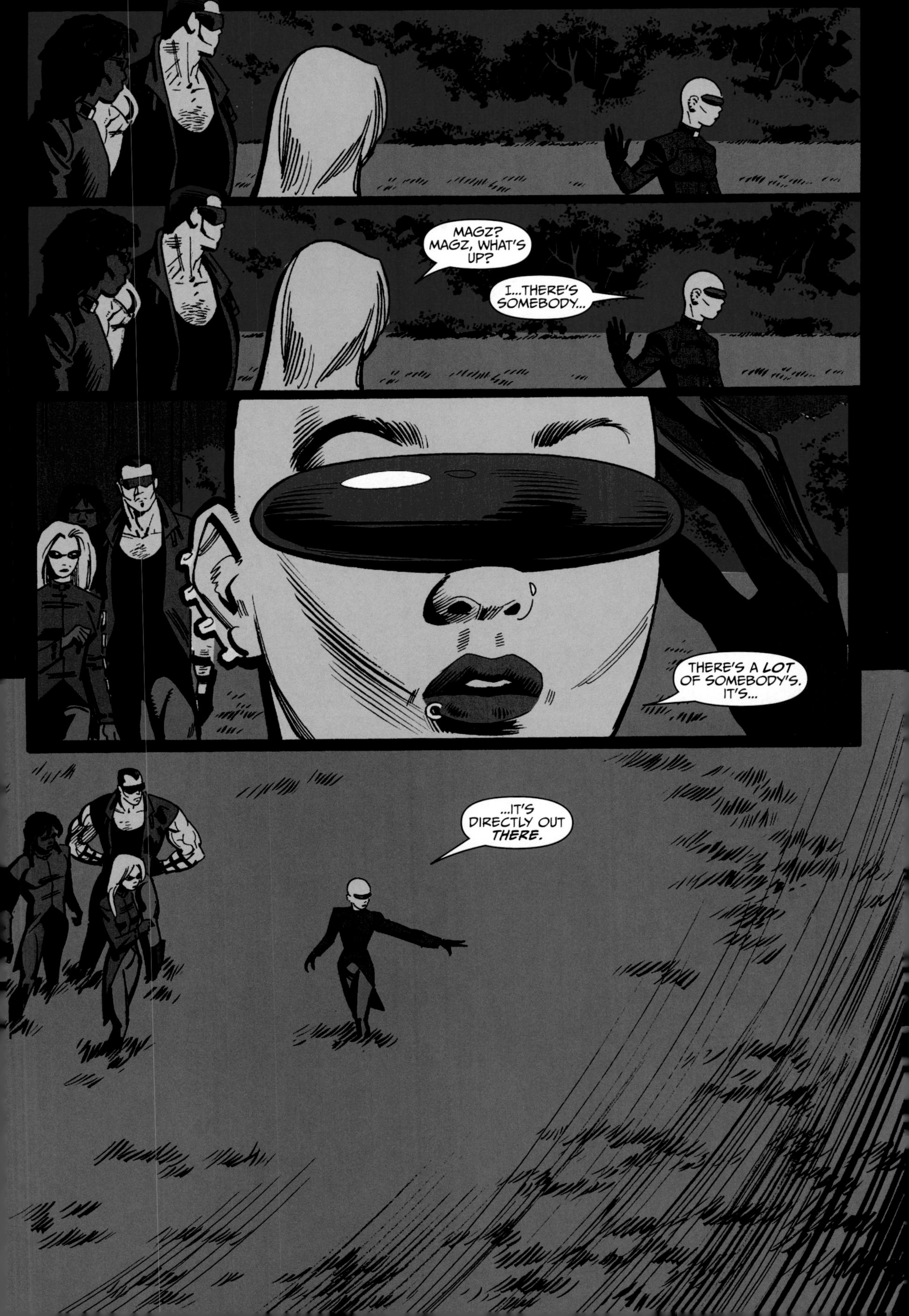
MAGZ? MAGZ, WHAT'S UP?
I...THERE'S SOMEBODY...
THERE'S A *LOT* OF SOMEBODY'S. IT'S...
...IT'S DIRECTLY OUT *THERE.*

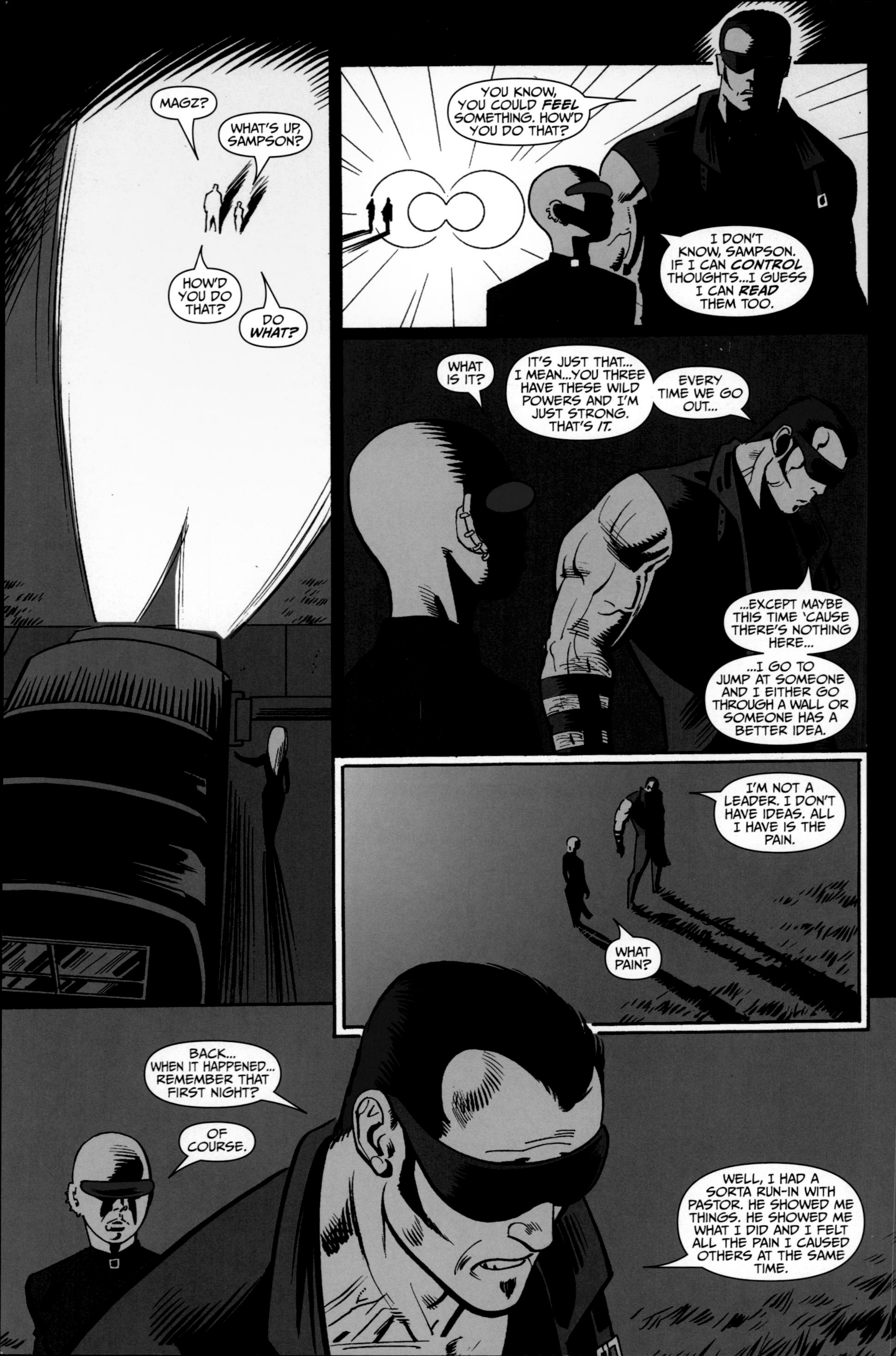
MAGZ?
WHAT'S UP, SAMPSON?
HOW'D YOU DO THAT?
DO *WHAT?*
YOU KNOW, YOU COULD *FEEL* SOMETHING. HOW'D YOU DO THAT?
I DON'T KNOW, SAMPSON. IF I CAN *CONTROL* THOUGHTS...I GUESS I CAN *READ* THEM TOO.
WHAT IS IT?
IT'S JUST THAT... I MEAN...YOU THREE HAVE THESE WILD POWERS AND I'M JUST STRONG. THAT'S *IT.*
EVERY TIME WE GO OUT...
...EXCEPT MAYBE THIS TIME 'CAUSE THERE'S NOTHING HERE...
...I GO TO JUMP AT SOMEONE AND I EITHER GO THROUGH A WALL OR SOMEONE HAS A BETTER IDEA.
I'M NOT A LEADER. I DON'T HAVE IDEAS. ALL I HAVE IS THE PAIN.
WHAT PAIN?
BACK... WHEN IT HAPPENED... REMEMBER THAT FIRST NIGHT?
OF COURSE.
WELL, I HAD A SORTA RUN-IN WITH PASTOR. HE SHOWED ME THINGS. HE SHOWED ME WHAT I DID AND I FELT ALL THE PAIN I CAUSED OTHERS AT THE SAME TIME.

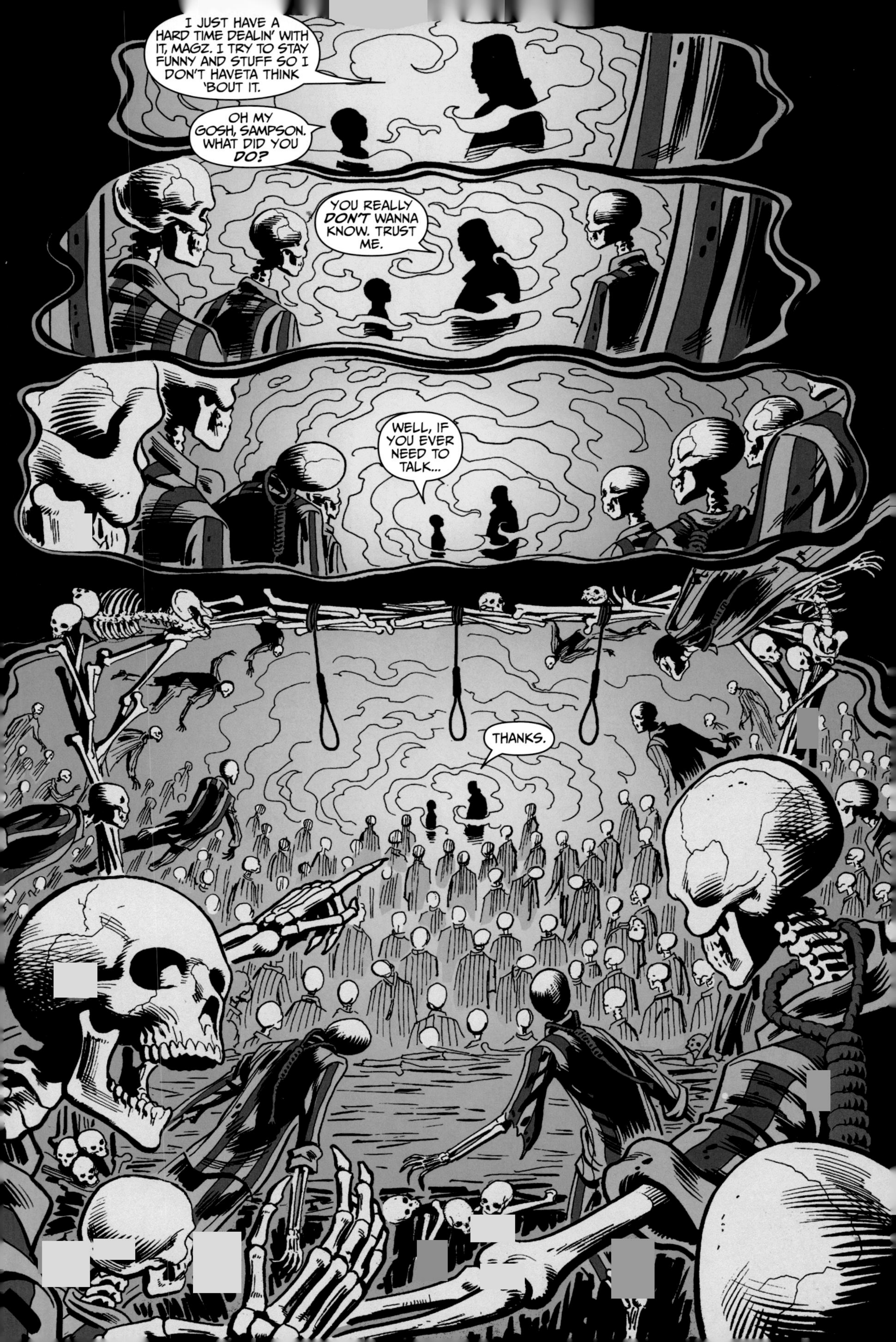

I JUST HAVE A HARD TIME DEALIN' WITH IT, MAGZ. I TRY TO STAY FUNNY AND STUFF SO I DON'T HAVETA THINK 'BOUT IT.
OH MY GOSH, SAMPSON. WHAT DID YOU *DO?*
YOU REALLY *DON'T* WANNA KNOW. TRUST ME.
WELL, IF YOU EVER NEED TO TALK...
THANKS.

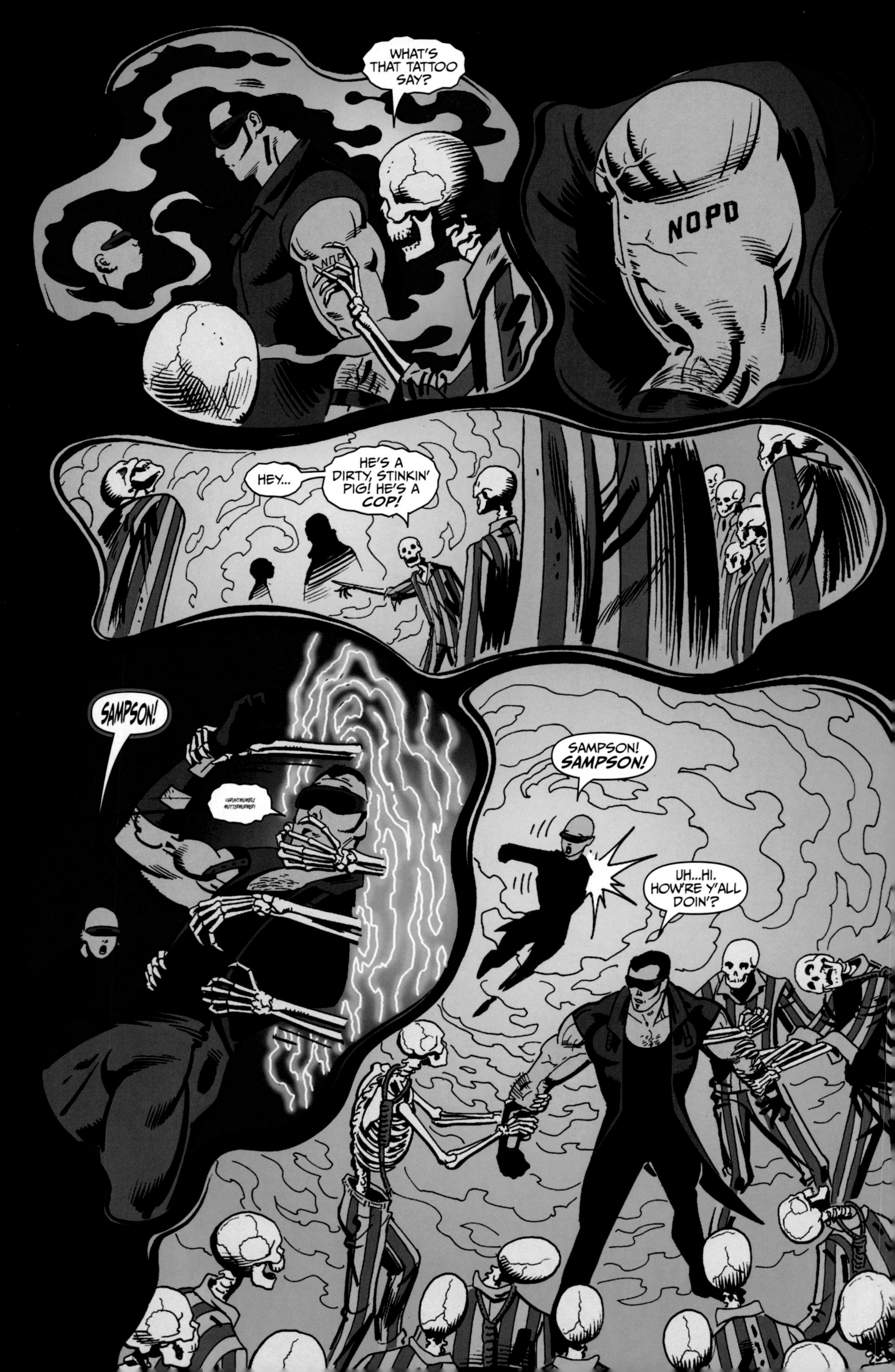
WHAT'S THAT TATTOO SAY?
NOPD
NOPD
HEY...
HE'S A DIRTY, STINKIN' PIG! HE'S A COP!
SAMPSON!
=GRUNTMUMBLE MUTTERMURMER=
SAMPSON! SAMPSON!
UH...HI. HOW'RE Y'ALL DOIN'?

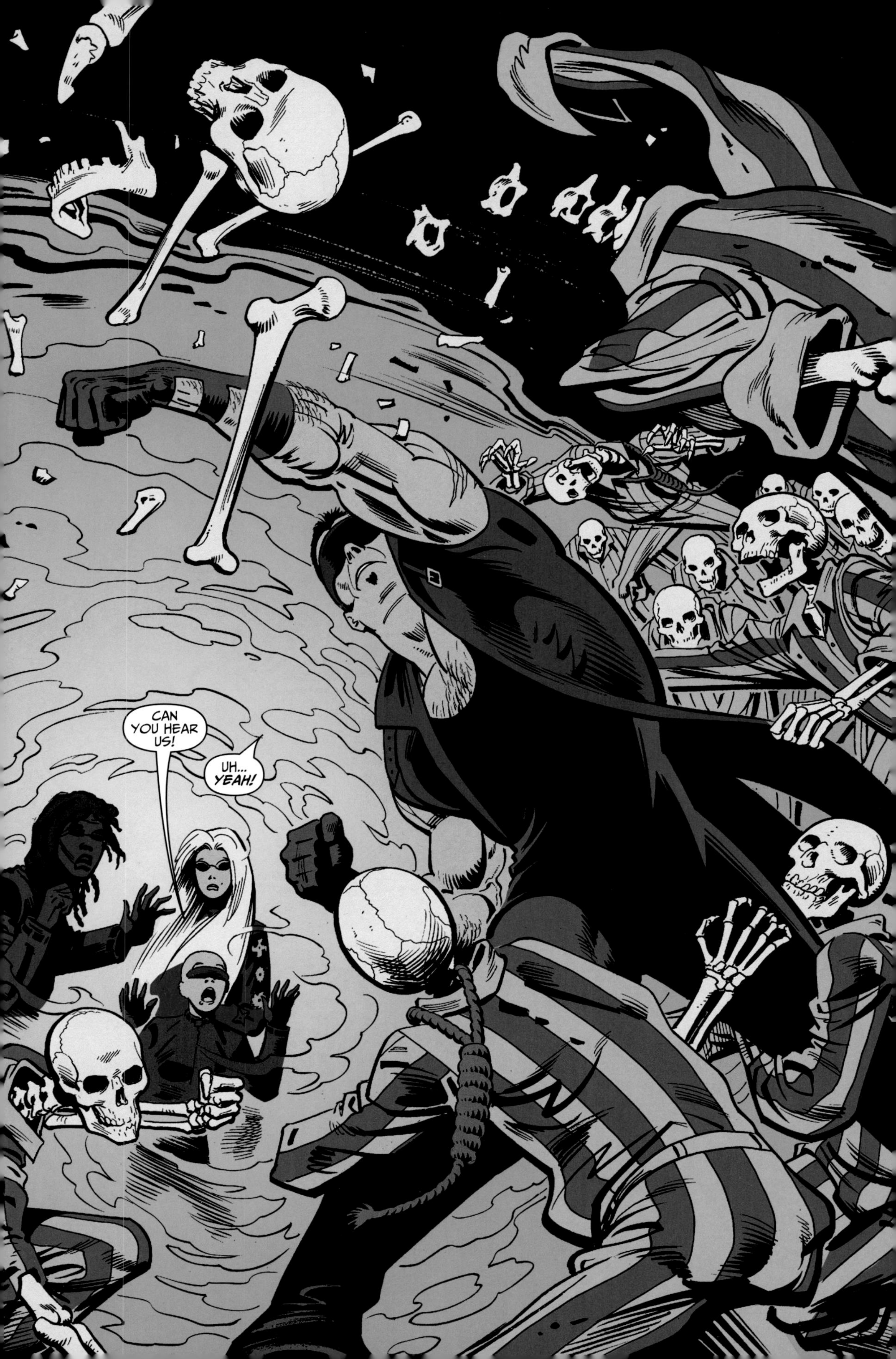
CAN YOU HEAR US!
UH... YEAH!

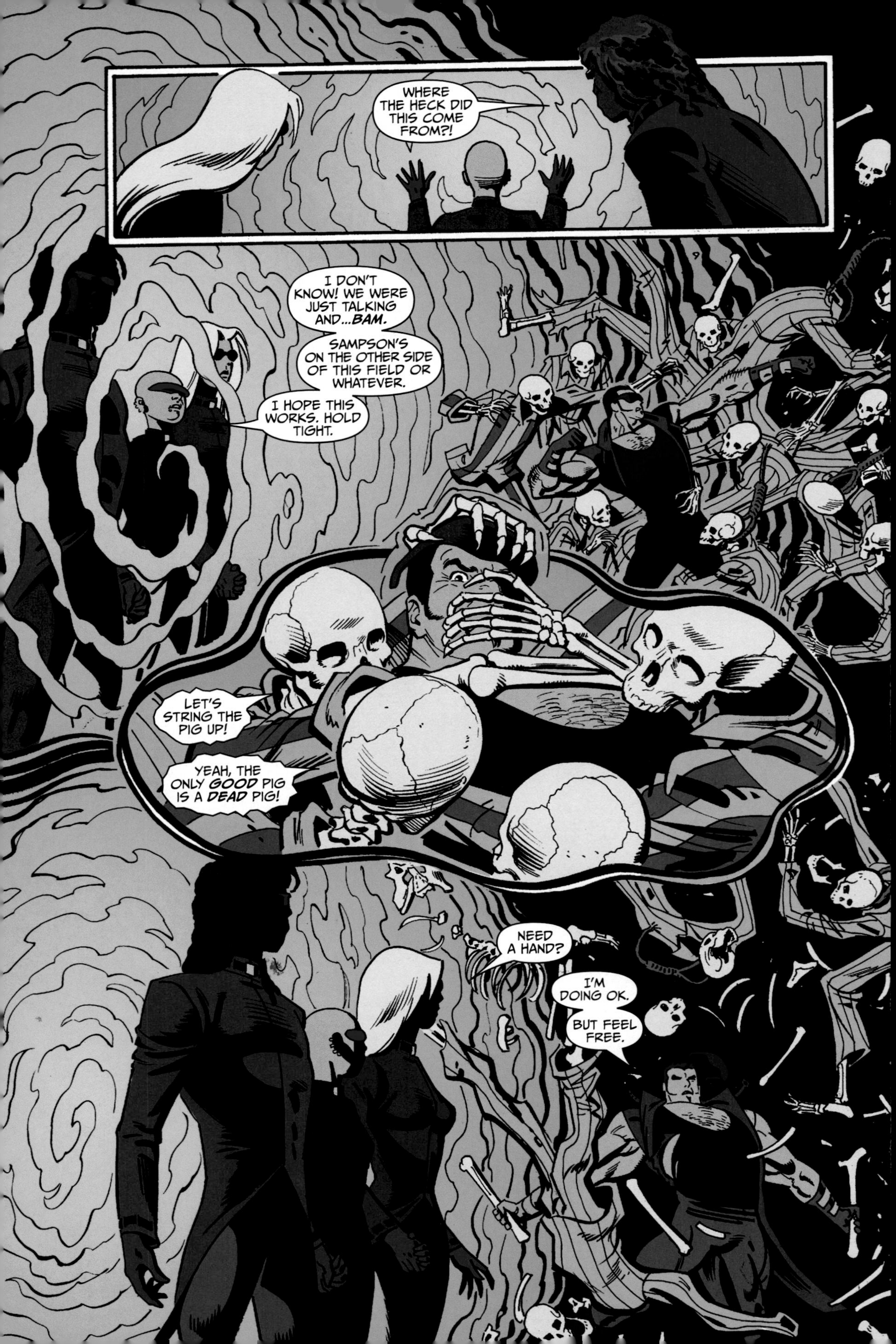

WHERE THE HECK DID THIS COME FROM?!
I DON'T KNOW! WE WERE JUST TALKING AND...BAM.
SAMPSON'S ON THE OTHER SIDE OF THIS FIELD OR WHATEVER.
I HOPE THIS WORKS. HOLD TIGHT.
LET'S STRING THE PIG UP!
YEAH, THE ONLY GOOD PIG IS A DEAD PIG!
NEED A HAND?
I'M DOING OK.
BUT FEEL FREE.

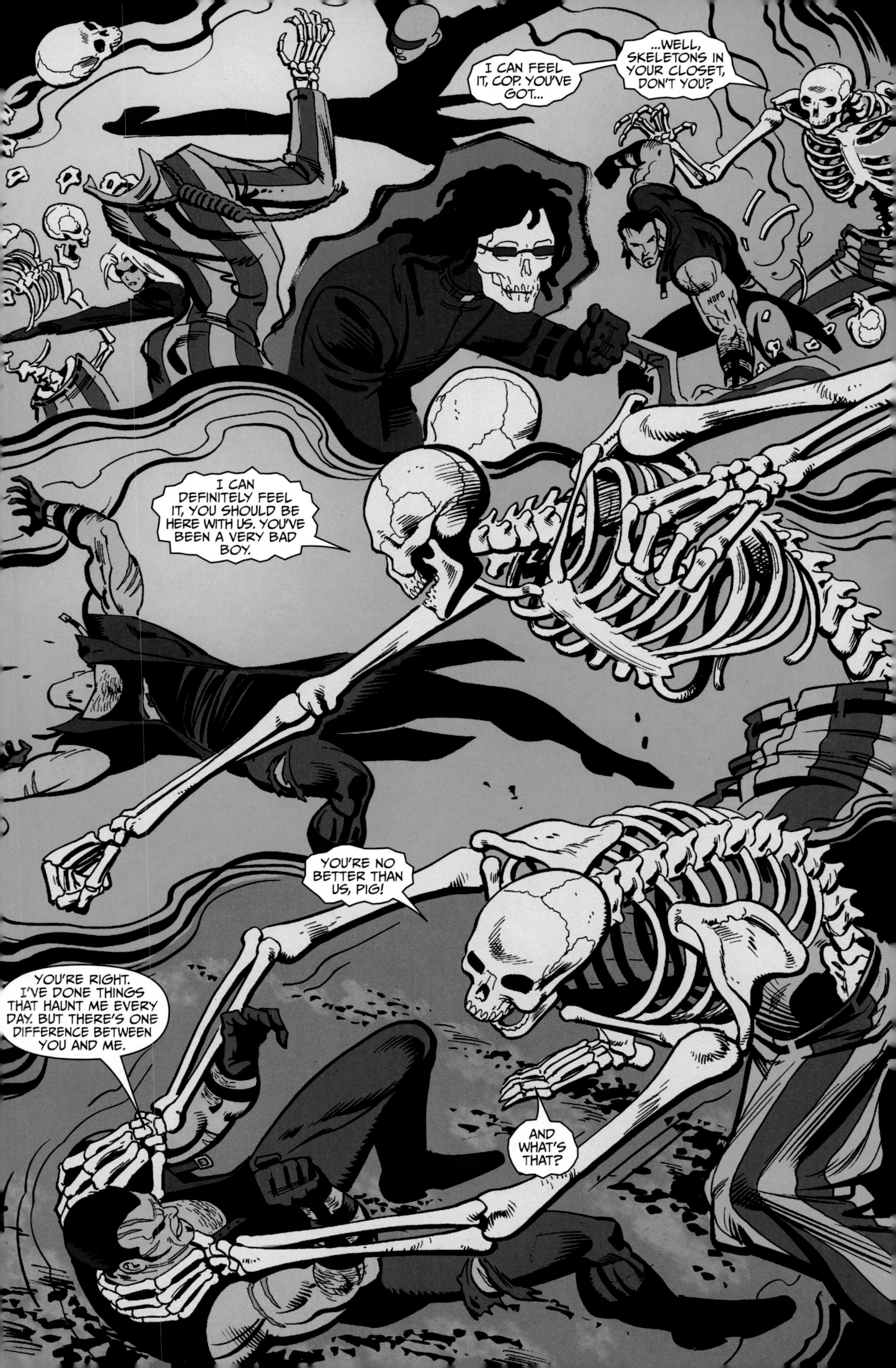
I CAN FEEL IT, COP. YOU'VE GOT...
...WELL, SKELETONS IN YOUR CLOSET, DON'T YOU?
I CAN DEFINITELY FEEL IT, YOU SHOULD BE HERE WITH US. YOU'VE BEEN A VERY BAD BOY.
YOU'RE NO BETTER THAN US, PIG!
YOU'RE RIGHT. I'VE DONE THINGS THAT HAUNT ME EVERY DAY. BUT THERE'S ONE DIFFERENCE BETWEEN YOU AND ME.
AND WHAT'S THAT?

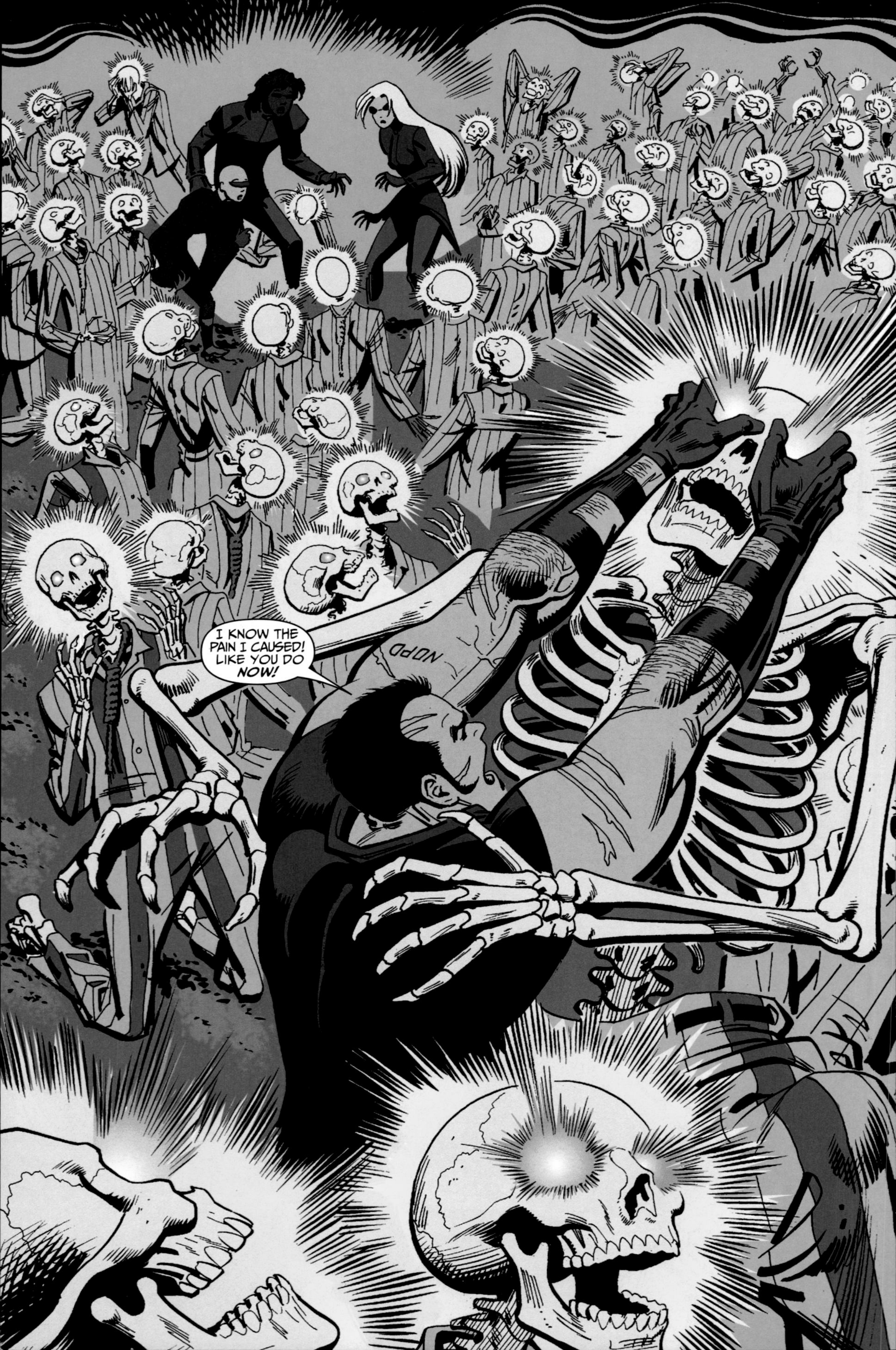
I KNOW THE PAIN I CAUSED! LIKE YOU DO NOW!

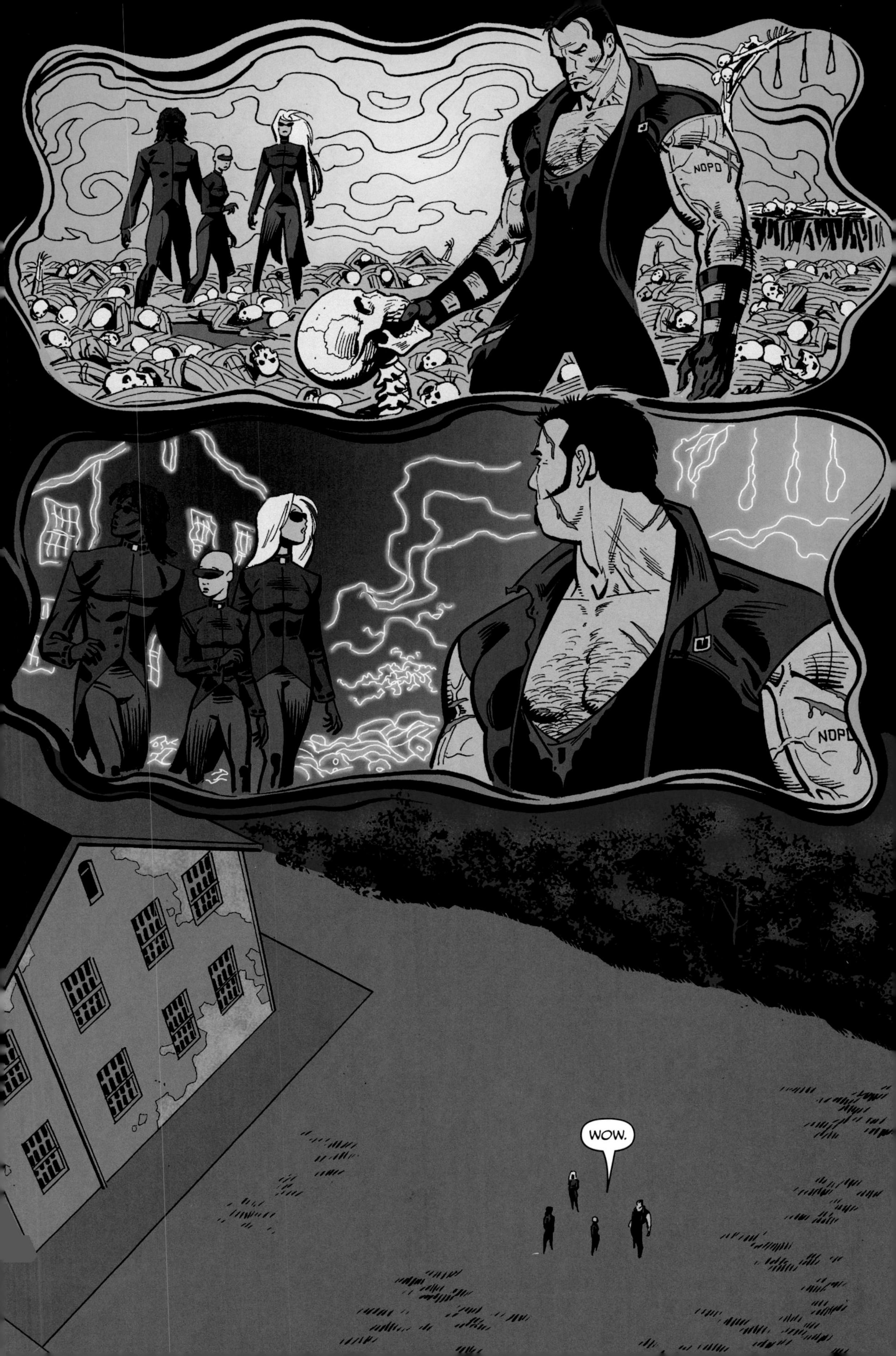
NOPD
NOPD
WOW.

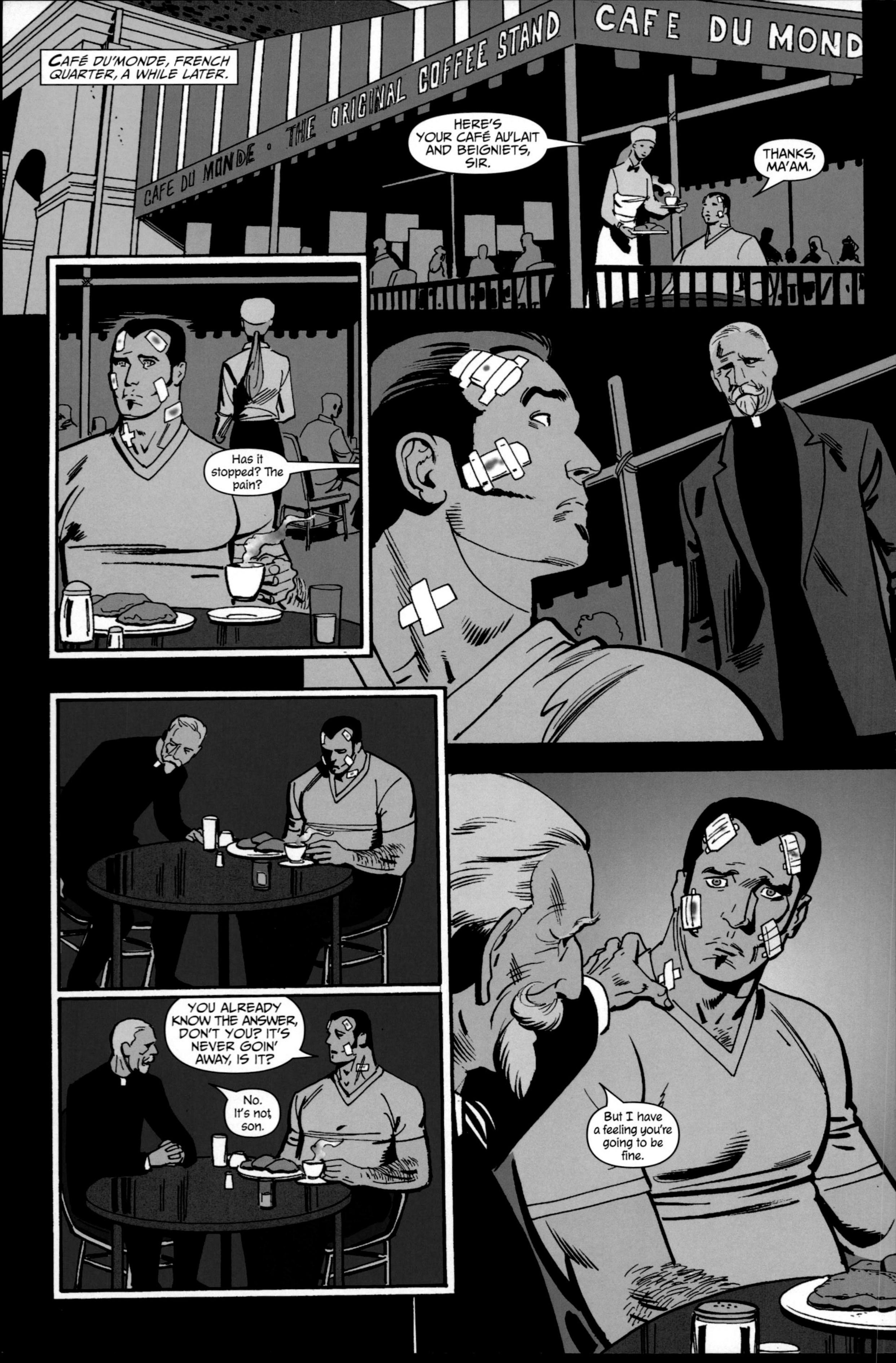
CAFÉ DU'MONDE, FRENCH QUARTER, A WHILE LATER.
CAFE DU MONDE · THE ORIGINAL COFFEE STAND
CAFE DU MOND
HERE'S YOUR CAFÉ AU'LAIT AND BEIGNIETS, SIR.
THANKS, MA'AM.
Has it stopped? The pain?
YOU ALREADY KNOW THE ANSWER, DON'T YOU? IT'S NEVER GOIN' AWAY, IS IT?
No. It's not, son.
But I have a feeling you're going to be fine.

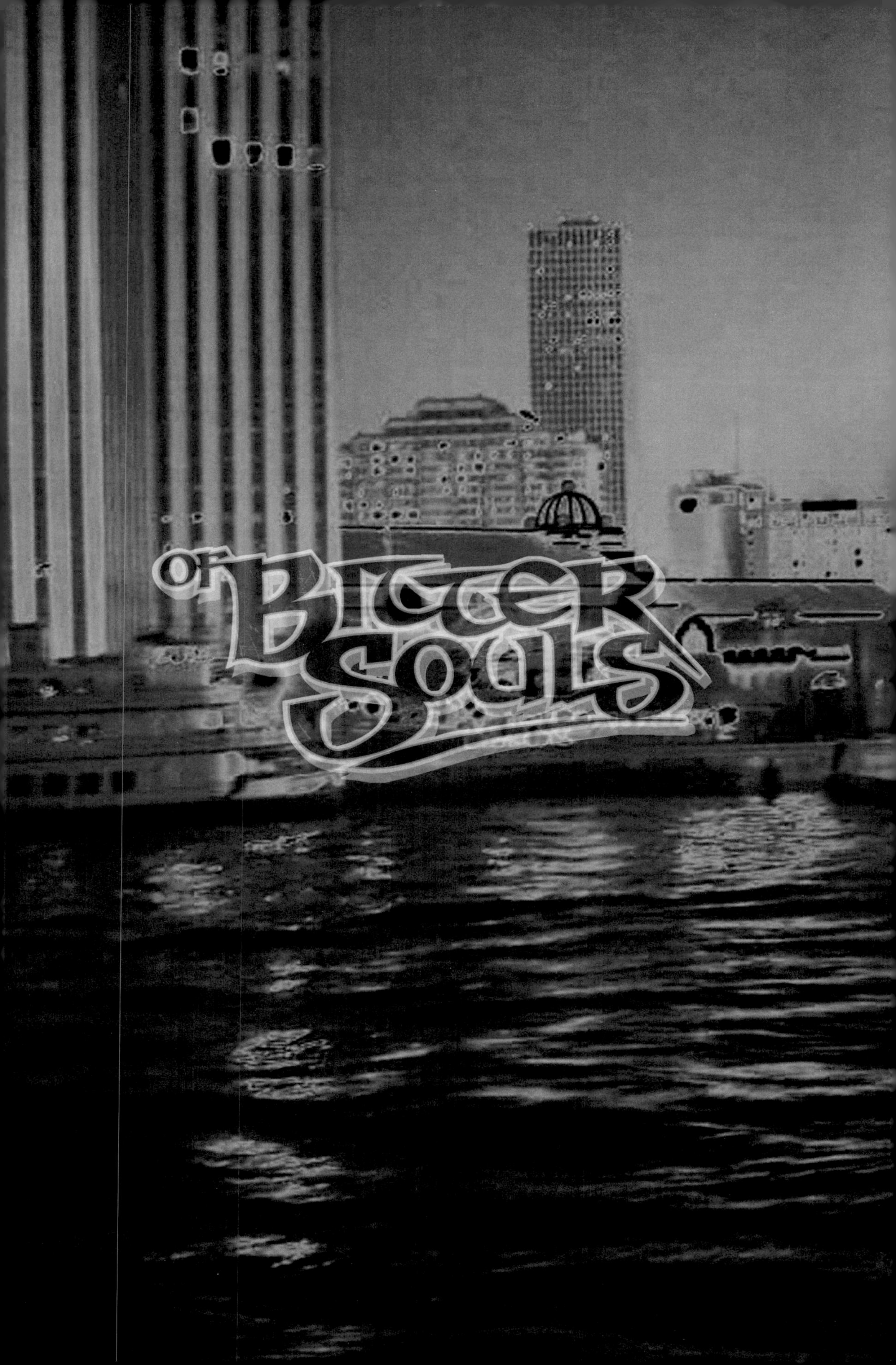
Of Bigger Souls

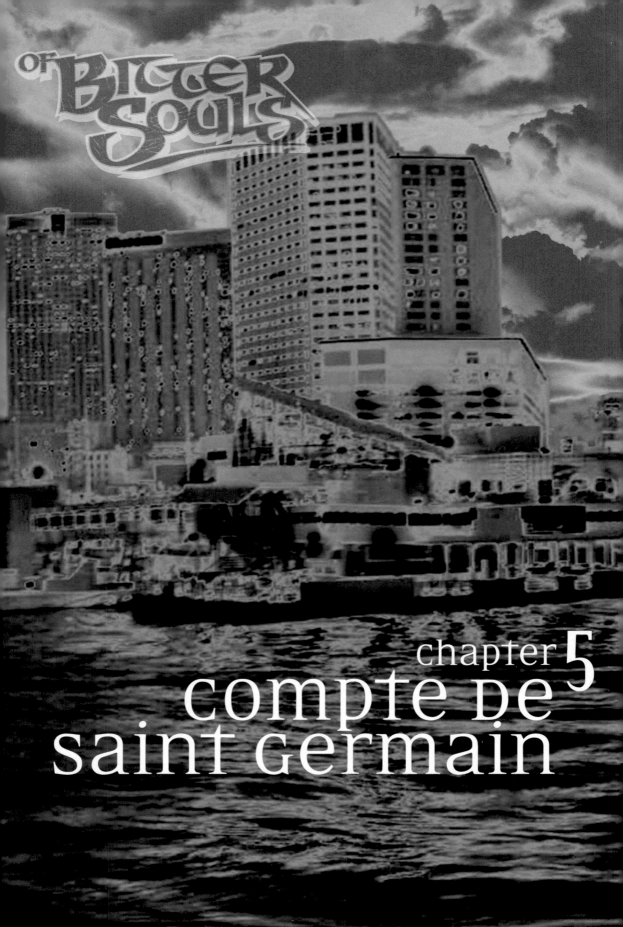

chapter **5**
compte de
saint germain

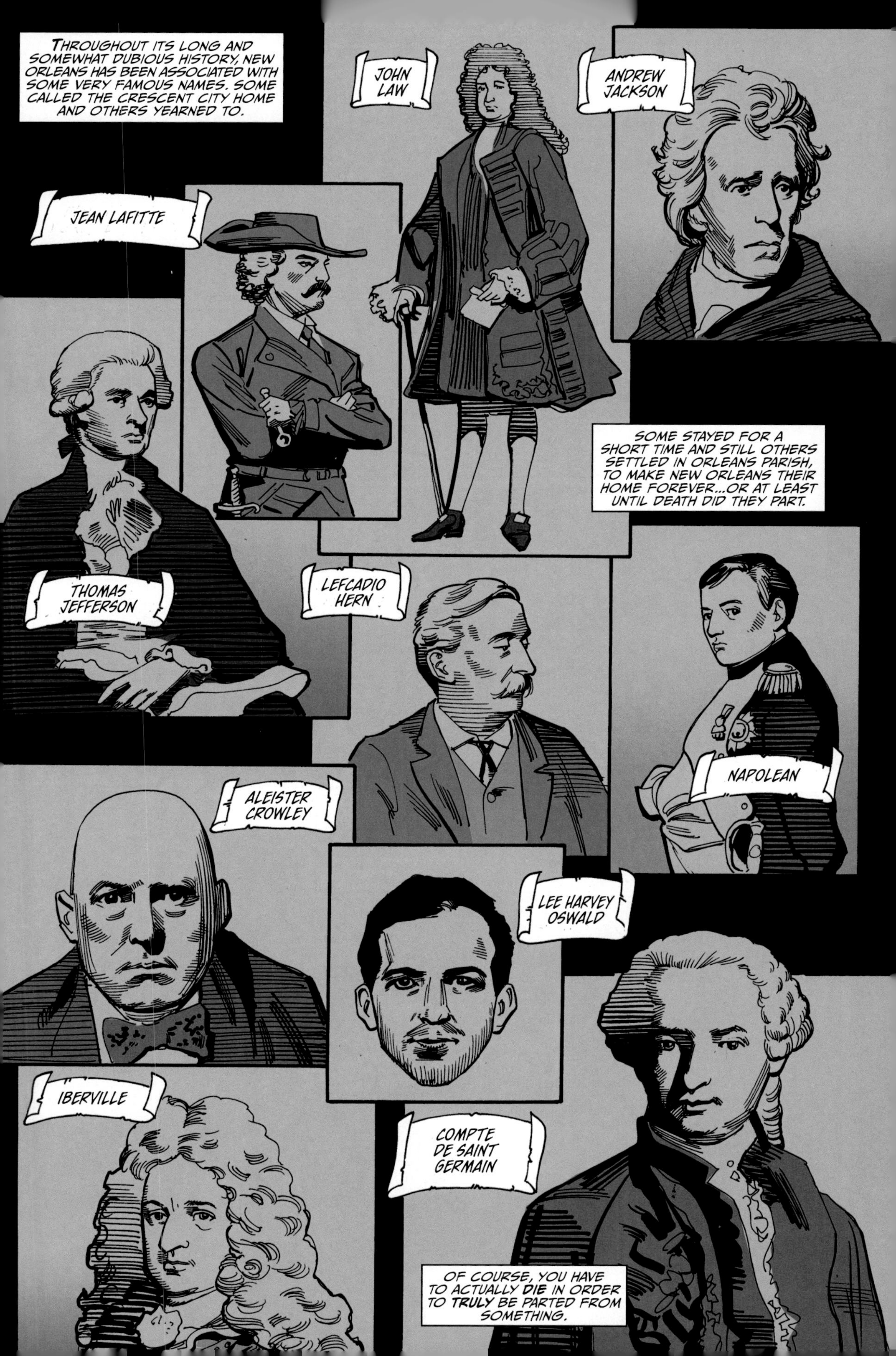

THROUGHOUT ITS LONG AND SOMEWHAT DUBIOUS HISTORY, NEW ORLEANS HAS BEEN ASSOCIATED WITH SOME VERY FAMOUS NAMES. SOME CALLED THE CRESCENT CITY HOME AND OTHERS YEARNED TO.
JOHN LAW
ANDREW JACKSON
JEAN LAFITTE
SOME STAYED FOR A SHORT TIME AND STILL OTHERS SETTLED IN ORLEANS PARISH, TO MAKE NEW ORLEANS THEIR HOME FOREVER...OR AT LEAST UNTIL DEATH DID THEY PART.
THOMAS JEFFERSON
LEFCADIO HERN
NAPOLEAN
ALEISTER CROWLEY
LEE HARVEY OSWALD
IBERVILLE
COMPTE DE SAINT GERMAIN
OF COURSE, YOU HAVE TO ACTUALLY DIE IN ORDER TO TRULY BE PARTED FROM SOMETHING.

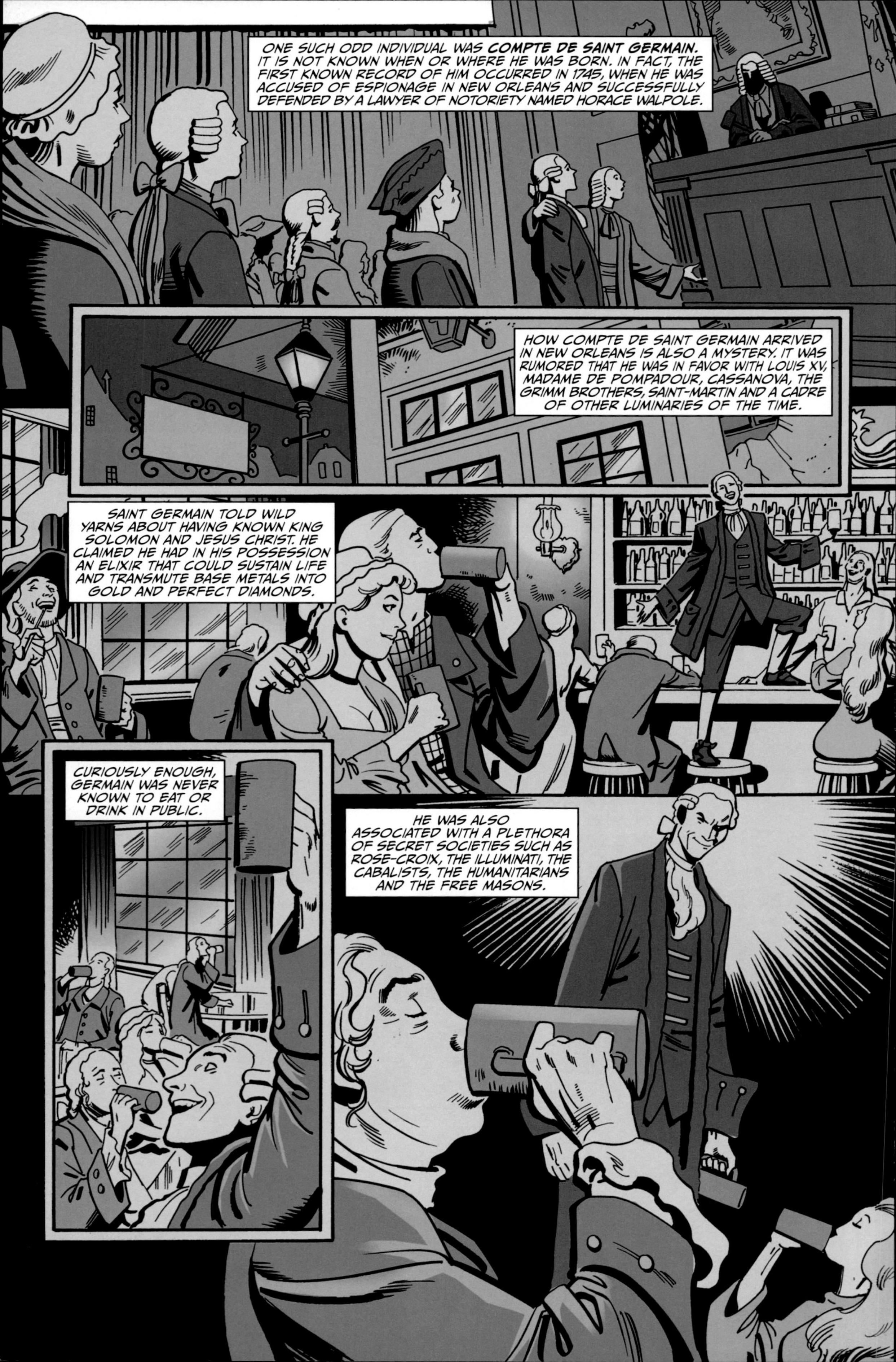
ONE SUCH ODD INDIVIDUAL WAS COMPTE DE SAINT GERMAIN. IT IS NOT KNOWN WHEN OR WHERE HE WAS BORN. IN FACT, THE FIRST KNOWN RECORD OF HIM OCCURRED IN 1745, WHEN HE WAS ACCUSED OF ESPIONAGE IN NEW ORLEANS AND SUCCESSFULLY DEFENDED BY A LAWYER OF NOTORIETY NAMED HORACE WALPOLE.
HOW COMPTE DE SAINT GERMAIN ARRIVED IN NEW ORLEANS IS ALSO A MYSTERY. IT WAS RUMORED THAT HE WAS IN FAVOR WITH LOUIS XV, MADAME DE POMPADOUR, CASSANOVA, THE GRIMM BROTHERS, SAINT-MARTIN AND A CADRE OF OTHER LUMINARIES OF THE TIME.
SAINT GERMAIN TOLD WILD YARNS ABOUT HAVING KNOWN KING SOLOMON AND JESUS CHRIST. HE CLAIMED HE HAD IN HIS POSSESSION AN ELIXIR THAT COULD SUSTAIN LIFE AND TRANSMUTE BASE METALS INTO GOLD AND PERFECT DIAMONDS.
CURIOUSLY ENOUGH, GERMAIN WAS NEVER KNOWN TO EAT OR DRINK IN PUBLIC.
HE WAS ALSO ASSOCIATED WITH A PLETHORA OF SECRET SOCIETIES SUCH AS ROSE-CROIX, THE ILLUMINATI, THE CABALISTS, THE HUMANITARIANS AND THE FREE MASONS.

REPORTS OF HIS DEATH SURFACED IN 1794.

ON OCCASION AFTER THAT, REPORTS SURFACED THAT SEEMED TO CONFLICT WITH THE DEATH REPORT.

THOSE RUMORS OF SAINT GERMAIN ALIVE AND WELL ULTIMATELY STOPPED COMING IN AND THEN, A LITTLE OVER ONE HUNDRED YEARS LATER, A MAN CLAIMING TO HAVE THE NAME JACQUES ST. GERMAIN MOVED INTO THE QUARTER. HE CLAIMED TO HAVE JUST MOVED FROM THE SOUTH OF FRANCE. HE ALSO CLAIMED TO BE A RELATION OF THE MYSTERIOUS COMPTE DE SAINT GERMAIN.

HE WAS THE SPITTING IMAGE OF COMPTE AND SOME BELIEVED IT WAS THE SAME MAN. THE STORIES OF HIS ESCAPADES A CENTURY EARLIER HAD BECOME LEGEND IN OCCULT CIRCLES.

IT IS SAID HE LIVED QUIETLY IN THE QUARTER FOR A FEW YEARS...

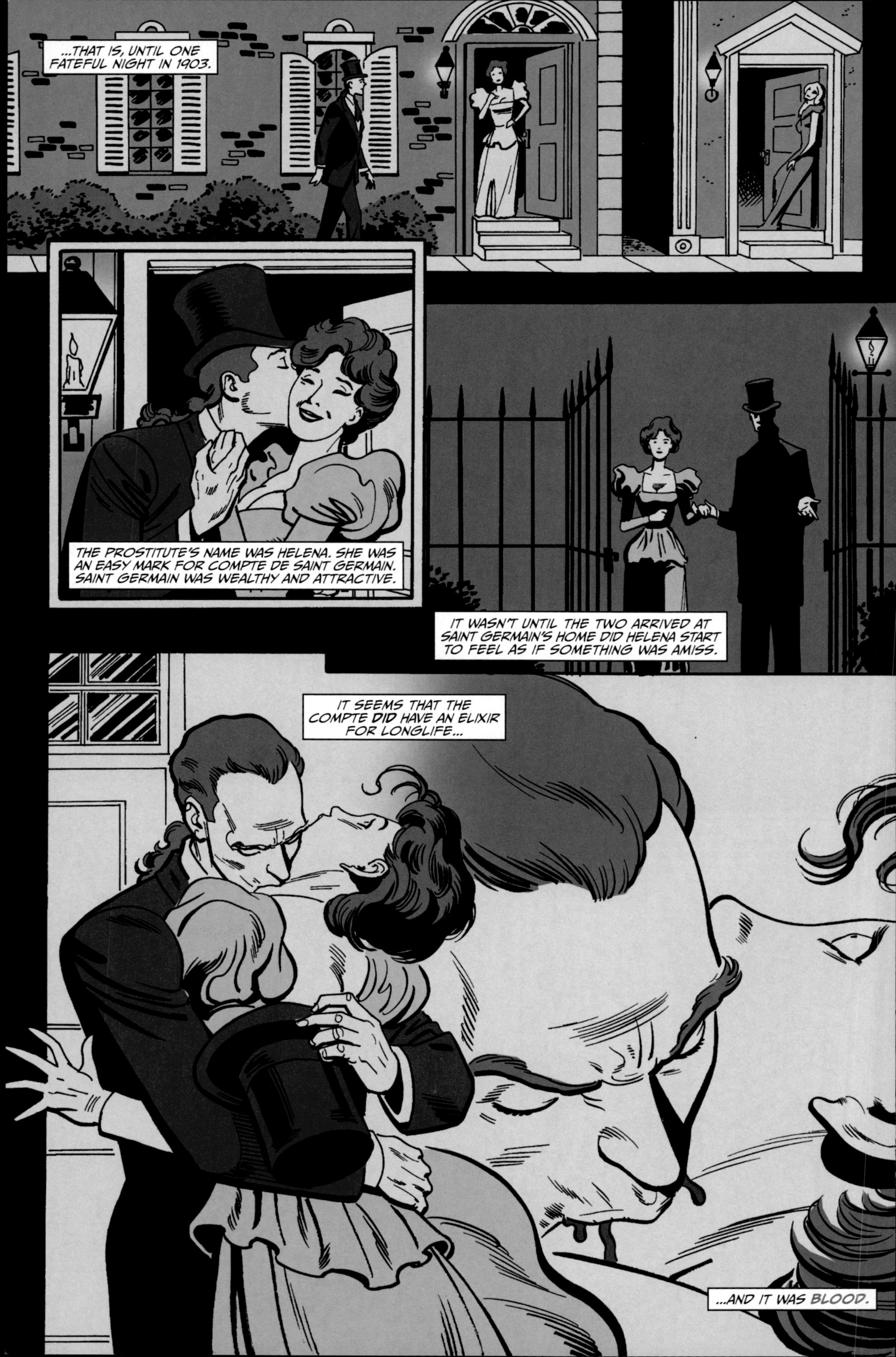

...THAT IS, UNTIL ONE FATEFUL NIGHT IN 1903.
THE PROSTITUTE'S NAME WAS HELENA. SHE WAS AN EASY MARK FOR COMPTE DE SAINT GERMAIN. SAINT GERMAIN WAS WEALTHY AND ATTRACTIVE.
IT WASN'T UNTIL THE TWO ARRIVED AT SAINT GERMAIN'S HOME DID HELENA START TO FEEL AS IF SOMETHING WAS AMISS.
IT SEEMS THAT THE COMPTE **DID** HAVE AN ELIXIR FOR LONGLIFE...
...AND IT WAS *BLOOD.*

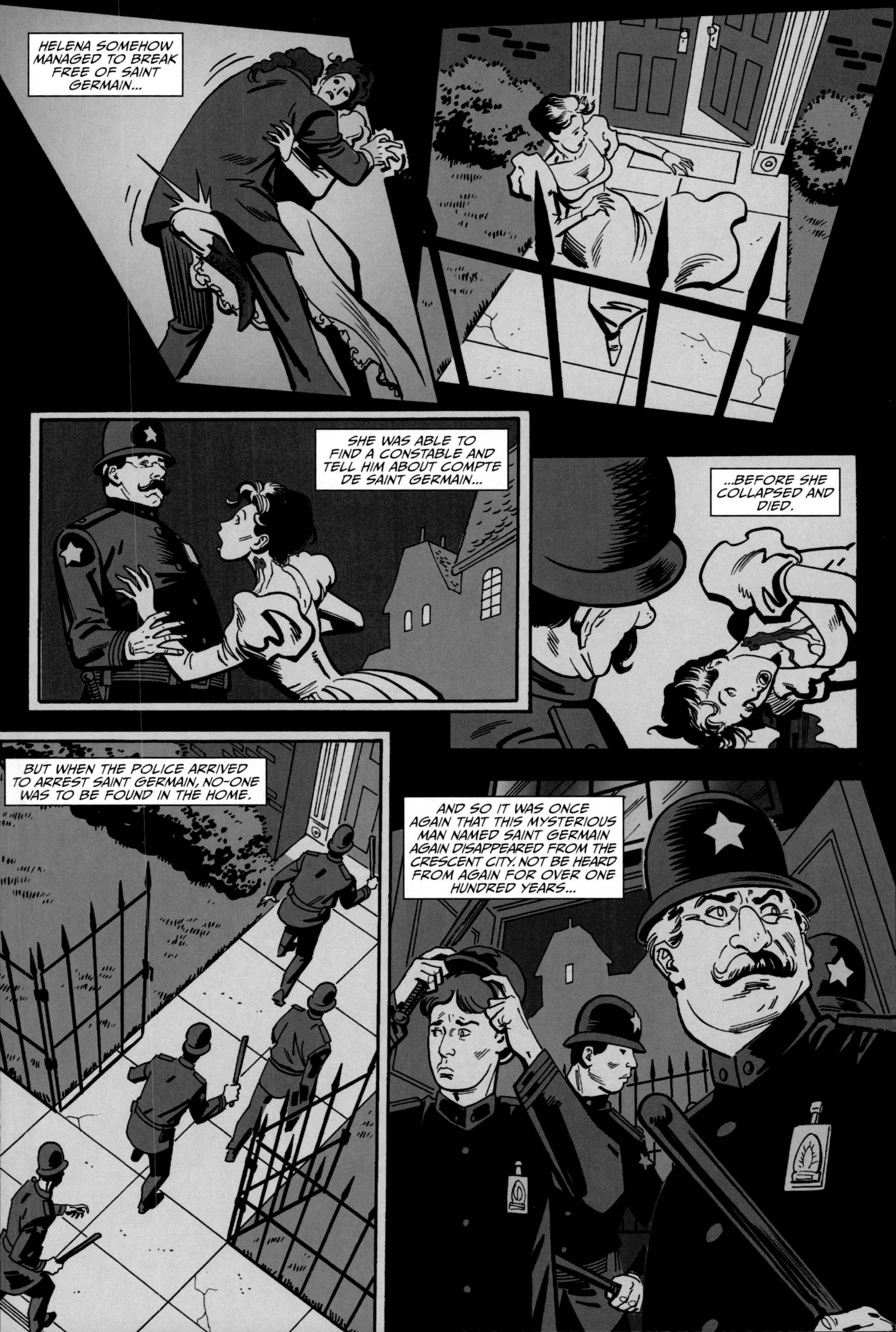

HELENA SOMEHOW MANAGED TO BREAK FREE OF SAINT GERMAIN...
SHE WAS ABLE TO FIND A CONSTABLE AND TELL HIM ABOUT COMPTE DE SAINT GERMAIN...
...BEFORE SHE COLLAPSED AND DIED.
BUT WHEN THE POLICE ARRIVED TO ARREST SAINT GERMAIN, NO-ONE WAS TO BE FOUND IN THE HOME.
AND SO IT WAS ONCE AGAIN THAT THIS MYSTERIOUS MAN NAMED SAINT GERMAIN AGAIN DISAPPEARED FROM THE CRESCENT CITY. NOT BE HEARD FROM AGAIN FOR OVER ONE HUNDRED YEARS...

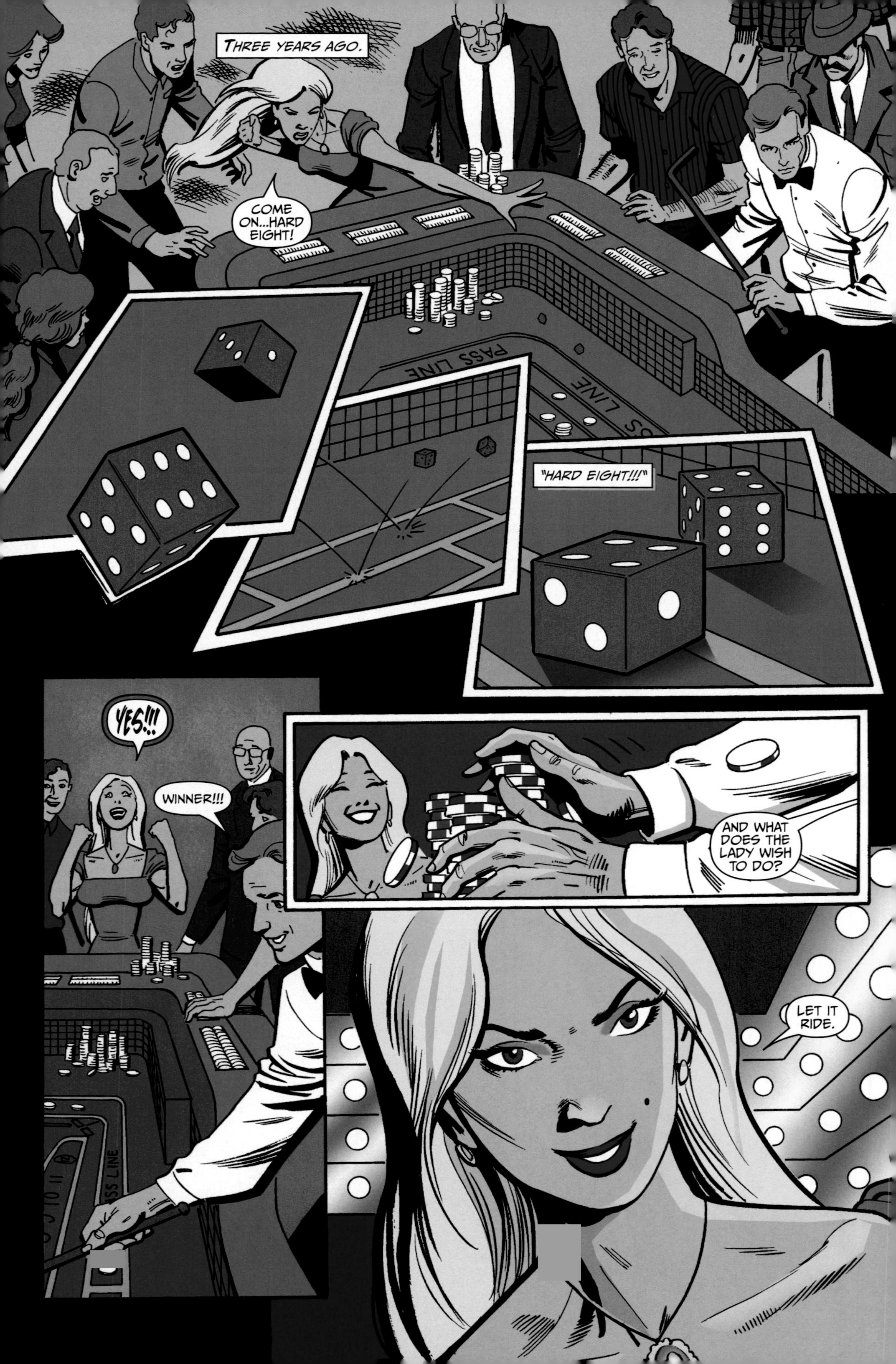
THREE YEARS AGO.
COME ON...HARD EIGHT!
PASS LINE
PASS LINE
"HARD EIGHT!!!"
YES!!!
WINNER!!!
AND WHAT DOES THE LADY WISH TO DO?
LET IT RIDE.

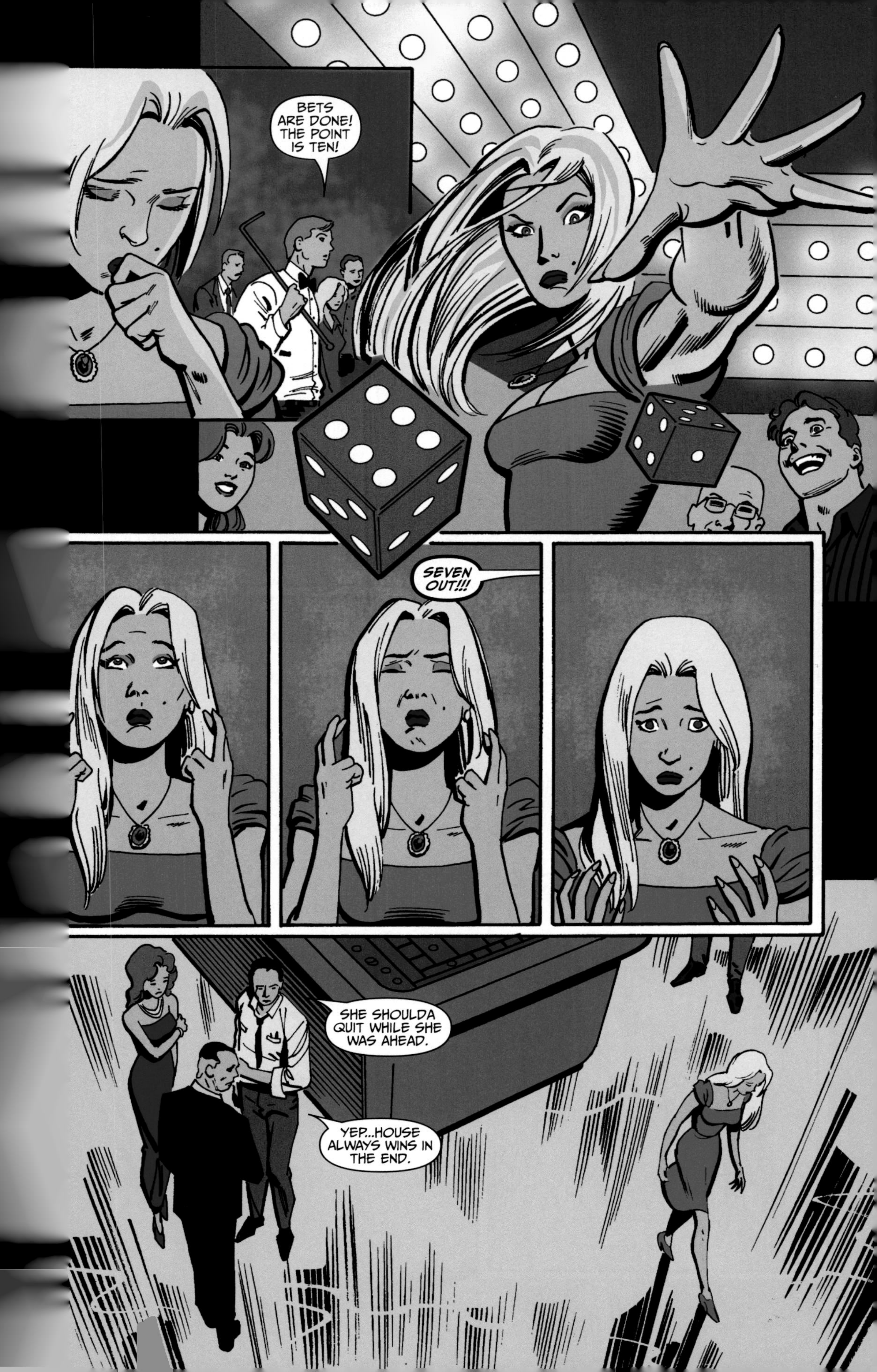
BETS ARE DONE! THE POINT IS TEN!
SEVEN OUT!!!
SHE SHOULDA QUIT WHILE SHE WAS AHEAD.
YEP...HOUSE ALWAYS WINS IN THE END.

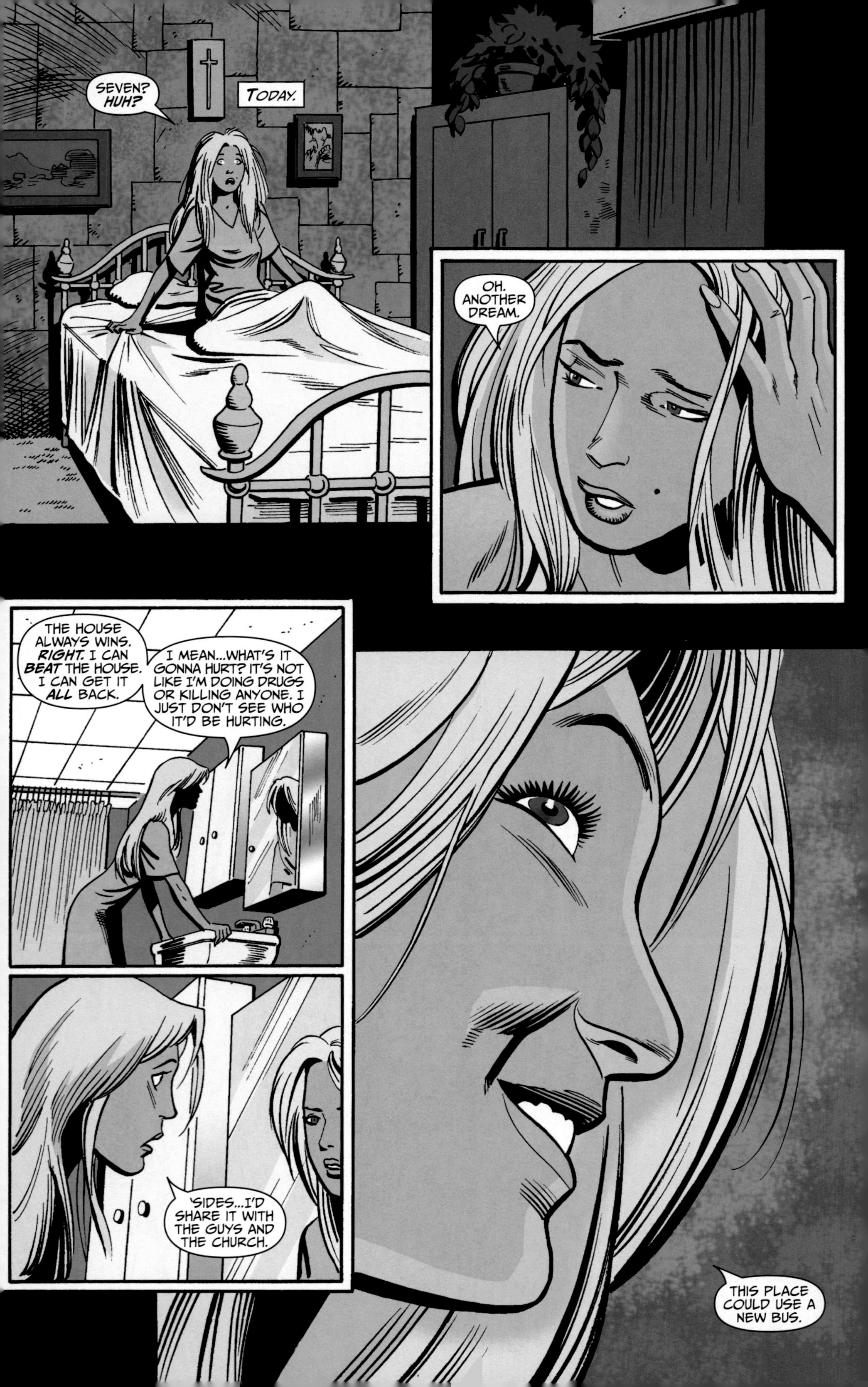
SEVEN? HUH?
TODAY.
OH. ANOTHER DREAM.
THE HOUSE ALWAYS WINS. RIGHT. I CAN BEAT THE HOUSE. I CAN GET IT ALL BACK.
I MEAN...WHAT'S IT GONNA HURT? IT'S NOT LIKE I'M DOING DRUGS OR KILLING ANYONE. I JUST DON'T SEE WHO IT'D BE HURTING.
'SIDES...I'D SHARE IT WITH THE GUYS AND THE CHURCH.
THIS PLACE COULD USE A NEW BUS.

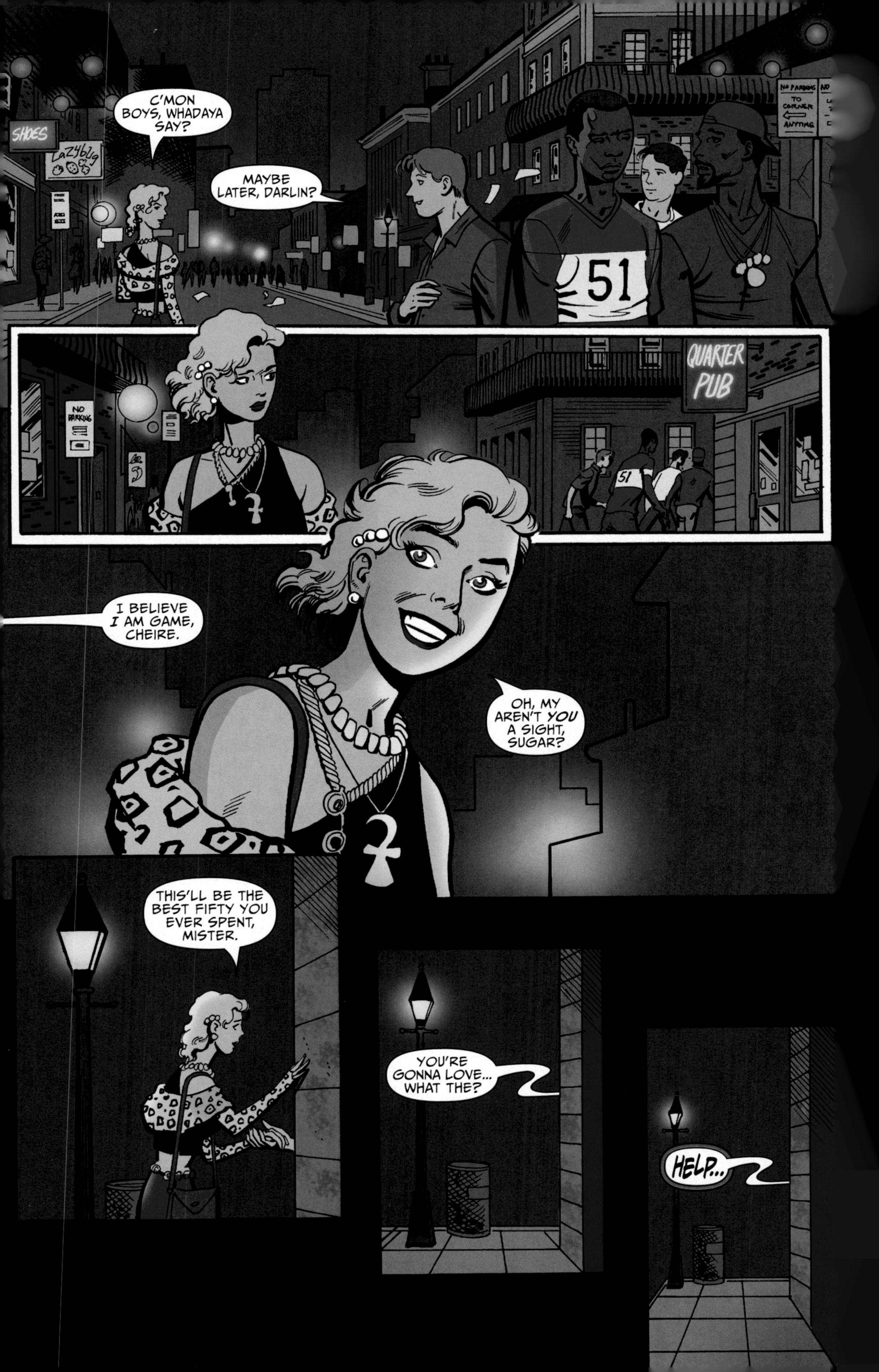

SHOES
C'MON BOYS, WHADAYA SAY?
MAYBE LATER, DARLIN?
51
QUARTER PUB
I BELIEVE I AM GAME, CHEIRE.
OH, MY AREN'T YOU A SIGHT, SUGAR?
THIS'LL BE THE BEST FIFTY YOU EVER SPENT, MISTER.
YOU'RE GONNA LOVE... WHAT THE?
HELP...

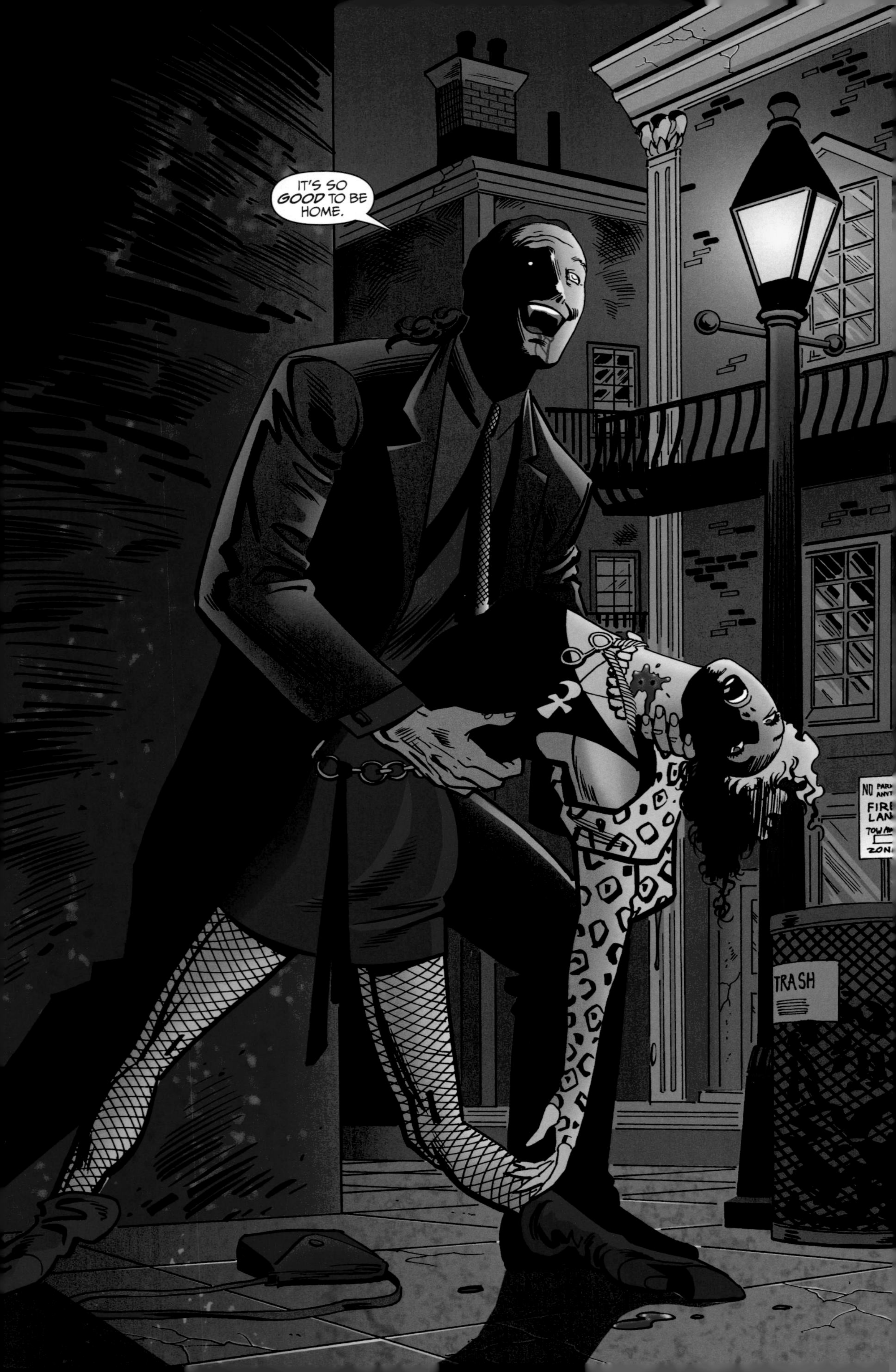
IT'S SO GOOD TO BE HOME.
TRASH

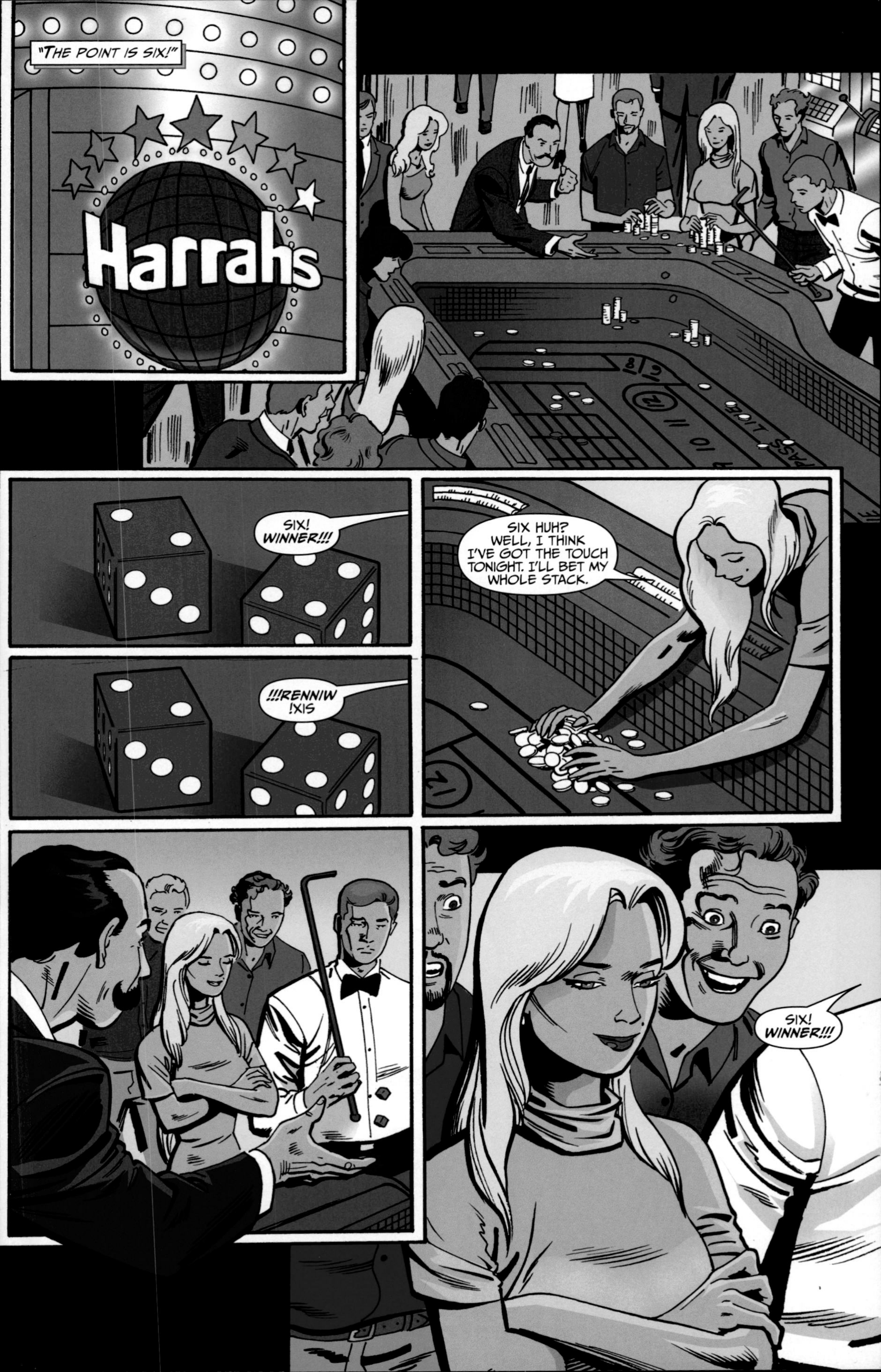
"THE POINT IS SIX!"
Harrahs
SIX! WINNER!!!
!!!RENNIW
!XIS
SIX HUH? WELL, I THINK I'VE GOT THE TOUCH TONIGHT. I'LL BET MY WHOLE STACK.
SIX! WINNER!!!

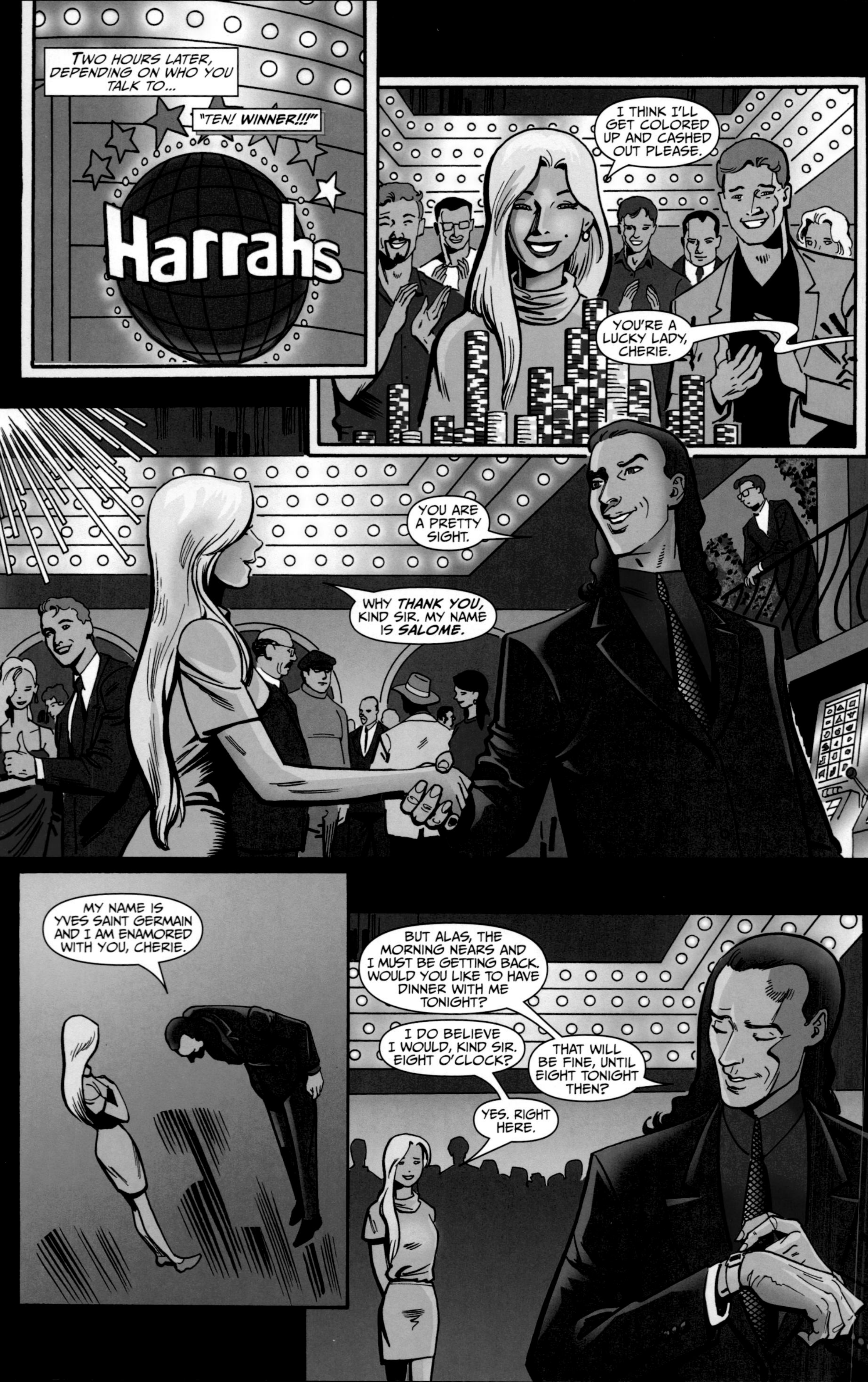
TWO HOURS LATER, DEPENDING ON WHO YOU TALK TO...
"TEN! WINNER!!!"
Harrahs
I THINK I'LL GET COLORED UP AND CASHED OUT PLEASE.
YOU'RE A LUCKY LADY, CHERIE.
YOU ARE A PRETTY SIGHT.
WHY THANK YOU, KIND SIR. MY NAME IS SALOME.
MY NAME IS YVES SAINT GERMAIN AND I AM ENAMORED WITH YOU, CHERIE.
BUT ALAS, THE MORNING NEARS AND I MUST BE GETTING BACK. WOULD YOU LIKE TO HAVE DINNER WITH ME TONIGHT?
I DO BELIEVE I WOULD, KIND SIR. EIGHT O'CLOCK?
THAT WILL BE FINE, UNTIL EIGHT TONIGHT THEN?
YES. RIGHT HERE.

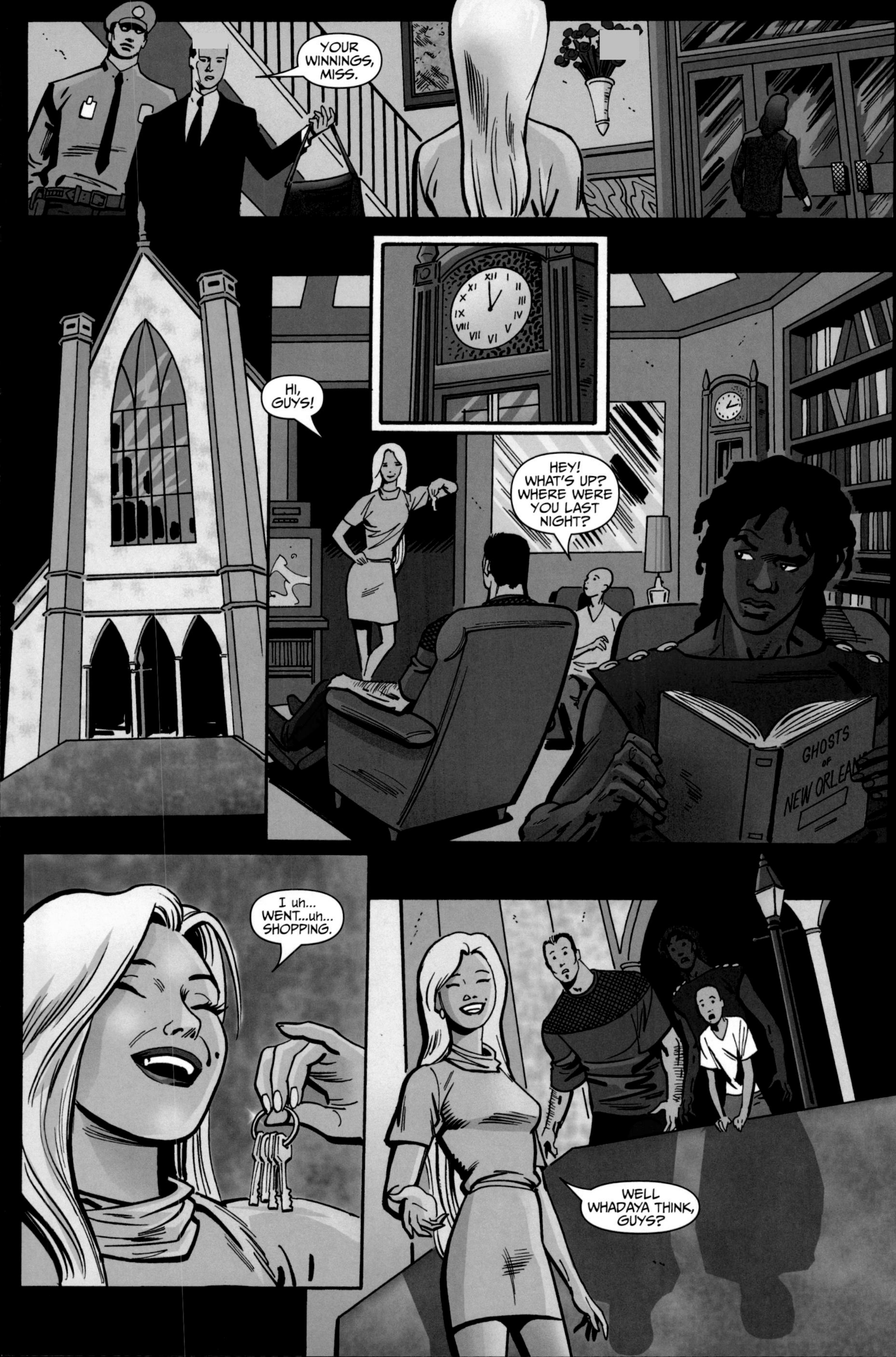
YOUR WINNINGS, MISS.
HI, GUYS!
HEY! WHAT'S UP? WHERE WERE YOU LAST NIGHT?
GHOSTS OF NEW ORLEA
I uh... WENT...uh... SHOPPING.
WELL WHADAYA THINK, GUYS?

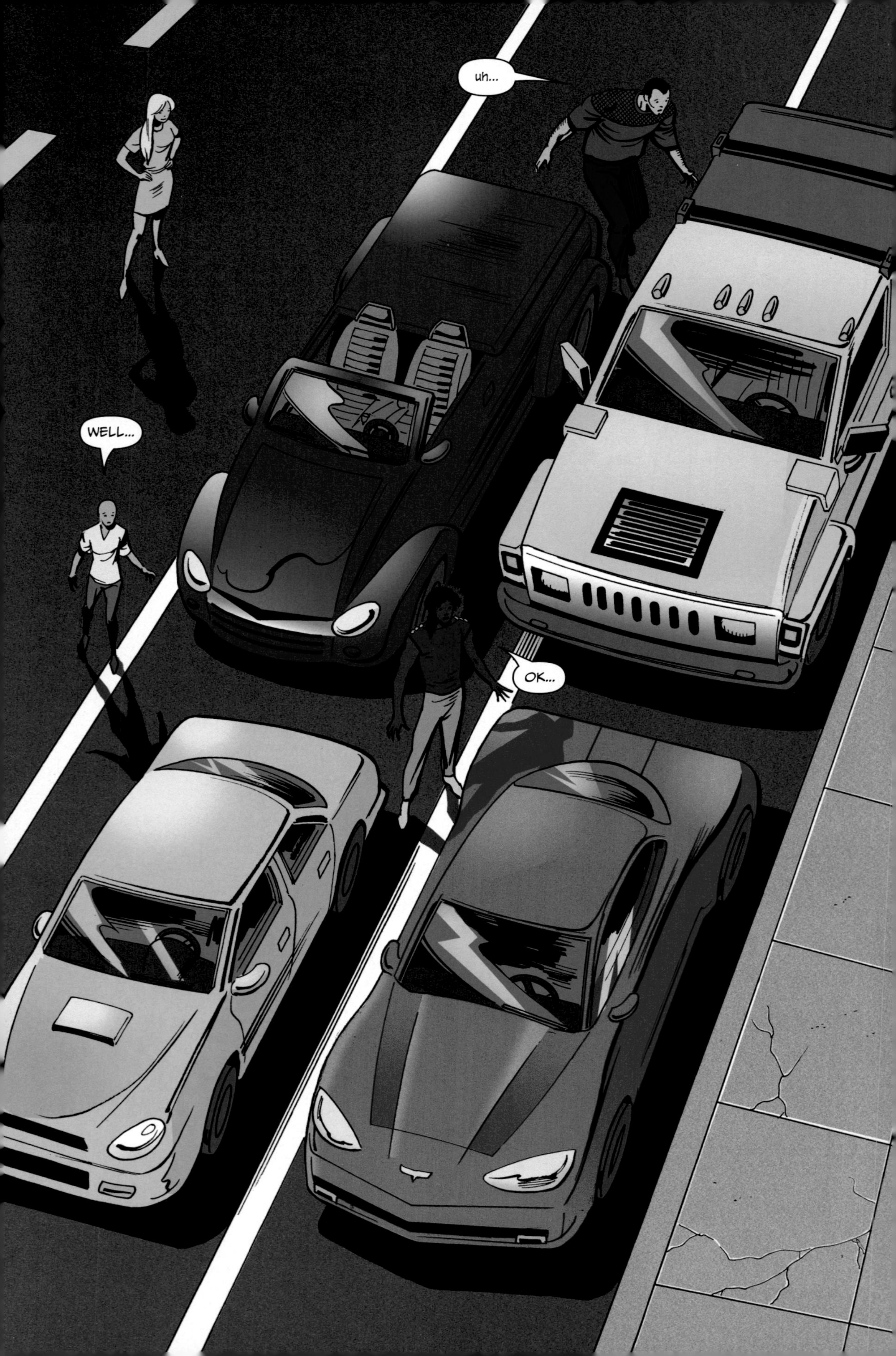
uh...
WELL...
OK...

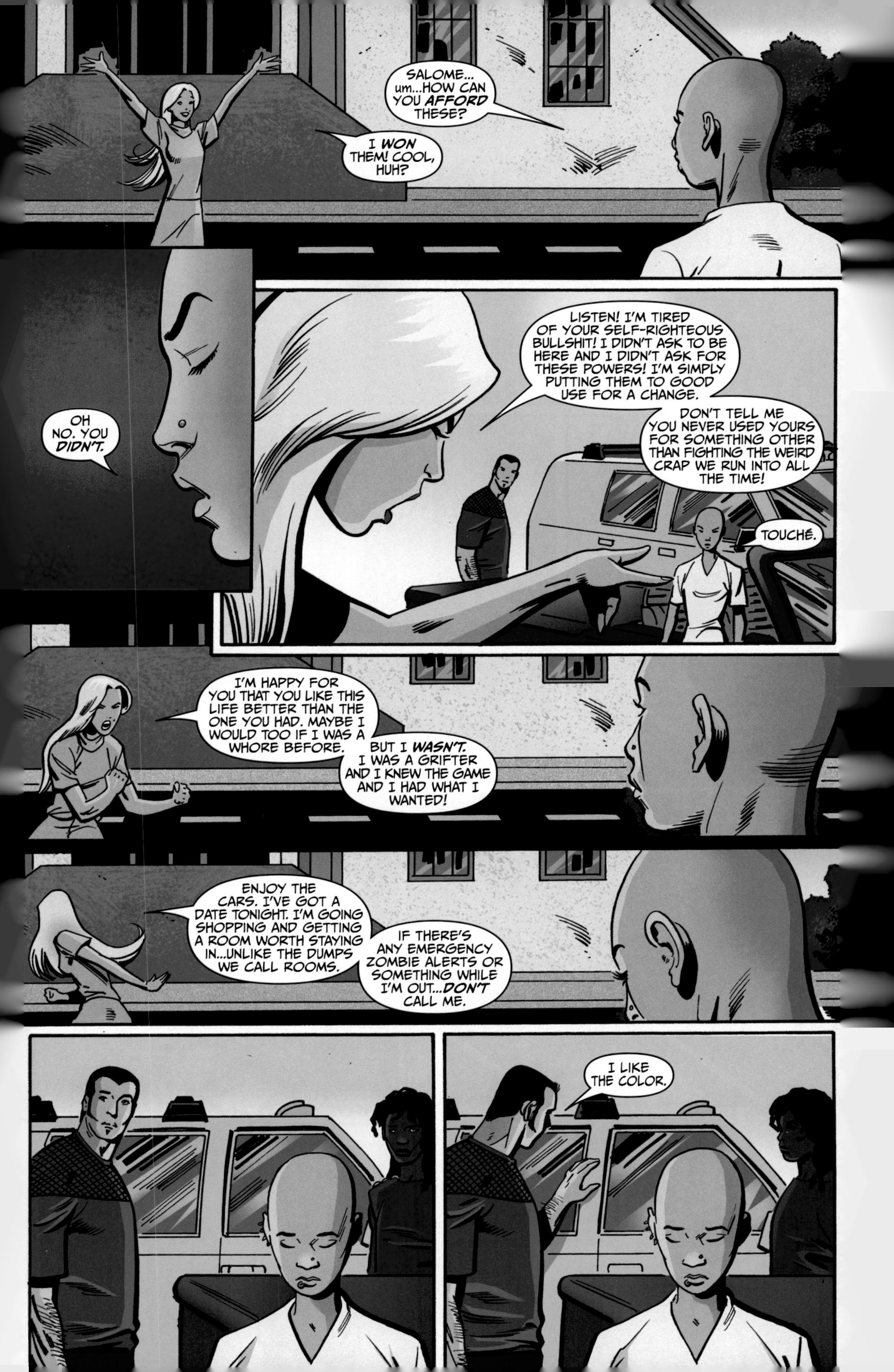
SALOME... um...HOW CAN YOU AFFORD THESE?
I WON THEM! COOL, HUH?
OH NO. YOU DIDN'T.
LISTEN! I'M TIRED OF YOUR SELF-RIGHTEOUS BULLSHIT! I DIDN'T ASK TO BE HERE AND I DIDN'T ASK FOR THESE POWERS! I'M SIMPLY PUTTING THEM TO GOOD USE FOR A CHANGE.
DON'T TELL ME YOU NEVER USED YOURS FOR SOMETHING OTHER THAN FIGHTING THE WEIRD CRAP WE RUN INTO ALL THE TIME!
TOUCHÉ.
I'M HAPPY FOR YOU THAT YOU LIKE THIS LIFE BETTER THAN THE ONE YOU HAD. MAYBE I WOULD TOO IF I WAS A WHORE BEFORE.
BUT I WASN'T. I WAS A GRIFTER AND I KNEW THE GAME AND I HAD WHAT I WANTED!
ENJOY THE CARS. I'VE GOT A DATE TONIGHT. I'M GOING SHOPPING AND GETTING A ROOM WORTH STAYING IN...UNLIKE THE DUMPS WE CALL ROOMS.
IF THERE'S ANY EMERGENCY ZOMBIE ALERTS OR SOMETHING WHILE I'M OUT...DON'T CALL ME.
I LIKE THE COLOR.

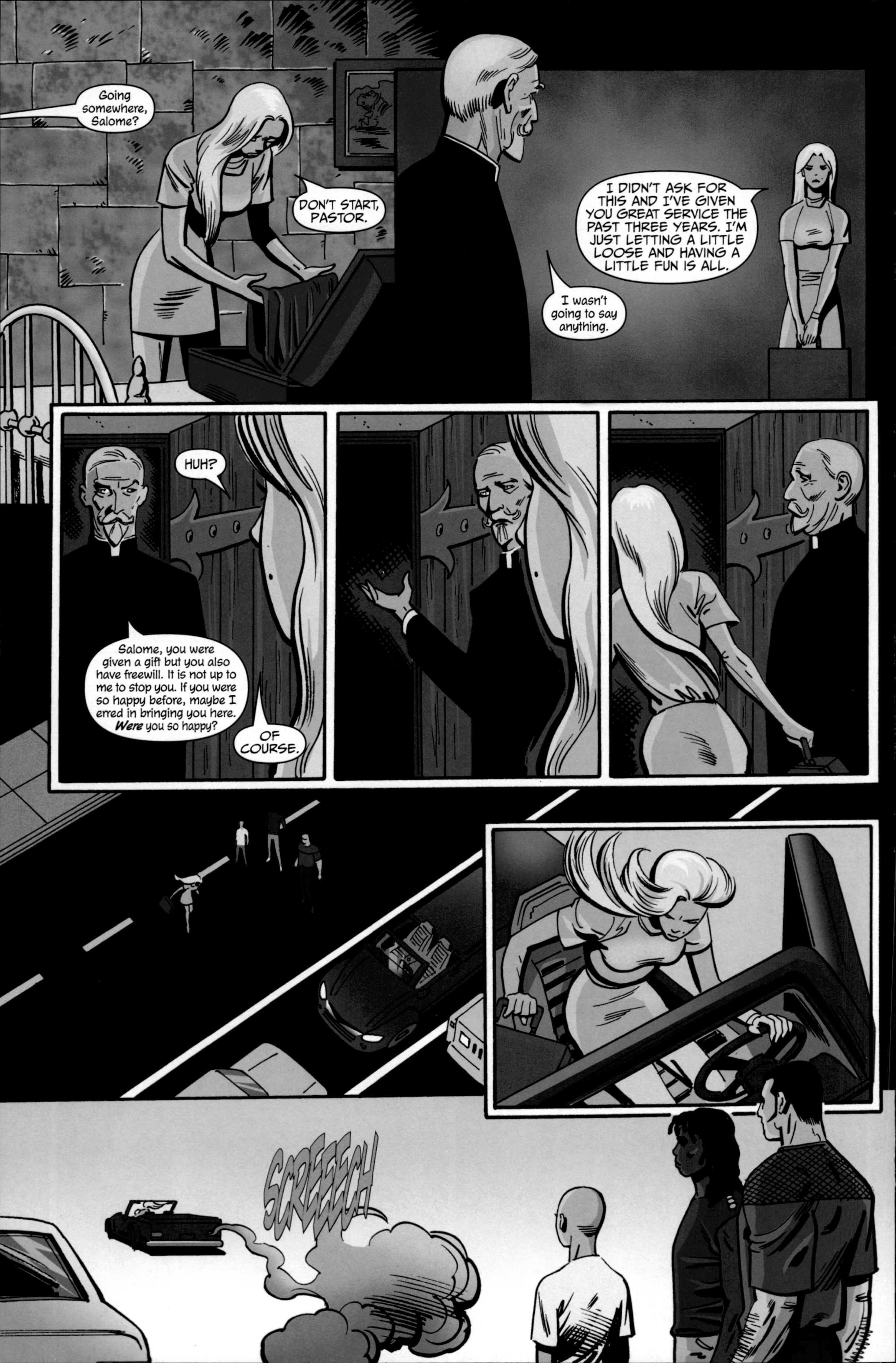
Going somewhere, Salome?
DON'T START, PASTOR.
I wasn't going to say anything.
I DIDN'T ASK FOR THIS AND I'VE GIVEN YOU GREAT SERVICE THE PAST THREE YEARS. I'M JUST LETTING A LITTLE LOOSE AND HAVING A LITTLE FUN IS ALL.
HUH?
Salome, you were given a gift but you also have freewill. It is not up to me to stop you. If you were so happy before, maybe I erred in bringing you here. ***Were*** you so happy?
OF COURSE.
SCREEECH

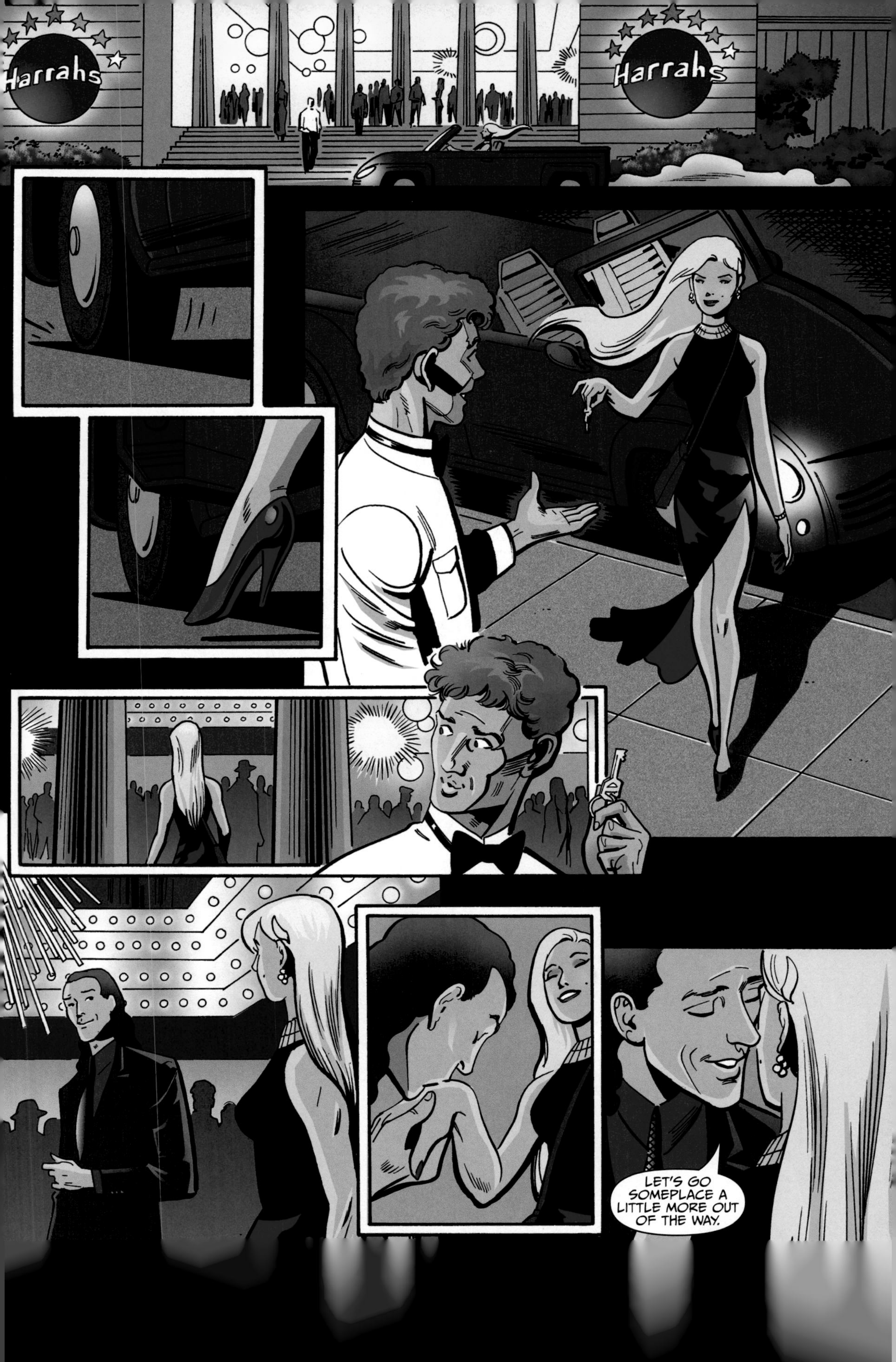
Harrahs
Harrahs
LET'S GO SOMEPLACE A LITTLE MORE OUT OF THE WAY.

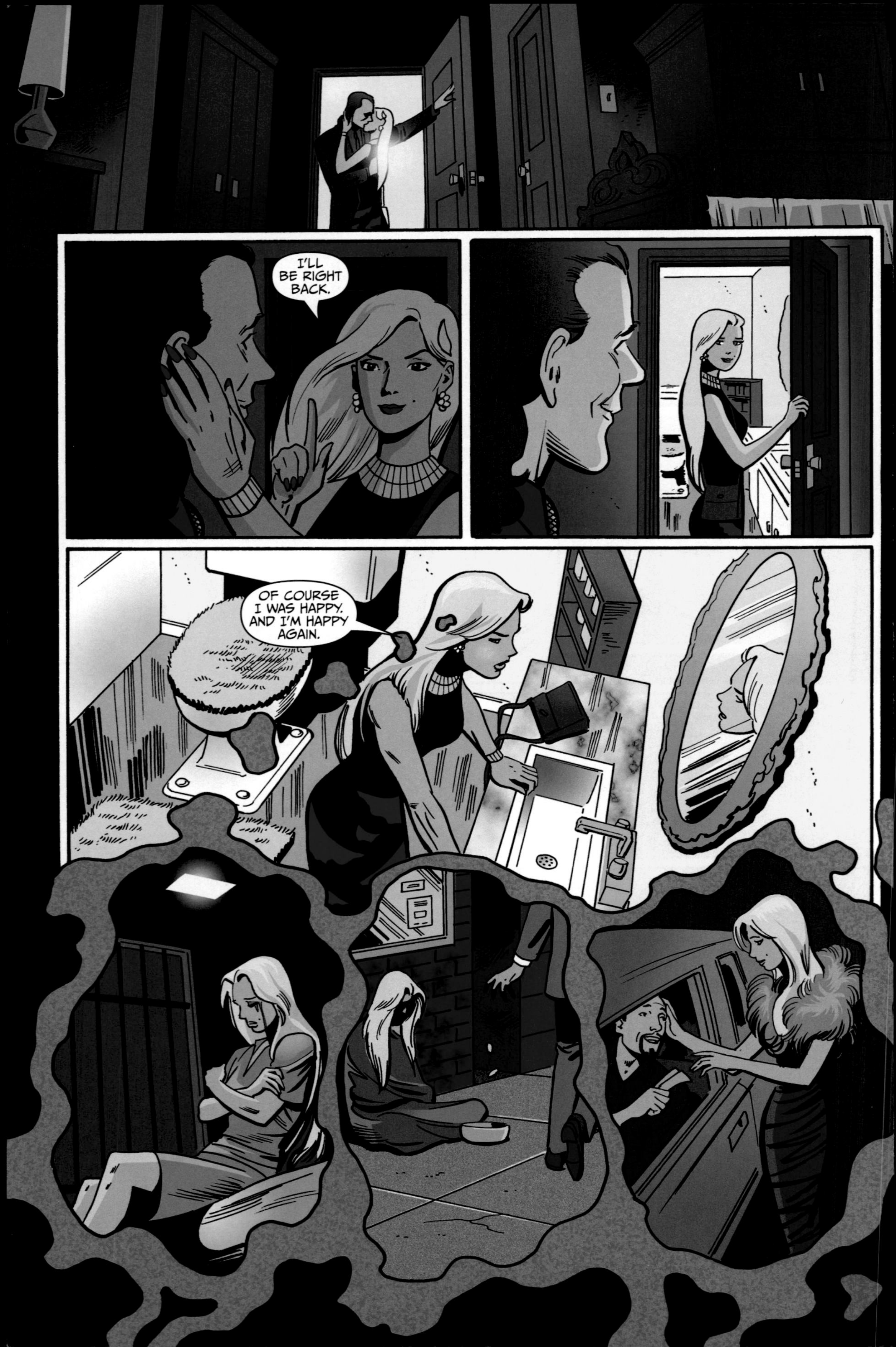
I'LL BE RIGHT BACK.
OF COURSE I WAS HAPPY. AND I'M HAPPY AGAIN.

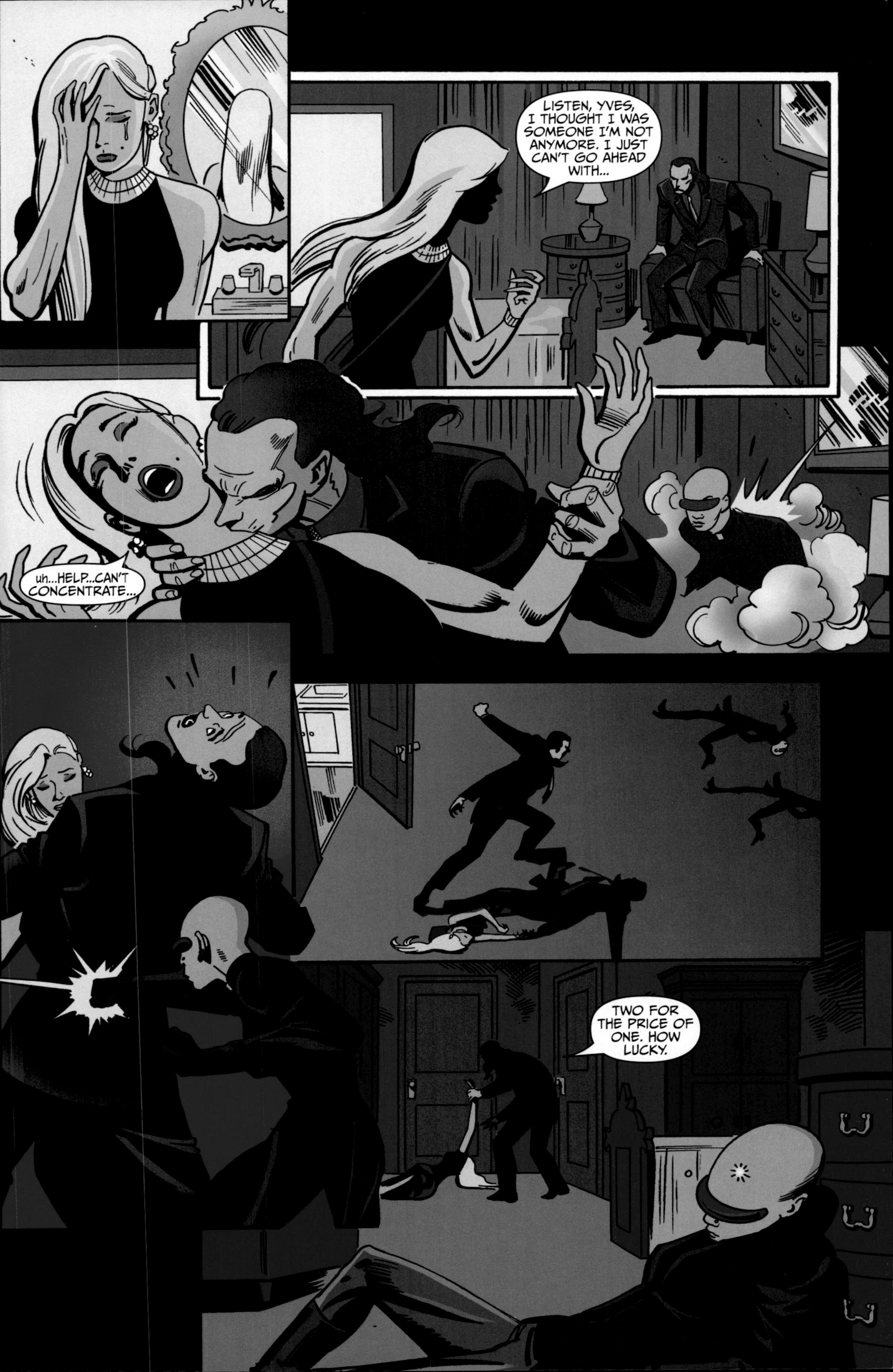
LISTEN, YVES, I THOUGHT I WAS SOMEONE I'M NOT ANYMORE. I JUST CAN'T GO AHEAD WITH...
uh...HELP...CAN'T CONCENTRATE...
TWO FOR THE PRICE OF ONE. HOW LUCKY.

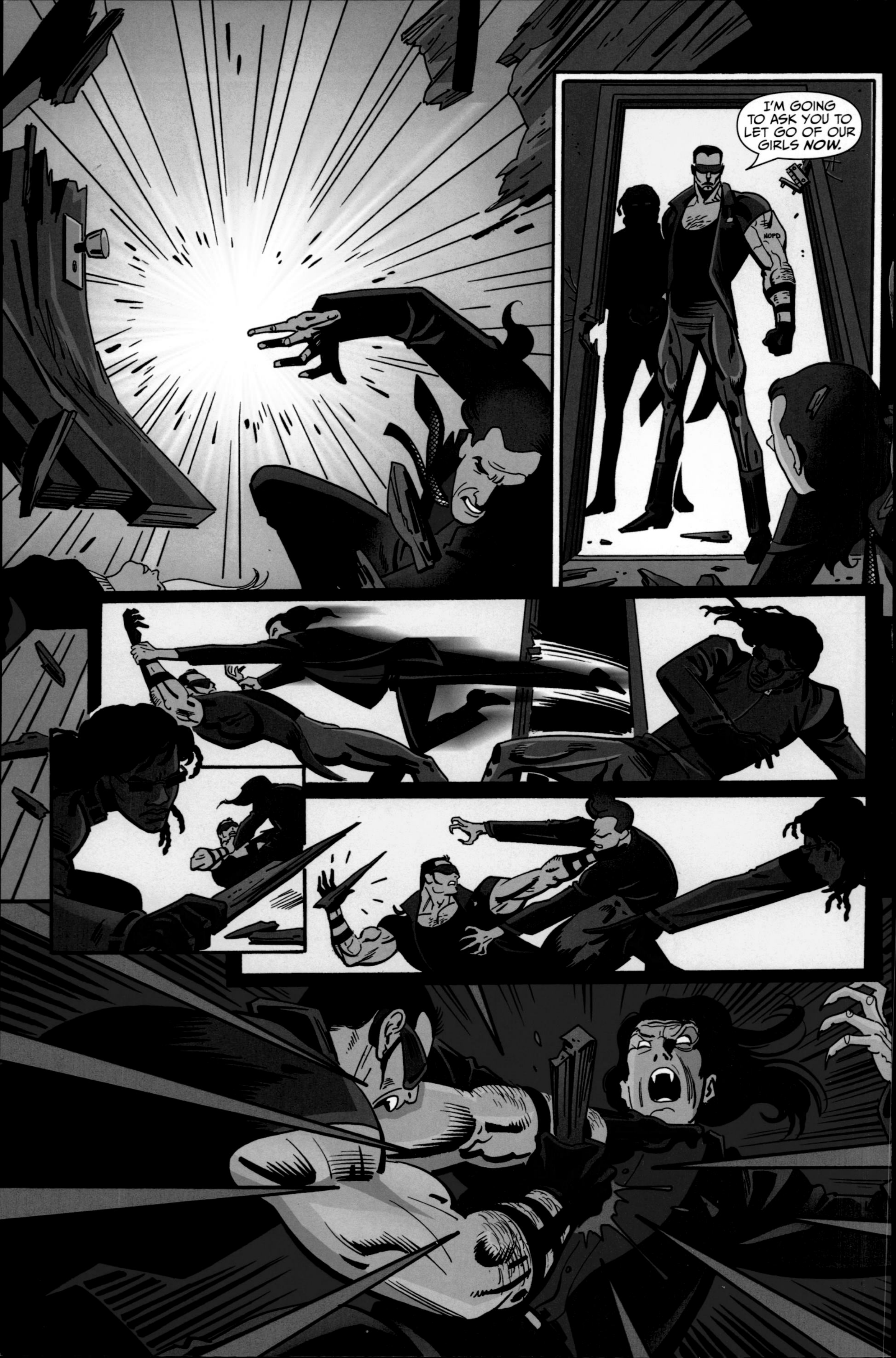
I'M GOING TO ASK YOU TO LET GO OF OUR GIRLS NOW.
NOPD

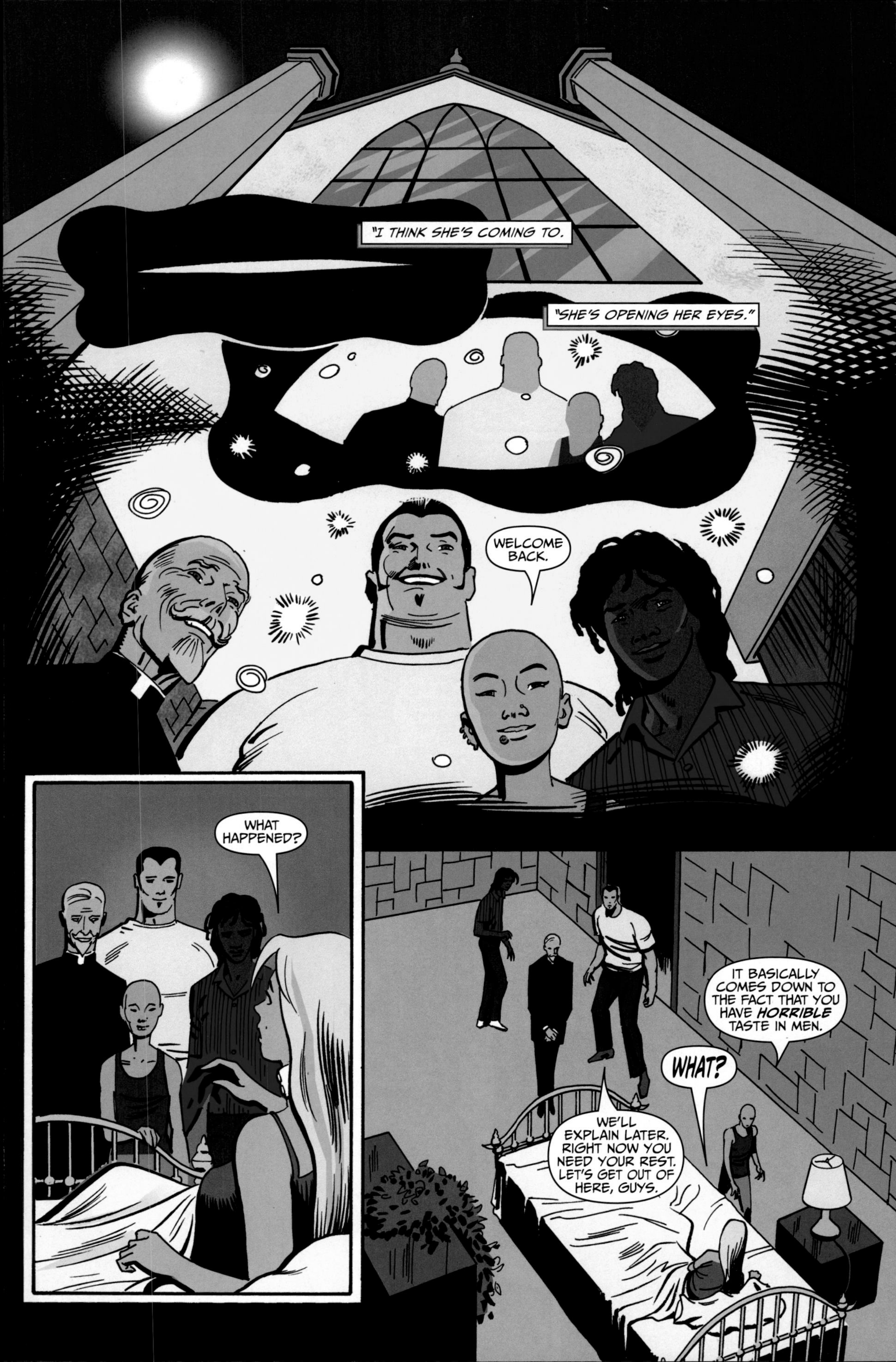
"I THINK SHE'S COMING TO.
"SHE'S OPENING HER EYES."
WELCOME BACK.
WHAT HAPPENED?
IT BASICALLY COMES DOWN TO THE FACT THAT YOU HAVE HORRIBLE TASTE IN MEN.
WHAT?
WE'LL EXPLAIN LATER. RIGHT NOW YOU NEED YOUR REST. LET'S GET OUT OF HERE, GUYS.

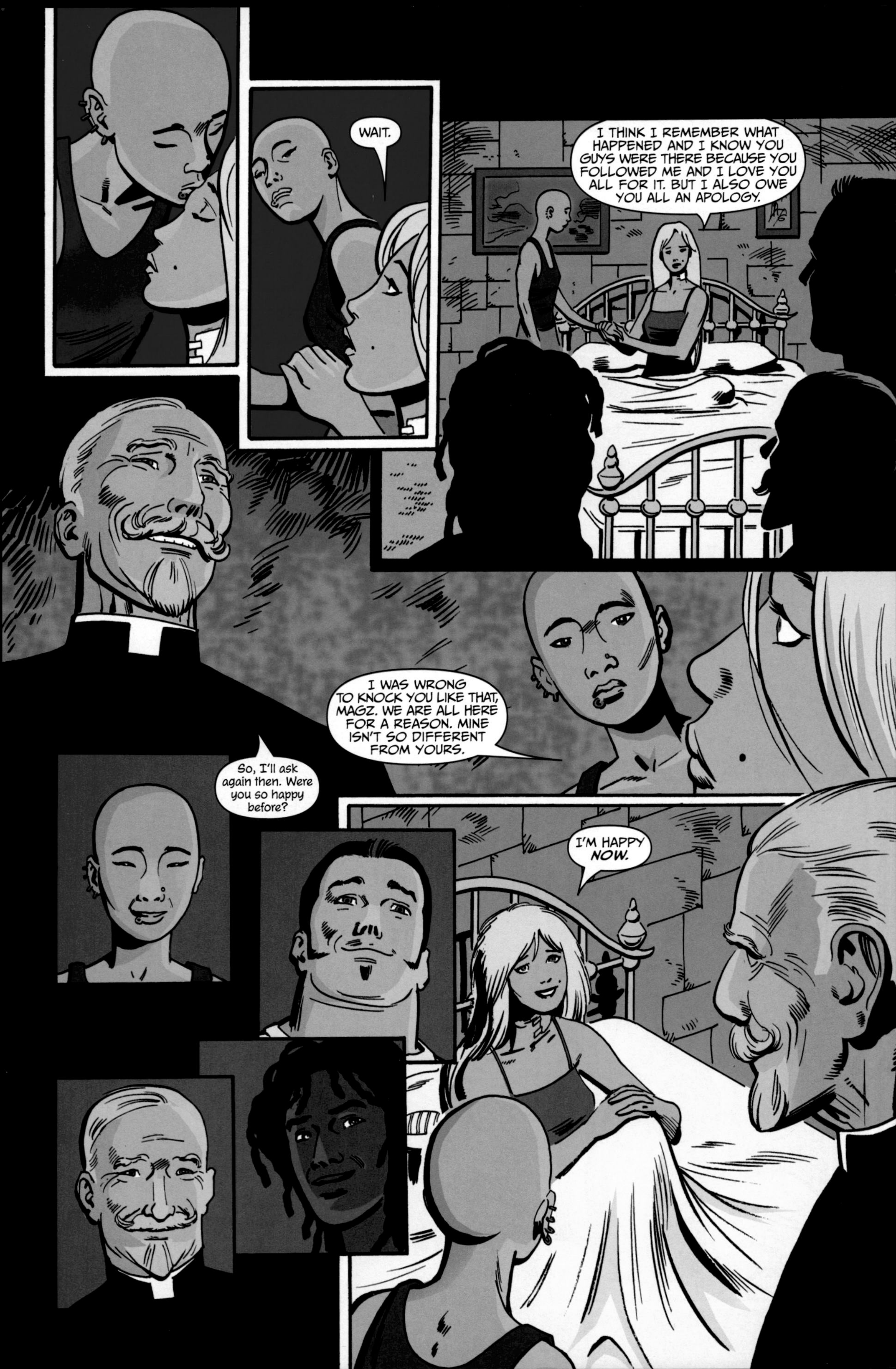
WAIT.
I THINK I REMEMBER WHAT HAPPENED AND I KNOW YOU GUYS WERE THERE BECAUSE YOU FOLLOWED ME AND I LOVE YOU ALL FOR IT. BUT I ALSO OWE YOU ALL AN APOLOGY.
I WAS WRONG TO KNOCK YOU LIKE THAT, MAGZ. WE ARE ALL HERE FOR A REASON. MINE ISN'T SO DIFFERENT FROM YOURS.
So, I'll ask again then. Were you so happy before?
I'M HAPPY *NOW.*

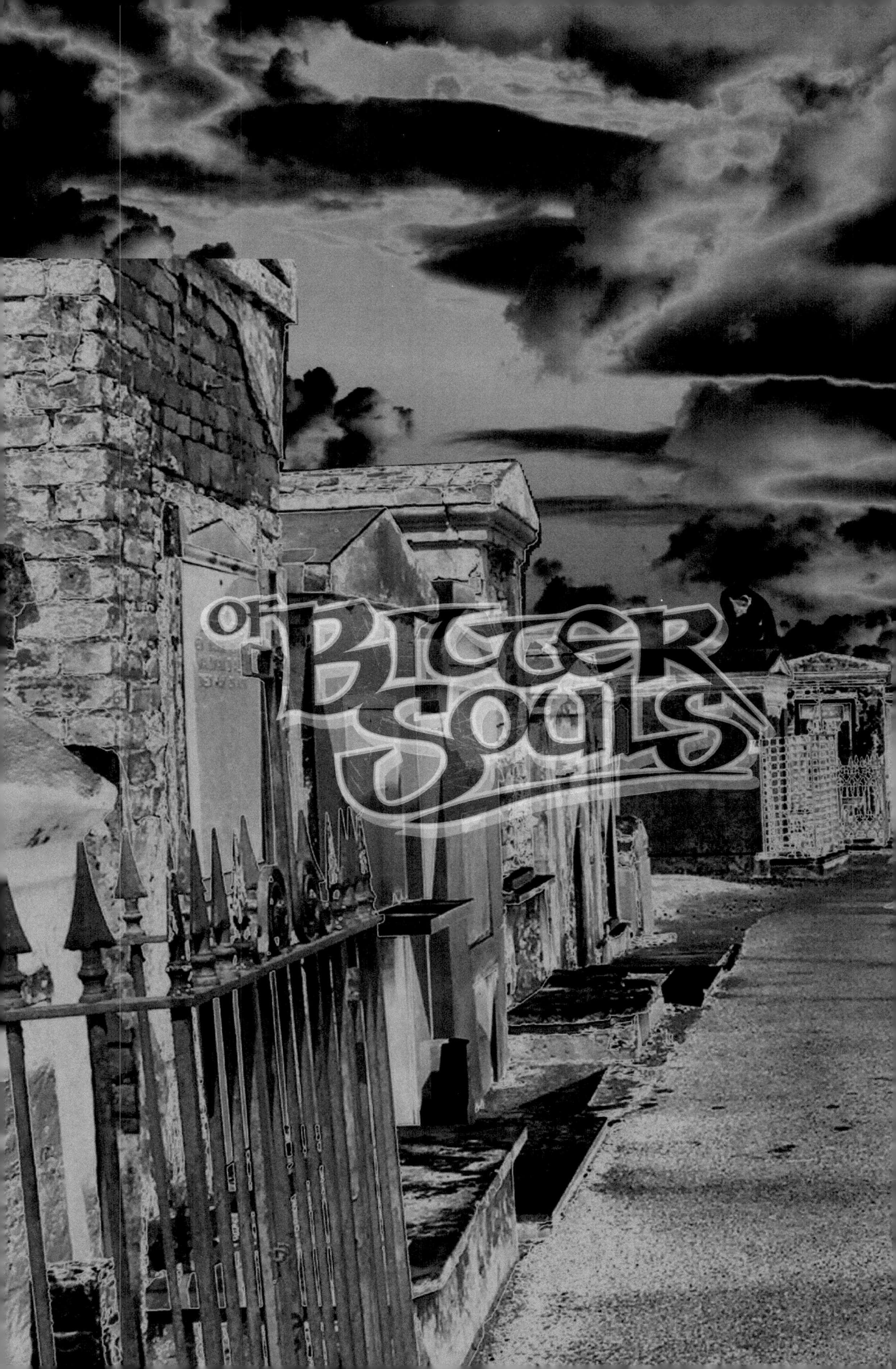
Of Bitter Souls

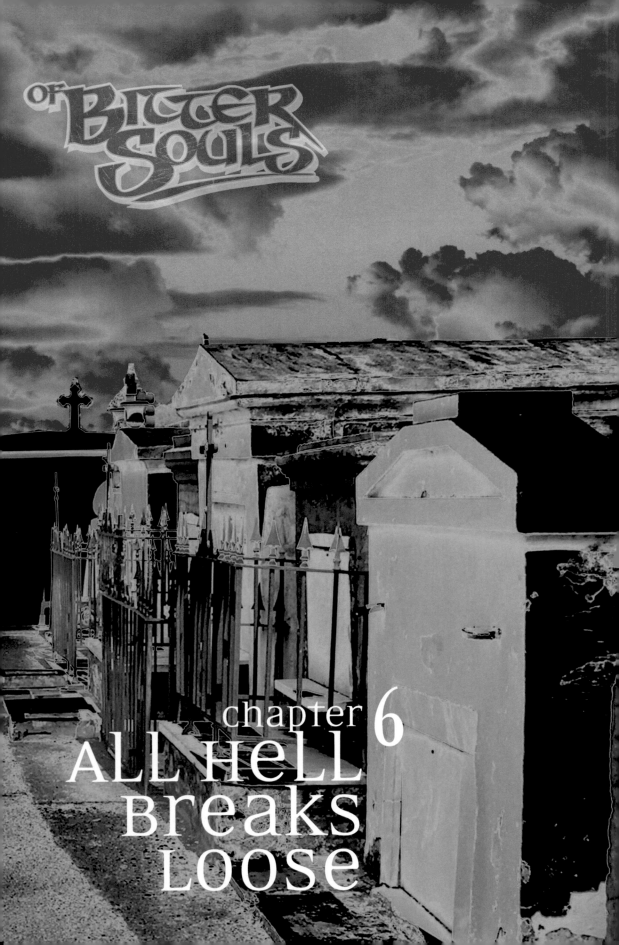

OF BITTER SOULS

chapter 6
ALL HELL
Breaks
Loose

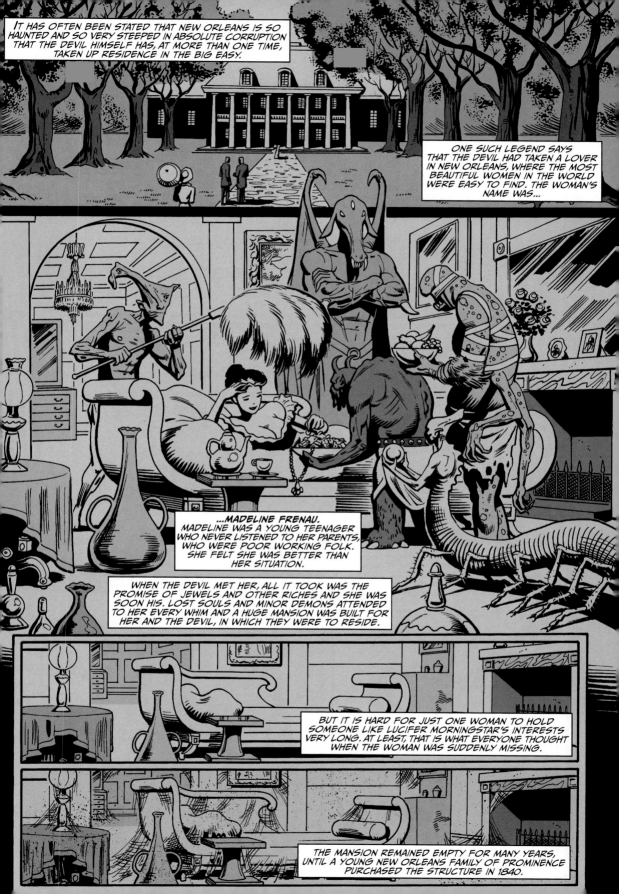

IT HAS OFTEN BEEN STATED THAT NEW ORLEANS IS SO HAUNTED AND SO VERY STEEPED IN ABSOLUTE CORRUPTION THAT THE DEVIL HIMSELF HAS, AT MORE THAN ONE TIME, TAKEN UP RESIDENCE IN THE BIG EASY.

ONE SUCH LEGEND SAYS THAT THE DEVIL HAD TAKEN A LOVER IN NEW ORLEANS, WHERE THE MOST BEAUTIFUL WOMEN IN THE WORLD WERE EASY TO FIND. THE WOMAN'S NAME WAS...

...MADELINE FRENAU. MADELINE WAS A YOUNG TEENAGER WHO NEVER LISTENED TO HER PARENTS, WHO WERE POOR WORKING FOLK. SHE FELT SHE WAS BETTER THAN HER SITUATION.

WHEN THE DEVIL MET HER, ALL IT TOOK WAS THE PROMISE OF JEWELS AND OTHER RICHES AND SHE WAS SOON HIS. LOST SOULS AND MINOR DEMONS ATTENDED TO HER EVERY WHIM AND A HUGE MANSION WAS BUILT FOR HER AND THE DEVIL, IN WHICH THEY WERE TO RESIDE.

BUT IT IS HARD FOR JUST ONE WOMAN TO HOLD SOMEONE LIKE LUCIFER MORNINGSTAR'S INTERESTS VERY LONG. AT LEAST, THAT IS WHAT EVERYONE THOUGHT WHEN THE WOMAN WAS SUDDENLY MISSING.

THE MANSION REMAINED EMPTY FOR MANY YEARS, UNTIL A YOUNG NEW ORLEANS FAMILY OF PROMINENCE PURCHASED THE STRUCTURE IN 1840.

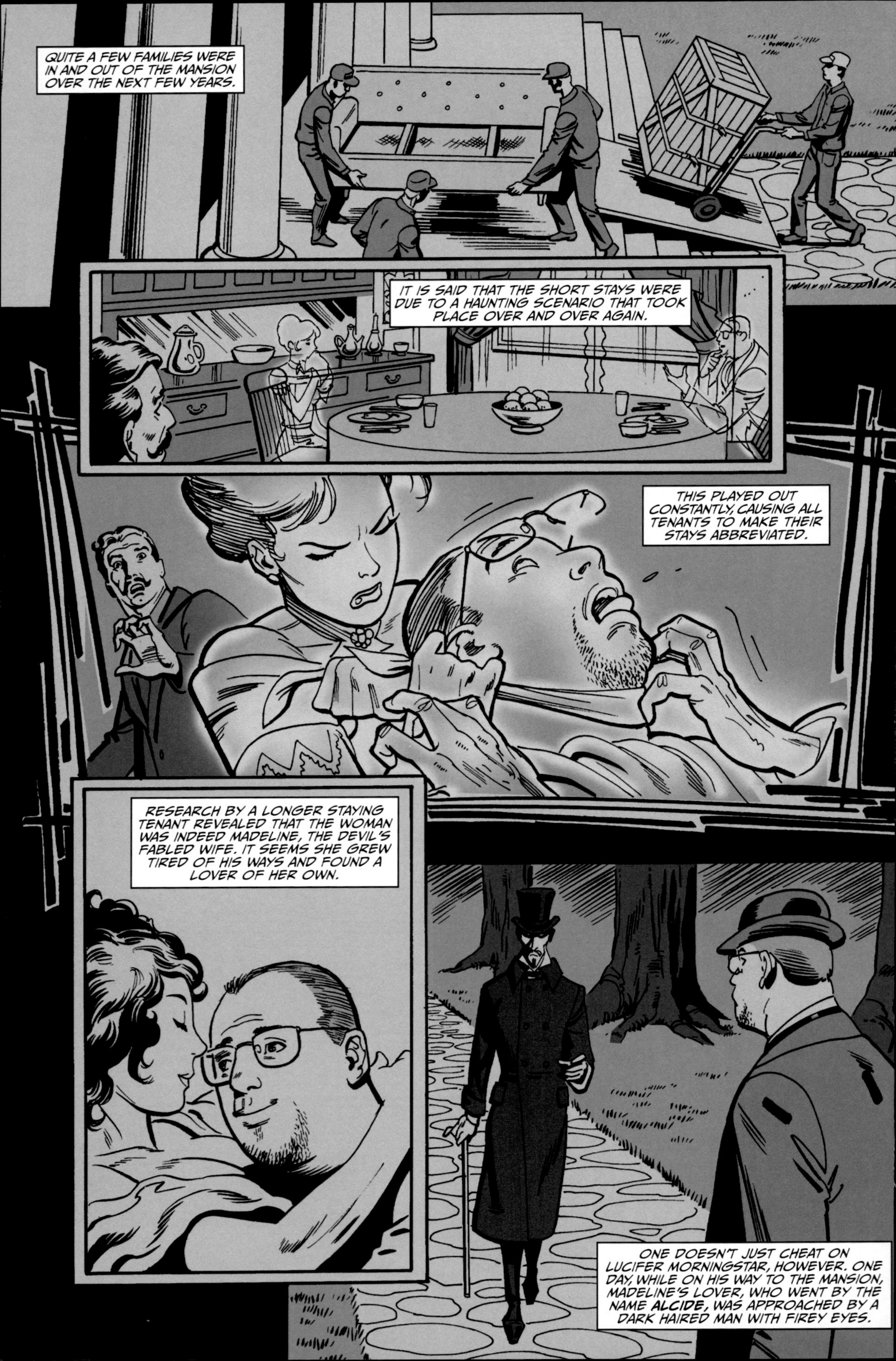
QUITE A FEW FAMILIES WERE IN AND OUT OF THE MANSION OVER THE NEXT FEW YEARS.
IT IS SAID THAT THE SHORT STAYS WERE DUE TO A HAUNTING SCENARIO THAT TOOK PLACE OVER AND OVER AGAIN.
THIS PLAYED OUT CONSTANTLY, CAUSING ALL TENANTS TO MAKE THEIR STAYS ABBREVIATED.
RESEARCH BY A LONGER STAYING TENANT REVEALED THAT THE WOMAN WAS INDEED MADELINE, THE DEVIL'S FABLED WIFE. IT SEEMS SHE GREW TIRED OF HIS WAYS AND FOUND A LOVER OF HER OWN.
ONE DOESN'T JUST CHEAT ON LUCIFER MORNINGSTAR, HOWEVER. ONE DAY, WHILE ON HIS WAY TO THE MANSION, MADELINE'S LOVER, WHO WENT BY THE NAME **ALCIDE**, WAS APPROACHED BY A DARK HAIRED MAN WITH FIREY EYES.

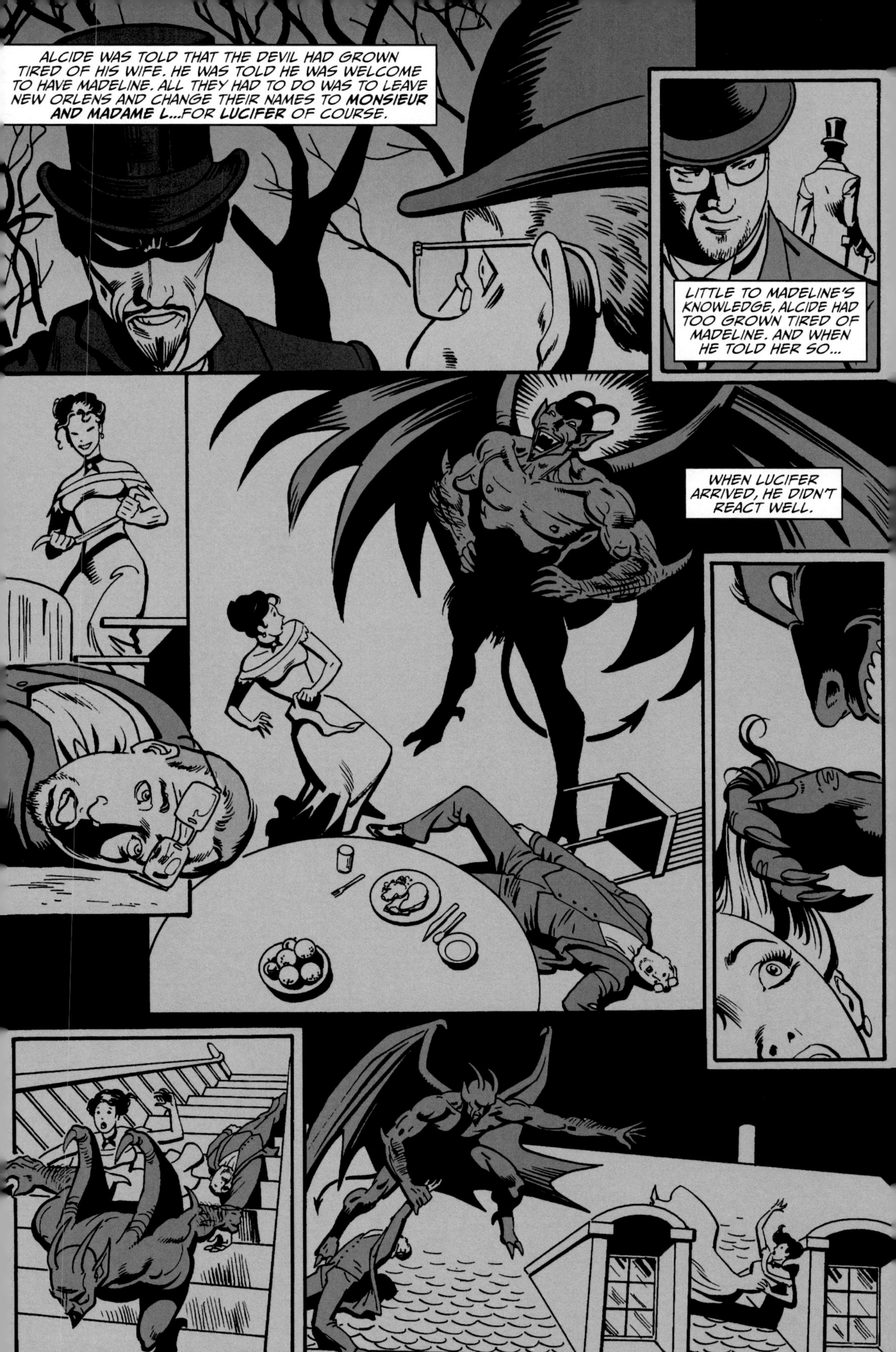
ALCIDE WAS TOLD THAT THE DEVIL HAD GROWN TIRED OF HIS WIFE. HE WAS TOLD HE WAS WELCOME TO HAVE MADELINE. ALL THEY HAD TO DO WAS TO LEAVE NEW ORLENS AND CHANGE THEIR NAMES TO MONSIEUR AND MADAME L...FOR LUCIFER OF COURSE.
LITTLE TO MADELINE'S KNOWLEDGE, ALCIDE HAD TOO GROWN TIRED OF MADELINE. AND WHEN HE TOLD HER SO...
WHEN LUCIFER ARRIVED, HE DIDN'T REACT WELL.

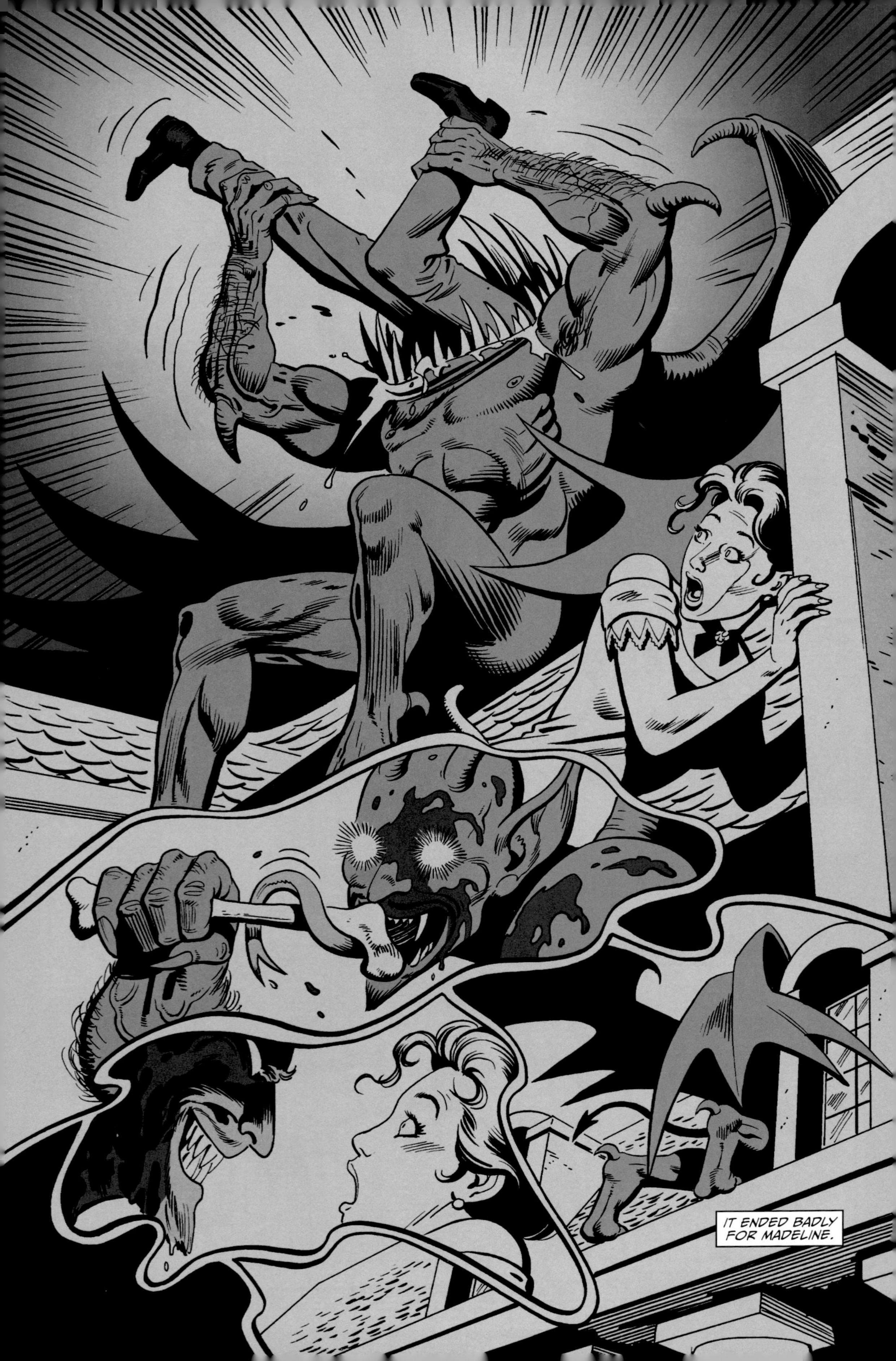
IT ENDED BADLY FOR MADELINE.

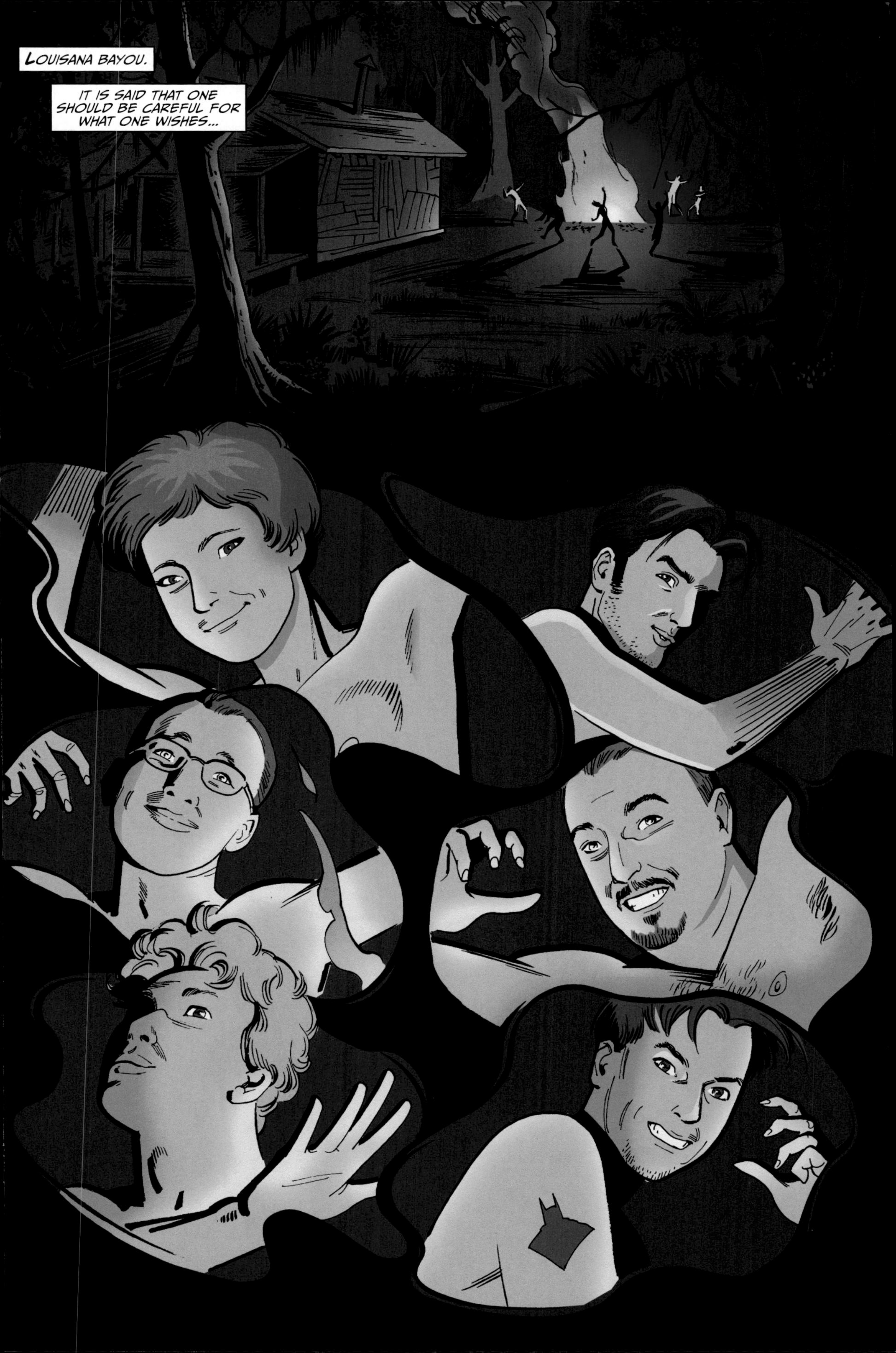
LOUISANA BAYOU.
IT IS SAID THAT ONE SHOULD BE CAREFUL FOR WHAT ONE WISHES...

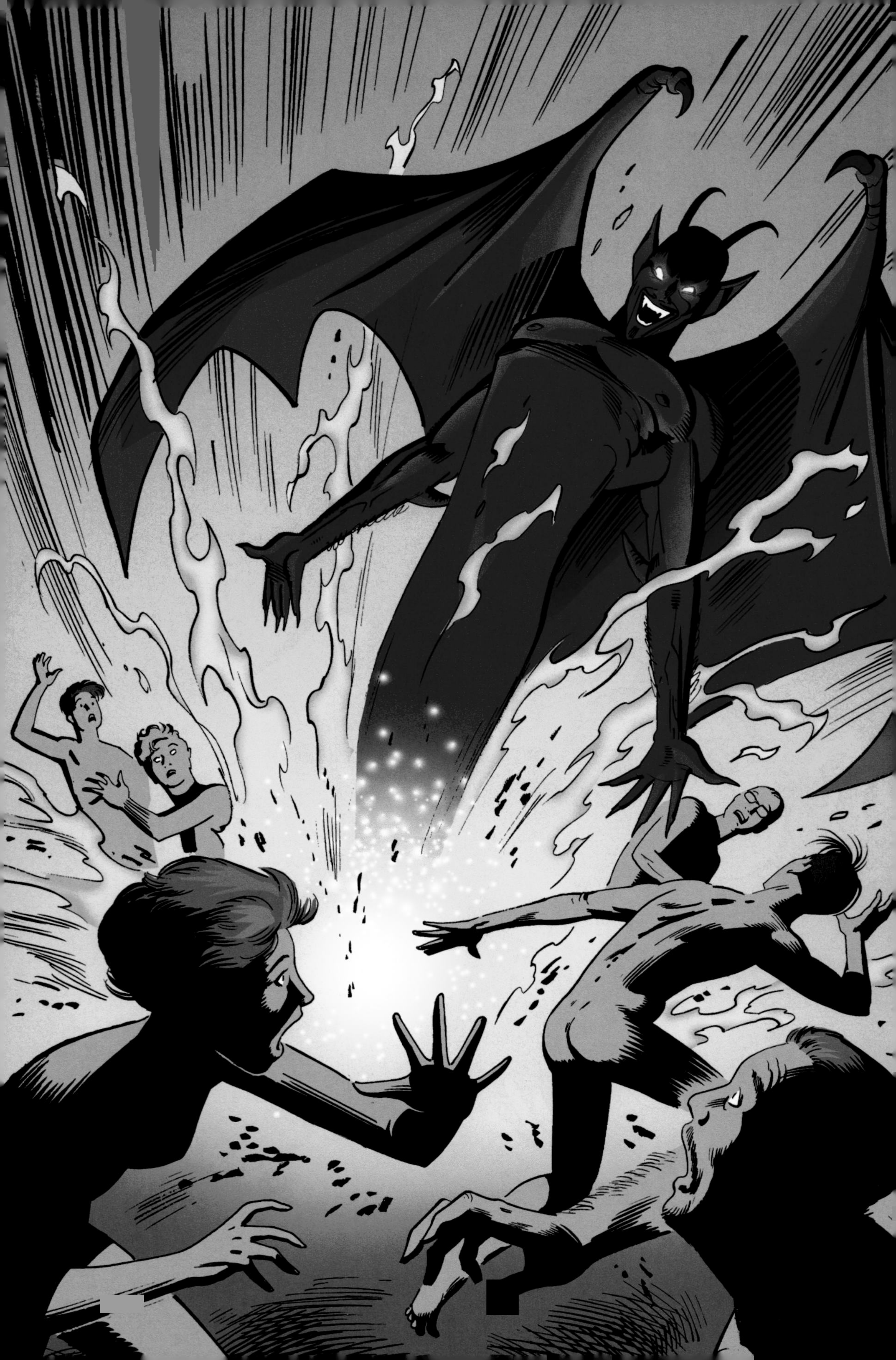

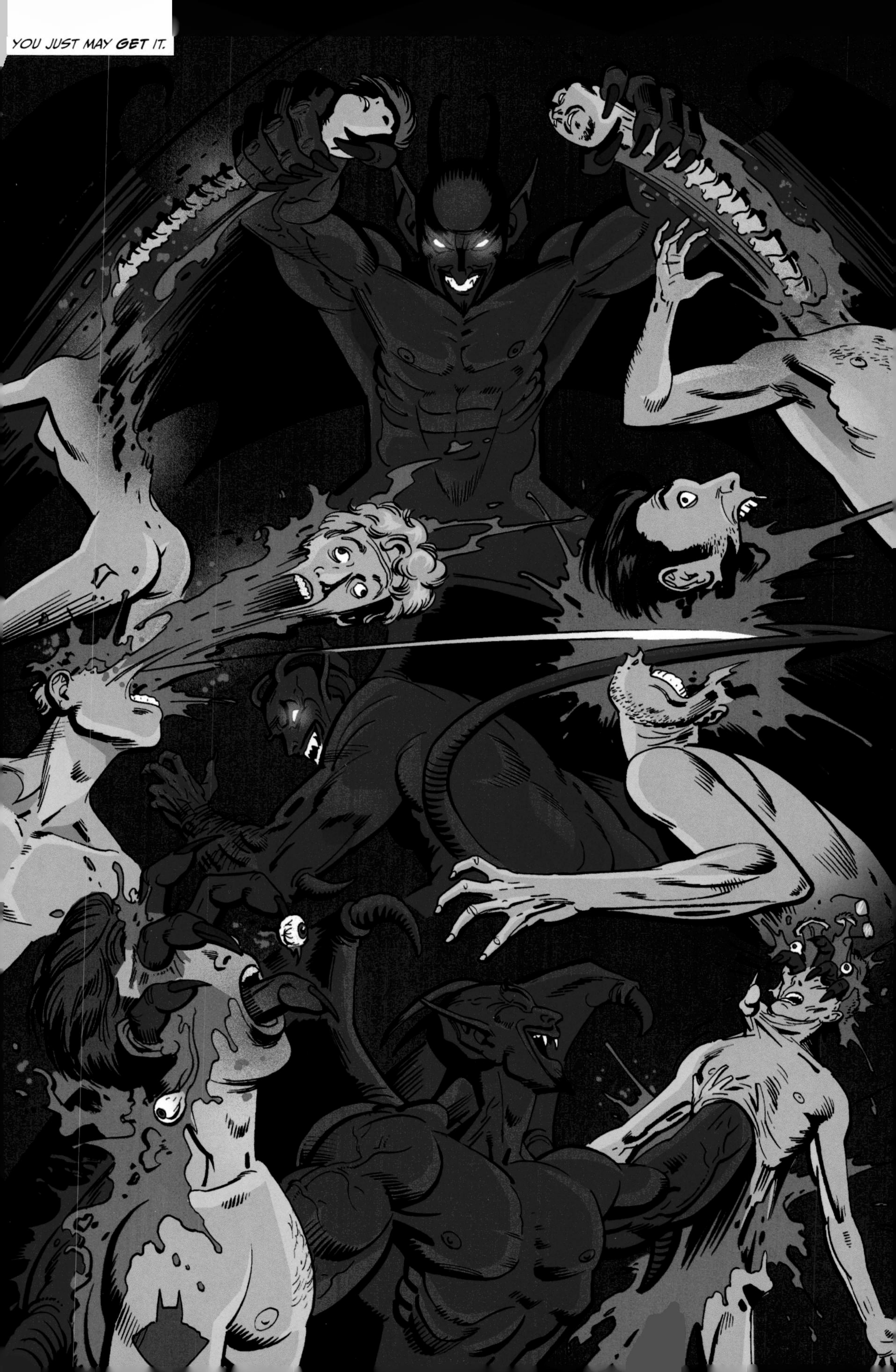
YOU JUST MAY GET IT.

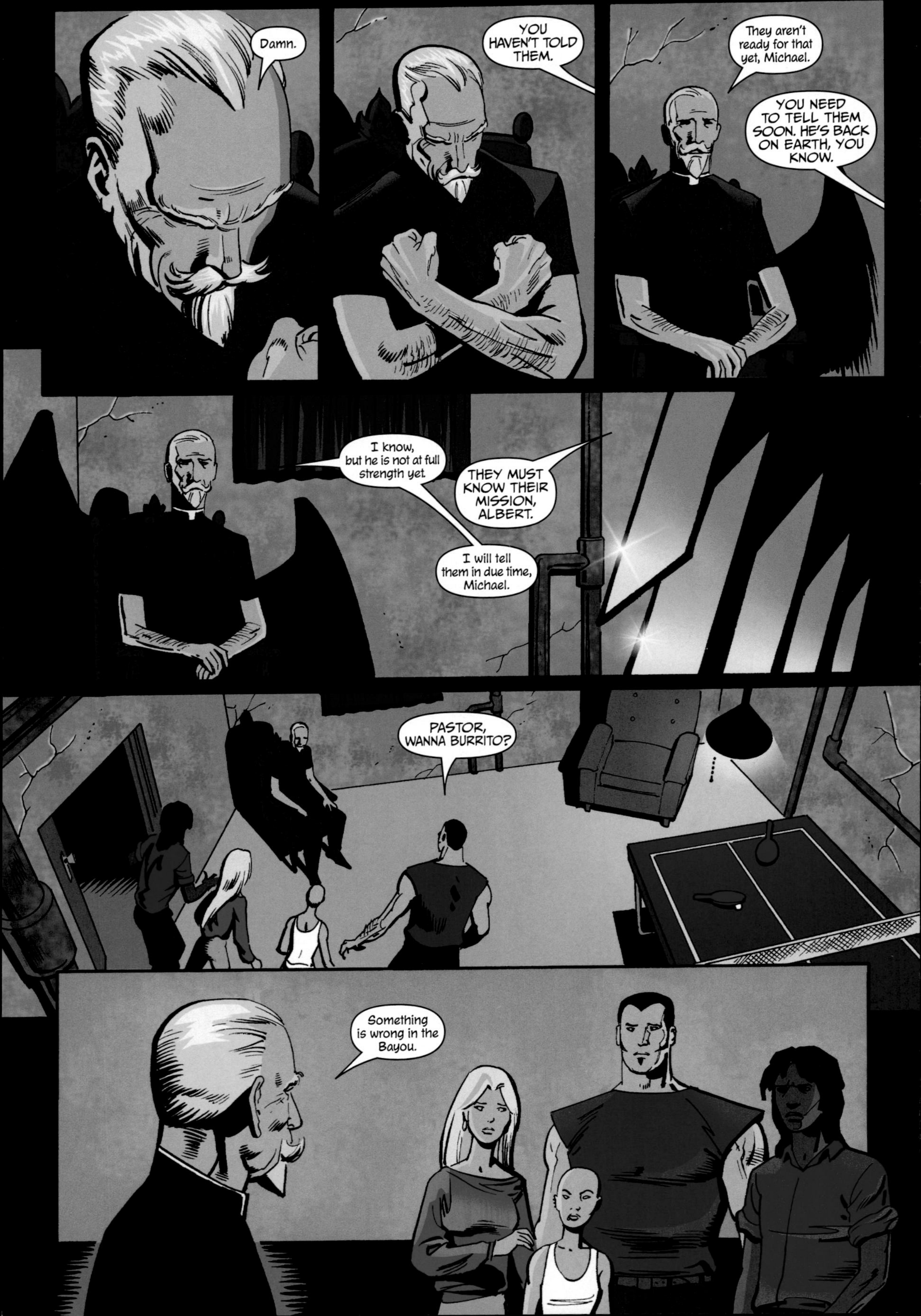
Damn.
YOU HAVEN'T TOLD THEM.
They aren't ready for that yet, Michael.
YOU NEED TO TELL THEM SOON. HE'S BACK ON EARTH, YOU KNOW.
I know, but he is not at full strength yet.
THEY MUST KNOW THEIR MISSION, ALBERT.
I will tell them in due time, Michael.
PASTOR, WANNA BURRITO?
Something is wrong in the Bayou.

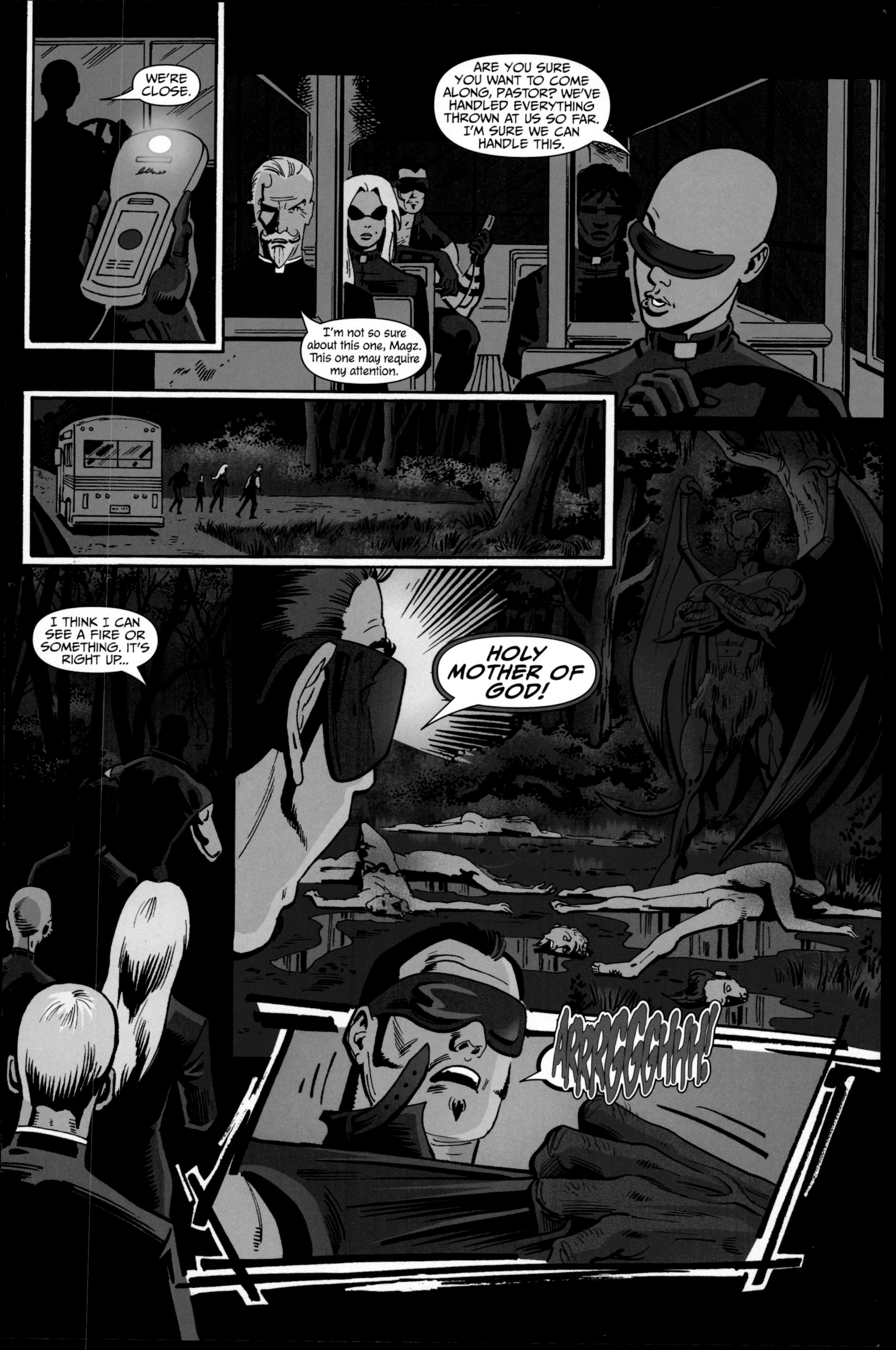

WE'RE CLOSE.
ARE YOU SURE YOU WANT TO COME ALONG, PASTOR? WE'VE HANDLED EVERYTHING THROWN AT US SO FAR. I'M SURE WE CAN HANDLE THIS.
I'm not so sure about this one, Magz. This one may require my attention.
I THINK I CAN SEE A FIRE OR SOMETHING. IT'S RIGHT UP...
HOLY MOTHER OF GOD!
ARRRGGGHH!

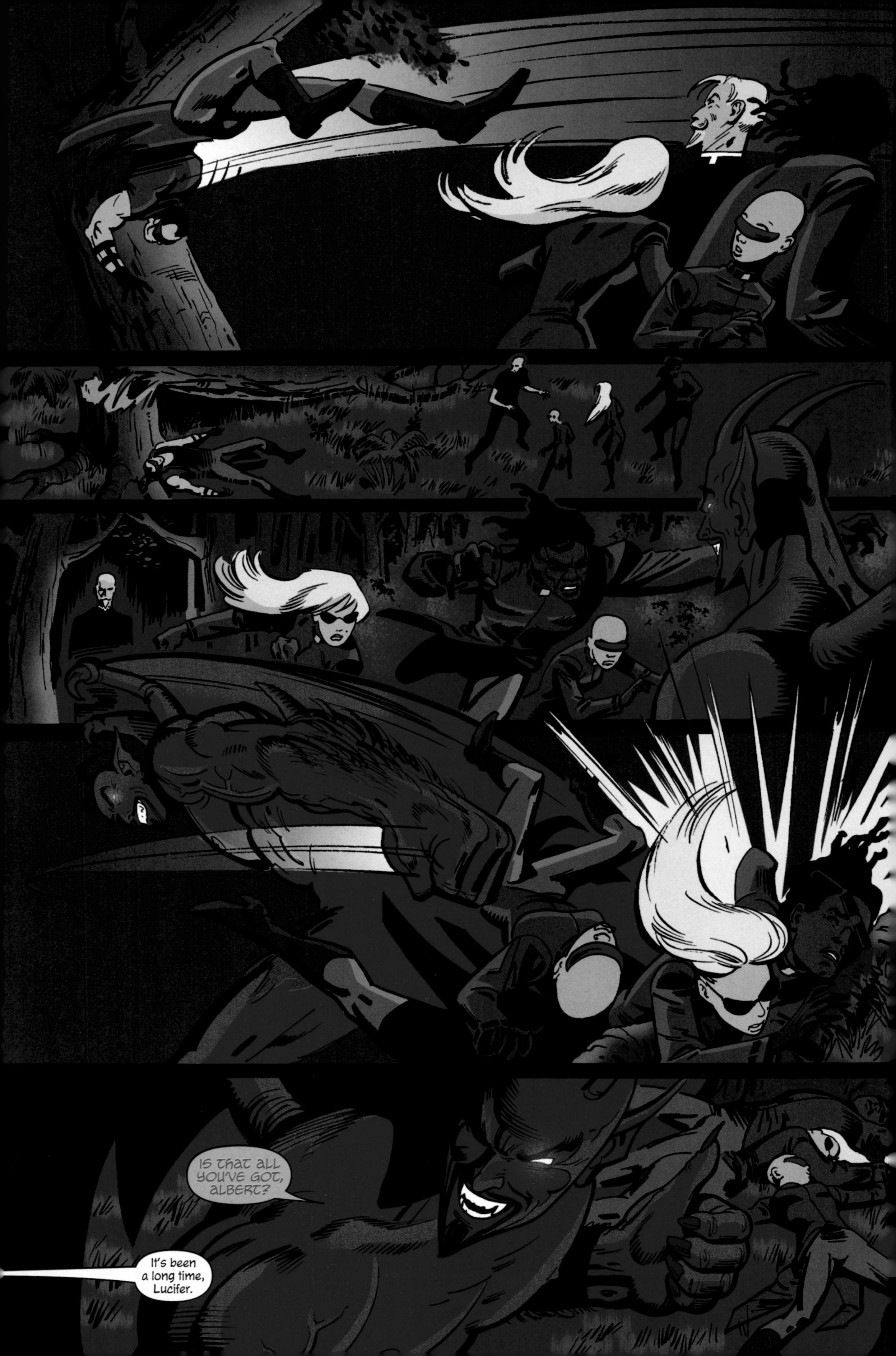
IS THAT ALL YOU'VE GOT, ALBERT?
It's been a long time, Lucifer.

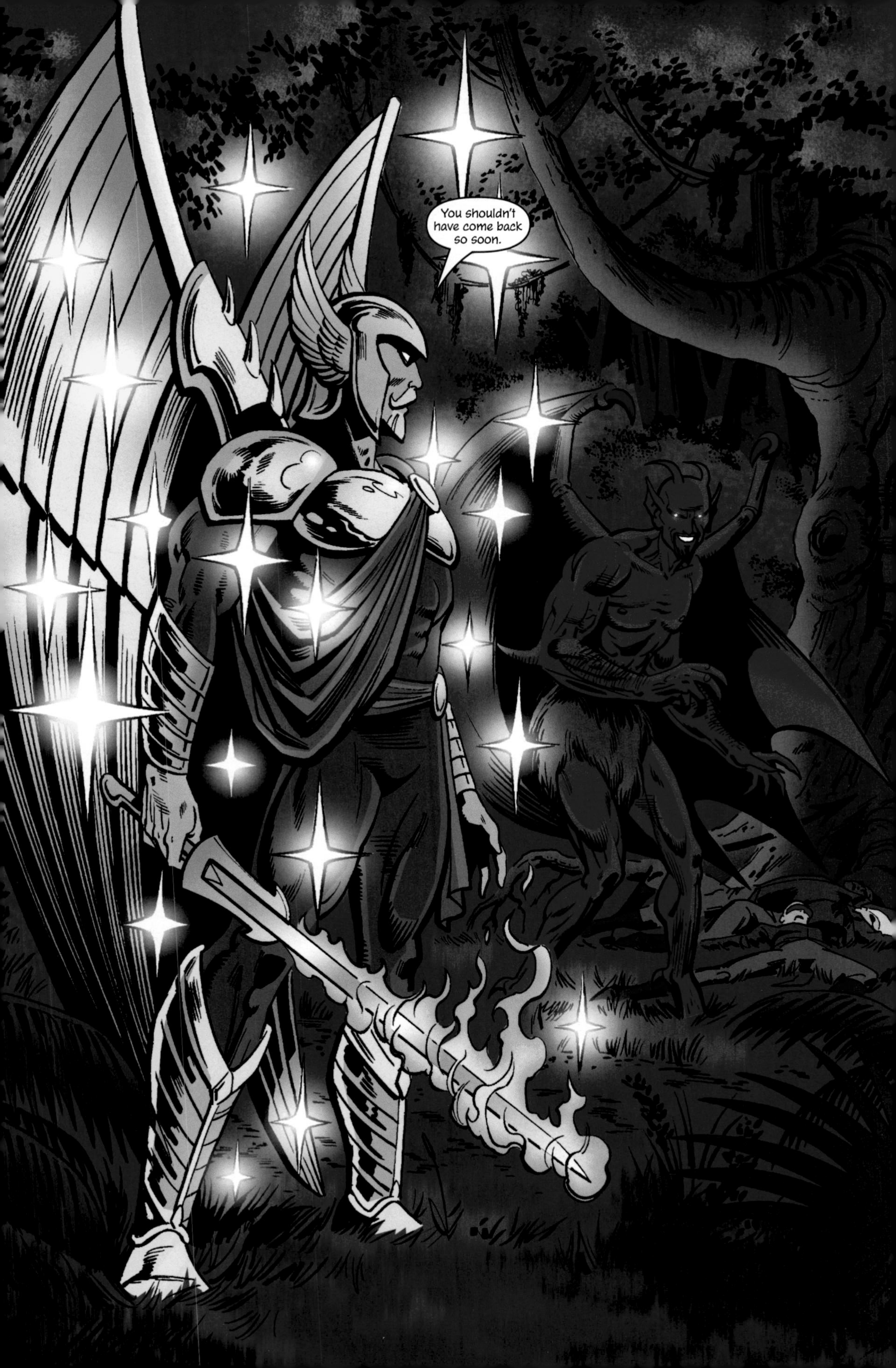
You shouldn't have come back so soon.

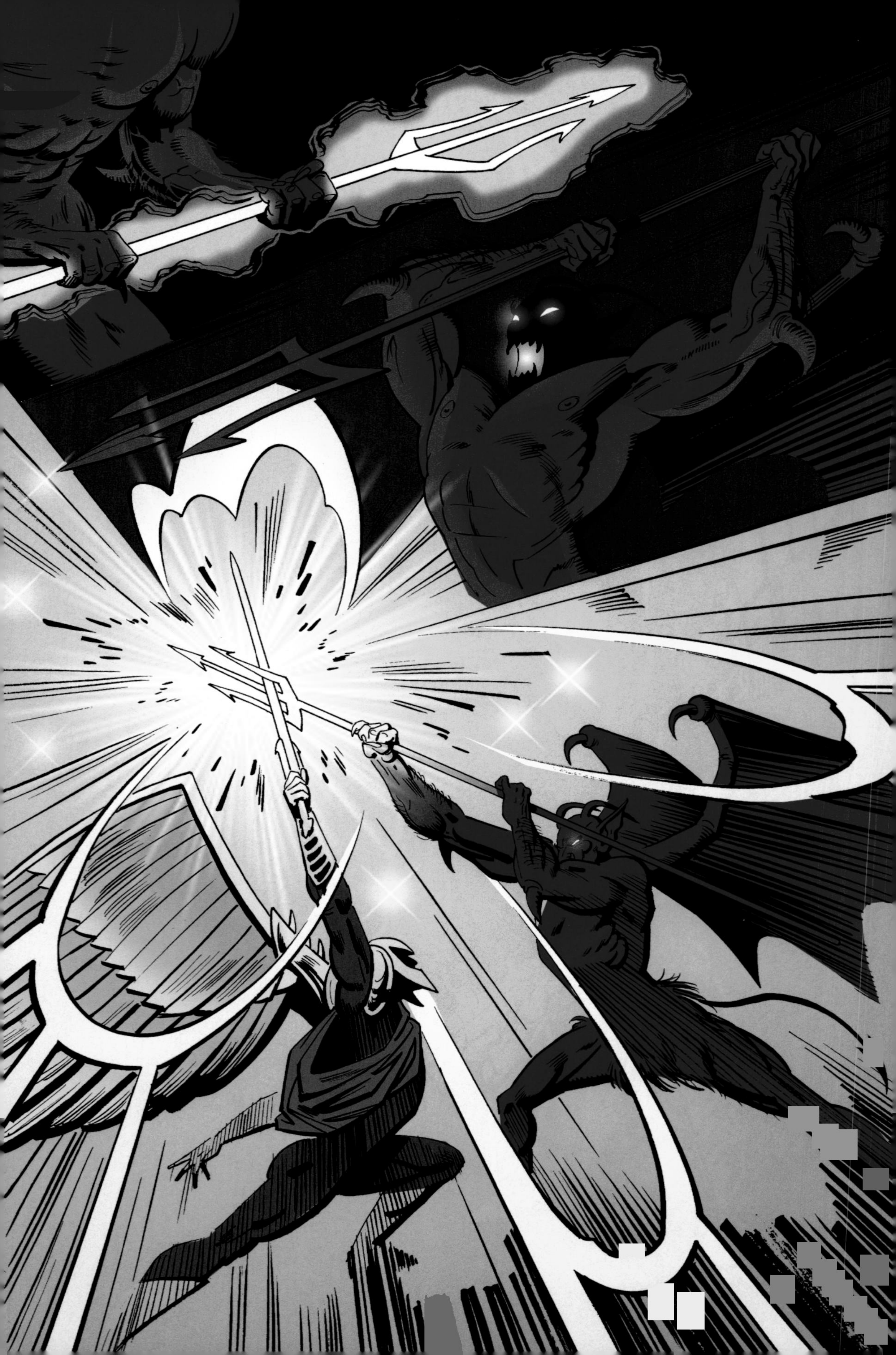

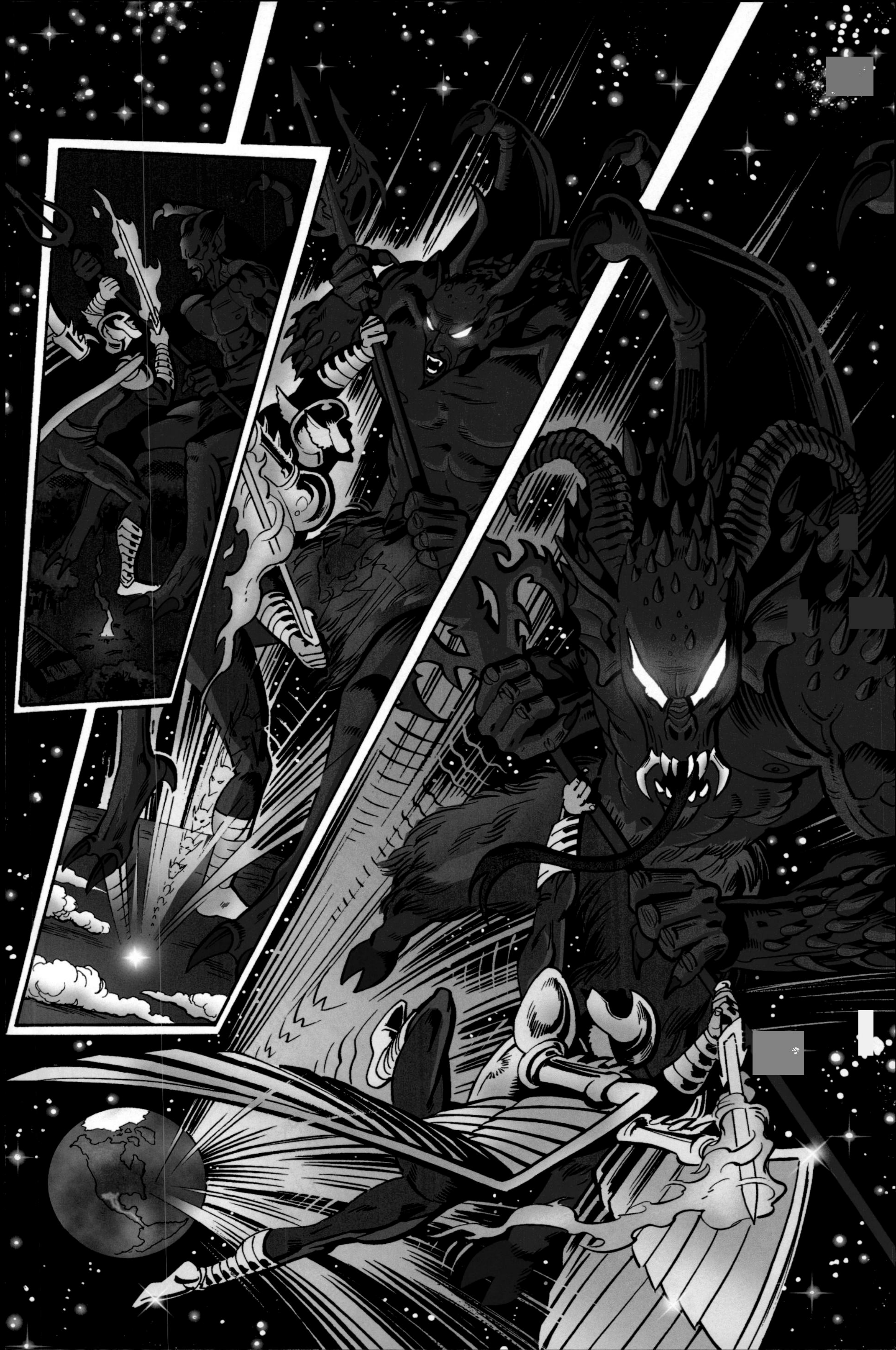

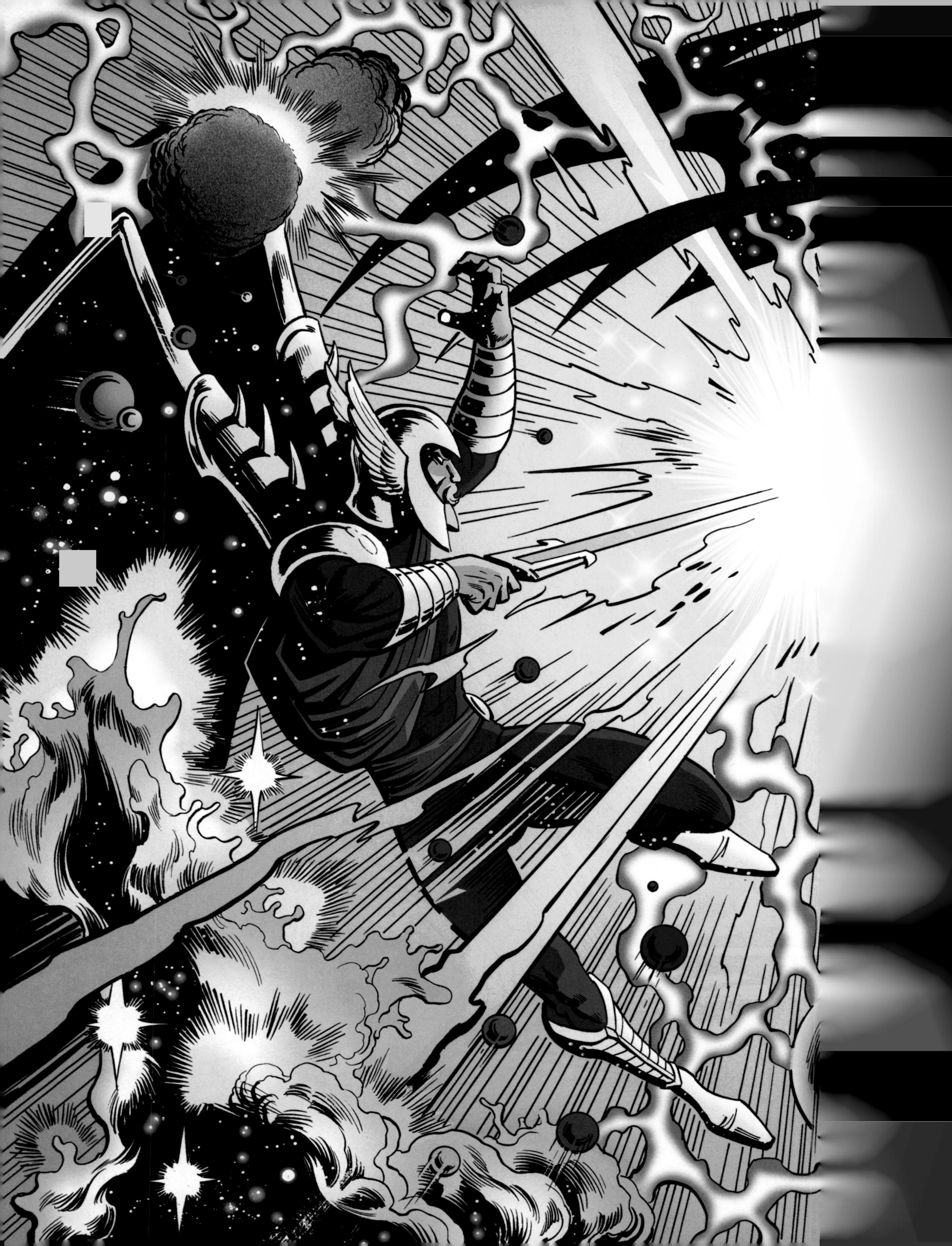

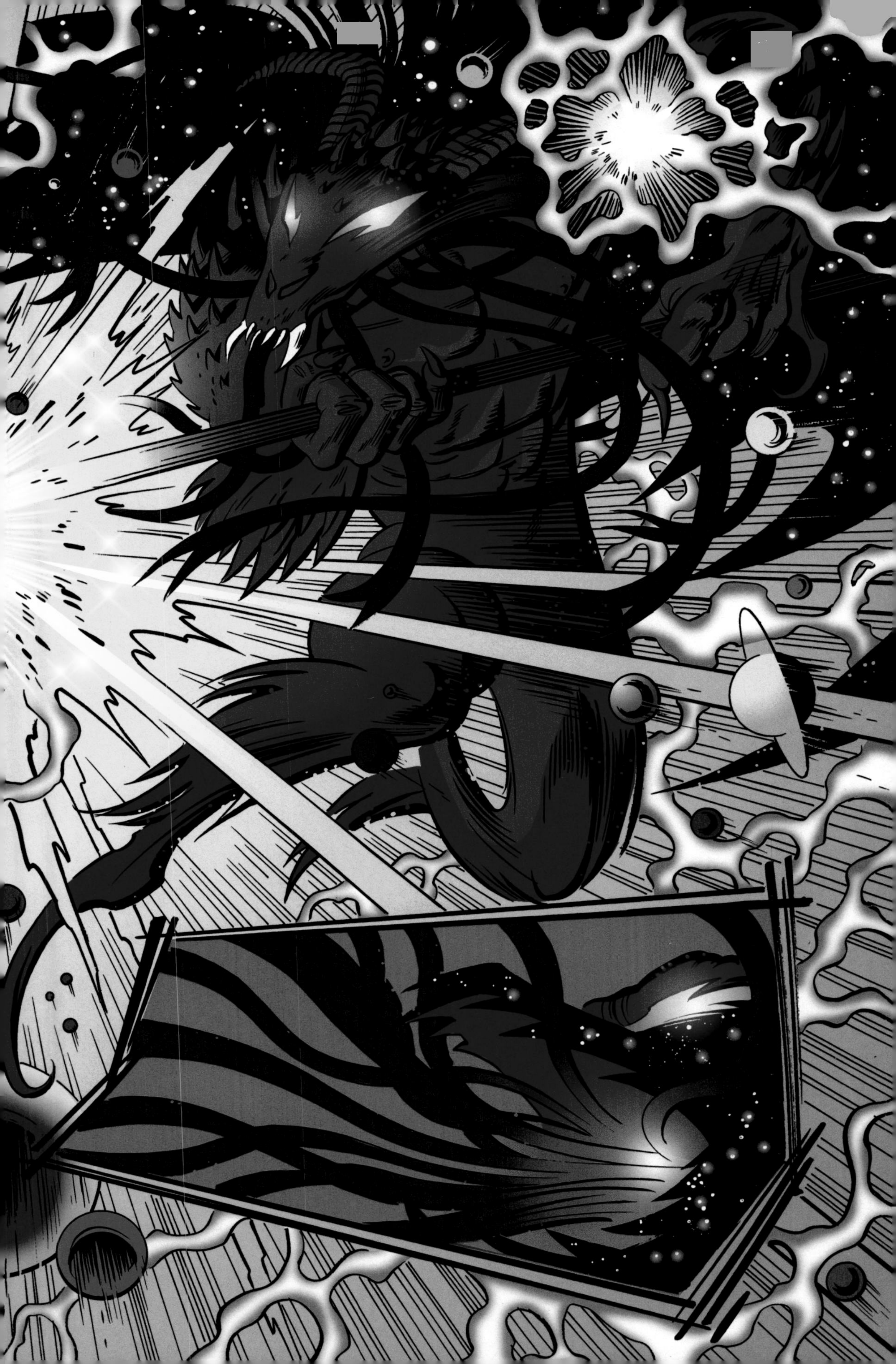

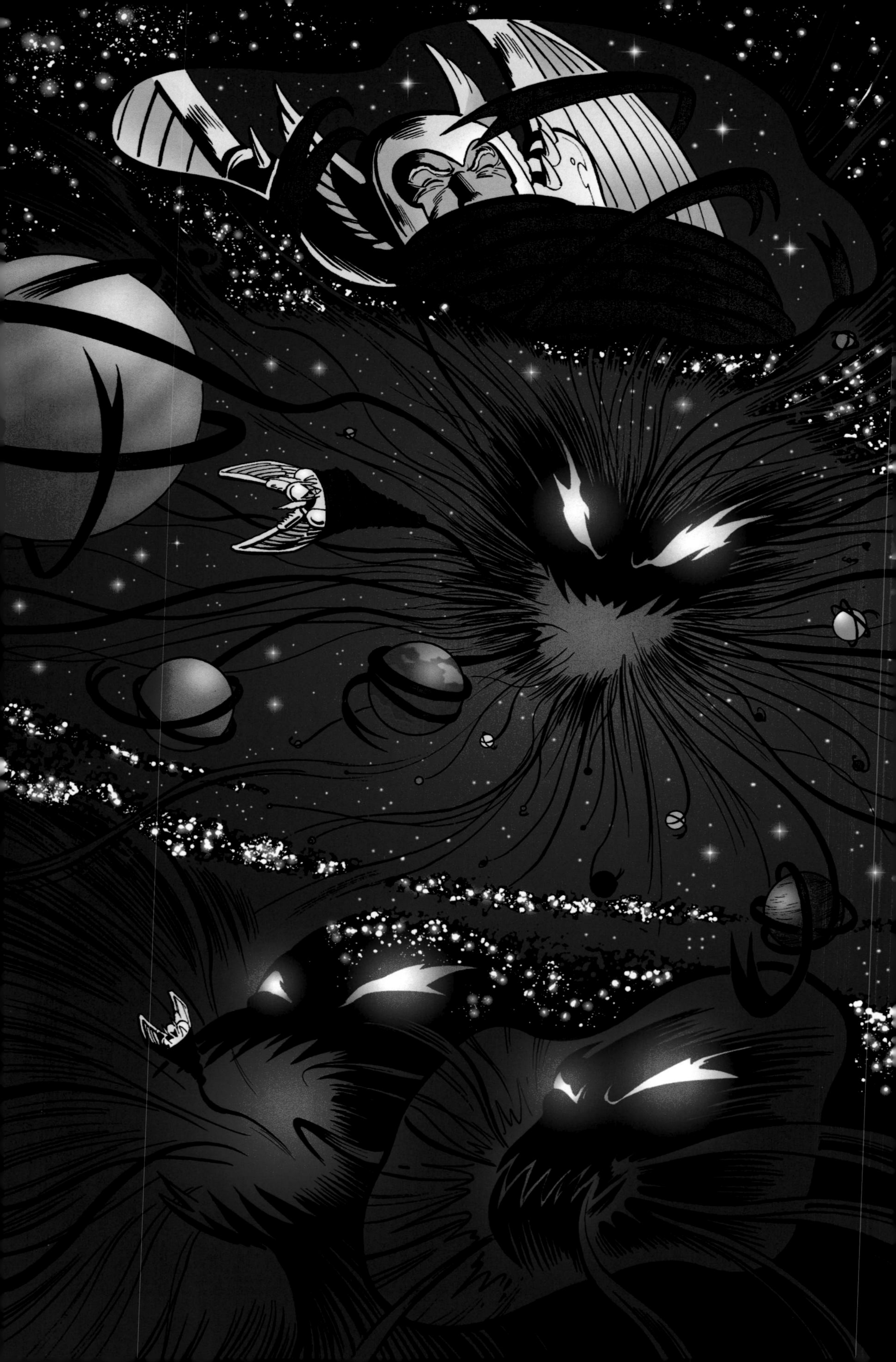

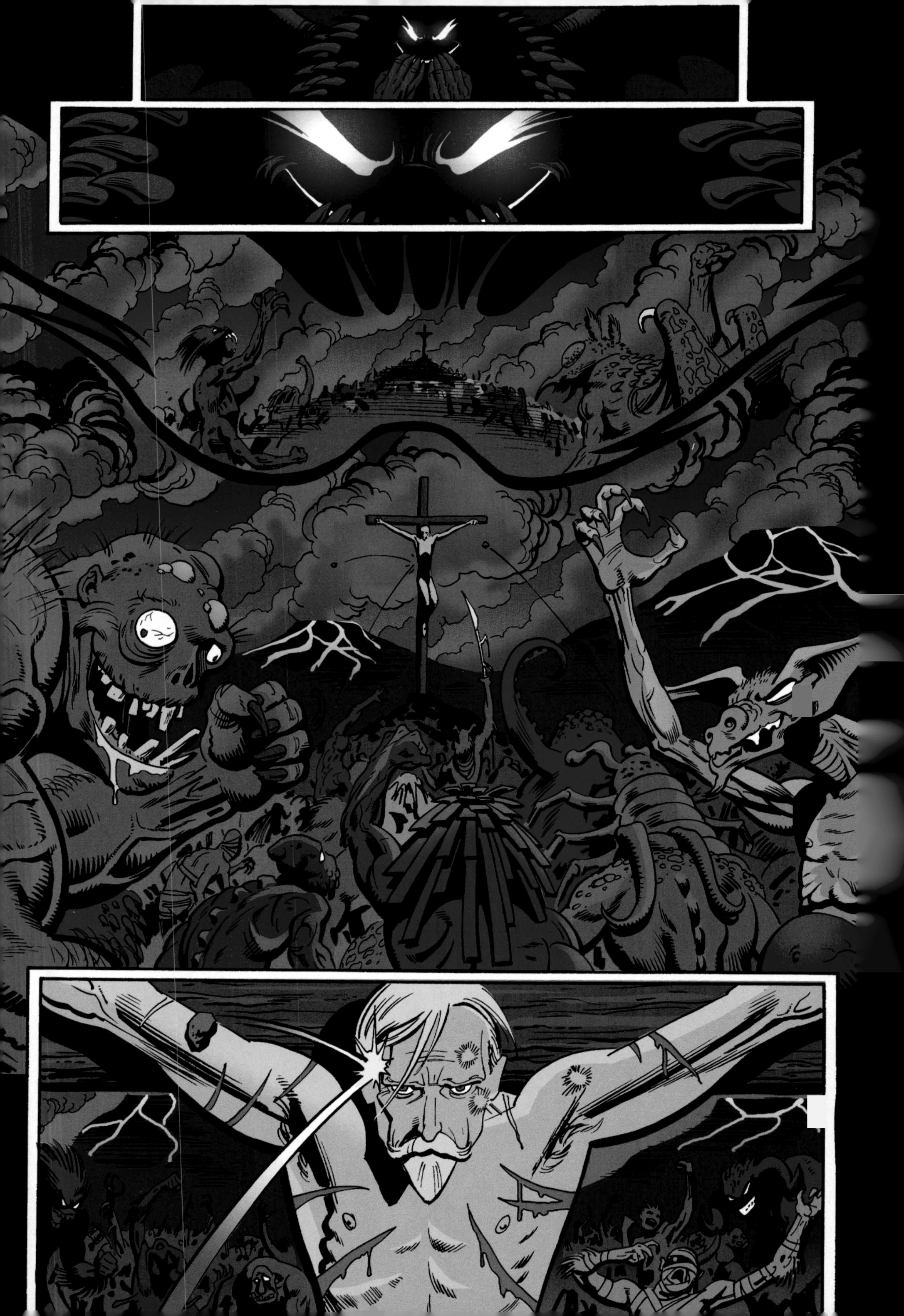

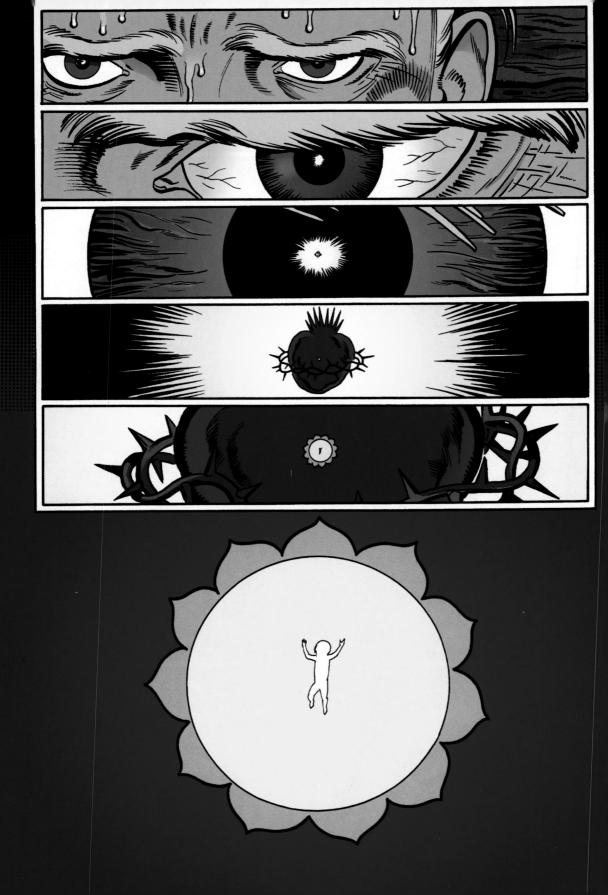

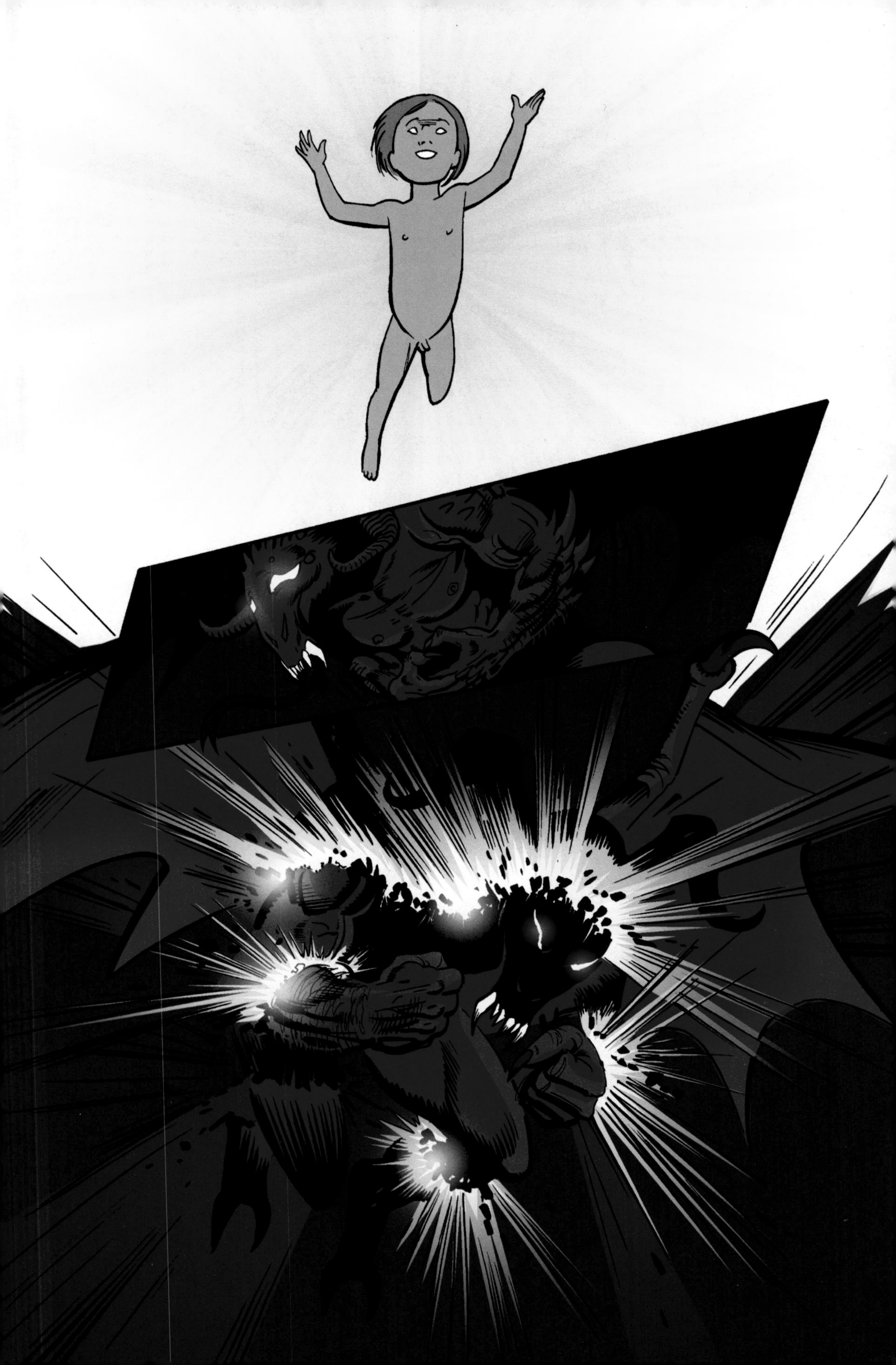

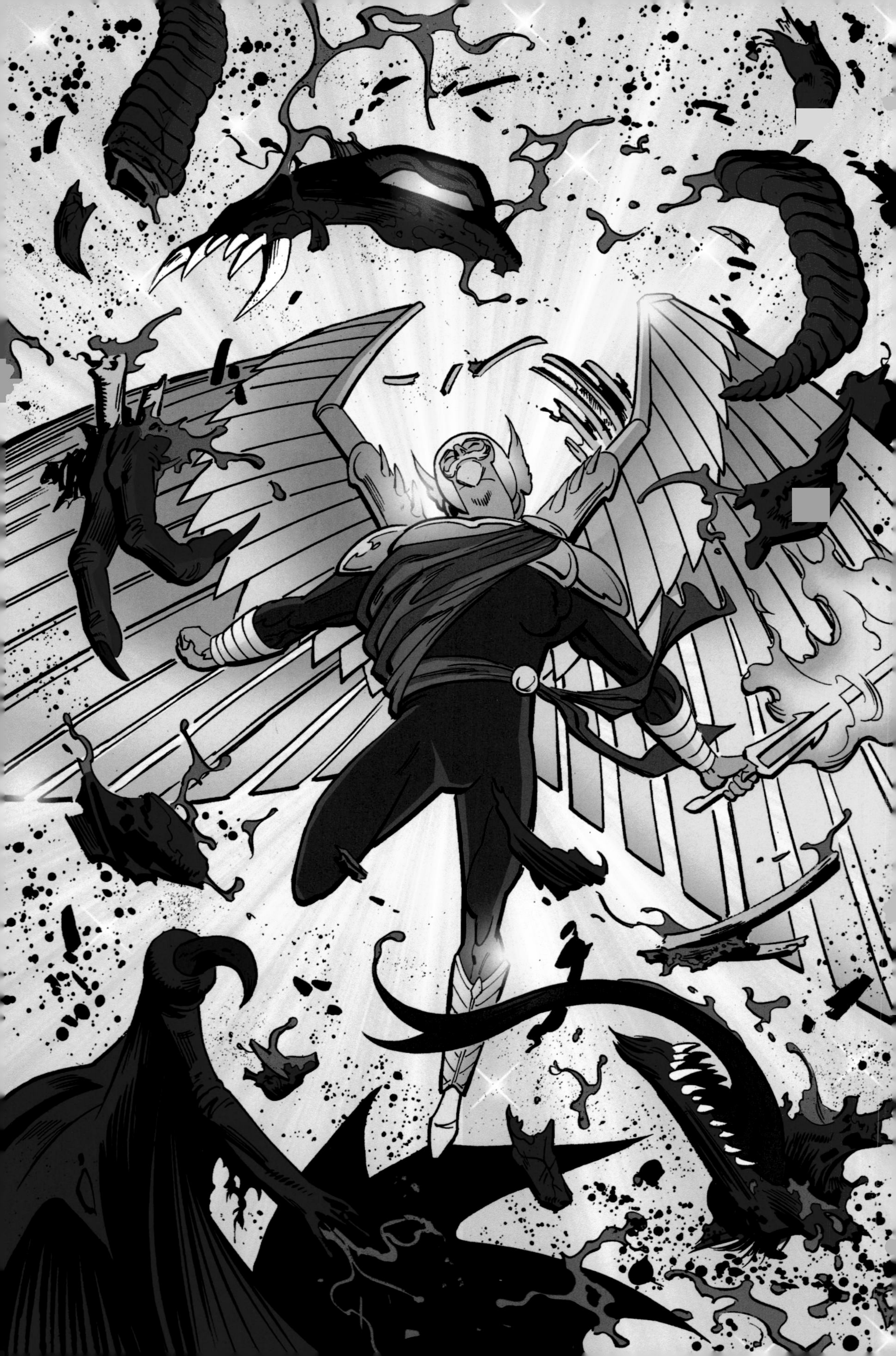

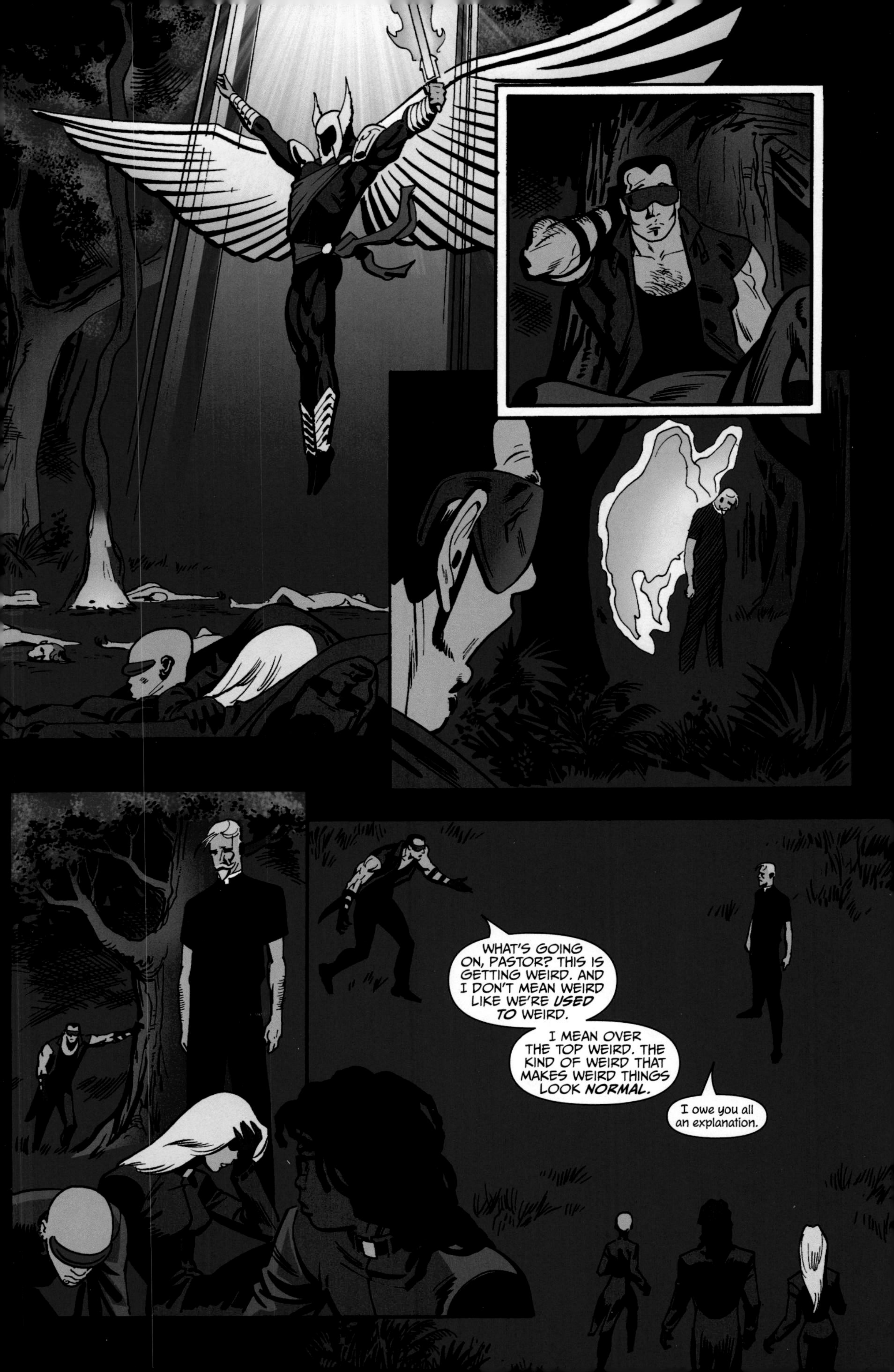
WHAT'S GOING ON, PASTOR? THIS IS GETTING WEIRD. AND I DON'T MEAN WEIRD LIKE WE'RE *USED TO* WEIRD.
I MEAN OVER THE TOP WEIRD. THE KIND OF WEIRD THAT MAKES WEIRD THINGS LOOK *NORMAL.*
I owe you all an explanation.

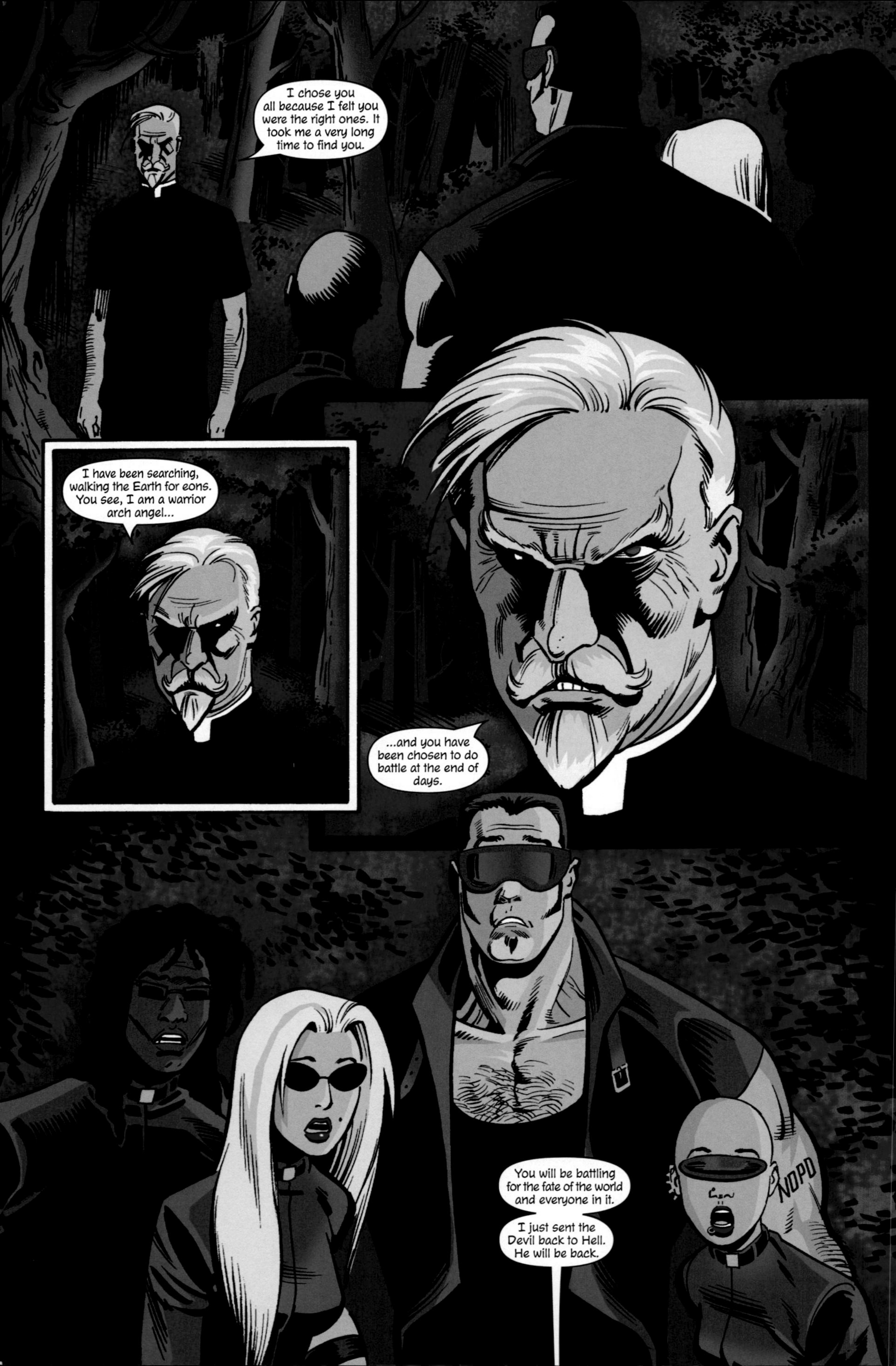

I chose you all because I felt you were the right ones. It took me a very long time to find you.
I have been searching, walking the Earth for eons. You see, I am a warrior arch angel...
...and you have been chosen to do battle at the end of days.
You will be battling for the fate of the world and everyone in it.
I just sent the Devil back to Hell. He will be back.
NOPD

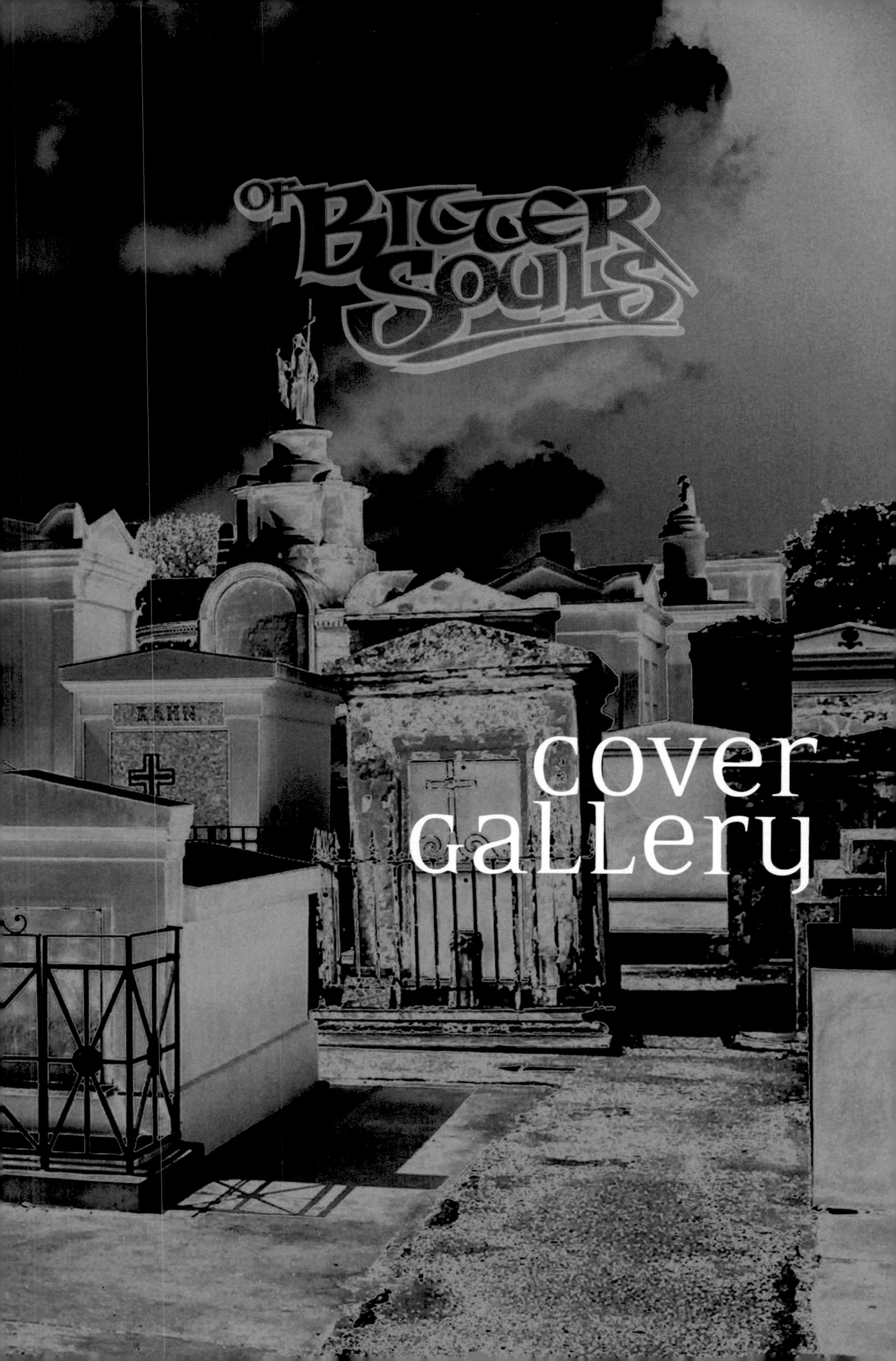
Of Bitter Souls
KAHN
cover
gallery

This cover was one of many sketches Norm submitted for the first ever 'Of Bitter Souls' cover. Norm used a photo taken by Chuck's wife Chris Satterlee while on vacation in New Orleans.

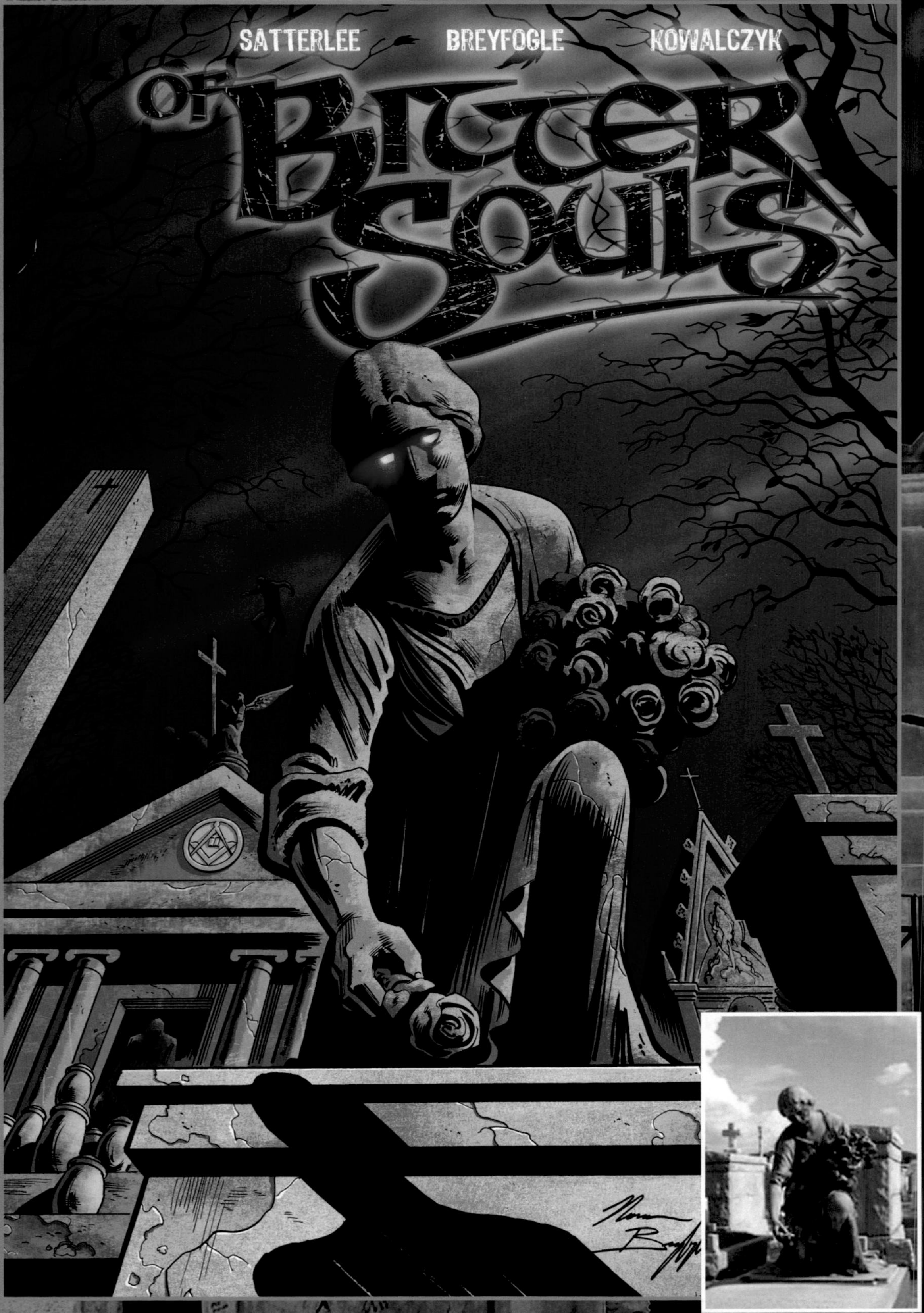
SATTERLEE
BREYFOGLE
KOWALCZYK
OF BITTER SOULS

his cover came from a sketch Norm did for issue one. We liked it so much we decided to use for issue two. Chuck decided to write in a scene at the end of issue two to match the cover.

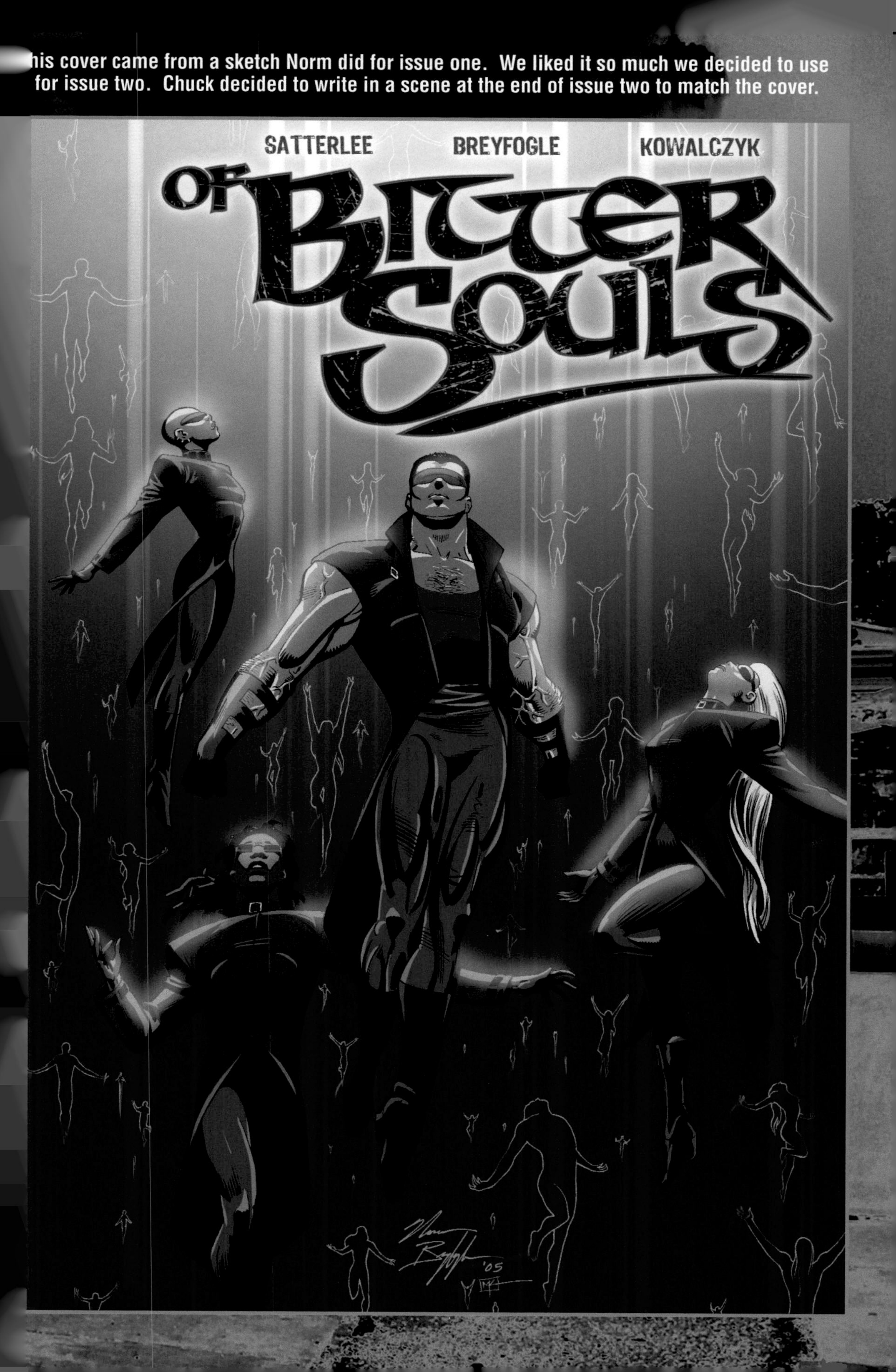
SATTERLEE
BREYFOGLE
KOWALCZYK
OF BITTER SOULS
'05

This cover was a no-brainer...so to speak.
Very few sketches were needed to arrive at this image.

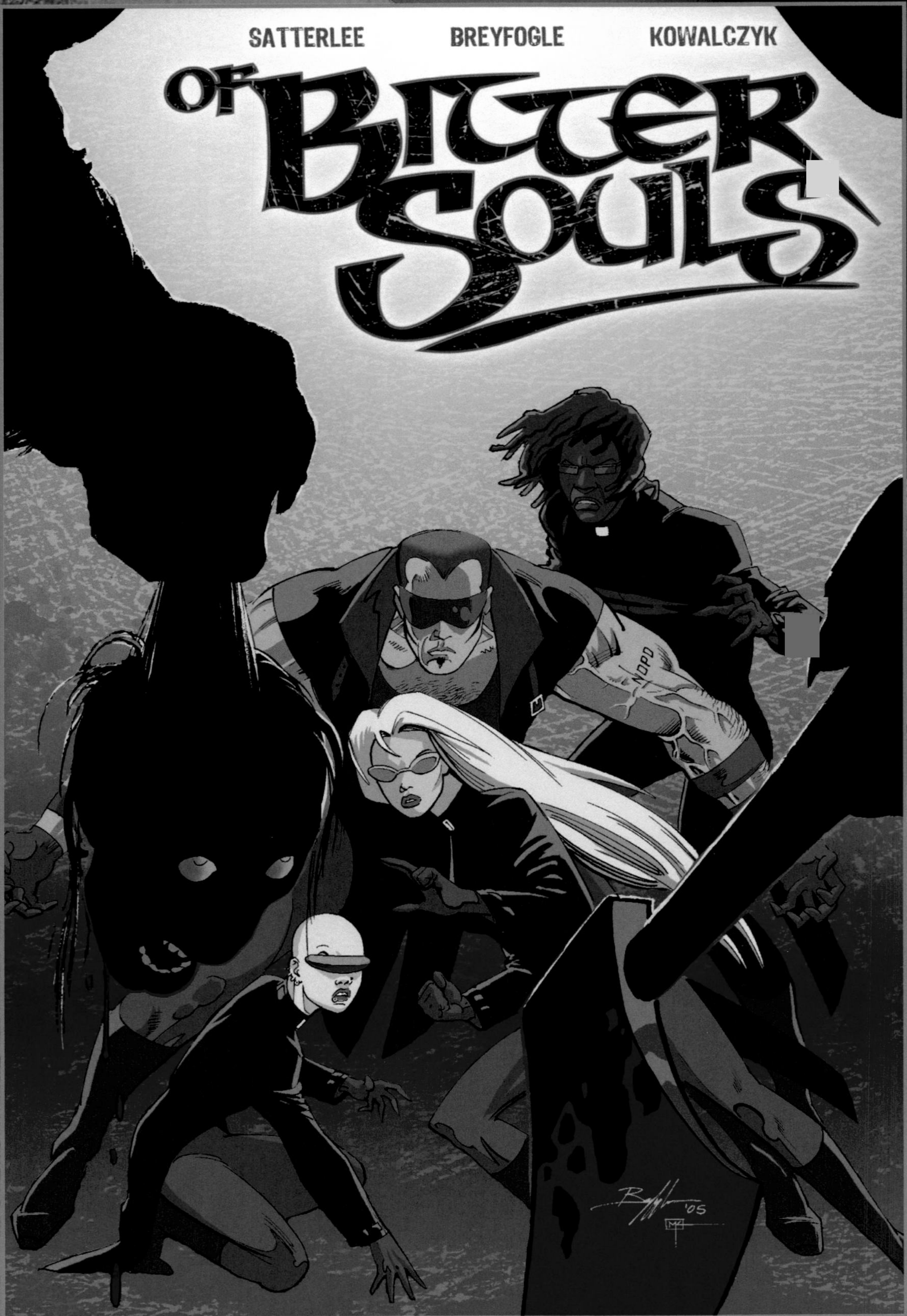
SATTERLEE
BREYFOGLE
KOWALCZYK
OF BITTER SOULS
NOPD

Chuck actually submitted the idea for this cover.
One idea…one sketch…one cover… This represents Chuck's first suggestion for covers on OBS.

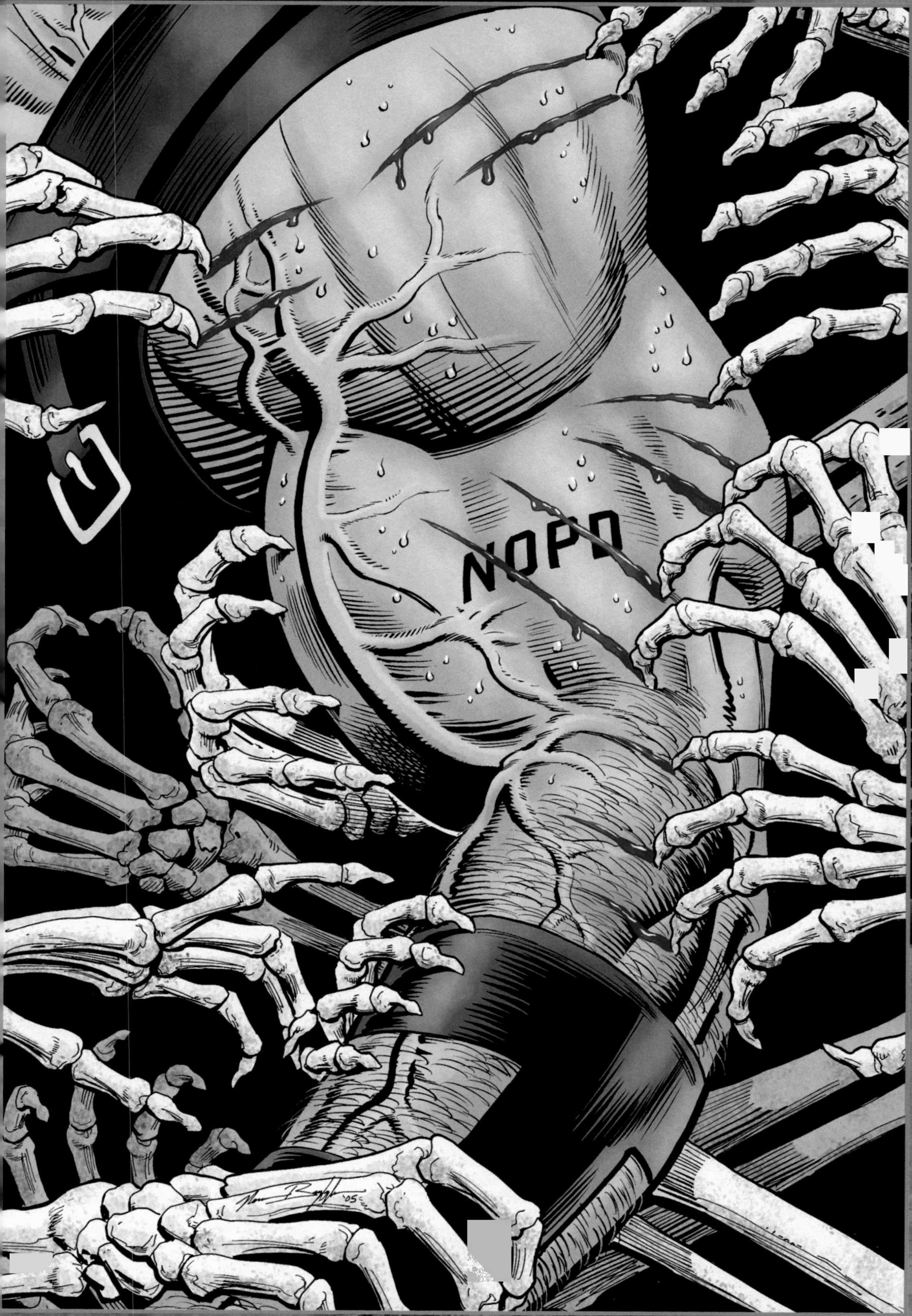
NOPD

Like issue four and six, this is published for the first time in this book.
Unlike the other covers, this one took quite a few sketches.

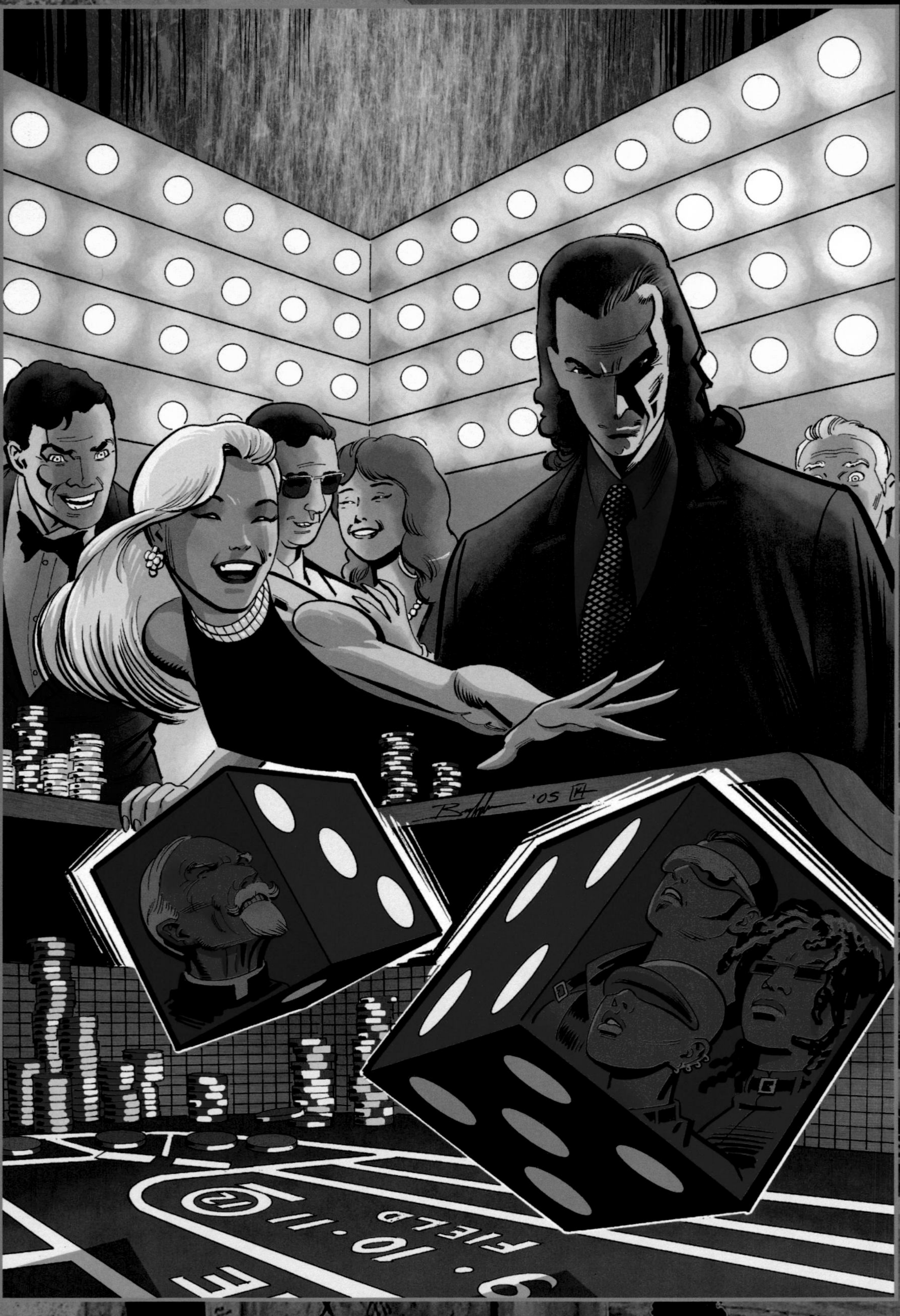
FIELD

Secord's true nature was still a secret by issue six, Chuck and Norm struggled with the question w much of the Devil to show in this cover. Since the issue never came out, it was a moot point.

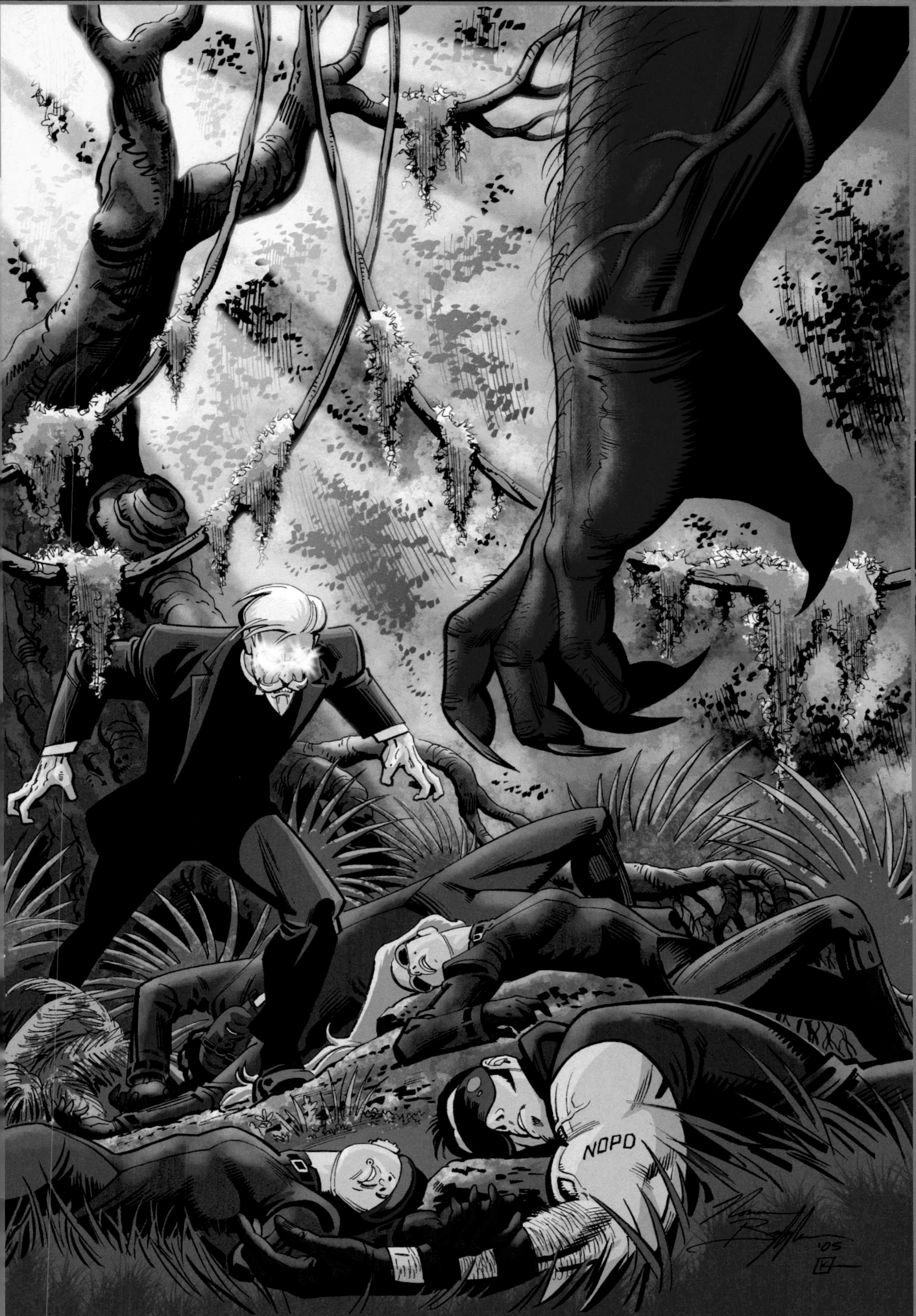
NOPD

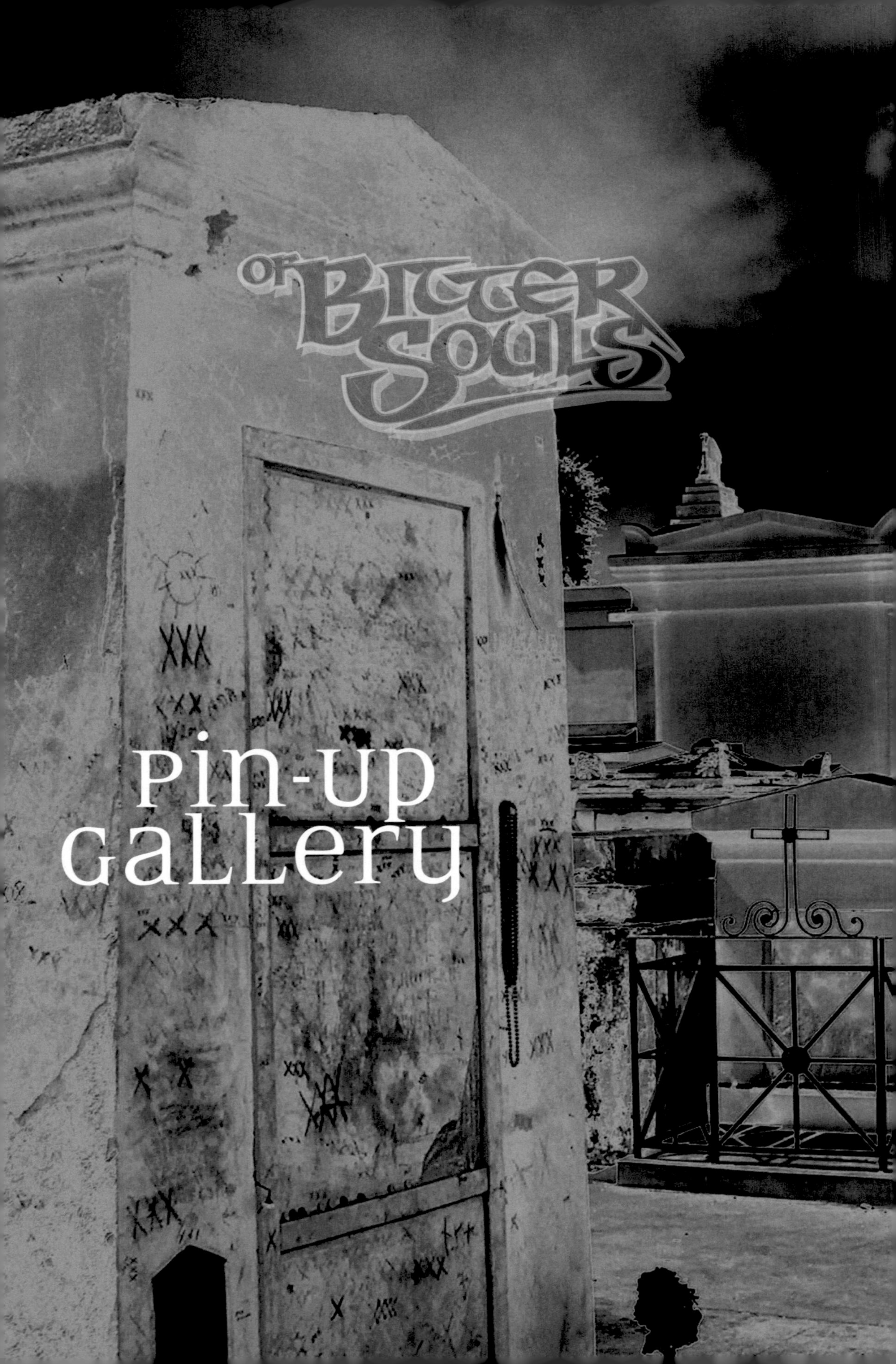
Of Bitter Souls
Pin-up Gallery

Norm Breyfogle *with colors by Mike Kowalczyk*

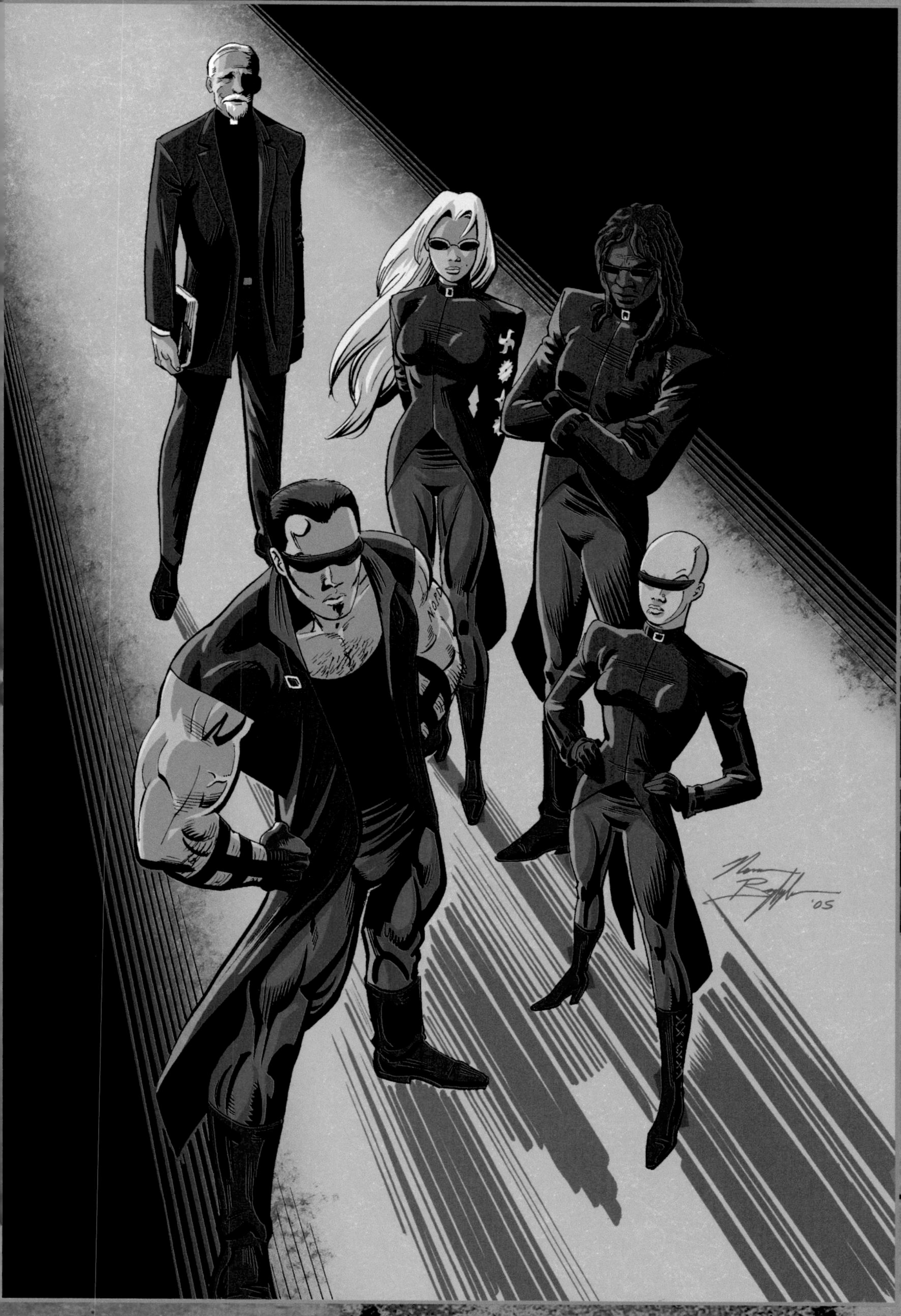

Norm Breyfogle *with colors by Mike Kowalczyk*

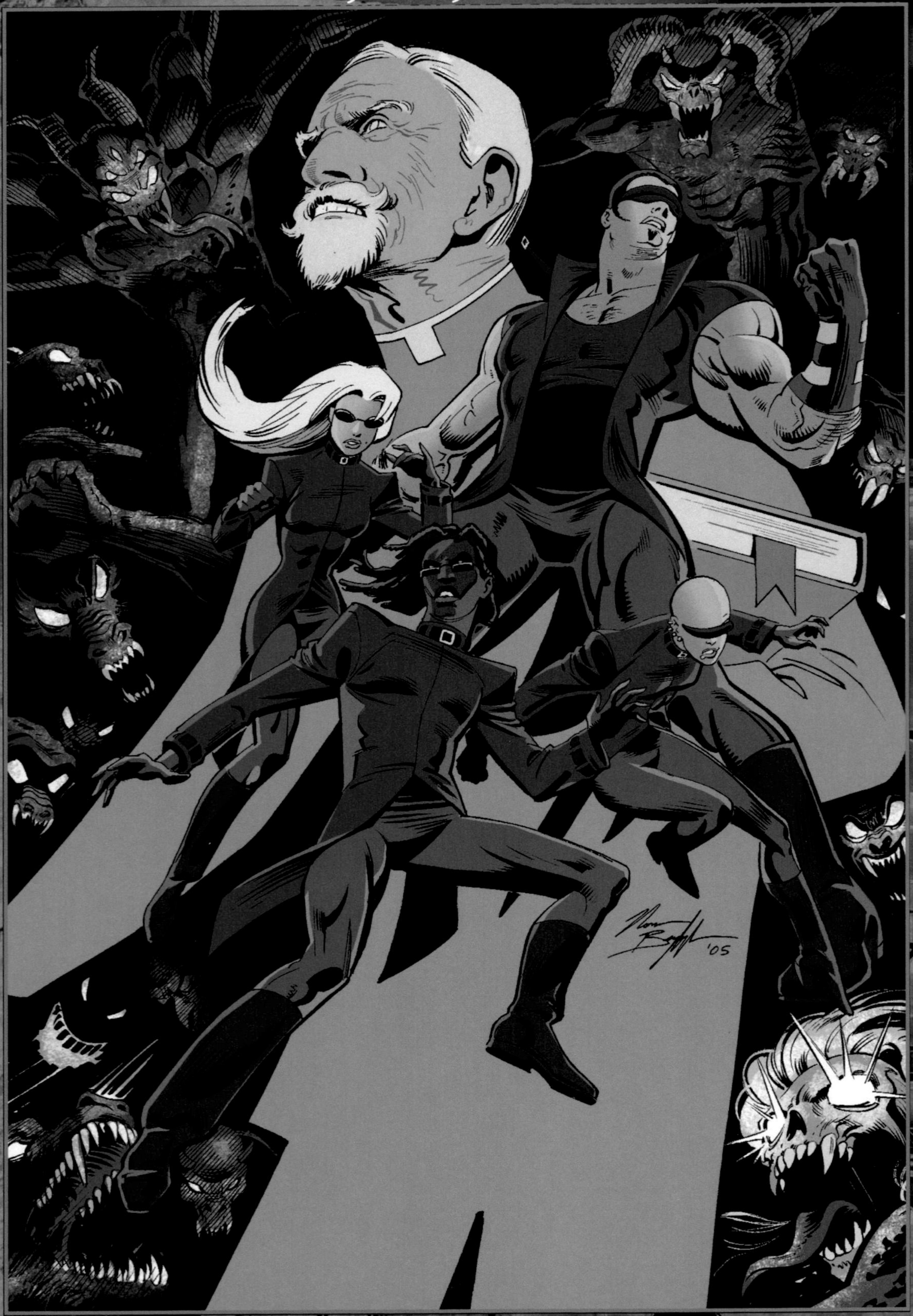
'05

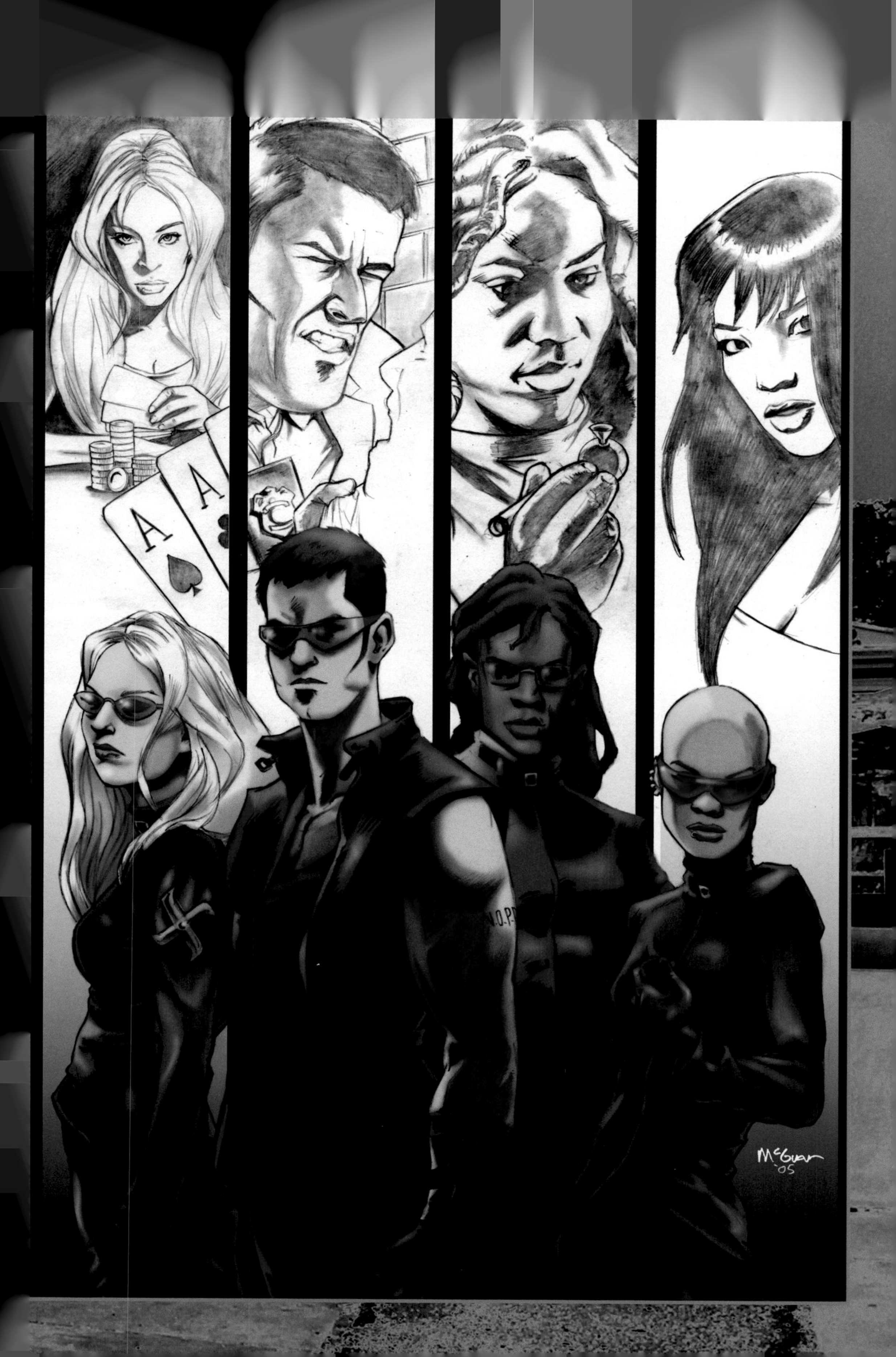

DICK GIORDANO *with colors by Mike Kowalczyk*

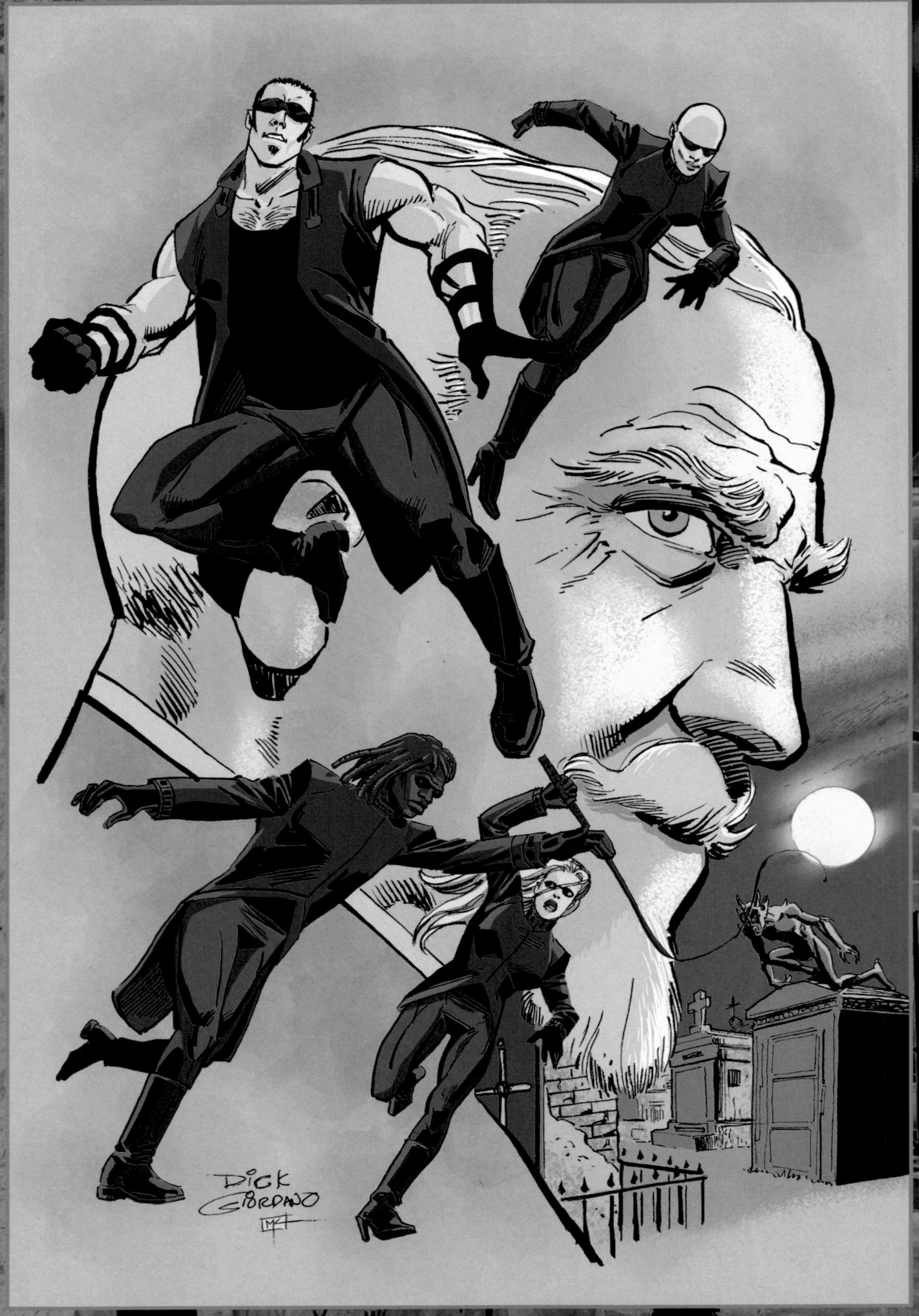
DICK GIORDANO

Kevin Breyfogle *with colors by Ian Sharman*

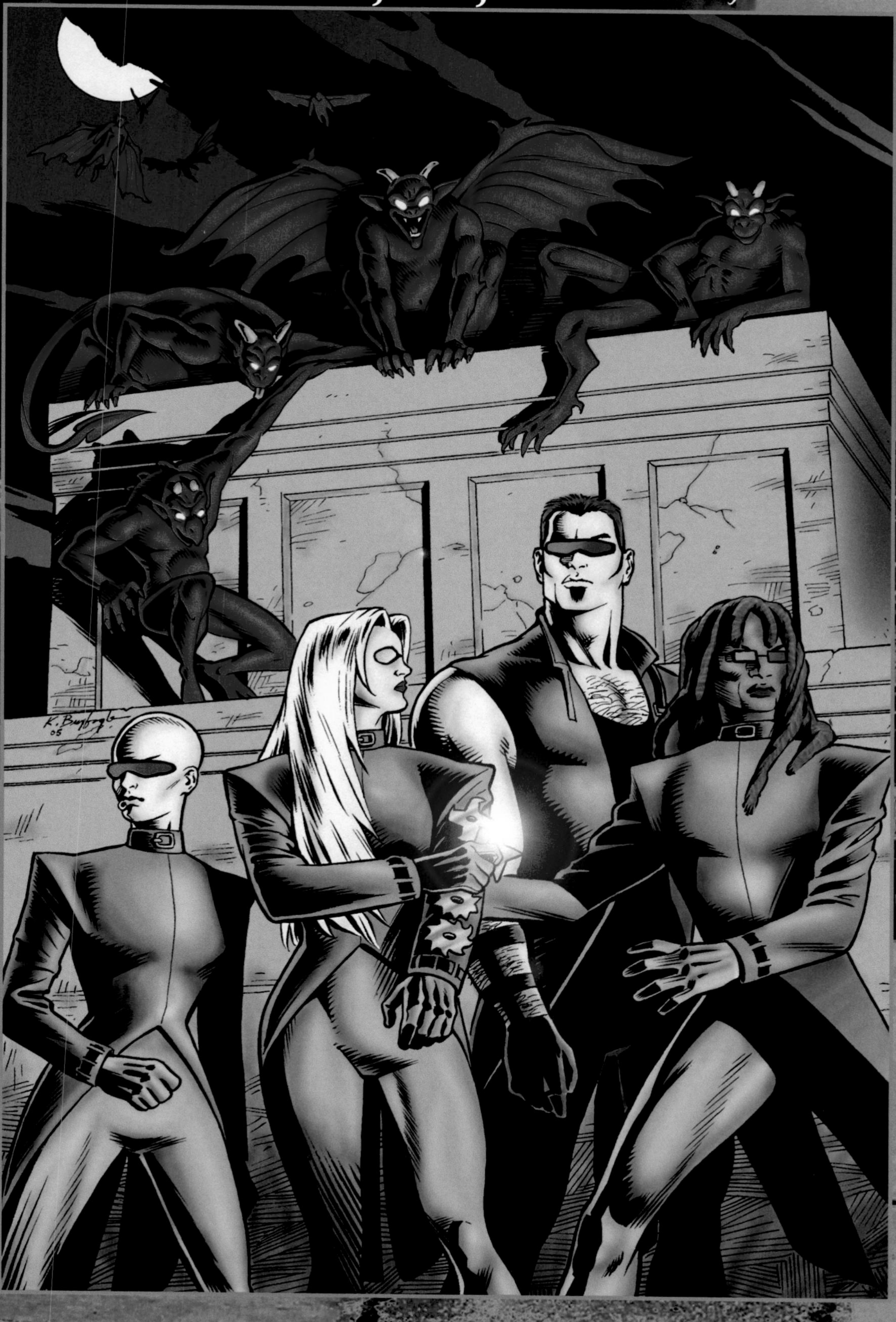

G. Gerald Garcia *with colors by Ian Sharman*

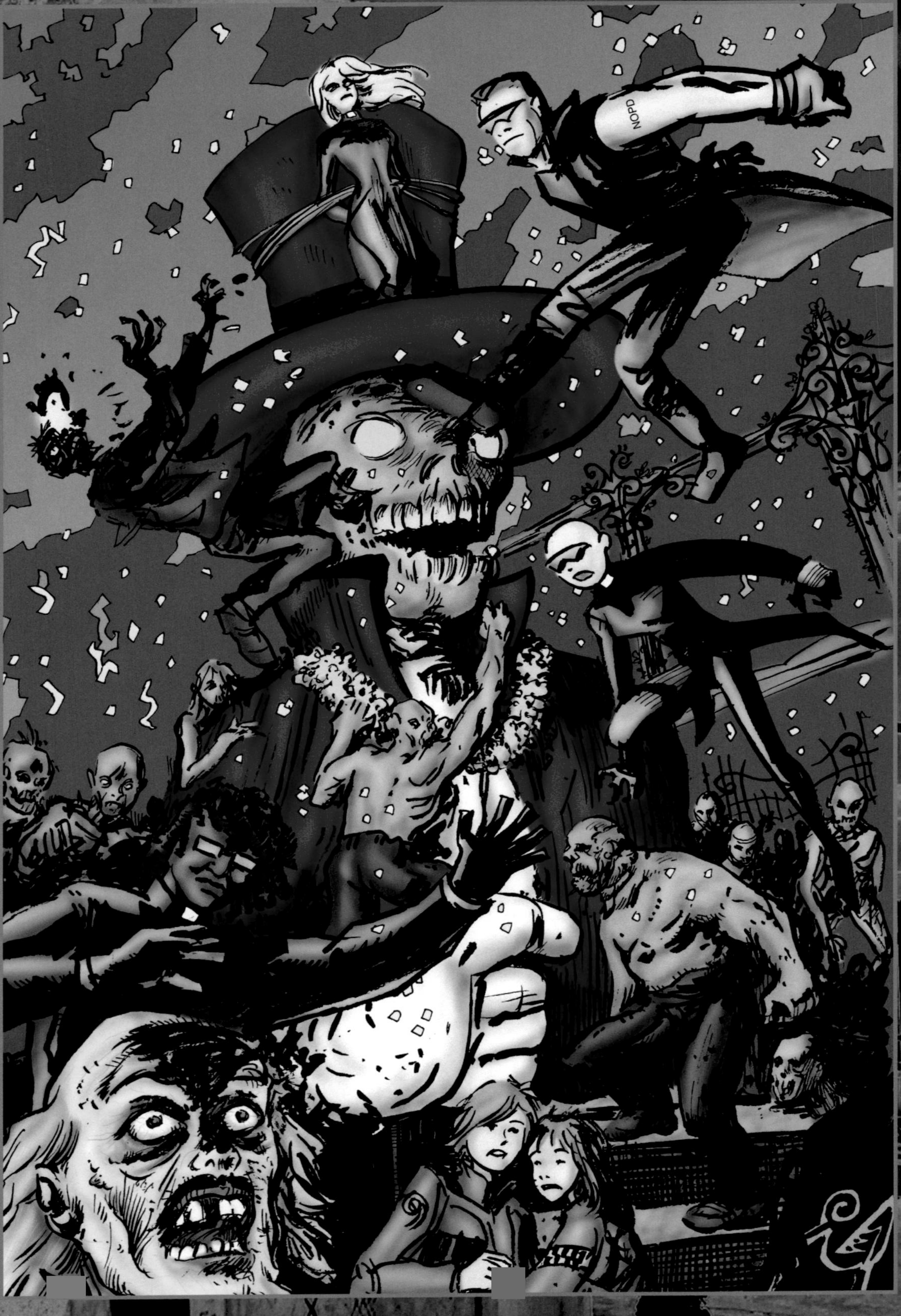

NOPD

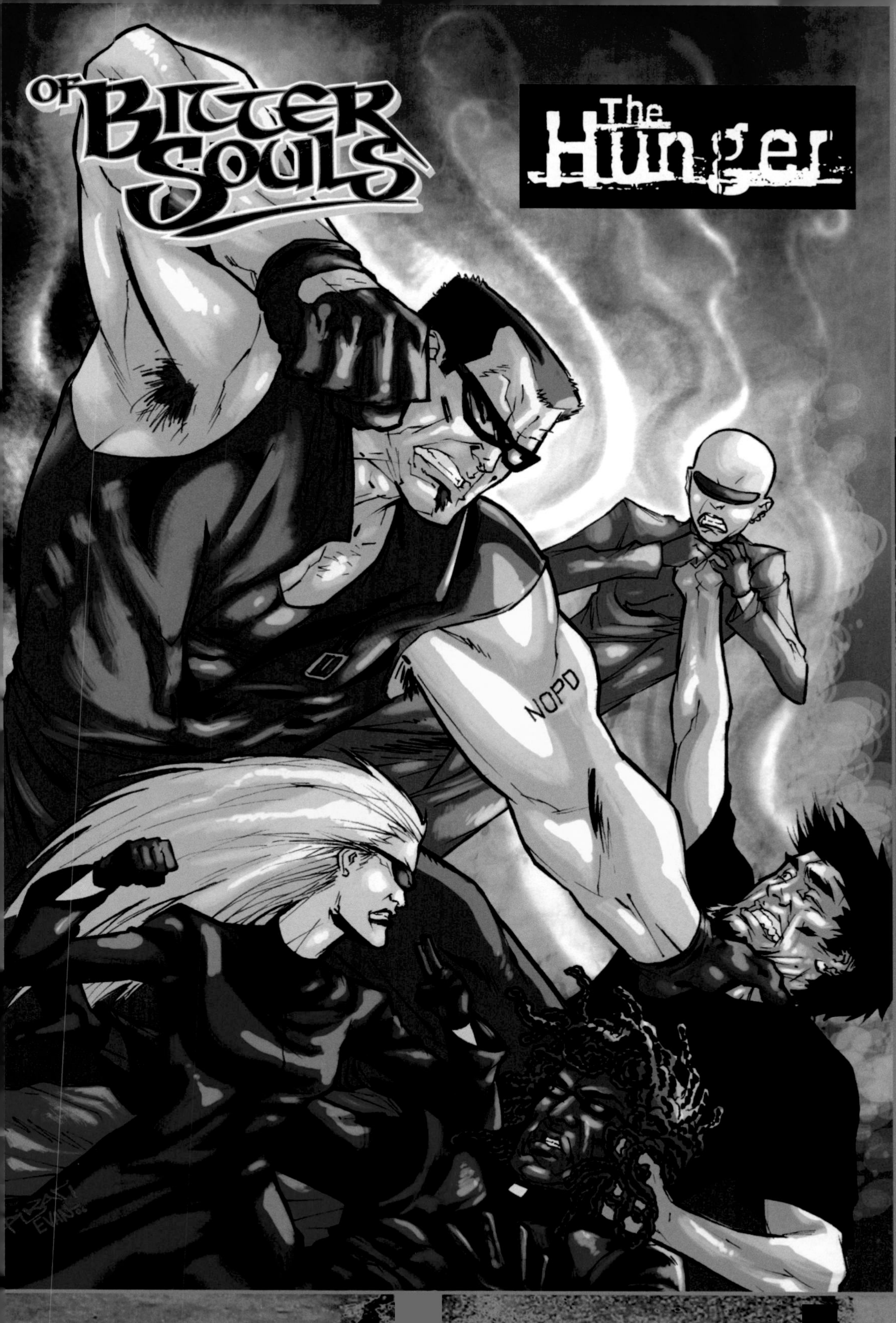
Of Bitter Souls
The Hunger
NOPD

scott Beaderstadt *with colors by Ian Sharman*

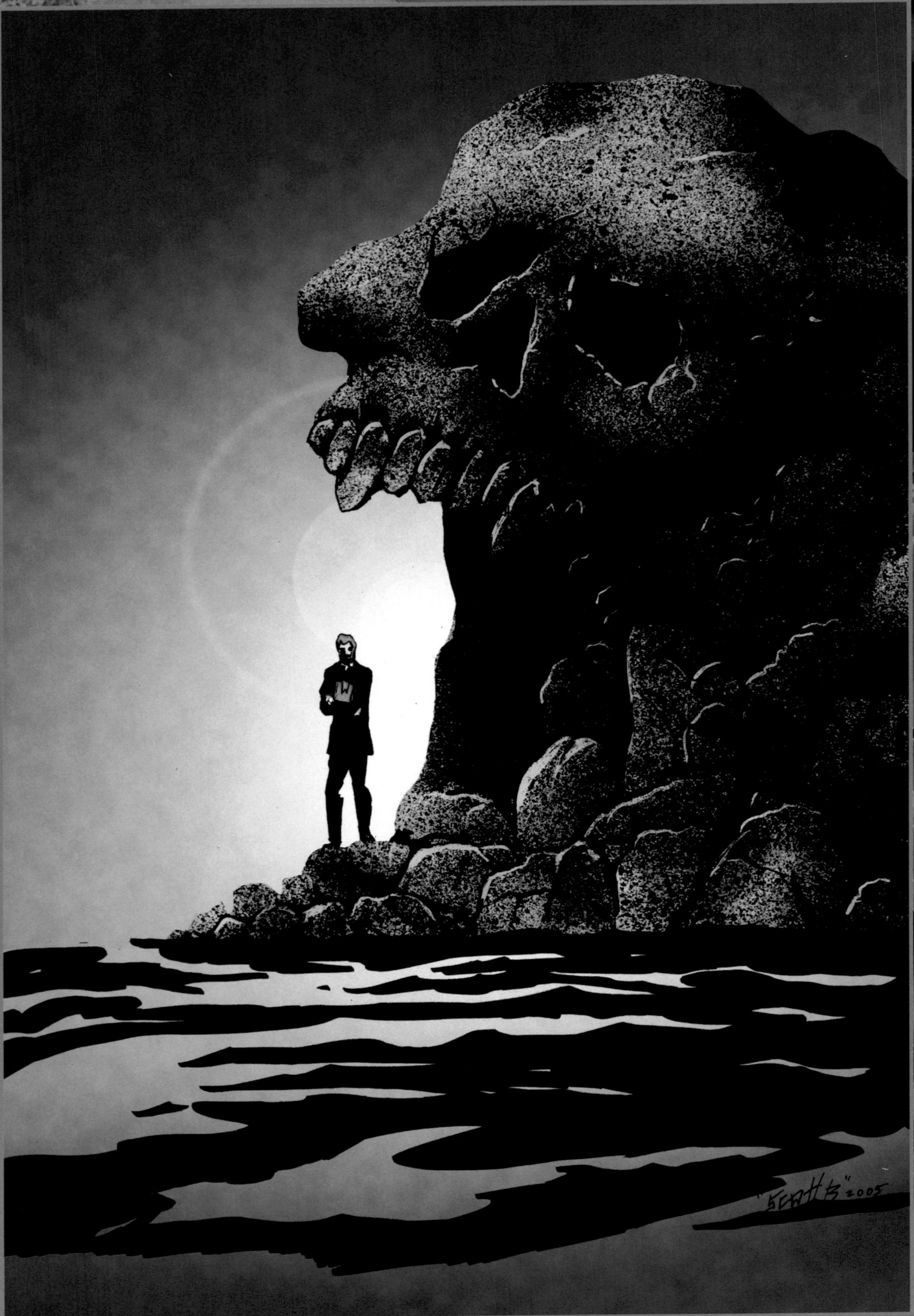

Mike Oeming *with colors by Mike Kowalczyk*

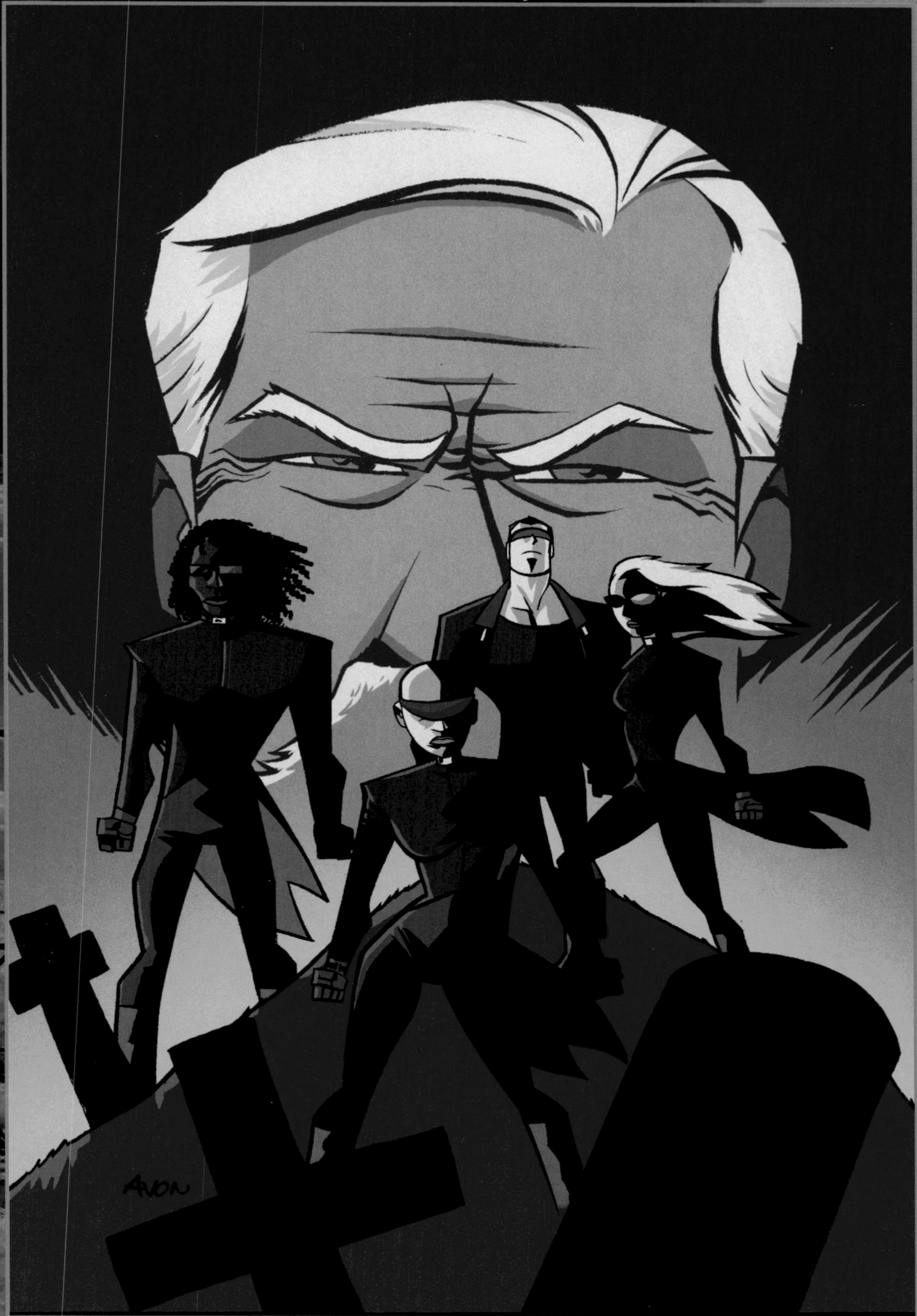
AVON

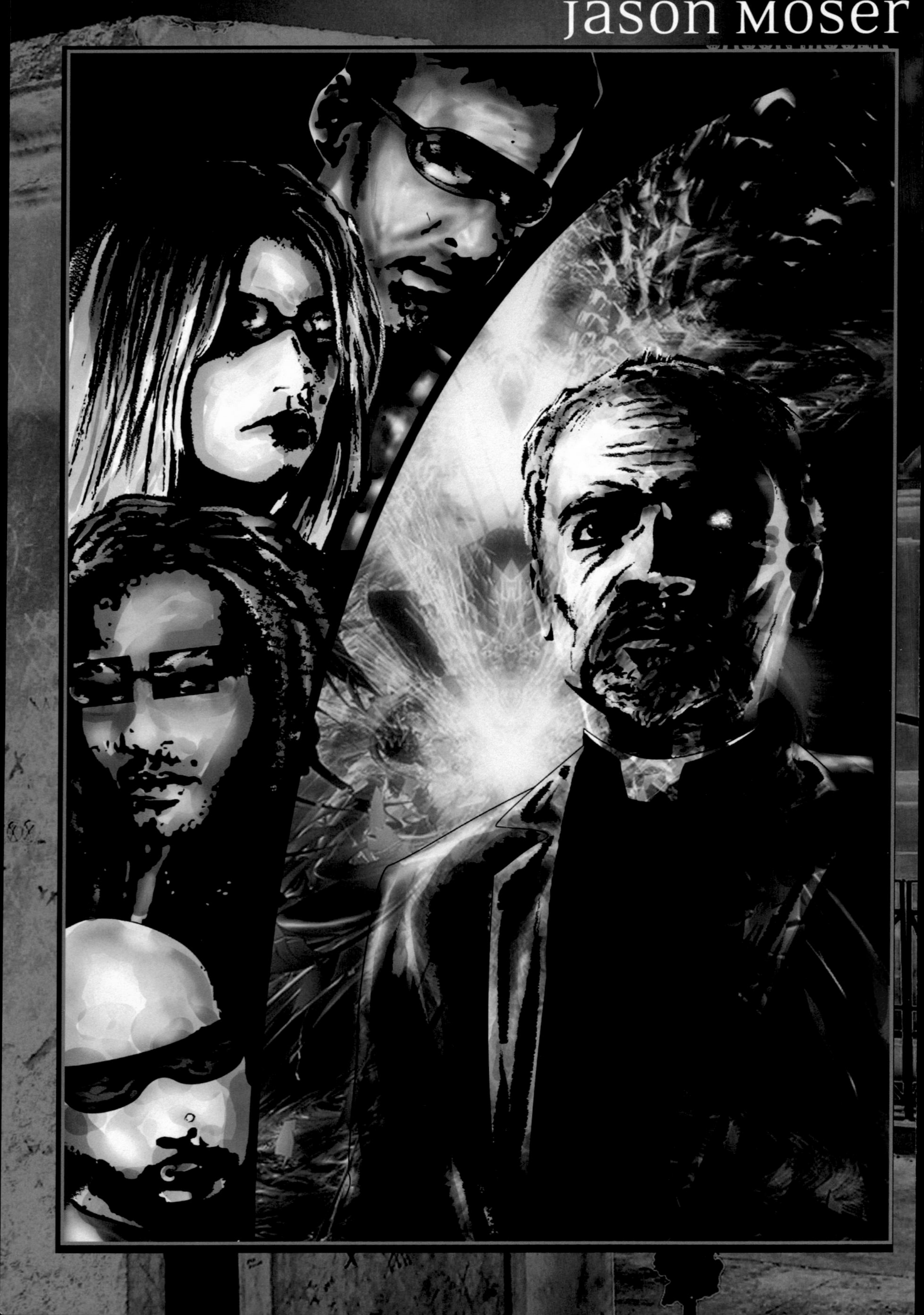
Jason Moser

Dan Bradford *with colors by Mike Kowalczyk*

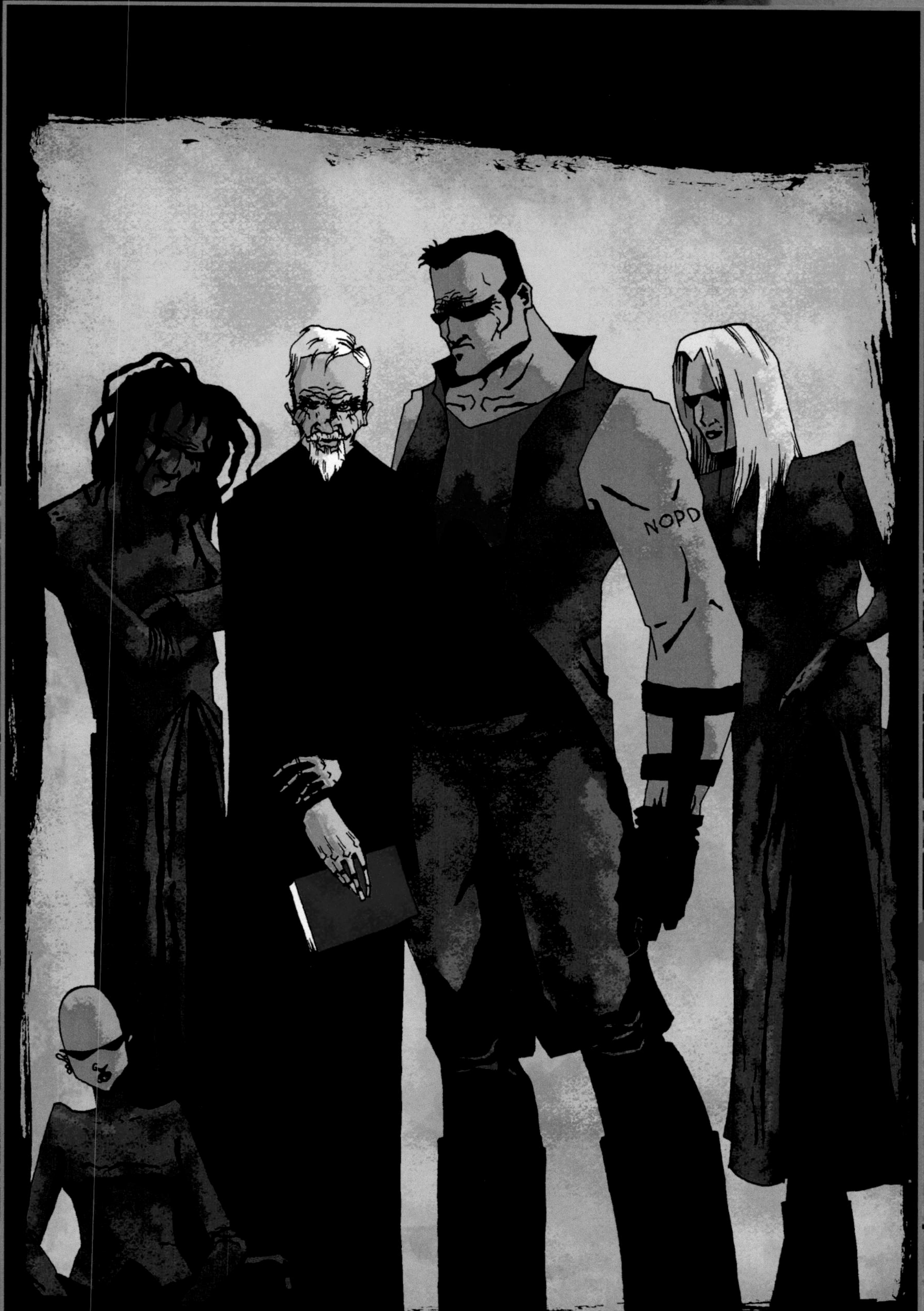
NOPD

Ryan Stegman *with colors by Kieran Oates*

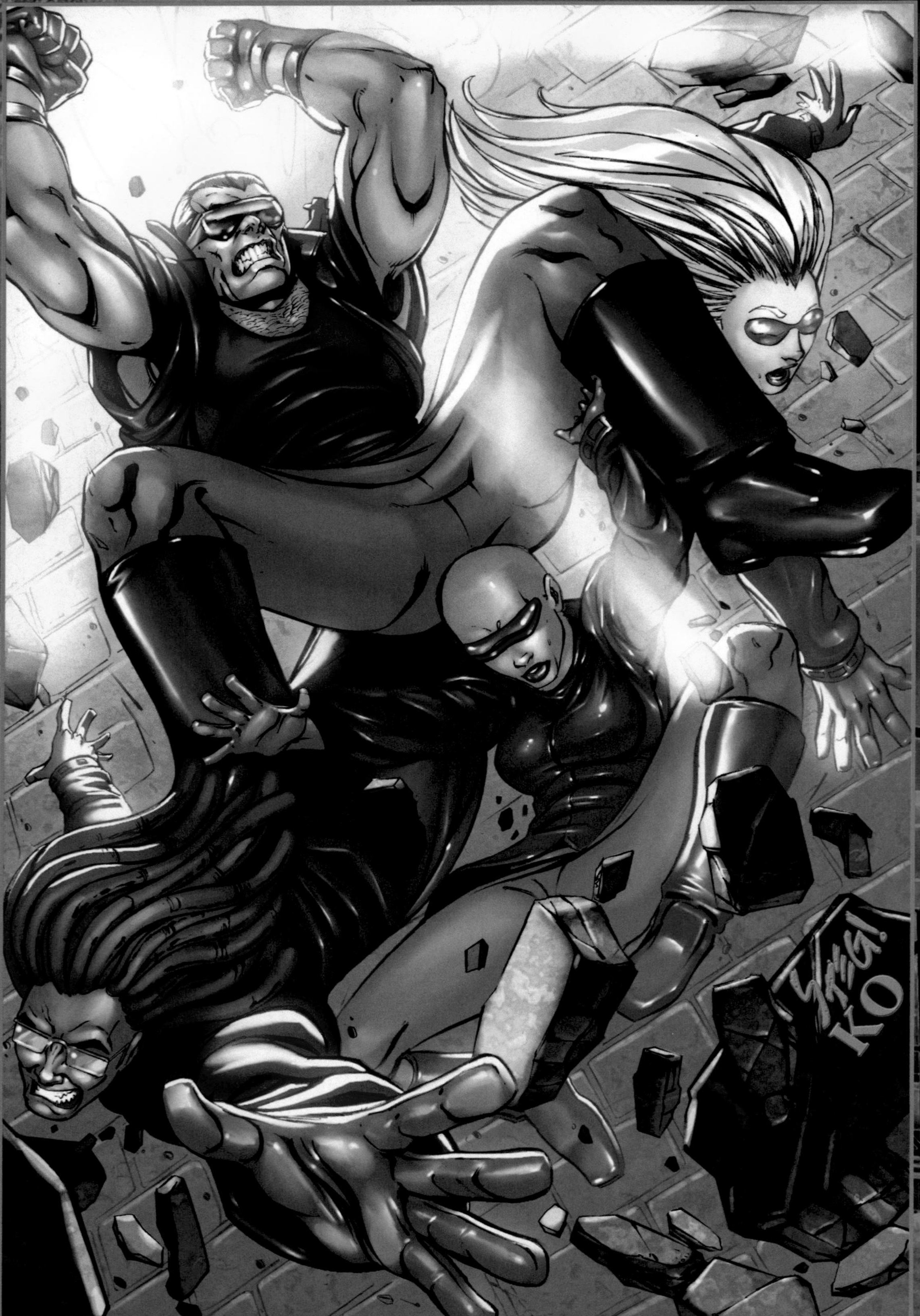
KO

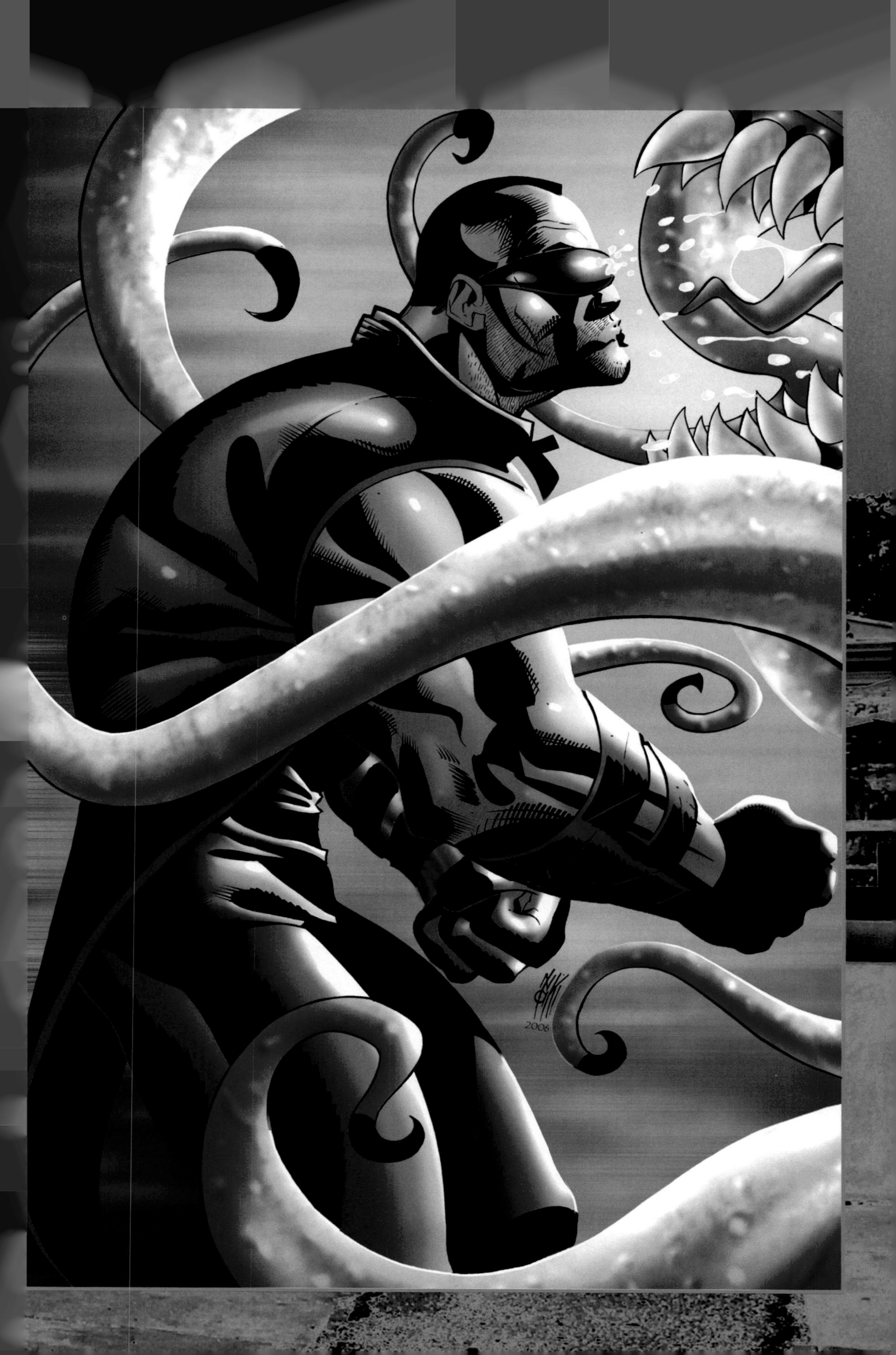

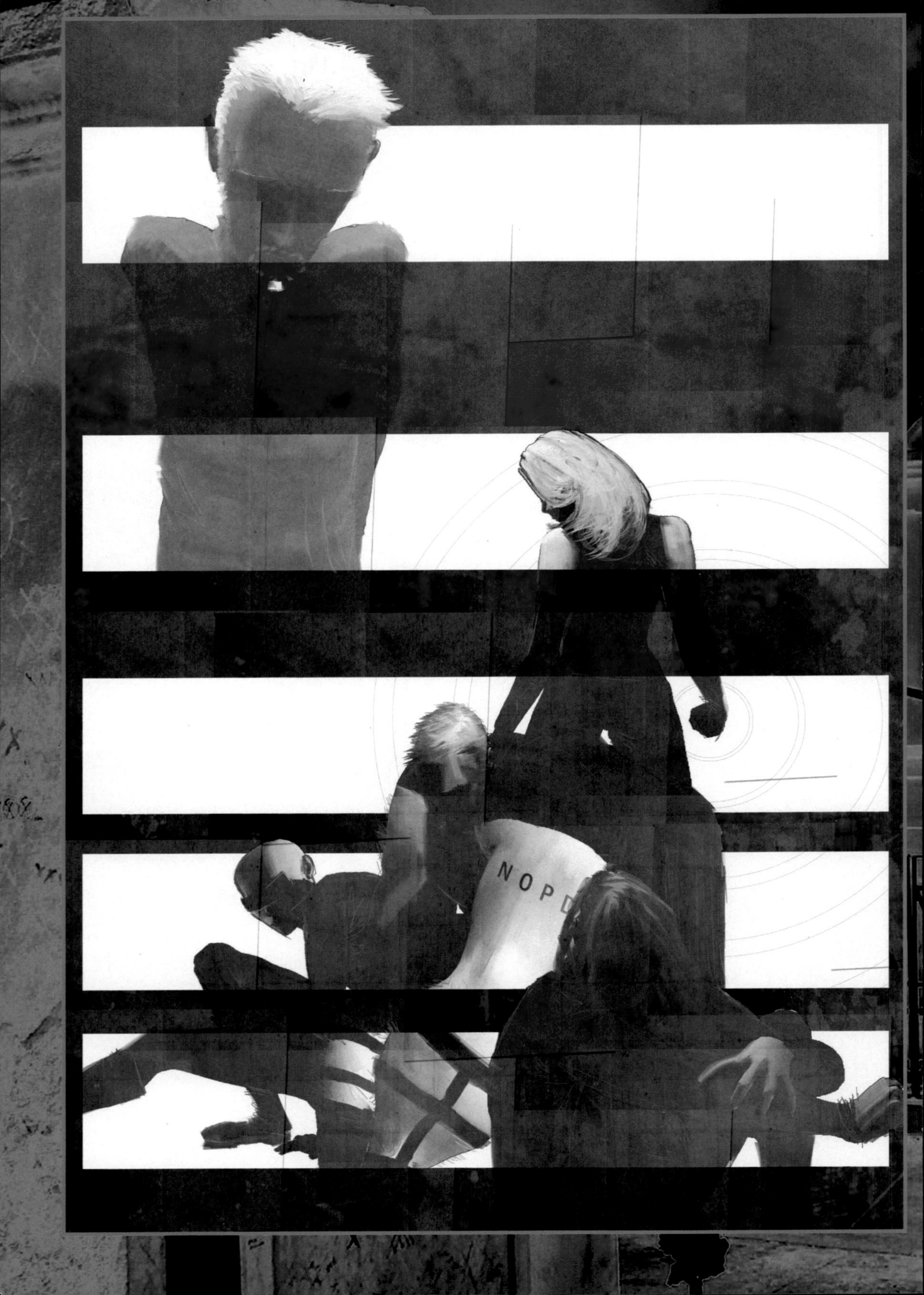
NOPD

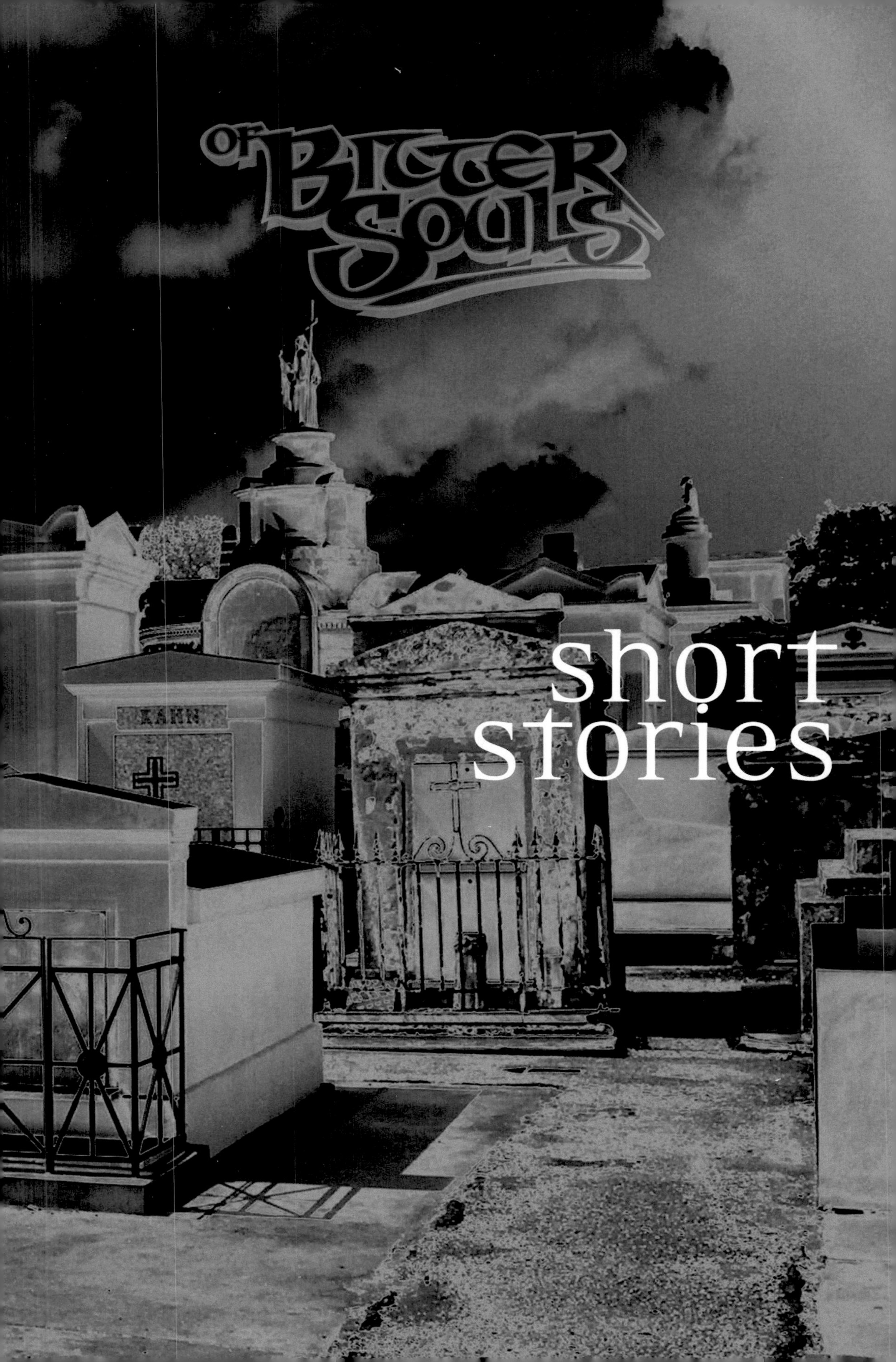
Of Bitter Souls
short stories
KAHN

THE IRON GATE

a story by BRIAN AUGUSTYN

Spring had come again to Germany that April in 1945, after a hard winter of the hell of war.

In the remote town of Alte Kirchenstadt, rumors were swirling like fluffs of pollen from the wild flowers gaily dotting the nearby hills. The Nazi regime was near collapse and the nation was in ruins.

The rumors reached even through the medieval stone walls of Eisernes Tor Krankenhaus on the ridge overlooking the town center. The Tor, a long abandoned hospital for the insane, had been seized by the Nazi soldiers and converted to a prison for dissidents and other local nuisances.

The man was tall and whip thin, with a head of backswept black hair and a matching, pointed beard. He wore the black shirt and white collar of a clergyman under a rather stylish gray suit coat. If being contained in the tiny cell for three weeks weighed upon him, it was not evident from his demeanor. Untroubled he stood at the barred window and sniffed contentedly as a soft breeze wafted the smell of new life and revived hope his way. A small brown bird sat on the sill and trilled happily, seemingly for the tall man's benefit alone. In turn, the man listened with rapt attention.

"Albert Secord!" a firm voice spoke the man's name like a curse. Before turning, the man smiled a secret smile.

"Yes, herr Thorwald? How may I serve our illustrious keeper?" Secord's German was excellent and his accent near perfect, but Thorwald knew the man was an American.

"You can do nothing for me, and I will do nothing for you, Secord. Orders have come through." Thorwald sneered his distaste for the prisoner.

Secord nodded slightly and continued to smile. Though imprisoned within this dank stone, there was little he did not hear. He had expected this day.

"I hear that the Nazi cause is all but lost, herr Thorwald. That the Russians will crush Berlin any day now. That even your noble Fhrer, herr Hitler, is in hiding." Secord did not gloat.

"I hear many things as well, how much is true is hard to judge. I doubt that the Fatherland is in so dire a condition, however."

Secord walked slowly toward to face the small, dapper man in the gray Nazi officer's uniform. He smiled, for he held no hatred for this functionary. Thorwald was an educated man, but was devoted to the Nazi cause and would follow his orders with ruthless precision.

"The war, your cause, herr Thorwald, are lost. Why not throw wide the gates and let these prisoners rejoin their loved ones?"

"I think not. Even if things are as you say, we still have standing orders on the treatment of detainees." Said Thorwald coldly.

"Yes, I imagine so. You will grant us only the freedom of the grave. You will kill clergymen, teachers and poets because of orders?"

"They are dissidents! You are a spy." Thorwald's temper rose suddenly, bringing color to his pale cheeks. He calmed himself immediately.

"Tomorrow at dawn all twenty-three of you will be executed." Thorwald was grim and determined.

"Yes," said Secord, "you have orders." He watched the dapper commandant walk stiffly away.

"Executed?" came the thin, high-pitched voice of young Eberhardt Koss in the adjoining cell. "They are going to kill us, Pastor?"

"They certainly intend to. But I believe they will fail."

"You are a man of God. I am only a writer-I could perhaps create a character that had such faith, but for myself" the young man's words trailed off.

Secord smiled fondly. Eberhardt's "crime" had been attempting to mount a production of a play he had written. An allegory entitled "The Boot," it envisioned the oppressed people of Europe as ants and the Nazis as a giant crushing boot. The play was dreadful and obvious, but Secord enjoyed the young man's passion. Eberhardt did not deserve to die. Neither did any of the rest of them.

Secord paused briefly and smiled his secret smile again. Perhaps, by the Nazi's standards, one among them did deserve death. Secord's smile broadened and became a low chuckle. Thorwald was right about one thing; Secord was a spy for God.

Time passed in silence within the Tor. The prisoners were all, in their own ways, attempting to understand their fates. As the afternoon sun slid slowly toward evening, Secord heard another voice call his name. This voice was mature and deep and, all things considered, quite calm.

"I hope you are right, Albert, I pray we will be spared, but I am ready too if things do not go well. I am ready to die as Christ died for me."

"I know you are, Helmut, and Jesus and I love you for your conviction. But we will survive, I promise you."

In his cell, the solidly built middle-aged man sat on the narrow bed and sighed. He too was dressed in clerical clothing and he held a small bible in his hands. For twenty-three years, Helmut Kaalstadt had pastored the old stone church that had given Alte Kirchenstadt its name. He had served without distinction and in silence for most of that time. There came a time, however, when he could no longer ignore what his country had become. Even Helmut's own Bishop had allowed himself to be co-opted by the heinous cause. Kaalstadt allied himself with a breakaway group of other concerned pastors and began to preach against the evils of Hitler and his dogs. Actually, Kaalstadt had preached a grand total of two and a half times before he was arrested and confined here. He had met Secord at a meeting of the dissident clergy a month before.

Kaalstadt closed his eyes and tried to envision the light of hope growing brighter in the distance, but could not. He had spoken the truth; he was prepared to die for his faith. Surviving to win more souls to Christ would also be preferable, but he was ready. He prayed all the harder that God's will be done.

Night filled the stone prison with cool darkness. No one slept, except Secord. Hours ticked away on a relentless journey to inevitable dawn. The black velvet of the sky slowly began to lighten as orange spread across the horizon. Morning was mere hours away, and already, the prisoners could hear the guards stirring, readying the courtyard below for the coming mass execution. Secord rose quietly, refreshed and ready for what he knew was to come.

"I will see you all outside these walls within hours my friends, on this side of the veil, I promise." Secord said with genuine brio.

"Amen." Came Helmut Kaalstadt's quiet answer.

The brightness of the dawn filled the cells with warm honey light. If hope could be grasped, it would be on a morning like this. The twenty-three men stood at their cell doors, silently awaiting whatever was to come.

At 5:33 a.m., they all heard a sudden sharp sound, like the tearing of a curtain not far away. Next came the sounds of raging wind and the rending of metal. None of the prisoners, save for Secord, could fathom what was happening.

Over the roar of rushing wind, they soon heard another sound; a high-pitched keening like animals in distress. It soon became evident that what they were hearing were human screams. There came then a crashing of stone and more ripping of iron and finally, the distant sound of a lone trumpet. Then silence fell heavily once again.

Within seconds, each of the cell doors popped open of its own accord. Not one of the prisoners questioned this as they stepped out to freedom. Secord faced his compatriots and spoke with quiet intensity.

"We are free, my friends. Nothing more will bar our way. But be prepared for what you will encounter on the way out. The power of God was not gentle with our jailers."

It was then the smell of smoke and charred meat reached them. Everyone reeled at the stench, knowing instinctively what it was that wafted on the breeze. Secord pointed grimly in the direction of the smoke.

"There is nothing for us but to go this way. Follow me."

Eberhardt Koss told himself he would look only at Pastor Secord's broad back and follow him out. But as they proceeded, he could not avoid catching involuntary glimpses of the carnage around them. Everywhere were greasy, charred lumps huddled against the wall. Several of these lumps still had bits of gray wool uniform, leather boots or belts. Eberhardt knew these were the guards he had so come to despise during his incarceration. The group moved on and Eberhardt began to pray again, now for the souls of his enemies.

Secord stopped at an open door and looked in. He smiled a tight, hard smile as he saw the occupant of the office was still alive for now.

"You are still with us, I see, herr Thorwald."

The commandant sat unevenly at his now shattered desk, leaning his weight on bloodied, arms. He looked down at the ruin of his midsection, a twisted tatter of uniform, flesh, blood and worse, and slowly raised his eyes to take in Secord's face. The once-neat man grimaced and croaked out his answer.

"Only for a moment, I think. It is my curse that I live this long already."

Secord looked down with no trace of sympathy. Such was the fate of all tyrants and those that serve them blindly. But, he strove to feel the mercy his God would have for the man.

Thorwald looked up again, his eyes already beginning to glaze over. He stammered out his final words.

"We have failed. Hell is our only destination." He slid wetly off his chair to the floor and died.

Pastor Albert Secord led his fellows through the broken iron gates of the prison to find the villagers already running up the hill to meet the liberated. There were tears of joy that washed away a great deal of the horror and pain of what had come before. Secord smiled as he saw life and love reasserting their dominance over the human spirit. God was in his heaven and all would soon be right again with the world.

For now, the pastor smiled, and he would be there when things went wrong again he knew. He had already given his life for master; it was his fate and duty to go on serving.

Eberhardt Koss looked around to thank Secord, but the tall man was already out of sight. Pastor Kaalstadt placed a gentle hand on the young man's arm and spoke quietly.

"He's gone, Eberhardt. Now it is for us to carry on."

"Yes." said Eberhardt as his eyes looked skyward to the bright warm sun overhead. On a morning such as this any good thing was possible. Even faith. ●

THE END

WHATEVER POSSESSED HER

A Tale Of Bitter Souls by Andrew Foley

The alley is a dark place, painted in strokes of black and grey. The rear doors of a tattoo parlor, a used bookstore, and a convenience store open out onto its East side, or used to, at least. Since the fire, no one wants to open those doors, to see the burnt-out husk of the building walling in the alley on the West. Condemned by authorities both mundane and sublime, it's easier to ignore that place, to pretend it never existed, to wish it out of history.

Most who knew this place have erased it from their memory. Most, but not all.

It is a dark place, this alley, but nothing in it is darker than the soul of the monster that makes it his home.

It was a life filled with blood and monsters, demons and death, a steady stream of horrors beyond mortal imagining. But with all that there was still hope, and for Magz, that made it a life worth living.

And then she awoke. The dream was over, and she was returned to the nightmare of life before Pastor Secord.

She whirled around, confused, taking in her surroundings. There were no windows, no way to know whether it was day or night. Metal fixtures in the walls suffused the incense-laden air with dim yellow light. A four-poster bed with pink sheets dominated the room. Folding Oriental dressing screens sat in one corner; behind them, Magz knew, were a variety of costumes designed to be shed as quickly as possible. The door was solid, and could only be opened from the outside. A dressing table sat near the door, numerous glass bottles spread across its surface, a large oval mirror ringed by lights above it.

Magz recognized the room. She could never forget this cell, this tawdry caricature of a Lady's bedchamber. It had been the backdrop to her personal hell for six years.

She did what came naturally, now: pictured the Pastor's church in her mind, saw its wooden pews, its stone floor, the stained glass saints looking down upon her. She willed herself there, but her surroundings did not blur and reconfigure themselves. That she could no longer teleport accompanied another awful realization. She was once again trapped, here, in the Bangkok Spa and Massage Parlor.

She took a deep breath, willed herself to relax. She wasn't the child she'd been three years before. She'd been trained for battle, stood toe to toe with evil incarnate. "You can handle this," she told herself. "You're Magz."

Then she saw the figure reflected in the mirror, and realized she was lying to herself.

The face looking out of the mirror wasn't hers.

The door opened. A gruff voice from the hallway outside said, "Ready or not, here I...come."

Magz had heard the joke many times before. It had never been funny.

Hea opened her eyes and tried to remember when she'd gone to sleep. Just a moment before she'd been in ... that room, waiting for the Spa's owner, Mr. Henry Lafleur. The other girls called the meeting an interview. She didn't share their sense of humor.

She awoke on a futon in small room. A single lightbulb dangled from the ceiling, flickering intermittently over walls unadorned by anything but a simple cross above the door.

She rubbed the sleep from her eyes and stood up slowly. She felt strange. The floor seemed further away than it ought to be.

With a start she realized her hair was gone. She ran her hands over her utterly bare head, terrified of what Lafleur might think of having a bald girl in his employ.

But Lafleur wasn't there. Nobody was there. She tried the door handle and was relieved when it opened for her.

The short hallway outside the door led to the front of a small church. A thin, white-haired man in a priest's collar stood at the podium. He turned to look at her as she exited the door. "Magz? Are you all right?"

He reached out; she reacted instinctively, stepping away from him. "What's wrong?" he asked. He stared at her, hard. She could feel his gaze boring through her, into her.

Without warning, his face twisted in anger. Bony fingers, strong and unforgiving as cold steel, wrapped around her throat. "Hellspawn!" he shouted. "What have you done with Magz?"

The Bangkok Spa and Massage Parlor's owner, Henry Lafleur, was a man of many and varied appetites. His massive frame showed he saw no virtue in denying himself. He towered over Magz's new body, his beady eyes groping her, examining his property in minute and intimate detail. She felt violated by his frankly appraising stare, but not as violated as she would if she let him have his way.

"You're a beautiful girl, Hea." He turned and walked toward the bed, unbuttoning his shirt.

"Hea?" asked Magz.

"We won't call you that when you work. We need something a little more … suggestive." The bedsprings squealed in pain as he sat on the four-poster's edge. "Maybe…Tawny. Anyway," he said, grunting with effort as he pulled his pants from around his ankles, "We'll think of something. Come over here."

The Priest held her hairless head still in his right hand as he pressed his left thumb into her forehead. She could feel the skin break under his thumbnail. He drew one line across and one down her brow.

"The Highest of Powers compels you!" yelled the Priest. "Tell me what you've done with Magz!"

"I don't know any Magz!" shrieked Hea. "I swear, I don't know what you're talking about, I was at the Spa and then I was here and I don't know anything, please don't hurt me, please!"

The Priest's eyes widened. "Oh," he whispered. "Oh, my child, I'm so sorry. I didn't know, I thought… " The words died on his tongue.

He guided her to a pew, gestured for her to sit. For a few moments, the only sound in the church was the sobs of a confused and frightened girl in a stranger's body.

He started to speak, stopped, then, after a moment, said, "It's all right, child. You're safe. Calm yourself." She looked up at the man who'd seemed to be the living incarnation of terror just moments before. His voice was calm and reassuring, his wrinkled face weathered but kind. How could this be the same person?

"What's happening to me?" she asked, then repeated the question, listening closely to the sound of her own trembling voice. She ran her hand again over her hairless head, traced fingers down her face to her trembling lips. Tears formed in her eyes. "What's happened to my face?"

The Priest sat beside her. "You're dreaming," he said. "You will awake, soon. But for now, you're safe. I promise you, no one will harm you here."

Betrayal was the one constant in Hea's life. Her parents put her on a boat and sent her to America to work off their debt, supposedly in a clothing factory, but what went on in the Spa had little to do with clothes. The other girls were callous in their disregard; their own suffering had left their feelings scabbed over with a hard shell. She had no reason to believe the Priest, or indeed any man.

But she did believe him.

It wasn't just that she had hair now. If the dream *had* been a dream, if Pastor Secord and the others had been a fantasy manufactured by her subconscious (and who could blame her for escaping however she could?), it still didn't explain the unfamiliar face in the mirror. There were similarities, to be sure; Magz's new body obviously shared her Korean heritage, but it wasn't a woman's body, it was a teenage girl's, little more than a child, something Magz had not been for many years.

She remembered the moment she'd taken her final step from childhood innocence, remembered the pain and the humiliation, the realization that what was happening, *what he was doing to her*, was all she had left to look forward to. It had happened in this very room, at the hands of the fat man in torn underwear and dress socks who sat on the edge of the bed, beckoning to her.

"What's the last thing you remember?" asked the priest.

Hea hesitated. Remembering life at the Bangkok was bad enough; she had no desire to talk about it.

"Whatever happened to you wasn't your fault. You were taken, weren't you? Taken from your family and shipped to America, to pay a debt, yes?

"I don't know you," he added quickly. "But I know someone like you. The person whose body you're in."

Hea looked down at the tall, leather-clad body that was hers, for now. She flexed its muscles, felt the strength within them, unfamiliar but exhilarating.

She could get used to this body. She could get used to this life. She could get used to any life

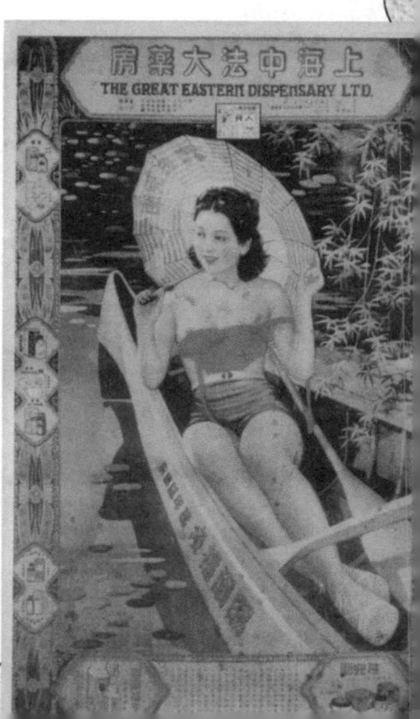
上海中法大藥房
THE GREAT EASTERN DISPENSARY LTD.

that didn't involve Henry Lafleur and the Bangkok Spa and Massage Parlor.

Lafleur grunted and wheezed as he let his bulk spread out face-down on the bed. Patches of black hair resembling mould grew on his shoulders. Magz stared at his back, revolted.

He twisted his neck to look back at her. "What're you waiting for?" he demanded. "Get over here!"

Magz's mind reached out, seeking Lafleur's consciousness. Nothing happened. If she ever had the power she imagined, it was lost to her now.

She was trapped. In this body, in this room. With him.

Lafleur rolled over onto his side, glaring at her through beady, piggish eyes. "Don't make me come over there," he said, his gravel voice laced with threat.

Horrified, Magz stepped back, bumping into the dressing table, upsetting glass-encased perfumes, jellies and oils.

Lafleur sighed. "Always the same…" He rolled off the bed, and reached for Magz.

This child's body wasn't hers, but the consciousness inhabiting it was. Three years had passed, years of training and battle against creatures more powerful than Lafleur, but no less vile. Her new hands, smaller, more delicate than the ones she was accustomed to, gripped the back of the chair. As his sausage fingers neared her, she swung the chair towards his head.

He caught a chair leg in one hand and jerked it from her grasp. Surprised, she stumbled forward. He seized a fistful of hair, yanked her head back.

"That's gonna cost you," he said.

Hea made it halfway down the Church's main aisle before becoming aware of her legs. They were long, much longer than she was used to. In letting the muscles remember how to move, she had the beginnings of a successful escape. The moment conscious observation overrode instinct, however, the moment she began thinking about the mechanics of running, the body rebelled. One leg hooked itself around the other; she fell to the Church floor in a heap.

The priest appeared above her. "There are some things you can't escape, no matter how fast you run," he said.

Magz flew threw the air. She landed hard on the floor and slid into the wall beside the dressing table. The mirror shook loose of its fittings and fell to the floor. Glittering glass fragments bounced through the air.

Lafleur moved towards Magz, faster than anything so large should be able to move. She grabbed a piece of the mirror, pushed it toward the fat man's throat. Lafleur grabbed the body's bony wrist in a meaty hand, twisted it down, forcing Magz to drop the glass to the floor.

He tossed her facedown on the bed. She scrambled to get away, but he was upon her in an instant, pinning her arms. The stench of cheap cologne, stale sweat and cigarette smoke filled her nostrils. Memories she'd tried desperately to forget flooded back. She'd been in this position before, trapped beneath this whale of a man. She knew what came next. He twisted her arms together, held them in one meaty fist. His other hand reached between her legs.

"I'm sorry," said the Priest. "I truly am. But the woman whose body you've possessed has a destiny. I've been charged with ensuring she fulfills it.

"She isn't--wasn't much different than you. But she's earned the power you feel coursing through you now. And you haven't.

"You can't stay in there. I think you know that."

She was ready to fight for a life away from the Bangkok Spa and Massage Parlor, away from the greasy paws of Lafleur and his cronies, ready to fight to the death, if necessary.

But she wouldn't fight the priest. Looking in the old man's eyes, she knew it was a fight she would never win.

"I don't know how I got here," she said. "I don't know how to get back. Can you help me?"

The priest smiled. "All you had to do was ask."

Magz cursed the prison of flesh and bone in which she found herself, cursed the girl Hea's body as much as the one laying on top of her. She squirmed beneath Lafleur, but he was too heavy, too much for this wretched body to move.

Magz was disgusted to realize her struggles were arousing him. With a triumphant grunt, Lafleur tore the panties from her legs. She didn't hesitate; her knee shot up, sinking deep in the fleshy folds of his groin.

Lafleur's body jerked forward, bending over as far as the bed would allow. The satisfaction of landing a blow evaporated as his full weight fell upon her.

She twisted her head, the only part of her not covered by hairy, sweating flesh, to the side, and clamped her teeth together over his ear. A salty warmth shot into her mouth. Lafleur screamed in pain.

"Magz's mind has considerable power," said the Priest. "It must have wandered while she slept, found you in a place like the one I found her."

"The Bangkok Spa and Massage Parlor," said Hea.

He nodded. "We need to go back." She inhaled, sharply. "It'll be all right. I won't let anyone hurt you. But I need you to concentrate, to picture the room you were in before you found yourself here…"

Lafleur rolled off the bed, clutching his groin in one hand, her arm held tight in the other. Crimson blood streamed from his masticated ear, spilling down his shoulder onto his chest.

Magz slammed into the dressing table and fell to the floor on the shattered mirror's remains. Glass crunched underfoot as he lunged forward, grabbed her by the hair (that damned hair!) and hauled her up to face him. "You're gonna die, you little slut! But first you're gonna suffer!" Pure malevolence burned bright in his piggy eyes. A strand of spittle hung from his puffy lips, swinging in the air above his chest.

Magz laughed. She couldn't help herself. She'd been so afraid of Lafleur, once, but those days were gone. Nothing he was capable of could compare to the horrors she'd witnessed standing beside Pastor Secord, horrors she'd fought, and vanquished. Lafleur was so small now, so very, very small.

Her laughter fanned the flames of the fat man's rage. He slapped her across the face, sending her spinning across the glass-strewn floor. Red streaks appeared on her arms and legs. She looked up at Lafleur, still laughing, but for a different reason, now.

Pastor Secord stood behind the fat man. Beside him was the body she no longer inhabited, her body, a cross carved in its forehead. The face below the bloody cross looked down at her, eyes widening in recognition…

…the world twisted, becoming a distorted blur that resolved itself into a different view of the same scene. Magz took it in in an instant: Lafleur, whirling around to face her and Pastor Secord, the bloody child lying in shattered glass, the four walls that had imprisoned her for six long years.

"Who the hell are you?" yelled Lafleur.

"I'll show you," said Magz. Without moving, she reached out. His body convulsed as she forced his mind open and pushed her life into it.

The tear-filled farewell to her Aunt; the weeks locked in the dank, claustrophobic confines of the boat's hold, surrounded by fifty-two others, forty-six of whom survived the journey to America; the countless degradations she suffered at the Bangkok Spa, many at Lafleur's own hands; all this flooded into the fat man's mind. She didn't stop there. Magz's memories of the past three years joined his own: Secord's rescuing her, the offer of salvation, training beside Jobe, Samson and Salome to face a darkness Lafleur had never imagined.

The sum of her life, each memory, every sensation, awful and holy, was seared into his consciousness. For the first time, Henry Lafleur understood, truly understood what he was. He would never forget it.

He fell at Magz's feet, begging forgiveness. She paid him no mind. He was beneath her.

Secord cradled Hea's body in his arms. "It's over," he said. "You're safe now." Through the pain, Hea found the strength to believe him.

Secord looked down at the snivelling creature wrapping its arms around Magz's ankles. "What did you do to him?"

"The last time I was here, you told me I abused my powers. I won't do it again." She put the toe of her boot below Lafleur's chin and levered his head up to look at her. "You know what you did. Live with it."

The words were a curse.

The Henry Lafleur who left that room was not the same one who entered it. The new Lafleur moved through the Bangkok Spa and Massage Parlor, ordering everyone within to leave.

Tears streamed down his face as he gave the girls what money was kept on the premises. He begged them to use it to start new lives. Many did, but not all. It was their choice.

As the fire spread through the building, he walked out into the alley behind it. That's where Henry Lafleur has been ever since, living with himself and the absolute, inescapable knowledge of what he is.

In his heart of hearts, he knows he's a monster that deserves nothing more than a swift and merciless death. But thanks to Magz, he also knows there are monsters far worse than him, awaiting him on the other side of existence.

He's in no rush to meet them.

LEARN ONE THING EVERY DAY

By Nickolas Allen (The Evolvist)

Have mercy on a shadow that dwells in the darkness, without a light to frame its existence. Ink on ebony, the shadow bumps into its self with every footfall, motivation, and notion that there is vagrant relevance to synchronicity, alone.

Parker. George Aaron Parker—shuffled like yesterday's concept into a jacked up warehouse where shadows call home. Even the walls of this establishment pay George little mind, though the ears that serve them are far more attuned to destiny's memory than the vagabonds scattered about the floor. They are lost monsters—and they are moving in directions without turning a wheel.

Crepusculum In Perpetuum…

Here, to George's left, in a niche of their own, a young couple, on all fours, are screwing their brains out. Something red and animalistic. And just beyond them, a middle-aged woman lay sprawled akimbo: eyes spooled back in her head, silver drool glossing her lips, and a thick rubber tube squeezing her upper arm. George felt the urge to roll her dress back down over her knees, but the sad odor perching in the air almost doubled him over, heaving a gut. The only thing to stop him from vomiting, however, was the sight of a familiar face. Not the face that George was searching for, but one that he would've never expected to catch so miserably corrupted—not even amongst the dimmest of shadow people.

It was a priest. And although George didn't know his name, nevertheless, the cleric was a fixture in George's neck of the woods, like ice cream trucks in June.

Flanked by two shipping crates and reciting rapid Hail Mary's between clenched teeth, it appeared the father had taken off the white centerpiece about his neck, and with one end in his mouth and the other ligating his bicep, the padre was slam-popping junk into the crook of his arm—sinking the needle, solely to swim. Further proof that a priest can never escape the cloth, but can always get a little higher.

But that's how all the people were in here: a score, or more, of shadows—dissimilar in every way, though all of them were riding off into the sunset on a black tar highway, astride funny white horses. Heroin is the game. The "shooting gallery" is the place. Yet George's only care was remaining lightless to the world and finding a baby amidst the noise.

This poor precious baby—Michael Moses Parker … A child stuffed in the skin of a man, who, although he had just turned twenty-two, would always be the baby brother to George.

The word on the corner was that after months of being invisible, George's brother, Michael, had turned up again and was seen frequenting the jivest junk joints in New Orleans. When the news finally reached Michael's mother, she shakily snubbed out her Pall-Mall on the bedpost, and before readjusting her oxygen mask, she whispered four words into George's ear: "fetch my baby home." What George heard, on the other hand, was something entirely different. It was a voiceover from a Saturday afternoon matinee of Kung Fu Theatre. His mother—or rather her elderly Asian doppelganger—said something more akin to, "fetch that stupid bastard"—a replacement to a mother's melodious verse that suited George's disposition towards his wayward sibling better, if not truer.

So when George Parker reached the warehouse that night, he didn't feel any more the guiding light than the shining knight. In fact, he was rattled and baffled. Spying the squad car parked at the edge of the warehouse, George would have usually high-tailed it, if it weren't for the odd way the policeman appeared. This one was one of them. A shadow, for sure. Standing in a slant of moonlight, the lone officer had evidently spotted the planet Pluto and was scratching the inside of his arm in the attempts to keep focused on celestial bodies (or maybe the cop was merely wondering how to get his next fix on a peacekeeper's pay).

Nonetheless, George was in now—and at every step, a stupid needle-freak became a study on the merits of Roe vs. Wade. It was a bleak way to view this gallery, yet searching through the shadows, and the shadows of the shadows, life through the business end of a syringe seemed more the like the end, instead of the means.

"Hey, brutha! China white will set you *right…*" came the voice at George's elbow; but George just glanced at the man who spoke to him. It wasn't George's "brutha" at all—just some hophead, with a scar running down his cheek that obviously didn't come from donating to charity.

In the far left corner of the warehouse, sitting next to heaps of moulded wool, Michael Moses Parker was reclining amongst the natives—casting no shadows, despite the glow of several candles encircling them.

Mixed emotions. George felt a ribbon of fear zip from the bottom of his guts to the back of his tongue as he walked to where his kid brother was seated. Nothing could make George feel any worse. Nothing could make Michael comprehend what George was doing there.

"Michael…" George began, but halted. Then George mustered the strength he needed. "Michael…momma says it time to come home now, so you'd best say goodbye to your playmates and let's go home."

To that, Michael burst out laughing: "What…? Do you *think…*? I mean, do you *really* think…?" Michael couldn't finish; his sides were near to splitting, swaggering as he made it to his feet.

"What the hell's so funny, Mike, huh?" George started to boil inside.

"Funny?" Michael put his hands on George's shoulders and looked him square in the eyes. "Funny, because momma would send *you* to get *me!* I mean, did you really think coming down here I would just walk out with you and pile up at home from now on out?"

The heat began to pool in the tips of George's ears.

"George. Look at me." Michael wasn't laughing anymore. In fact, his face was a granite mask. "Look at me and tell me you see 'high' in my eyes. Hell, bro, I've been clean for five months now, and—"

"—You lie!" George shot back.

"Oh, I'm lying now, George?" Michael put his hands on his hips. "Okay, yeah, I'm lying; and you can't see a damn thing wrong with me, 'cos I'm as clean as a bean and you know it! So, why don't you just walk back out of here and go home alone—or *wherever* it is you go—and tell momma that Michael is *aces.* You think you can do that, Georgie boy?"

"Then why are you here? George said inaudibly.

"What?"

George screamed: "I said…why are you *here*, Michael!"

Then: *Crepusculum In Perpetuum:* Forever Twilight.

Silence.

Michael merely wrapped his arms around his brother in a slow embrace that could only mean the meekest of mercies.

"I'm here, George…" Michael whispered in his ear. "I'm here to do for them what nobody could do for daddy, George—to take him out of the gutter. To show them that what I did, they can do. I'm here for me, George…and I'm here for you, too."

And with that, Michael quickly dipped his hand into George's jacket pocket—the jacket that had belong to their father, when daddy was in the army—and Michael pulled out what he knew was in George's pocket all along.

Taking a step back, Michael held up a glass crack pipe in front of George. The look on George's face was an amalgam of woe and regret, as he felt the shadows quicken around his shoulders, and the hungry urge to either run for the door…or dash for the pipe.

George moved a bit forward, as Michael moved a bit back—the kid wearing a thin, knowing smile that would not have been available to him this time last year.

"Now you go home to momma, George." Michael said. You could've heard the sound of pupils dilating, the warehouse was a hush. "And next time, big brother…next time, remember to remove the pipe out of your own eye, before you reach for the needle in mine.

"Now, goodbye now."

…George Parker…It's time to go.

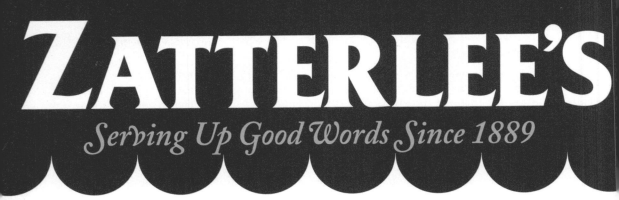

ZATTERLEE'S

Serving Up Good Words Since 1889

Thank you for taking a look at our little funnybook. You know, as I write this, I am also the Director of Operations for this publishing company. Do I know what the future brings? No. I sure hope we'll be around...but who knows? Regardless, I am here now; I am creating comics and a bunch of my friends have the chance to do the same. I am so thankful for the opportunity to do **Of Bitter Souls**. Working with Norm is a dream come true. He is a master and to work on this with him means I could quit comics now and have already achieved one of my biggest goals.

I want to thank my wife for her support. If you knew her, you would also know how hard a previous attempt at writing comic books hurt our family. I owe Chris the world and I am trying very hard to deliver it.

This book is dedicated to her and to my son Luke.

If I do anything with this book, I hope it's entertain people getting them thinking about their own gifts and whether they are using those gifts for their own glory...or the greater good. That is what OBS is all about.

There is a long list of people I want to thank. Those people are:

Charles Abbott (my Father), Dottie Abbott (my step-Mother), Janette Satterlee (My Mother), Scott Abbott, Norm Breyfogle, Harry Markos, Rich Emms, Adam Fortier (he gave this book a chance), Janice Binder (without whom this would not have been possible), Mike Kowalczyk, Erik Enervold, Jason Newcomb, Phil Hester, Brian Augustyn, Mark Waid, Dave Riske, Calude St. Aubin, Dan Bradford, Tom & Mary Hall, Tom & Christine Gonyo, Shawn McGuan, Frank Espinosa, George Singley, Ethen Beavers, Erin Tapken, Gahl Bushlov, Wookie & Buger, Art & Barb Keown, Linda & Ron Knutson, Wanda Bellich, Jim & Jackie Bellich, Ryan, Jen and Julie, Art & Emily, Eric & Laura, Kevin Breyfogle, Joe Disanto, Ken F. Levin, Mike Gold, Dick Giordano, G. Gerald Garcia, Nick The Evolvist, Tom Mauer, Ron Zoso, Ken Lillie-Paietz, Ian Sharman, Ryan Stegman, Freddie E. Williams II, Supreme Knight, Chuck Sellner, Fran & Kevin McGarry, Stacy Korn, Dean Phillips & the crew at Krypton Comics, supportive retailers, Diamond Comics, Jim Kuhoric, Dylan Lange, Neal Adams, Tom Mandrake, Vito DelSante, Bill Martin, Alisa Carter-Binder, Jim & Tracey Wetzstein, Becky & Jeff Witzke, Erick Hogan, Chris Stone, Andrew Foley and his beautiful wife Tiina (who put this book together with her great creativity) and last but first...God.

Chuck Satterlee, Bethlehem, Pa, May 2006

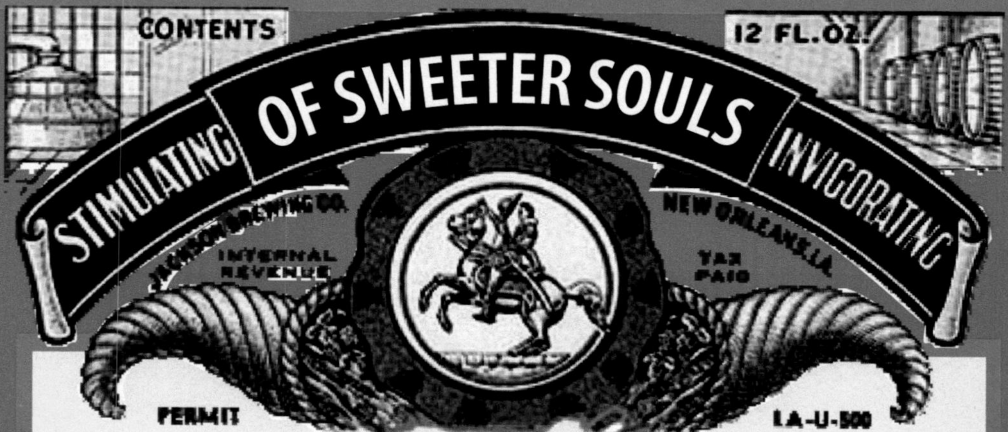
CONTENTS
12 FL.OZ.
STIMULATING
OF SWEETER SOULS
INVIGORATING
NEW ORLEANS, LA
INTERNAL REVENUE
TAX PAID
PERMIT
LA-U-500

There was a bitter man who had a bitter soul. He lived in a bitter nation and in a bitter house and he drove a bitter car to his bitter little job and he had a bitter wife, a couple of bitter children, and many bitter friends.

But he was happy, in spite of his bitterness!

This bitter man dearly loved his bitter soul, nation, house, car, job, wife, children, and his bitter firends. He loved his entire bitter life, for he knew that bitterness was a relative matter. You see, he was a philosopher and so he knew that no matter how bitter one was, someone else was always bitterer, so he was content with his level of bitterness. After all, it could certainly be worse!

Then one day this bitter man met the sweetest person that had ever existed, and his old life was ruined by the chance encounter. No longer could the bitter man be happy and content in his bitterness, for his eyes had been opened and the truth had blown his brains out: he didn't have to be bitter at all!

Thanks, Mom, for allowing and encouraging my freedom of thought. Thanks for your love and for the faith you had in my abilities. All my work is dedicated to you, even when it's also dedicated to others. See you soon.

Thanks, Dad, for the gift of my main talent.

Thanks to all my family, my friends, my relations, my loves, my peers, my fans, my enemies, my angels and my demons. Without all of you, I'd be in greater danger of becoming a bitter soul.

Thanks, Chuck, for writing stories I truly enjoy illustrating. Thanks for your friendship, your faith, your enthusiasm and for your tireless salesmanship.

Thanks, Harry Markos, for having faith in our effort.

And thanks to you, reader, for picking up this publication. Stick around for the on-going series; Chuck has only begun to tell this tale, and my pencils and my pointed head are sharpened and itching for the next leg of the saga.

How I love the smell of shaved lead and ink in the morning!

***Norm Breyfogle,** March 2006, Houghton, Michigan*

GENUINE

GENUINE

EVERY PENCIL SHARPENED

Sketchbook

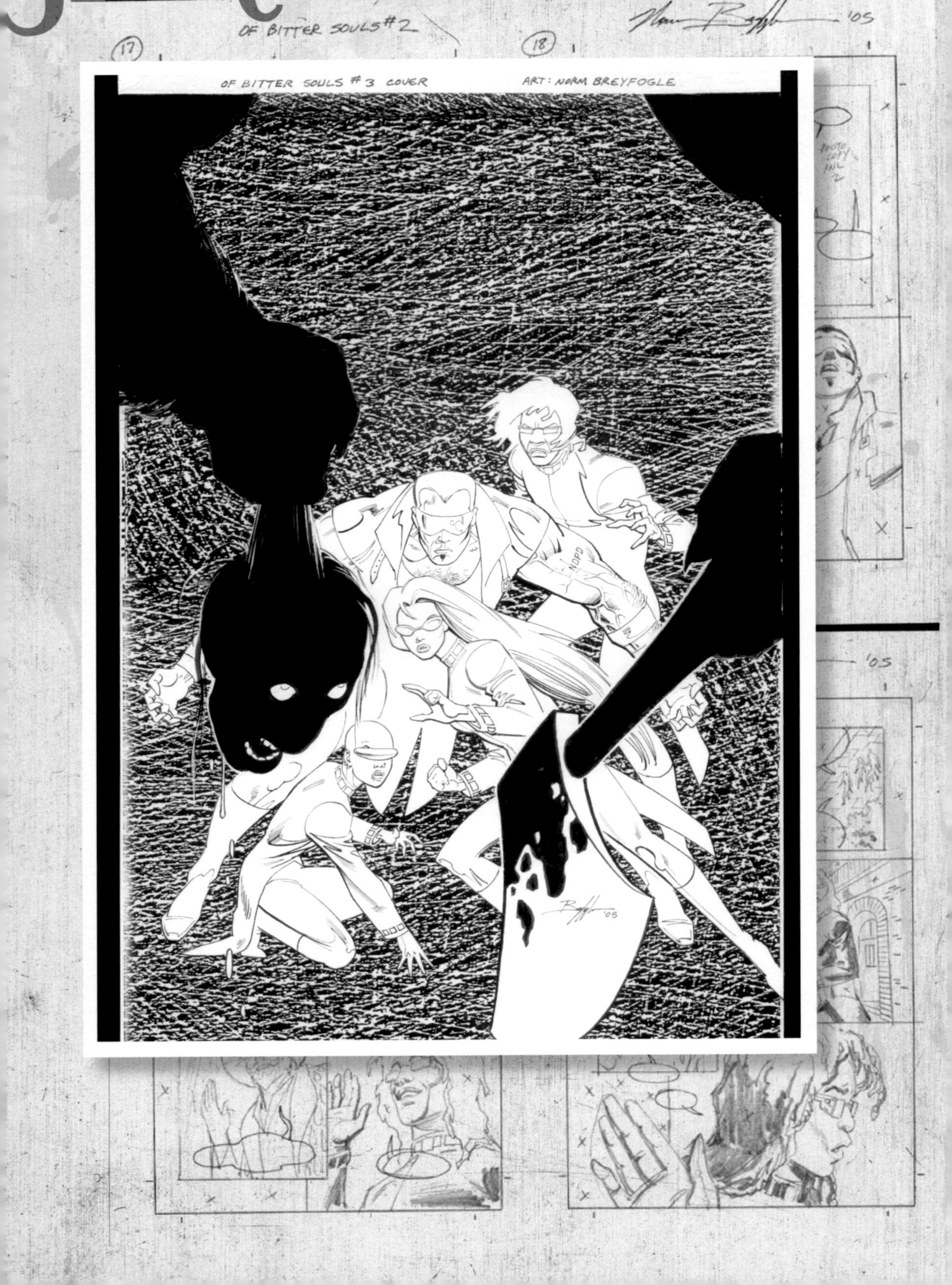

OF BITTER SOULS #2
'05
17
18
OF BITTER SOULS #3 COVER
ART: NORM BREYFOGLE
NOPD
'05

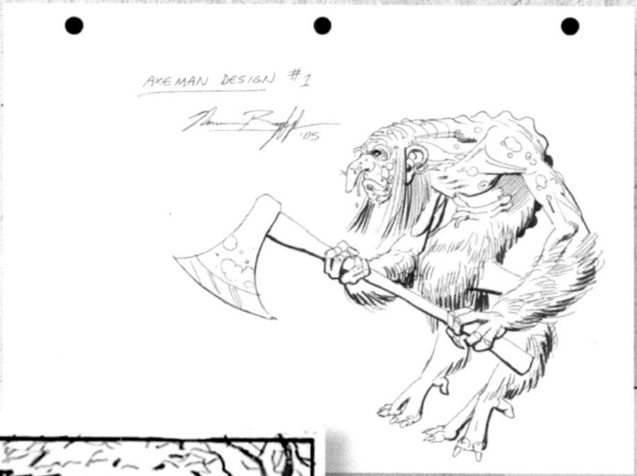
AXEMAN DESIGN #1
'05

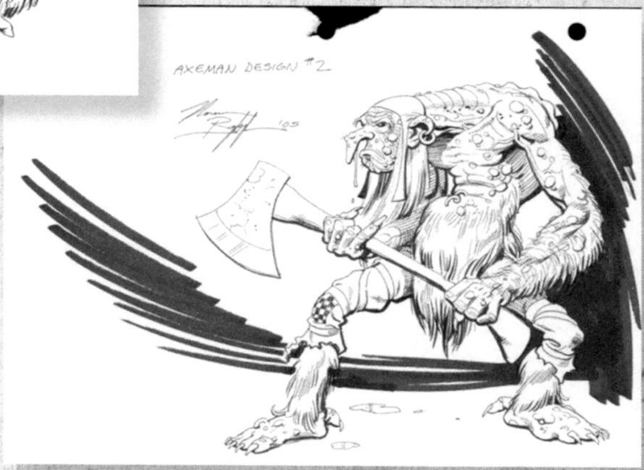
AXEMAN DESIGN #2
'05

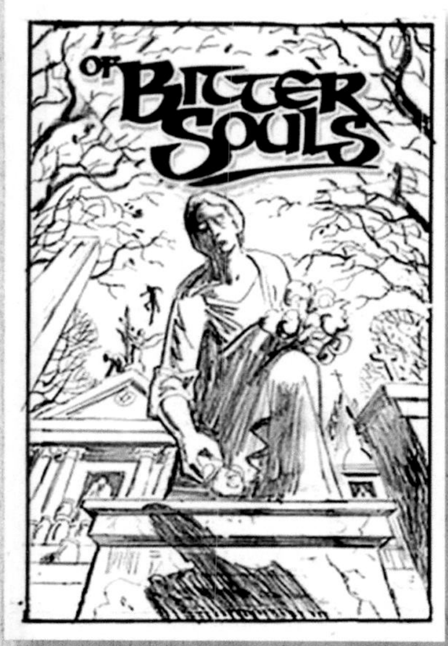
OF BITTER SOULS

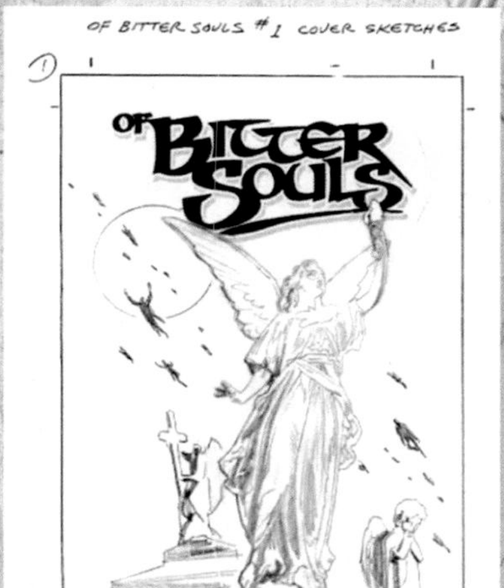
OF BITTER SOULS #1 COVER SKETCHES
OF BITTER SOULS

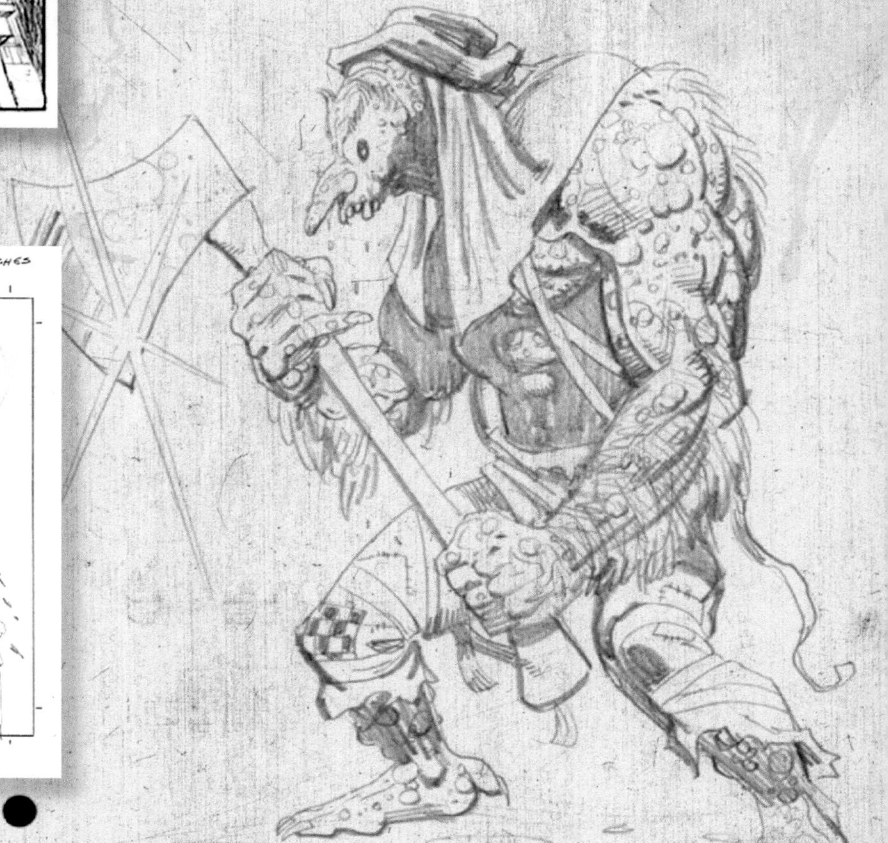

Sketchbook

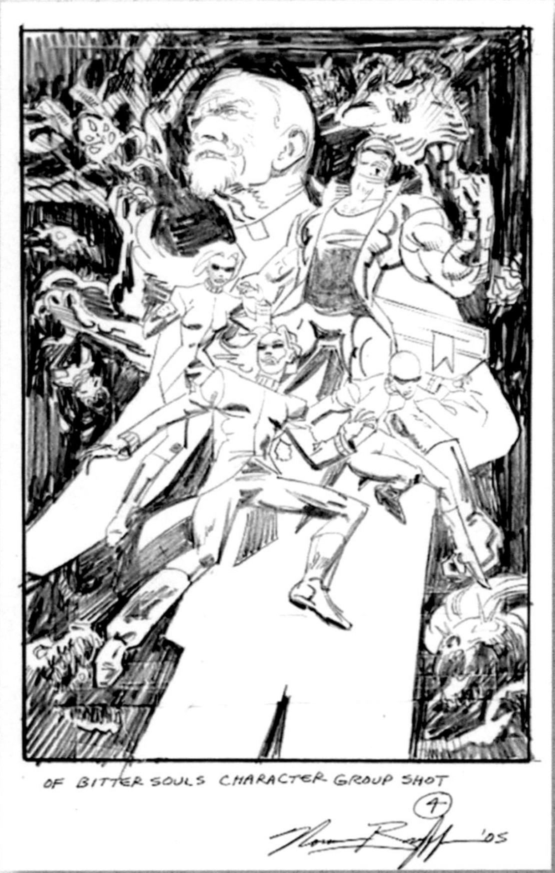
OF BITTER SOULS CHARACTER GROUP SHOT
4
'05

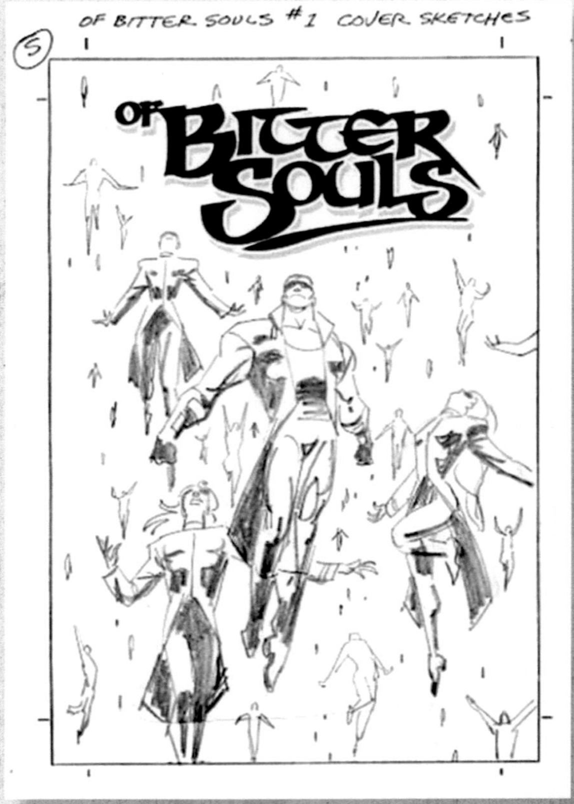
OF BITTER SOULS #1 COVER SKETCHES
5
OF BITTER SOULS

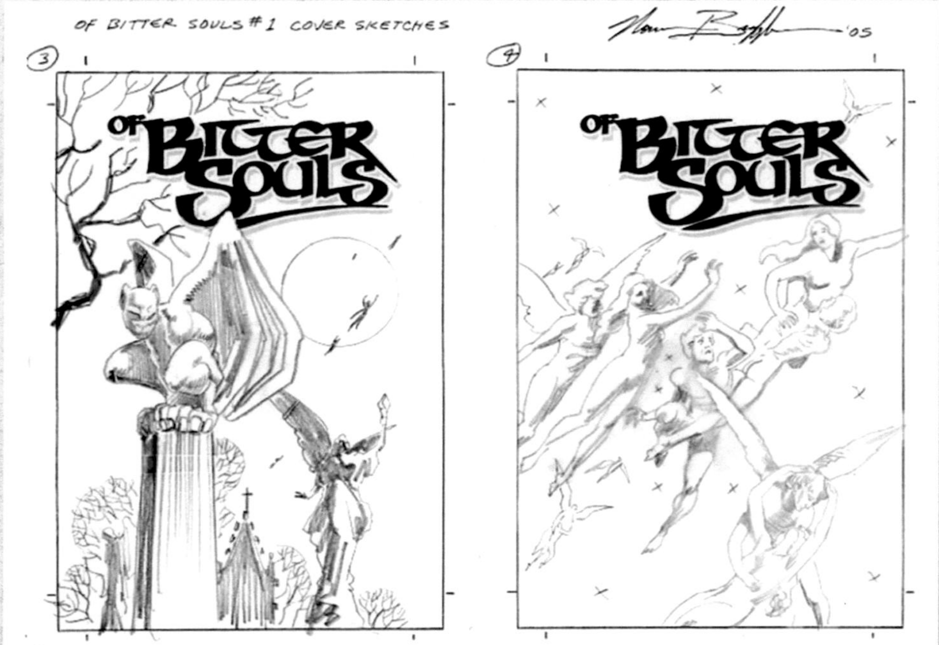
OF BITTER SOULS #1 COVER SKETCHES
'05
3
OF BITTER SOULS
4
OF BITTER SOULS

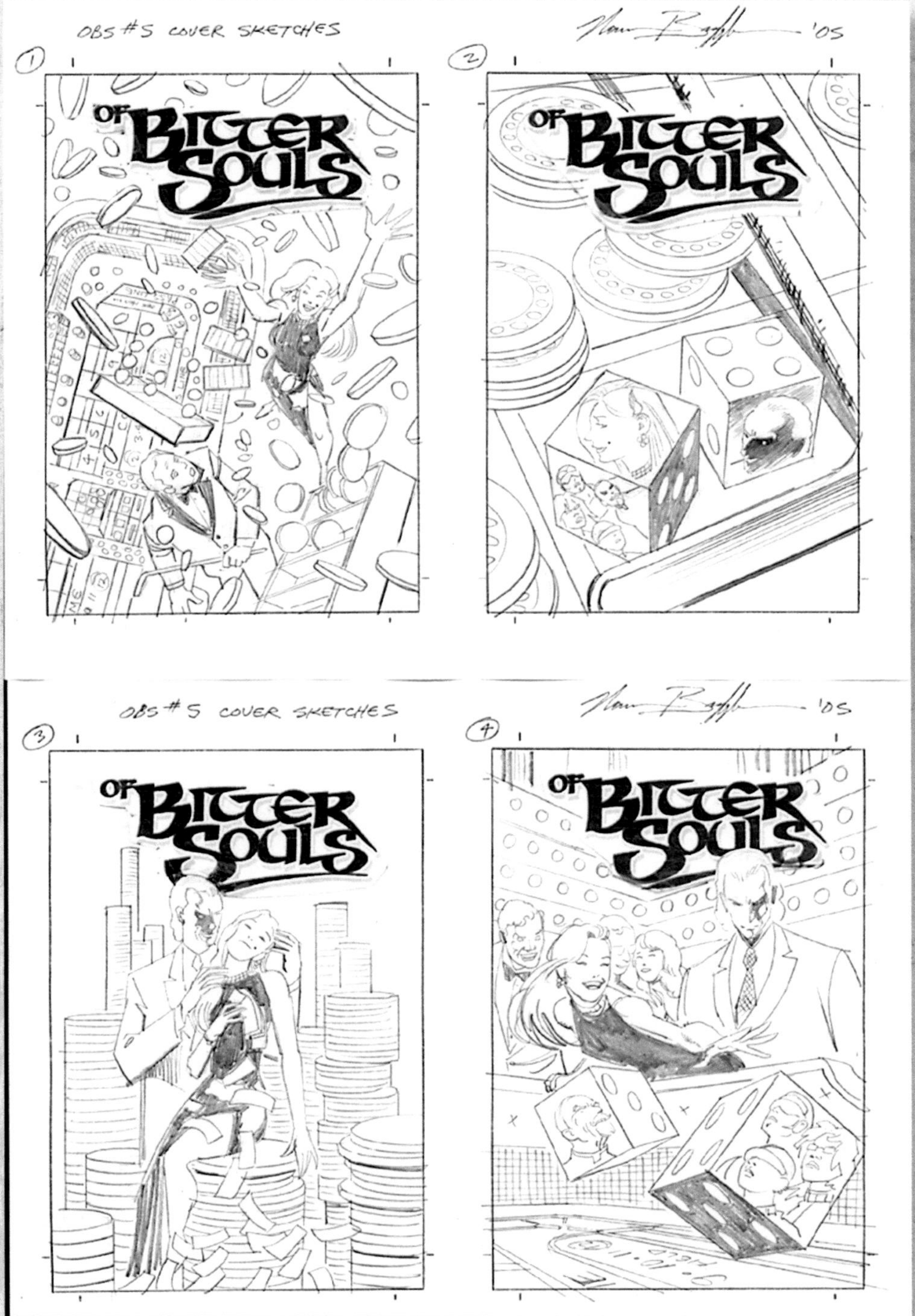
OBS #5 COVER SKETCHES
'05
1
OF BITTER SOULS
2
OF BITTER SOULS
OBS #5 COVER SKETCHES
'05
3
OF BITTER SOULS
4
OF BITTER SOULS

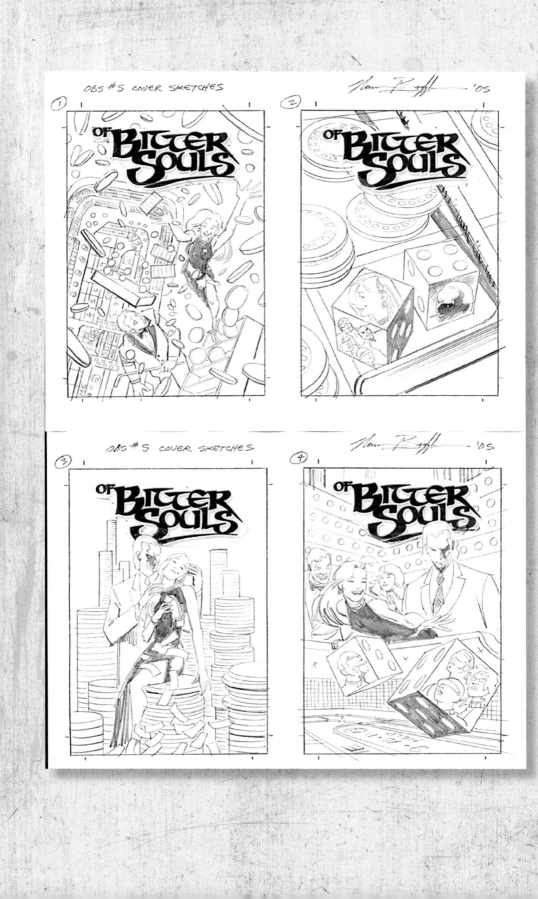

Sketchbook

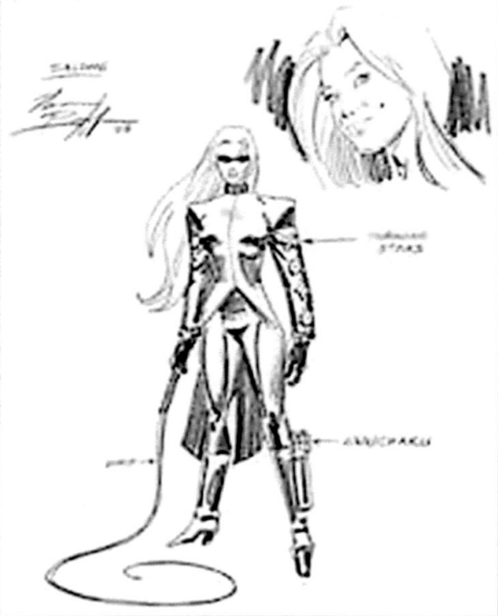
STARS

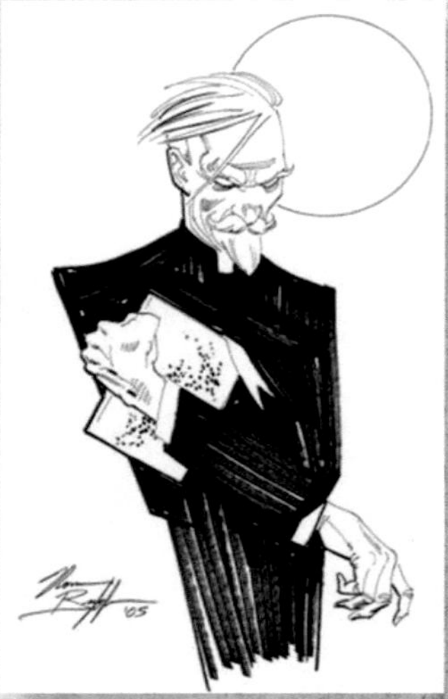

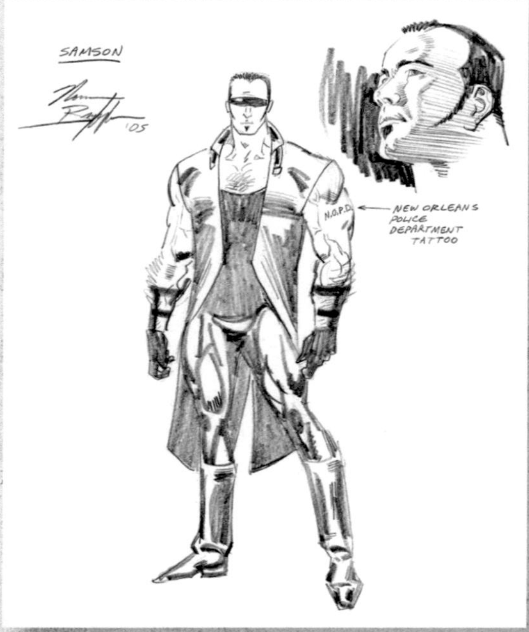
SAMSON
'05
N.O.P.D.
NEW ORLEANS POLICE DEPARTMENT TATTOO

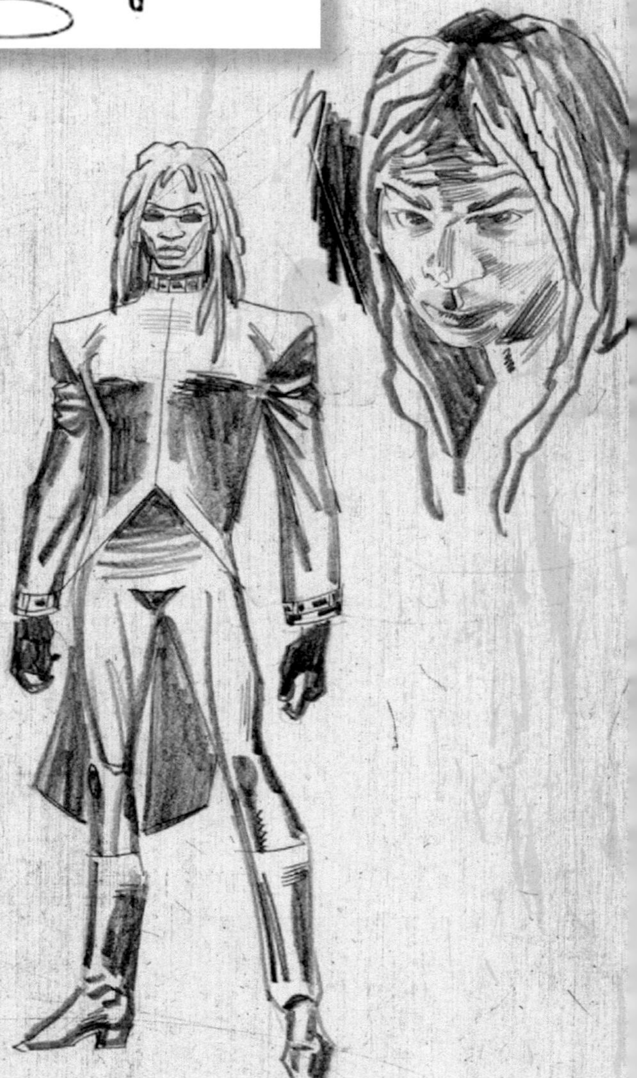

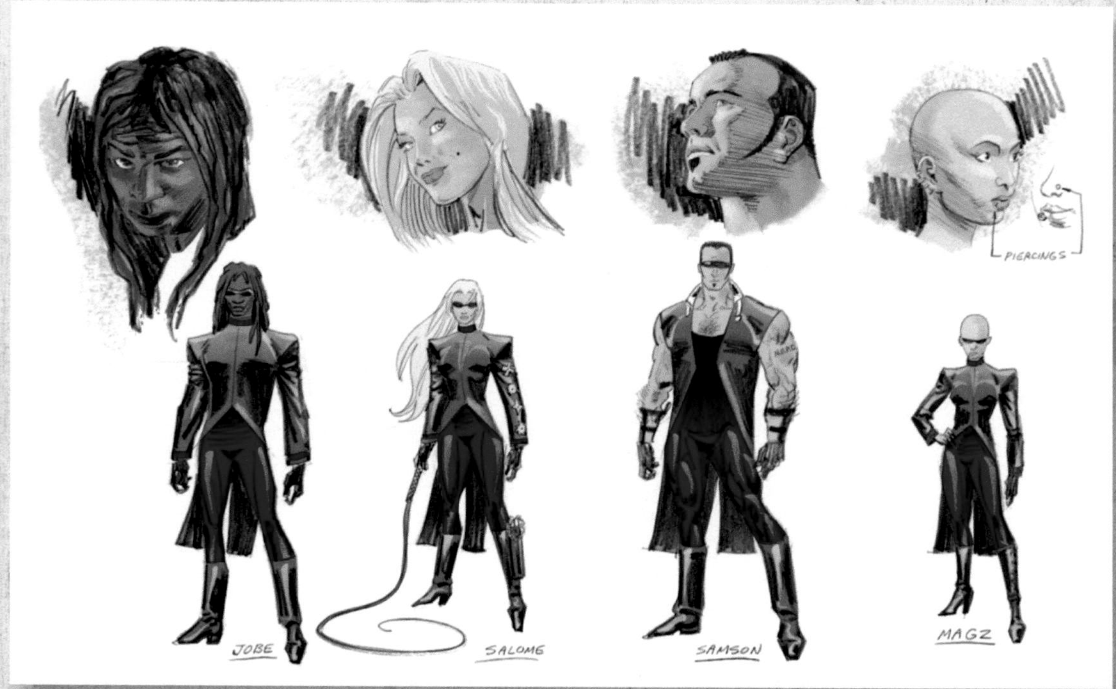
PIERCINGS
JOBE
SALOME
SAMSON
MAGZ

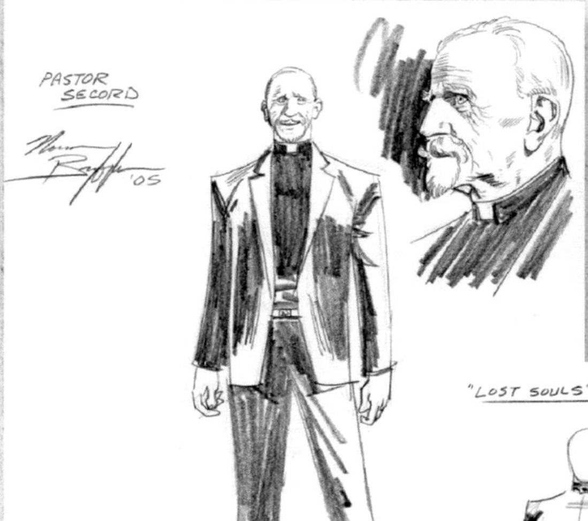
PASTOR SECORD
'05

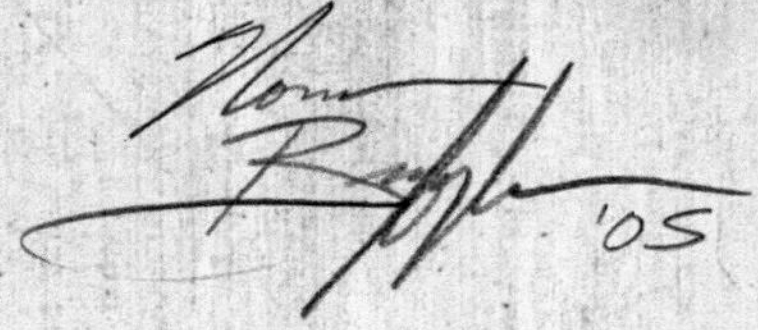
'05

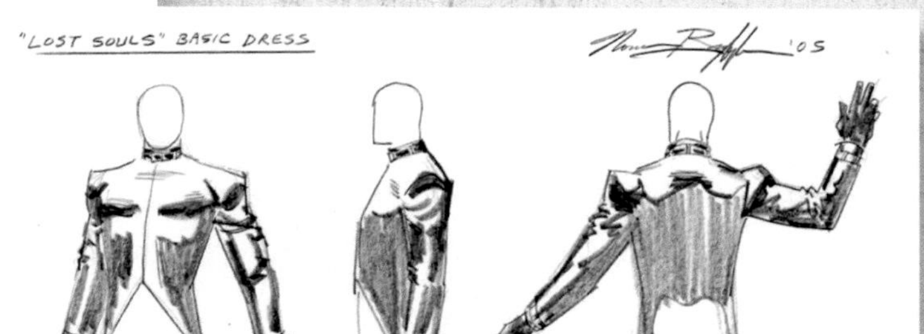
"LOST SOULS" BASIC DRESS
'05
BLACK LEATHER LONG COAT, BELTED AT NECK AND WRISTS
BLACK GLOVES
SEAM DOWN COAT FRONT OPENS BUT SHOWS NO FASTENING
PADDED SHOULDERS

Sketchbook

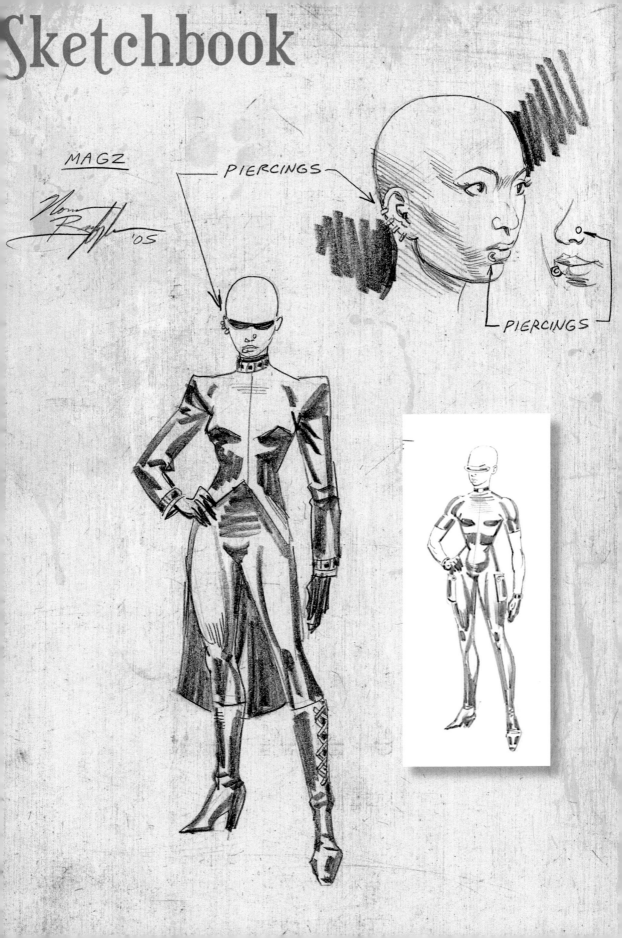

MAGZ

PIERCINGS

PIERCINGS

'05

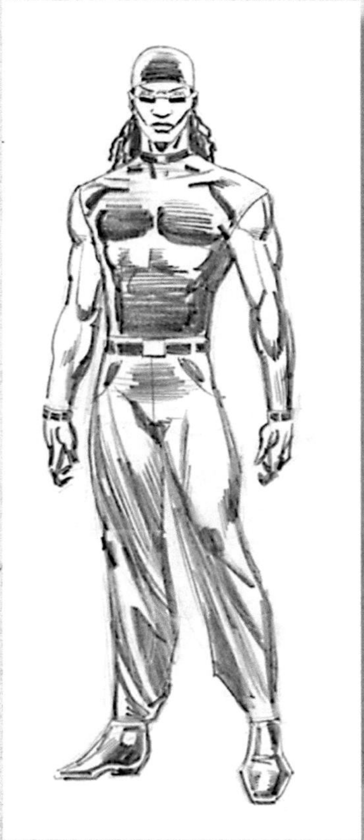

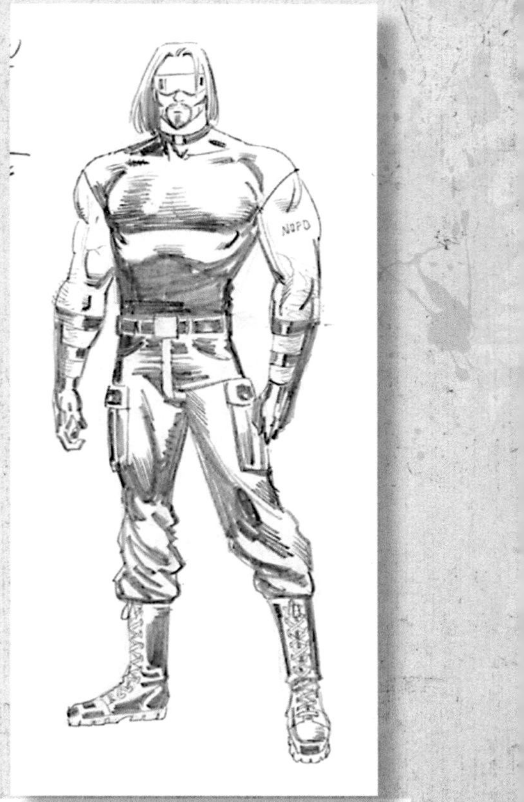
NOPD

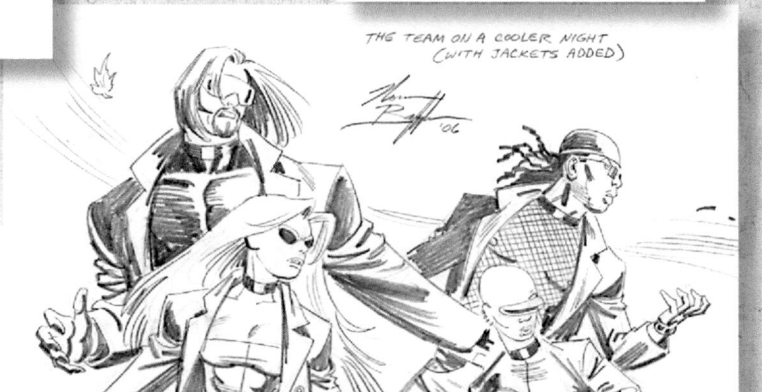
THE TEAM ON A COOLER NIGHT
(WITH JACKETS ADDED)
'06

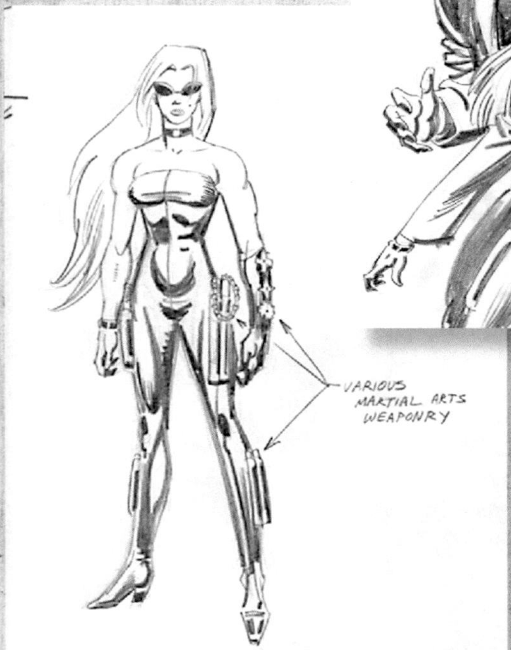
VARIOUS
MARTIAL ARTS
WEAPONRY

Brian Augustyn
afterword:

So, pretty cool, huh?

If you're already a fan of **Of Bitter Souls,** you knew going in that this was going to be one seriously fun roller coaster ride, but if this was your first exposure to Chuck and Norm's great comic, I bet you're a fan now. Hard not to be, I think.

What's not to love about a comic with a bunch of very flawed folks cosmically charged with the task of saving the world by kicking vampire butt--along with demon booty, werewolf tail and the occasional monster heinie? Too cool, right?

How can you avoid being excited by the art work by comic great, Norm Breyfogle? Come on, the guy's a genius and he's been knocking us out for years. Whisper, Batman, Prime, Anarky... and so on and so on. A terrific artist doing some of his best work here! What more could you want?

You certainly noticed that OBS also has a great premise and terrific characters – thanks to the very talented creator-writer, Chuck Satterlee. Chuck's got a very twisted imagination and a gift for action storytelling. He also writes his characters down to their souls, bitter and otherwise. Hard not to like that.

Then there's the dramatic and beautiful New Orleans setting. The Crescent City never looked so good or so mysterious. Chuck and Norm have captured our most mystical, magical American city perfectly. And, in a time when the Big Easy is on the road to recovery from the terrible devastation of Hurricane Katrina, it's heartening to find folks who love the place as much as the creators do. It's plain inspirational.

I have to say that the big draw for me, though, is the wonderfully conceived Pastor Secord. I mean, there are plenty of clergy characters in comics, but how many can claim to also be an all-powerful avenging angel in their spare time? Our beloved cleric can; he's the coolest. In fact, I'm prepared to boldly state that Pastor Secord is my very favorite Lutheran minister/avenging angel character in comics. Period. The others don't even come close. OBS satisfies!

So, we can agree, we're all fans for life of OBS, right? Even though we all read our comics mostly while we're alone, think of all of us as being part of one community – a funky, colorful, often wild and wacky community to be sure, but a group of fans united in our enjoyment of this terrific comic.

Welcome to the fold, the fun of **Of Bitter Souls** is just beginning in this collected edition. There's a new number one and way more excitement out there waiting for us...

See you in the comics!

Brian Augustyn

—Can I have my Mardi Gras beads now?

Brian Augustyn is a veteren comics writer and editor, and, in the interests of full disclosure, a former Chicagoan and long-time pal of Chuck Satterlee's.